VICE PRESIDENTS

A BIOGRAPHICAL DICTIONARY

Fourth Edition

Edited by

L. Edward Purcell

An imprint of Infobase Publishing

Vice Presidents: A Biographical Dictionary, Fourth Edition

Facts On File, Inc.
An imprint of Infobase Publishing
132 West 31st Street
New York NY 10001

Library of Congress Cataloging-in-Publication Data

Vice presidents : a biographical dictionary / [edited by] L. Edward Purcell.—4th ed.
    p. cm.
  Includes bibliographical references and index.
  ISBN 978-0-8160-7707-6 (hc : alk. paper) 1. Vice-Presidents—United States—Biography—Dictionaries. I. Purcell, L. Edward.

  E176.49.V52 2010
  973.09'9—dc22   2009026068

Text design by Annie O'Donnell
Composition by Hermitage Publishing Services
Cover printed by Art Print, Taylor, Pa.
Book printed and bound by Maple Press, York, Pa.
Date printed: May 2010
Printed in the United States of America

10 9 8 7 6 5 4 3 2 1

CONTENTS

ACKNOWLEDGMENTS

Many people and institutions helped accomplish the tasks of putting this volume together, and especially important were those who suggested authors. In alphabetical order, the following are very gratefully acknowledged: Irving H. Bartlett, Marvin Bergman, Roger Bridges, the George Bush Presidential Materials Project, John Catanzaritti, the Cowles Library at Drake University, Todd Culbertson, Ken Davidson, William C. Davis, Virgil Dean, the Des Moines Public Library, the Grace Doherty Library at Centre College, John Dumville, George C. Edwards, H. Roger Grant, John Robert Greene, Peter Harstad, Mary Holt, Loren N. Horton, Ludwell Johnson III, the M.I. King Library at the University of Kentucky, Richard Kirkendall, James Klotter, John Kolp, the Lexington Public Library, the Library of Congress, Frank Mackaman, Madison House Publishers, Robert McCown, Martin Medhurst, Susan Naulty, the Richard Nixon Library and Birthplace, Nick Noyes, Nancy Osborne, Mark Palmer, Bradley Patterson, Jr., Frances Pollard, Sarah J. Purcell, the Dan Quayle Center and Museum, Janet Rassweiler, the Regents Press of Kansas, Donald Ritchie, George Robinson, Richard Ryerson, Elizabeth Safly, Edward L. Schapsmeier, Leonard Schlup, Ann Shaller, Robert M. Sutton, Brent Tarter, Tim Walch, Robert Waller, Shirley Anne Warshaw, Clyde Wilson, and Dan Wilson. Special thanks to Amy Drake, who updated the Chronology of Events for this edition.

INTRODUCTION

This is a book of reference, and it is not intended, nor is it likely, that the biographies of all forty-seven American vice presidents will be read through from start to finish, from John Adams to Joseph Biden. Should readers choose to do so, however, they will discover much about the political history of our nation and the role played by the vice presidents. They will also, of course, discover a wealth of interesting facts about these men, from the titillating public innuendo about William Rufus King's sex life to the otherworldly dreams of Henry Wallace.

One of the most striking conclusions to be drawn from considering the lives of the vice presidents is the extremely high quality of the men who have borne that title.

When they devised the Constitution of the United States after the American Revolution, the Founding Fathers intended that the vice presidency go to whomever the electoral voters thought was presumed to be the second-best man in the nation and deserving of a high and mighty office. The writers of the Constitution gave the vice president only the specific task of presiding over the Senate, thus conceiving of the vice presidency as primarily a working legislative office with the major proviso that the vice president would take over the presidency if the chief should die or become incapacitated, what author Richard Zuczek calls the vice president's "ultimate function."

In the more than 200 years since John Adams was sworn in, we have come to view the vice presidency somewhat differently. In fact, in the popular mind, before the vice-presidential term of Dick Cheney demonstrated otherwise, the vice president has been often a figure of fun, someone who has no meaningful role in life other than to check on the president's health each morning.

Cheney, of course, transformed the office of the vice president when he aggressively seized control of both national policy and decision-making. His role is aptly described by the title of a new 2009 study by Shirley Anne Warshaw: *The Co-Presidency of Bush and Cheney*. Whether Cheney's version of the vice presidency will outlive his terms in office remains to be seen.

Otherwise the very idea of the vice presidency calls forth a flow of derision—just look at the titles of the most popular books about the vice presidents. Worse yet, the incumbents themselves have done much to demean the office in what must be an unparalleled tradition of public self-loathing. Except for Dick Cheney, virtually all the vice presidents, beginning with Adams, have sooner or later said or written something in public that indicated their viciously low self-opinion: John Nance Garner's pithy comparative reference to a warm bodily fluid was unusual only in its stark directness.

It is not too difficult to comprehend where this negative view comes from. The actual duties of the office of vice president, unless the incumbent is taken into the confidence of the president and given real work to do (as was frequently the case in the twentieth century), are slight and boring. Active politicians who find themselves thus sidelined, often at the height of their powers, have not taken kindly to the situation.

Yet it seems very clear with only a little serious examination that it is the *office* of the vice president that should be the butt of jokes and not the people elected to it.

There is little profit in protesting the opinion that vice presidents are historical ciphers, but it is quite contrary to historical fact. If the list of vice presidents was presented in some neutral context, without the fatal "vice presidents" label, it would be mistaken for an honor roll of significant American political leaders.

It will probably come as a shock and surprise to most American general readers and even many political scientists and historians who consult the biographies in this volume to learn that the great majority of U.S. vice presidents have been men of extraordinarily high ability and achievement. Even individual authors, all of whom are experts, of the biographies in this volume frequently hint that only *their* subjects were accomplished leaders and therefore must be aberrations.

Nothing could be further from the truth. Only a handful of the forty-seven vice presidents have been nonentities, mostly those serving during the so-called Gilded Age, when American politics in general may have hit a historic low. During most of our national history, however, it would have been impossible for politically unimportant men to come to the vice-presidential nomination and election. For example, the list of vice presidents is filled with men who were Speakers of the House of Representatives, distinguished and powerful senators, governors of the most important states, powerful mayors, and military heroes. Even many of the less distinguished came to the office with impressive credentials: Charles Dawes, who performed poorly as vice president, was an international expert on finance and had a Nobel Peace Prize in his portfolio when nominated.

Anyone who doubts the quality of the vice presidents should pause to consider John Adams, Thomas Jefferson, John C. Calhoun, Theodore Roosevelt, Harry Truman, and Lyndon Johnson. Slipping down a notch still produces a list with names such as George Clinton, John Nance Garner, Henry Wallace, Hubert Humphrey, and Nelson Rockefeller. No matter what their overall job rating, Martin Van Buren, John Tyler, Millard Fillmore, Andrew Johnson, Chester Arthur, Calvin Coolidge, Gerald Ford, and George Bush all were presidents of the United States. Even the most notorious of vice presidents, Aaron Burr, Richard Nixon, and Dick Cheney, had immense impact on the nation.

Overall, the following forty-seven biographical essays demonstrate the vigor of the office of vice president and of American political life since the founding of the republic, and they will, one hopes, provide ample information and interpretation about the individuals who have served.

JOHN ADAMS
(Library of Congress)

By Jack D. Warren

Amajor figure in the patriot cause in Massachusetts before the American Revolution, a leader in the Continental Congress during the Revolutionary War, and one of the United States's first diplomats in Europe, John Adams served for eight years as the first vice president of the United States before succeeding George Washington to become the second president of the United States. Although his career as vice president was overshadowed by his accomplishments as congressman, diplomat, and president, John Adams was among the most important vice presidents in American history. The precedents established during his eight years in office continue to shape the vice presidency more than 200 years later, and his tie-breaking votes in the Senate were decisively important to the establishment of a strong national government during the Washington administration.

John Adams was a man of brilliant intellect, enormous personal integrity, and high principles. He was also ceaselessly ambitious— for professional and political advancement, wealth, and mostly for lasting fame. From the outbreak of the Revolution, he devoted himself to the patriot cause with an industry matched by few of his contemporaries. Although Adams spent most of his adult life in politics, he was temperamentally ill suited to the accommodations and compromises required by political life. Always fiercely independent, he could be stubborn and self-righteous and was often blunt, undiplomatic, impatient, and demanding. He was apparently awkward in social situations and possessed an unfortunate talent for alienating people. Unsparingly critical of himself, he was equally quick to point out shortcomings in those around him. Adams's political principles and his passion for fame and advancement often dictated contradictory actions, and it is a credit to him that at decisive points in his career he consistently sacrificed his ambitions to his principles. He refused to compromise his convictions for popularity or political office, a characteristic that ultimately cost him reelection to the presidency.

John Adams was born on October 19, 1735, in Braintree (later renamed Quincy), Massachusetts, the eldest son of John Adams, a yeoman farmer, and his wife, Susanna Boylston Adams. Educated at Harvard College, from which he graduated in 1755, he then took up the study of law and was admitted to the bar in Boston in November 1758. On October 25, 1764, he married Abigail Smith, the daughter of a Weymouth, Massachusetts, minister. Although she lacked formal education, she was vivacious and possessed a sparkling intellect that made her an ideal partner for Adams through his long and varied public career. During the next ten years the couple had four children: John Quincy, Thomas, Charles, and Abigail II.

John Adams became a major public figure in Massachusetts during the decade-long controversy between Britain and its American colonies that preceded the outbreak of the American Revolution. During the Stamp Act controversy, Adams drafted resolutions of protest for Braintree that were imitated all over Massachusetts. As a lawyer, he was involved in a number of legal cases arising out of the pre-Revolutionary crisis: He defended John Hancock against smuggling charges but also defended the British soldiers involved in the Boston Massacre against charges of murder, an action that marked him as a man of personal integrity, devoted to his principles regardless of personal cost.

In June 1774, Adams was chosen to be one of the three delegates from Massachusetts to the Continental Congress, meeting in Philadelphia. In the First Continental Congress, he counseled moderation and publicly supported reconciliation with Britain, but privately he was becoming impatient with British intransigence; in the Second Continental Congress, he emerged as a most outspoken and determined advocate of independence. Congress adopted a resolution in May 1776, with a preamble written by Adams, that called on the states where no adequate colonial government remained to adopt constitutions independent of British authority. This virtual declaration of independence was followed immediately by a resolution calling for independence, foreign alliances, and a confederation of the states. Adams was appointed to committees to prepare a declaration of independence and to prepare a plan for treaties with foreign powers.

Although Thomas Jefferson wrote the Declaration of Independence, Adams accepted the difficult task of securing its adoption on the floor of Congress, where, according to Jefferson, he "supported the Declaration with zeal and ability, fighting fearlessly for every word of it."

On November 28, 1777, Congress appointed Adams to join Benjamin Franklin as an American commissioner to France, launching Adams on a diplomatic career that would last more than ten years. Adams's first mission to Europe was a frustrating and largely unproductive experience. By the time he reached Paris in April 1778, France had already recognized the United States, and war between France and Britain was imminent, leaving Adams with little to do. He spent most of this first trip abroad reorganizing the U.S. mission, establishing an orderly system of correspondence, and recommending changes in the conduct of American diplomacy to Congress.

Adams returned to the United States in the summer of 1779 and was immediately elected to represent Braintree at the Massachusetts state constitutional convention. The constitution adopted by that convention in 1780 was largely his work, and its principal features—a bicameral legislature, single executive, and an independent judiciary—served as a model for the framers of the federal constitution in 1787.

But Adams was called away from the convention before its work was complete, having been chosen by Congress as a commissioner to negotiate a peace treaty with Great Britain. After this, he was to serve as American minister to Great Britain and to conclude a commercial treaty with the British. Arriving in Paris in February 1780, Adams soon found himself caught up in intrigues with the French ministry and Franklin and then functioned as sole American minister to France. At French Minister Vergennes's urging, he kept his peace mission secret but soon regretted the decision, concluding that the French wished to prolong the war for their own advantage. Adams found himself in the delicate position of intruding on Franklin's prerogatives and soon alienated himself from Vergennes.

In July 1780, Adams went to Holland to seek a loan for the United States. Although this effort met with no immediate success, he was appointed minister to the Dutch republic by Congress in December 1780. Two years later, Adams concluded a treaty with the Dutch republic and made proposals that resulted in the first Dutch loan to the United States. At the same time, Franklin and John Jay were concluding preliminary articles for a peace treaty with Great Britain. Hastening to Paris, Adams made important contributions toward concluding the final peace treaty, signed September 3, 1783.

The British court received Adams as minister from the United States in May 1785. He spent more than two years in fruitless efforts to resolve matters arising out of the peace treaty, but the British, lacking faith in the United States government under the weak Articles of Confederation, paid little attention to these matters or to Adams. Unable to accomplish his primary mission, Adams spent much of his time in London studying the principles of government, publishing the results in a massive, three-volume work entitled *A Defense of the Constitutions of Government of the United States* (1787–88) that was praised by contemporaries as the most thorough disquisition on the principles of American constitutionalism yet published. The work was also criticized by many in the United States as too favorable to monarchical forms in government. Having been frustrated in his tenure as U.S. minister to Britain, Adams was recalled at his own request in February 1788.

Adams returned home to find that he had been chosen as a delegate to the Confederation Congress, but he never took his seat in that expiring body. His future seemed clouded: In his absence, eleven of the original states had ratified the new federal Constitution, drafted by a convention in the summer of 1787. Despite being one of the nation's most important political thinkers, Adams had not been able to participate in this convention. His distinguished record as a lawyer, legislator, and diplomat marked him as a suitable candidate for a position in the new federal government—as vice president, senator, Supreme Court justice, or secretary of state—but his long absence from the domestic political scene made his advancement to any of these posts uncertain.

In the first election under the federal Constitution, George Washington was the universal choice for president, but Adams was just one of several prospective candidates for the vice presidency. In the absence of political parties and a formal nominating method, the process of selecting and advancing candidates for vice president was conducted in private correspondence and behind-the-scenes maneuvering by established political leaders. Eighteenth-century political principle, which held that public servants should be above self-interested motivations, precluded candidates from actively seeking office. At the end of the eighteenth century, candidates for office were typically brought forward by their political allies, agreed upon quietly within coalitions of like-minded men, and then publicly advanced in newspapers.

This manner of selecting a candidate for vice president put Adams at a disadvantage. Although he enjoyed widespread respect, his long absence from domestic politics left Adams with few allies to champion his candidacy. In particular, his absence during the crucial deliberations that produced the federal Constitution and the political struggle over its ratification further hampered his prospects; although his support of the federal Constitution was assumed, he was not associated with the triumphant nationalist leadership that had worked through the 1780s to establish the federal government on a strong basis. Other men were better positioned than Adams to be chosen vice president. With some justification, he regarded his prospects for being elected vice president as poor.

Through the summer of 1788, several possible candidates for vice president were discussed in private correspondence and the press. Benjamin Franklin was widely advanced as the most distinguished American after Washington, but even his most ardent supporters recognized that he was too old. Adams, John Jay of New York, John Rutledge of South Carolina, and John Hancock of Massachusetts were the other candidates most frequently mentioned. Hancock's distinguished record in the Revolution, highly visible public role in New England politics, and extraordinary popularity in Massachusetts, of which he was governor, made him the leading contender, as did the widely held principle that the major offices in

the new government ought to be distributed geographically to secure attachment to the new government. Rumors circulated, however, that Hancock had refused to accept second place to any man, and his supporters seem to have held out hope that he would be elected president in the event Washington declined the office.

Adams seemed a suitable New England alternative to Hancock, but leading Federalists, including Alexander Hamilton and James Madison, were uncertain where Adams stood on some most critical political issues. Madison, in particular, was concerned that Adams had "made himself obnoxious to many particularly in the Southern states by the political principles avowed in his book. Others recollecting his cabal during the war against General Washington." The latter was the main concern of Hamilton, who had served as Washington's military secretary during the Revolution and believed that Adams was "unfriendly in his sentiments to General Washington." In Adams's defense, Massachusetts Federalist Theodore Sedgwick assured Hamilton that Adams was "a man of unconquerable intrepidity & of incorruptible integrity" fully deserving the confidence "of those who wish energy in government." Mollified, Hamilton decided to support Adams for vice president, partly, he explained to Madison, to prevent Adams from being "nominated to some important office for which he is less proper" as well as to prevent him from becoming a "malcontent." Hamilton was then careful to orchestrate, through private correspondence with other Federalist leaders, the disposition of votes in the electoral college to ensure that Adams did not receive more votes that Washington.

During the months of political maneuvering leading up to Adams's election, George Washington did not publicly endorse a candidate for the vice presidency, explaining to a friend that "Whosoever shall be found to enjoy the confidence of the States so far as to be elected Vice President, cannot be disagreeable to me," adding that:

Supposing myself to be connected in that office with any gentleman of character, I would most certainly treat him with perfect sincerity and the greatest candor in every respect. I would give him my full confidence & use my utmost endeavours to cooperate with him, in promoting and rendering permanent the national prosperity—this should be my great—my only aim—under the fixed & irrevocable resolution of leaving to other hands the helm of the State, as soon as my services could possibly with propriety be dispensed with.

This statement, combined with Washington's expressed determination to retire from the presidency after a single term, suggested that he would regard the vice president as his natural successor in the presidency. In January 1789, Washington wrote privately that it was clear "that Mr. John Adams would be chosen Vice President. He will doubtless make a very good one: and let whoever may occupy the first seat, I shall be entirely satisfied with that arrangement for filling the second office."

When Congress convened in New York City on April 6, 1789, Washington was found to have received a vote from each of the sixty-nine electors. Adams received the vote of thirty-four electors, including all ten from Massachusetts, all five from New Hampshire, five of seven from Connecticut, one of six from New Jersey, eight of ten from Pennsylvania, five of ten from Virginia. Other second votes were widely scattered. John Jay received nine votes. Robert H. Harrison of Maryland and John Rutledge of South Carolina received six votes each, all from their respective states. The Antifederalist candidate, George Clinton, received only three votes, all from Virginia.

Adams arrived in New York City on April 20, 1789, and took the oath of office the next day. He then presented a brief address, anticipating the difficulties that lay ahead. Adams noted that he was "unaccustomed to refuse any public service, however dangerous to my reputation, or disproportioned to my talents." He added that he was "not wholly without experience in public assemblies," but that "I have been more accustomed to take a share in their debates, than to preside in their deliberations" and asked the forbearance of the members: "If from inexperience, or inadvertency, any thing should ever escape me, inconsistent with propriety, I must entreat you, by imputing it to its true cause, and not to any want of respect, to pardon and excuse it."

Adams's conduct as president of the Senate was governed by rules adopted before he arrived to take his seat. These rules made it clear that the senators expected Adams to conduct himself much like the presidents of the Continental Congress, managing the flow of business and maintaining order but not actively participating in debates. This would prove to be a role for which Adams—a brilliant intellectual, skilled in debate but also opinionated and lacking in tact—was to prove temperamentally ill suited. Yet, unlike some later vice presidents, Adams took his duties as president of the Senate very seriously and was rarely absent from the chair. During his first six months in office, Adams's attention to the business of the Senate was, in his wife's words, "close and unremitting." He privately acknowledged that he was unsuited to his task: "My office," he wrote to his son John Quincy in July 1789, "requires rather severe duty, and it is a kind of duty which, if I do not flatter myself too much, is not quite adapted to my character—I mean it is too inactive and mechanical." Even when he believed he could throw light on a matter under consideration, "it cannot be done." To a friend, Adams wrote dismally that his new office left him without "the smallest degree of power to do any good either in the executive, legislative, [or] judicial departments."

He had become, he complained, a "'head of wood,' a mere mechanical tool to wind up the clock." To the Senate, he made his contempt for his new post abundantly clear: "I am Vice President," he said during one contentious debate, and "in this I am nothing."

Adams's frustration was compounded by his conviction that the union of the states, and indeed even American independence, remained in jeopardy and depended upon the wisdom of precedents established at the outset by the new government. He had returned to the United States in a mood of black pessimism about the future of the new nation. His experience as a member of Congress during the Revolution had convinced Adams that the American people lacked sufficient willingness to sacrifice enough of their selfish, private interests for the good of the whole. From Europe, he had observed the confederation's gradual disintegration from the unwillingness of the states to provide funds for the payment of U.S. financial obligations at home or abroad. He had experienced, at first hand, the wiliness and duplicity of European diplomats, and he doubted that the federal government would be able to protect the new nation from their machinations. He had little faith that the federal Constitution, in the absence of broad-based public willingness to sacrifice for the country's good, could provide the basis for long-term government stability and fully expected the Union to be torn apart by the competing interests of the different states and sections.

His frustrations were also personal. At the outset of his tenure, he found that Congress had not yet voted a salary for the vice president and he was virtually without funds. He considered resigning and wrote home to Abigail not to join him until he received some assurance of a decent salary. When Congress finally voted a salary, it was only half of what was to be paid to the president, despite the fact that the vice president found himself under a public obligation to entertain nearly as many guests as Washington.

Adams's tenure as vice president was shaped both by his personal relationship with Washington and by Washington's conception of the vice presidency. Adams and Washington had first met as delegates to the Continental Congress, before Washington assumed command of the Continental Army. He had supported Washington's appointment to that post; later he had been openly critical of the defensive strategy adopted by Washington and of the congressional policy of vesting the commander in chief with extensive powers, and he was privately critical of Washington's generalship. At least some of these criticisms probably came to Washington's attention, but relations between the two men remained cordial while Adams was serving in Congress. Between the time Adams first departed for Europe and their meeting in New York in 1789, Washington and Adams do not seem to have had any contact. Adams was thus not one of Washington's circle of advisors, a group that included Jay, Hamilton, and Madison. Washington seems to have consulted Adams infrequently during the early months of the administration. The evidence of such consultation may simply not exist; the two men were in regular contact and would have had infrequent need to resort to letters. Yet, the silence of the documentary record suggests that Adams had little influence in executive appointments or policy. Even on foreign affairs, a subject about which Adams possessed considerable expertise, Washington does not often seem to have appealed for his advice.

One matter about which Washington did seek Adams's advice, along with that of Hamilton, Madison, and Jay, involved the adoption of formal procedures regulating access to the president. Shortly after arriving in New York, Washington was deluged with invitations and visitors. It soon became obvious that he would have to institute formal measures regulating his social life or else have all his time consumed in receiving and returning visits and attending public and private functions. These, he feared, would not only prevent him from accomplishing public business, but would also diminish the dignity of the presidential office. Adams shared Washington's belief that the new government's success relied, to a large extent, on the respect its officials could command. In his reply to Washington, Adams wrote that "neither Dignity, nor Authority, can be Supported in human Minds collected into nations or any great numbers without a Splendor and Majisty, in Some degree, proportioned to them."

Adams approved of Washington's proposal to insulate the presidency from the public and supported his proposal to institute regular levees at which to receive visitors. But Adams went even further than Washington in his efforts to elevate the presidency in the public mind, proposing to endow the president and other high federal officials with formal titles reminiscent of the forms and usages of monarchical governments. The president, Adams maintained, should be referred to as His Excellency or by some other appropriate title and that relations between the Senate and the president should be conducted with the same formality that characterized relations between the House of Lords and the British monarch. Adams first made these proposals in the Senate on April 23, 1789, before Washington arrived in New York (the nation's capital at that time), when the Senate was considering arrangements for Washington's inauguration; the issue was referred to a committee and discussed inconclusively on the floor until May 1, when debate began in earnest.

Most of what is known about this debate, as well as others that occurred in the Senate during the First Congress, comes from the private diary of William Maclay, a senator from Pennsylvania. Maclay had supported Adams for vice president, but the debate over titles made him one of Adam's harshest critics: He took the lead in attacking Adams's proposals on the grounds that they were repugnant to the principles of republican government. "We have lately had a hard struggle for our liberty against Kingly Authority," Maclay reminded Adams, and "everything related to that Species of Government is odious to the People." At this, Maclay wrote, Adams "expressed the greatest Surprize, that any thing should be objected to on account of its being taken from the Practise of that Government under which we had lived so long and so happily formerly, that he was for a dignifyed and respectable Government, and as far as he knew that sentiments of People they thought as he did. That for his part he was one of the first in the late

Contest and *if he could have thought of this, he never would have drawn his Sword.*" Maclay replied that "there had been a Revolution in the Sentiments of the People, respecting Government, equally great as that which had happened in the Government itself," and that the people now abhorred "all the trappings and Splendor of Royalty."

Maclay and other plain republicans may have regarded the idea of endowing government officials with titles with varying degrees of amusement or scorn, but to Adams the matter involved immutable precedents that ought not be established without thoughtful consideration. To his opponents, Adams insisted that titles were essential to the successful administration of the government: "You are against Titles," he said, "but there are no People in the World so much in favour of Titles as the People of America and the Government never will be properly administered, until they are adopted in the fullest manner." Debate over the question lasted until May 14.

Ultimately, the Senate rejected Adams's proposals altogether. The decision was a defeat for Adams, but it also heightened concerns, raised by some readers of Adams's *Defense of the Constitutions,* that the vice president had abandoned his former republicanism and favored the establishment of an American monarchy and a hereditary aristocracy. Thomas Jefferson, commenting about the titles controversy to James Madison, wrote that it confirmed Benjamin Franklin's assessment of Adams: "always an honest man, often a great one, but sometimes absolutely mad." Reaction in the press was uniformly hostile. Federalists who only a short time before had supported Adams's election began to view the vice president as a political liability who might bring the new government into popular disrepute.

The controversy seems to have cast a shadow over the relationship between the president and the vice president. Washington offered Adams no support during the titles debate, writing later that "the question was moved before I arrived, without any privity or knowledge of it on my part, and urged after I was apprized of it contrary to my opinion; for I foresaw and predicted the reception it has met with, and the use that would be made of it by the adversaries of the government." Frustrated by the storm of criticism, Adams apparently made uncomplimentary remarks in private about Washington, implying hat it was the president, rather than himself, who was fond of aristocratic display. Some of these intemperate remarks may have made their way to Washington's ears, and he was particularly sensitive to charges that he was conducting himself like a republican monarch. Washington's official coolness toward Adams may also have been prompted by concerns that the titles controversy had given critics of the new government fresh reasons for opposing the measures of the administration. A close friend and political confidant, David Stuart, reported to Washington that the debate over titles had rendered Adams "unpopular in the extreme" and "highly odious" in Virginia. Stuart was certain that Adams would "never get a vote from this State again."

Washington's decision not to consult with the vice president did nothing to diminish Adams's determination to support the establishment of a strong executive branch. During Adams's first term as vice president, the Senate adopted legislation creating the executive departments, establishing the foreign service, and fixing the permanent location of the nation's capital; the Senate also adopted a series of controversial measures proposed by Secretary of the Treasury Alexander Hamilton establishing tariffs, providing for the funding of the national debt and the assumption of the Revolutionary debts of the states, as well as creating a national bank and a federal excise tax. Although he remained silent during most of the debates over these measures, Adams was called upon repeatedly to use his tie-breaking vote to push legislation through the Senate. In every case, Adams supported vesting the president with broad authority and backed the measures for ordering American finance rec-

ommended by Hamilton. In all, Adams cast fifteen tie-breaking votes during the First Congress alone; five of these votes were cast in the debate over the location of the nation's capital and three in the debate over funding the national debt. During his eight years in office, Adams cast his tie-breaking vote more than any subsequent vice president.

Adams's first opportunity to determine a question in the Senate by tie-breaking vote came in the summer of 1789 on the question of whether the Senate would acknowledge a presidential power to remove, without the consent of that body, officeholders who had been previously confirmed by the Senate. The question was raised in debate over a provision of the bill establishing the department of state. To senators nervous about the accumulation of power in the hands of the president, granting him the power to remove appointees at will threatened to unhinge the balance of power between the branches of government. Adams regarded this power as essential to executive branch operations and believed that opponents were engaged in a transparent attempt to extend the Senate's authority at the president's expense. Although he remained silent during formal debate, between sessions he drew members aside, trying to persuade them to vote in favor of acknowledging the president's power to remove. When the question was called on July 16, 1789, he had enough votes. The six members from south of the Potomac, as well as Maclay, Johnson of Connecticut, and the two senators from New Hampshire, voted against admitting the power; the remaining ten voted for it. With the Senate divided 10–10, Adams cast the deciding vote in favor of acknowledging the president's authority to remove his subordinates at will. Adams later noted that this vote, among all those he cast as vice-president gave him the most pleasure, but the pleasure came at considerable political expense. His growing number of enemies accused him of using the vote to build up the power of the presidency merely because he hoped to inherit the job from Washington.

Criticism of Adams's conduct as president of the Senate continued in the press without pause through the fall recess of 1789 and into 1790. In addition to continuing accusations that he favored the establishment of an American monarchy, opponents charged that he constantly interfered in Senate debates. Adams denied the charge, asserting that he had spoken at length only once, on the issue of the removal power, and that he did not wish to involve himself in any future debate. The attacks disturbed Adams so deeply that he considered resigning, suggesting to his friend John Trumbull in March 1790 that his personal unpopularity might endanger the government, particularly if Washington died or resigned the presidency, leaving the office in his hands.

Whether Adams actually came close to resigning the vice presidency in spring 1790 is not known, but the prospect that he would succeed to the presidency by Washington's death became a real possibility a few weeks later. In the spring of 1790, Washington contracted a case of influenza. The illness apparently developed into pneumonia; Washington's condition deteriorated quickly between May 12 and May 15, and by the evening of the fifteenth his doctors were convinced that Washington was dying. His fever was very high and he was coughing blood. Abigail Adams, who seems to have been present, recorded that early in the evening Washington "was Seazd with Hicups & rattling in the throat so that Mrs Washington left his room thinking him dying." For a few hours, it was expected that Adams would soon become president, but by late evening the crisis had passed and Washington began to recover. By the end of May, he was well enough to resume his duties.

Fortunately for the country, this episode was brief and occurred at a time when national affairs were relatively quiet. The country was spared a constitutional crisis, but the incident nonetheless set important precedents. During the weeks that Washington was unable to perform his duties, the executive department heads continued to manage their business without significant direction. The immediate business of the president's office was handled by William Jackson, one of Washington's private secretaries. Adams was not called upon, and no evidence has been found to indicate that anyone in the administration or in Congress suggested turning the responsibilities of the presidency over to him—particularly while the Senate was still in session. But the possibility of an invalid president had apparently occurred to some members of Congress. Earlier in the spring, when Washington's lingering illness began to raise comment and concern, Georgia Congressman Abraham Baldwin had written that:

> Our great and good man has been unwell again this spring. . . . If his health should not get confirmed soon, we must send him out to mount Vernon to farm a-while, and let the Vice manage here; his habits require so much exercise, and he is so fond of his plantation, that I have no doubt it would soon restore him.

This situation, ultimately, did not arise, and the vice president's role in the case of the president's long-term incapacity—a matter that would come up again in the nineteenth century but that was not resolved until recently—remained undetermined during the remainder of Adams's tenure.

After Congress recessed in August 1790, Adams devoted himself to writing a series of essays on politics, entitled "Discourses on Davila," which were published serially in the *Gazette of the United States*. The essays, which constitute one of Adams's most important political works, were constructed as a series of commentaries on the work of Henrico Caterino Davila, an Italian who had been involved in the French civil wars of the sixteenth century and wrote a history of the events. By comparing the civil wars with the French Revolution, Adams intended to demonstrate that the contemporary revolution, like its predecessor, was doomed to failure because neither revolution sought to establish a truly balanced government like the one that people of the United States enjoyed under the federal Constitution. Adams also sought to refute the ideas of universal equality and human perfectibility upon which the French Revolution was based and to justify his own position in favor of titles, ceremonies, and formalities.

Adams based his *Discourses on Davila* on the argument that man was everywhere and at all times motivated mainly by a desire for distinction "to be observed, considered, esteemed, praised, beloved, and admired by his fellows." This was the motive, Adams argued, behind the accumulation of wealth and the pursuit of political and social authority and was, in fact, the basis for most of the great achievements of human history. By attempting to abolish distinctions between individuals and establish government on the false idea of universal equality, Adams contended, the French revolutionaries were stifling the most natural and vital of human desires. In a properly ordered society, the desire for public acclaim should be "gratified and encouraged, and arranged on the side of virtue." Rather than frustrate the passion for distinction, then, governments should channel men's efforts to achieve superiority into useful pursuits by rewarding men of merit and accomplishment with titles and other honors. Without distinctions to award, governments would be despised, and men would seek acclaim in other spheres. Ultimately, they would overthrow the government and replace it with one that recognized and rewarded superiority.

Public reaction to Adams's *Discourses on Davila* was hostile, as he apparently expected. Opponents denounced him as a friend to monarchy and an enemy of the rights of man and the principles of American Revolution. Critics, some of whom called Adams the "Duke of Braintree," charged that he had been seduced by aristocratic corruption during his years in Europe and converted into a reactionary. John Fenno, the editor of the *Gazette of the United States,* found himself under a hail of criticism for printing the essays and decided to stop publishing the series. This put an end to Adams's efforts to present his political ideas for public discussion for the remainder of his vice presidency.

Although Adams had made himself a focus of controversy during his first term, Federalist leaders were content to support his reelection in 1792. His critical votes for administration measures had earned him the grudging support of Hamilton, who was also determined to defeat George Clinton, an old political opponent proposed by the emerging Republican opposition as an alternative to Adams. Clinton had the support of New York, Virginia, and North Carolina; Adams could expect the support of New England and solidly federalist South Carolina. The election hinged on the vote of the Middle States, most important of which was Pennsylvania, where the Republican opposition was well organized and active in promoting Clinton's election. Under these circumstances, Hamilton urged Adams, who had withdrawn to his farm in Quincy, to return to Philadelphia. Adams, who was determined to avoid the appearance of campaigning for office, refused. Hamilton's concern increased when he learned that Republican leaders were considering dropping Clinton as their candidate in favor of Aaron Burr. He implored Adams to come to Philadelphia immediately, but the vice president was unmoved.

The burden of securing Adams's reelection fell largely to Hamilton and his associates. When the electoral votes were counted in February 1793, Washington was reelected by a unanimous vote; Adams was reelected vice president with seventy-seven electoral votes. Clinton received fifty electoral votes, including all of those from New York, Virginia, North Carolina, and Georgia, and one from Pennsylvania. Jefferson received the four votes of Kentucky, and Aaron Burr received one vote from South Carolina. Adams received all the rest, including all the votes of New England, New Jersey, Delaware, and Maryland; fourteen of fifteen from Pennsylvania; and seven of eight from South Carolina.*

During his second term as vice president, Adams conducted himself with caution and circumspection, avoiding the kinds of controversies that had embroiled his first term. In the process, he isolated himself from partisan politics at the very moment when the national government was dividing into Federalist and Republican camps. By the beginning of 1793, the national government was deeply divided between Federalists, who supported Hamilton's financial program and American neutrality in the European conflict caused by the French Revolution, and the Republican opposition, which was violently opposed to Hamilton's financial system and sympathetic to the principles of the French Revolution. Although Adams had long since made his views on these matter abundantly clear, he refused to give his opponents further grounds for criticism and declined to make a partisan stand with the Federalists.

The controversy came to a head in 1793, when the new French minister to the United States, Edmond Genêt, sought to invoke the French-American alliance to draw the United States into France's war against Britain. Washington received conflicting advice from his cabinet on dealing with Genêt. Jefferson argued that Genêt should be received as the legitimate representative of France, while Hamilton urged the president to decline to receive him. Both men agreed that American neutrality should be declared, but Jefferson argued that this was the responsibility of Congress, while Hamilton contended that the president was empowered to issue a neutrality proclamation. When Hamilton's subordinate, Tench Coxe, wrote to Adams seeking support for Hamilton's position, Adams refused to become involved, writing that "I have no constitutional vote in it" and adding that "I therefore protest against taking any side

in it or having my name or opinion quoted about it."**

As Adams's reticence increased, the barrage of public criticism of him declined. As early as 1792 opponents of the administration had begun to focus their harshest blows on Hamilton rather than Adams, and by the beginning of 1794 even Washington, formerly immune to public criticism, came under attack. Adams seems to have taken a certain wry pleasure in this change. "I have held the office of libellee-general long enough," he commented; "the burden of it ought to be participated and equalized, according to modern republican principles." Yet, with his determination not to wade into the political struggle, Adams began to feel even more irrelevant. In December 1793, he complained to Abigail that "My country has in its wisdom contrived for me the most insignificant office that was the invention of man . . . or his imagination conceived."

Adams's second term as vice president, was, in many ways, the true twilight of his career. His health, never robust, had been deteriorating since his return from Europe. He had experienced repeated bouts of illness, lost several of his teeth, and suffered increasingly from rheumatic symptoms. Repeated inflammations of the eyes at times rendered him almost blind. Abigail's health was failing as well, and Adams endured frequent separations from her when her ills confined her to the farm in Quincy while he journeyed to Philadelphia to attend the Senate. In 1794, he recorded that his routine during one of these solitary periods consisted of going to the Senate each day, seeing a few friends once a week, and going to church on Sundays. For amusement and intellectual stimulation, he turned increasingly to his books, although after the hostile reception of his *Discourses on Davila,* he no longer sought to express his political ideas in the public press. Instead, he became increasingly eccentric and

---

*Editor's note: See George Clinton for further explanation of this election.

**Editor's note: See George Clinton for further explanation of the Genêt Affair.

reclusive and also suffered from bouts of depression, during which he tended to be particularly gloomy about the future of the country.

Adams's private pessimism about the future of the nation did not diminish his ambition to succeed Washington as president. Adams regarded his succession to the presidency as natural, due to him by seniority and long service in the second post. When he had assumed the presidency, Washington seems to have regarded the vice president as his natural successor, but as the election of 1796 approached, he studiously avoided endorsing any of the potential candidates. Thomas Jefferson was the candidate of the Republicans and Adams's principal competitor, but neither Adams nor Jefferson actively campaigned for the office. The Republicans supported Aaron Burr for the vice presidency. Federalist leaders settled on Thomas Pinckney of South Carolina for vice president, but some, including Hamilton, worked behind the scenes to secure Pinckney's election as president by making sure that he received the second votes of electors from all sections. Some southern electors could be expected to vote for Pinckney and Jefferson and thus deliver the presidency to the South Carolinian and leave Adams with the vice presidency. This possibility occurred to Adams's supporters in New England, and some of them cast their second votes for candidates other than Pinckney. When the ballots were counted, Adams received seventy-one electoral votes, while Jefferson received sixty-eight, Pinckney fifty-nine, and Burr thirty. Adams was thus elected president by only three electoral votes.

Adams was inaugurated as president on March 4, 1797. By the time Adams assumed the presidency, relations with France had reached their lowest point since the Revolution. The French government, infuriated by Jay's Treaty and the recall of James Monroe as minister, had issued decrees permitting attacks on American shipping and refused to permit Monroe's successor, Charles C. Pinckney, to remain on French soil. The ensuing diplomatic crisis with France completely dominated Adams's presidency. Although Adams managed to preserve peace with France, the effort ultimately cost him his political career. It also undermined the unity of the Federalist party and delivered the presidency to Adams's Republican opponent in the election of 1800, Thomas Jefferson.

Adams's conduct throughout the crisis in relations with France—and indeed his whole administration—was shaped by the personal, political, and intellectual isolation that had gradually overtaken him during his eight years as vice president. Although his principles were consistently Federalist, Adams had not established himself as a leader of the Federalist Party. The principal members of his cabinet—Secretary of State Timothy Pickering, Secretary of the Treasury Oliver Wolcott, and Secretary of War James McHenry—were retained from the Washington administration and were close political allies of Hamilton, to whom they looked for guidance and leadership. Adams made no effort to cultivate their loyalty to him or to build a loyal following among others in the government. He preferred to make important decisions on his own, and his failure to consult with his cabinet or other members of the government often made his decisions appear erratic and impulsive. This tendency, combined with his touchiness and vanity, alienated him from the members of his own party and led ultimately to his political downfall.

Shortly after taking office, Adams dispatched a special commission to France to reestablish cordial relations. The commission quickly ran into difficulty: French foreign minister Talleyrand saw that he could take advantage of the crisis in relations between the two countries to embarrass the Adams administration, thus helping the American friends of France in the Republican Party. He consequently sent three unofficial agents to demand payments from the commissioners before beginning negotiations. When the attempts by Talleyrand's agents (dubbed X, Y, and Z) to extort these bribes from the commissioners became known in the United States, the public was outraged. Adams, with widespread public support, announced that he would not send another minister to France without assurances that he would be received with courtesy and began preparations for war.* Congress declared the existing treaties with France void and ordered the construction of new ships for the navy and the establishment of a large provisional army. Encounters between French and American warships off the American coast and in the Caribbean, including several full-scale engagements, pushed the United States and France to the brink of war.

Having provoked the crisis, Talleyrand was prepared to appear conciliatory, by stages, in order to divide the Federalist Party between advocates of peace and war. In trying to preserve peace, Adams fell victim to this strategy. In the fall of 1798, Adams embraced reports that the French were prepared to renew negotiations. Members of the cabinet, however, argued against sending another minister to France without assurances that he would be received with honor. Adams initially agreed, but when he learned in February 1799 that the French had retracted their maritime decrees, he decided to nominate William Vans Murray as minister to France. When this decision encountered hostility in the Senate, Adams proposed sending a peace commission to France, of which Murray would be a member, as soon as the French indicated a willingness to receive them. The Senate grudgingly approved the plan, but many Federalists believed that Adams's efforts to avoid war only invited further national humiliation. Pickering, Wolcott, and McHenry privately blamed Adams for dividing the Federalist Party, arguing that this could only benefit the French and their American friends in the Republican Party. Within the government, they worked to prevent the departure of the commissioners, contending for months that the French had not provided adequate assurances that they would be received with respect.

Adams unwittingly obliged his opponents by retiring to Quincy for several months, conducting public business by correspondence, and deferring many important decisions to cabinet members. Federalist leaders, including Hamilton, met with Adams when he returned to the capital in October, imploring him to delay the mission indefinitely. Unmoved, Adams ordered the commissioners to depart for Europe. "We have succeeded," Talleyrand boasted in a confidential report to his superiors, "in dividing the party of Mr. Adams himself."

The commission opened negotiations with the French in April 1800, but the talks proceeded at a frustratingly slow pace. Talleyrand was not inclined to make Adams a hero by allowing the commissioners to return home quickly with a treaty meeting all or even most of the American demands. Instead of a definitive treaty, the two sides ultimately agreed to a modest convention, signed on October 3, 1800. In it, the parties agreed to return captured naval vessels and all captured property not yet condemned, and they effectively agreed to dissolve the alliance signed in 1778, as well as the consular convention of 1788. The new convention renewed the maritime principle of the treaty of 1778, discarded by the French in their campaign against American shipping, that free ships make free goods. In this sense the convention was a diplomatic success for the Adams administration, but it came too late to save Adams's political career.

Federalist leaders meeting in May 1800 had decided to support Adams's reelection and chose Charles C. Pinckney as their candidate for vice president. Despite their hostility to Adams, Hamilton and his associates realized that supporting a war candidate would divide the party in the election and ensure the victory of Jefferson. Hamilton's reluctant support of Adams's reelection soon turned to open hostility, however, and in the closing weeks of the campaign he made a savage attack on Adams in the press that all but ensured Federalist defeat. While the Federalists quarreled, Republicans, united behind the candidacy of Thomas Jeffer-

*Editor's note: See Elbridge Gerry for further explanation of the XYZ Affair.

son, staged a well-organized and effective campaign. When the electoral votes were counted. Jefferson and the Republican vice presidential candidate, Aaron Burr, received seventy-three votes each; Adams received sixty-five, and Pinckney sixty-four. John Jay received one vote. Adams retained the support of New England, New Jersey, and Delaware, as well as five of ten votes from Maryland, seven of fifteen from Pennsylvania, and four of twelve North Carolina. The tie between Jefferson and Burr threw the election into the House of Representatives, where Jefferson was ultimately elected.

Adams's defeat ended a career in public service that had lasted some twenty-six years. He lived for more than twenty-five more years but never again held public office. In the first years of his retirement, Adams was blamed for the defeat of the Federalists by the Hamilton wing of the party, although he continued to enjoy the esteem of many moderate New England Federalists. Although out of office, he maintained a keen interest in politics and political philosophy untinged by partisanship. After Jefferson left the presidency, the two old friends were reconciled and engaged in a lively correspondence that lasted until both men died. Abigail Adams died on October 28, 1818, depriving Adams of his closest friend. John Adams lived long enough to see his eldest son, John Quincy, elected president in 1824. John Adams's own death occurred on July 4, 1826, just a few hours after the death of Thomas Jefferson.

REFERENCES

James Grant, *John Adams: Party of One* (New York: Farrar, Straus, and Giroux, 2005); John P. Diggins, *John Adams* (New York: Times Books, 2003); David McCullough, *John Adams* (New York: Simon & Schuster, 2000); Page Smith, *John Adams,* 2 vols. (Garden City, N.Y.: Doubleday & Co., 1963); John Ferling, *John Adams: A Life* (Knoxville, Tenn.: University of Tennessee Press, 1992); Peter Shaw, *The Character of John Adams* (Chapel Hill, N.C.: University of North Carolina Press, 1976); Joseph J. Ellis, *Passionate Sage: The Character and Legacy of John Adams* (New York: W.W. Norton & Co., 1993); Stanley Elkins and Eric McKitrick, *The Age of Federalism* (New York: Oxford University Press, 1993); Alexander DeConde, *The Quasi-War: The Politics and Diplomacy of the Undeclared War with France, 1797–1801* (New York: Charles Scribner's Sons, 1966); Edmund S. Morgan, *The Meaning of Independence: John Adams, George Washington, Thomas Jefferson* (Charlottesville, Va.: University of Virginia Press, 1976); Gordon S. Wood, *The Creation of the American Republic, 1776–1787* (Chapel Hill, N.C.: University of North Carolina Press, 1969); *The Diary and Autobiography of John Adams,* Lyman H. Butterfield et al., eds., 4 vols. (Cambridge, Mass.: Harvard University Press, 1961); *The Papers of John Adams,* Robert J. Taylor et al., eds., 6 volumes to date (Cambridge, Mass.: Harvard University Press, 1977–); *Adams Family Correspondence,* Lyman H. Butterfield et al., eds., 7 volumes to date (Cambridge, Mass.: Harvard University Press, 1963–); *New Letters of Abigail Adams, 1788–1801,* Stewart Mitchell, ed. (Boston: Houghton Mifflin, 1947); *The Adams-Jefferson Letters,* Lester J. Cappon, ed. (Chapel Hill, N.C.: University of North Carolina Press, 1959); *The Diary of William Maclay and Other Notes on Senate Debates,* Kenneth R. Bowling and Helen E. Veit, eds. (Baltimore, Md.: Johns Hopkins University Press, 1988); *The Papers of George Washington,* W. W. Abbot et al., eds., multiple vols. to date (Charlottesville, Va.: University of Virginia Press, 1983–).

JACK D. WARREN is executive director of the Society of Cincinnati and was formerly assistant editor of *The Papers of George Washington* and a member of the faculty of the University of Virginia. He specializes in politics in the Federalist era and is the co-author of *A Covenanted People: The Religious Tradition and the Origins of American Constitutionalism* (Providence, R.I., 1987) and the author of several articles on the Early Republic.

THOMAS JEFFERSON (1743–1826)
Vice President, 1797–1801
(President John Adams)

THOMAS JEFFERSON
(Library of Congress)

By Eugene R. Sheridan

A true Renaissance man, Thomas Jefferson combined the skills of an astute political leader with the vision of a dazzling intellectual virtuoso to a degree that is unsurpassed in American history. In the course of four critical decades of public service, during which he played a key role in the disruption of the First British Empire and the emergence of the new American nation, Jefferson distinguished himself as a member of the Continental Congress, Virginia legislators and governor, minister to France, secretary of state, Republican Party leader, vice president, and president. As a political philosopher, he eloquently proclaimed in the Declaration of Independence the core values of liberty, equality, and natural rights that constitute the heart of the American experiment in self-government. As the author of the epochal Virginia Statute for Religious Freedom, he set forth the pattern of complete religious liberty through strict separation of church and state that eventually became standard throughout the United States. As a leading man of science, he wrote a pioneering work in natural history, *Notes on the State of Virginia,* was a proficient archaeologist and inventor, and served for almost two decades as president of the nation's most prestigious scientific institution, the American Philosophical Society. As the most accomplished American architect of his time, his designs for his home at Monticello, the Virginia state capitol, and the University of Virginia helped to inspire the revival of classical architecture in the new republic. As an educator, he was a strong champion of public education and the main founder of the University of Virginia. As a devoted bibliophile and accomplished linguist, he amassed an extraordinarily varied library of almost 7,000 volumes that served as the nucleus of the new Library of Congress after the destruction of the old one during the British attack on Washington in 1814. Finally, he was the first person in American history to engage in one of the key developments in modern biblical criticism, the quest for the historic Jesus. In view of this extraordinary record of accomplishment, President John F. Kennedy spoke only half in jest when he hailed a group of Nobel laureates in various fields as the "most extraordinary collection of talents that has ever gathered together at the White House, with the possible exception of when Thomas Jefferson dined alone."

The central theme of Jefferson's career was his fervent commitment to the establishment of a lasting republican social and political order in the United States. Jeffersonian republicanism was a dynamic blend of Lockean liberalism and civic humanism that rejected all vestiges of monarchy and hereditary privilege and sought to promote liberty, advance enlightenment, and unleash the creative energies of the American people within the framework of limited government, popular sovereignty, and an agrarian society guided by a natural aristocracy based on virtue and merit rather the birth and wealth. To ensure that government respected the natural rights of man and guaranteed to free men the fruits of their labor, Jefferson insisted that its powers must be sharply limited and made strictly accountable to the people through written constitutions, institutional checks and balances, and frequent elections. In Jefferson's view, the central theme of history was the perpetual struggle between power and liberty, and he rarely wavered in his conviction that the government's powers had to be limited in order to make people's liberties secure. That Jefferson never extended liberty and natural rights to include African Americans exemplified one of the central paradoxes of American history.

In the end, however, Jefferson believed that the survival of republicanism in the United States depended more on the character of its people than the structure of the U.S. government. In his opinion, a republic could only survive among a virtuous people who were independent, frugal, temperate, industrious, ready to fight for their liberty, and willing when necessary to subordinate their private interests to the greater public good. Convinced that these qualities were best exemplified by farmers and planters, whose ownership of land endowed them with the personal independence he considered absolutely essential for politically responsible citizenship in a republican polity, he hoped to preserve agrarian dominance of American society indefinitely by seeking foreign markets to absorb surplus agricultural production and by supporting the westward advance of American settlement. By thus inhibiting the development of manufacturing and urbanization, which he feared would undermine republican virtue by creating increasing webs of economic and social dependence among the American people, Jefferson hoped that expansion across space would delay the corruption over time to which, according to his reading of history, republics were invariably subject.

Jefferson was born into a Virginia gentry family on April 13, 1743, the eldest son and the third of eight surviving children. He attended the College of William and Mary from 1760 to 1762 and then studied law for five years with

George Wyth. Until his retirement from the legal profession in 1775, Jefferson enjoyed a successful legal practice in Virginia. Among other things, this helped him to contract an advantageous marriage in 1772 with a young widow, Martha Wales Skelton, who before her untimely death ten years later bore him six children, only two of whom, Martha and Mary, reached adulthood. Between what he inherited from his father and acquired through marriage, Jefferson was one of the wealthiest Virginians of his time, owning about 10,000 acres of land and 150 slaves, with the centerpiece of his estate being the elegant Palladian villa of Monticello, set high atop a 987-feet-high mountain overlooking the town of Charlottesville. It was the greatest irony of Jefferson's life that his career as a defender of republican liberty was based upon an economic system in which his own freedom and prosperity depended upon depriving black people of theirs. To add personal irony, Jefferson likely had a long-term sexual relationship with one of his slaves Sally Hemings, who was also his wife's half sister (Jefferson's father-in-law was Sally's father and her mother was a slave). Hemings lived both at Monticello and with Jefferson in Paris between 1787 and 1789. Modern DNA testing has led to the conclusion that Jefferson fathered Hemings's six children, whom he later freed—unlike almost all of his other slaves, including Sally herself, who remained his property.

Jefferson's belief that British efforts to reorganize the Empire after 1763 were part of a systematic conspiracy to destroy American liberties launched a political career that lasted for forty years and left a decisive mark on American history. He entered the House of Burgesses in 1769 and within a few years emerged as a strong proponent of unified colonial resistance to British imperialism. In 1774, he placed himself in the vanguard of the radical movement with the publication of *A Summary View of the Rights of British America,* a pamphlet that denied parliamentary authority over the colonies and argued that the colonies were only bound to Britain by their allegiance to the king. As a member of the Continental Congress during the final throes of the imperial crisis in 1775–1776, he made his greatest contribution to the revolutionary cause through his authorship of one of the fundamental charters of American freedom, the Declaration of Independence.

After the congressional decision for independence, Jefferson turned his attention to the task of laying secure foundation for the emerging republican order in the new nation. As a member of the Virginia House of Delegates from 1776 to 1779, he sought with only partial success to replace the traditional aristocracy of birth and wealth in his native state with a natural aristocracy of virtue and merit to guide an enlightened citizenry. In consequence of the role he played in revising the entire structure of Virginia law so as to rid it of all vestiges of monarchy and make it compatible with republican principles, Jefferson served as governor of Virginia from 1779 to 1781. Though a capable administrator, he dealt ineffectually with two British invasion of the state in 1781, and the resultant criticism led him to retire to private life in June of that year.

Jefferson returned to public service in reaction to the tragic death of his wife in 1782, which shattered his dream of spending the rest of his life at Monticello pursuing his scientific interests. Before this devastating loss, however, he had taken advantage of his first retirement from public life to write the manuscript of his first book, *Notes on the State of Virginia,* an eloquently written essay on natural history, published in 1785, in which he vigorously disputed the contention of European naturalists that human, animal, and plant life had degenerated in America because of the New World's allegedly insalubrious climate. Jefferson also argued that racial hierarchy was "natural": Native Americans could be civilized through education, but African American were naturally inferior and subordinate.

Resuming his legislative career on the national level, Jefferson served in the Confederation Congress from 1783 to 1784. During this period he made a profound contribution to

American political and social development with a report on territorial government whose basic principles were incorporated into the more celebrated Northwest Ordinance of 1787. By providing procedures for the admission of new states into the Union on the basis of equality with the original thirteen, Jefferson sought to promote rapid settlement of the American West by farmers in order to preserve and extend the agrarian social base that he regarded as necessary for the success of the American experiment in republicanism.

Jefferson's second term in Congress was followed by his entry into diplomatic service. Between 1784 and 1789 he served Congress in Paris, first as a commissioner to negotiate commercial treaties with various European powers and then as American minister to France. This experience convinced him that the United States needed a stronger central government to achieve its foreign policy objectives, so he generally supported the Constitution of 1787; however, he criticized its lack of a bill of rights and its failure to limit the number of presidential terms. His criticisms played a small part in convincing Federalists to remedy the former omission. He left France in the fall of 1789, convinced that a new day of liberty was dawning in Europe and that France was the only nation on which the United States could rely as an effective counterweight to Britain. Even though he hoped to return to his ministerial post in Paris, he reluctantly agreed in 1790 to serve instead as George Washington's first secretary of state.

During Jefferson's tenure as secretary of state from 1790 to 1793, he became involved in a titanic struggle with Secretary of the Treasury Alexander Hamilton over the future of the American republic. In the great trinity of Hamiltonian finance—funding, assumption, and the national bank—Jefferson eventually detected a vast system of special privilege that he believed enriched the few at the expense of the many, encouraged an unhealthy speculative spirit among the people, upset the balance of property, and corrupted the national legislature. In the Hamiltonian call for federal encouragement of a wide range of U.S. manufacturing, Jefferson perceived a grave threat to the agrarian social order he considered essential for the health of American republicanism. In the Hamiltonian insistence on loose construction of the Constitution, Jefferson espied a source of constitutional degeneration that was designed to aggrandize the powers of the central government at the expense of the states' authority and the people's liberty. In the Hamiltonian support of a pro-British foreign policy, Jefferson perceived an effort to align the United States with the forces of monarchy and aristocracy in their conflict with revolutionary France. Viewing these policies cumulatively, Jefferson detected nothing less than a concerted Federalist effort to establish a monarchical form of government in the United States along British lines.

Convinced that Federalist centralism was a mortal threat to his vision of the United States as a virtuous agrarian republic, Jefferson joined James Madison in creating the Republican Party as an effective counterweight to Federalism. After collaborating in 1791 to establish the *National Gazette* in Philadelphia to promote the Republican cause, the two Virginians followed a natural division of labor with respect to the emerging opposition: While Madison organized Republicans in the House of Representatives and articulated their position in the columns of the *National Gazette,* Jefferson opposed Hamilton in the cabinet and in a series of remarkable private communications in which he sought to persuade President Washington that the treasury secretary and his policies were undermining American republicanism. Jefferson's efforts to mobilize opposition against Hamiltonian Federalism reached a climax early in 1793, when he secretly engineered an abortive attempt by capital Republicans to drive Hamilton from office by censuring his management of the Treasury. Although thereafter Jefferson continued to be involved in formulating Republican Party strategy, he felt so ambivalent about acting as a party leader that he retired from office on the final day of 1793, determined to remain a private citizen for the rest of his life.

The imperatives of party politics drew a reluctant Jefferson back into the political arena only three years after beginning what he fondly hoped would be a lifelong period of retirement at Monticello. Frustrated by Congress's failure to enact the program of commercial retaliation against Britain he had recommended shortly before leaving office as secretary of state, Jefferson then lost confidence in the president after Washington denounced the Democratic Republican Societies in the wake of the Whiskey Rebellion and approved the Jay Treaty, an agreement that Jefferson viewed as a surrender of vital American national interests to the British. Unable to persuade Madison to stand as Republican candidate for president, Jefferson reluctantly allowed Republicans to cast him in this role after Washington announced that he would not serve a third term. Jefferson took no active part in the campaign and actually hoped that the moderate Federalist John Adams would prevail, in large part because the francophile Jefferson was disinclined to serve as president when American relations with France were rapidly deteriorating in the wake of French dissatisfaction with the Jay Treaty. Jefferson received the second-highest number of electoral votes after Adams, and because at that time electors did not cast separate votes for president and vice president, the Virginia leader won the latter office.

Jefferson was the first vice president in American history to preside over a Senate dominated by an opposing party. From 1797 to 1801, Federalists held solid majorities in the Senate, and if Jefferson viewed Federalists as covert monarchist conspirators, they regarded him as an unregenerate Jacobin fanatic who threatened their vision of the United States as an orderly, centralized, hierarchical republic. Federalists made no secret of their contempt for Jefferson, and it was not unusual for Federalist senators to make sharp verbal attacks on the Virginia leader even as he presided over the Senate. As a result of this situation, Jefferson as vice president carefully confined himself to serving as the Senate's presiding officer and made no official effort to use this office to shape that body's legislative agenda.

Federalist control of the Senate accounts in no small measure for Jefferson's pattern of attendance as vice president. Except for the first session of the Fifth Congress, which met from May 15 to July 10, 1797, Jefferson arrived in the Senate several weeks after the legislative opened, and apart from the first session of the Sixth Congress, which met from December 2, 1799, to May 14, 1800, he left a few days before it closed. In response to public criticism that he was thereby neglecting his public duty, Jefferson contended that there was no need for him to attend during the first three weeks of the legislative session because the Senate rarely considered any bills during that time. At the same time he argued that it was essential for him to leave early and enable the Senate to choose a president pro tempore because under the Presidential Succession Act of 1792 that official stood next in line for the presidency after the vice president. Although these factors were undoubtedly operative, it also seems clear that Jefferson deliberately delayed his arrival at the beginning of each legislative session so that he did not have to affix his signature as vice president to the inevitably laudatory replies that the Federalist-dominated Senate made to President Adams's opening addresses to Congress. He had fallen into this trap during the emergency legislative session called by Adams during the summer of 1797 but thereafter avoided committing the same political error.

Jefferson was involved in two dramatic episodes in senatorial history during his tenure as vice president. In the first, he presided over the Senate trial of William Blount, a Republican senator for Tennessee who had been expelled in 1797 for conspiring to establish British control over the Spanish provinces of Louisiana and West Florida and then had been impeached by the House. Jefferson, who at this point in his career was fearful of impeachment as a tool that

Federalists might abuse in the heat of partisan warfare with their Republican adversaries, privately advised Senators Henry Tazewell of Virginia and Samuel Livermore of New Hampshire that it would be preferable to have Blount tried by a jury. Jefferson's advice was disregarded, but in the end he was mollified by the Senate's decision that senators were unimpeachable civil officials.

In addition to presiding over the first impeachment trial in Senate history, Jefferson was apparently instrumental in frustrating a Federalist effort to try the noted Republican editor, William Duane, for contempt of the Senate. In 1800, Federalist senators sought to try Duane for contempt in retaliation for his unauthorized publication in the Philadelphia *Aurora* of a Senate bill that provided for the creation of a special commission to rule on the validity of disputed presidential election votes and for his depiction of it as a blatant partisan maneuver to ensure Federalist success in the forthcoming national election. With Jefferson's covert support, Duane refused to appear before the Senate for trial because of that body's refusal to allow his counsel to question its jurisdiction in this case. Changing tack, the Senate then requested President Adams to have Duane prosecuted for seditious libel under the Sedition Act, a maneuver that Jefferson himself deflected after he became president.

Jefferson's most lasting contribution as vice president was the compilation and publication of his *Manual of Parliamentary Practice for the Use of the Senate of the United States*. The orderly conduct of parliamentary business had been a central concern of Jefferson's ever since his early days as a Virginia colonial legislator. Upon taking office as vice president, he was accordingly distressed to encounter what he regarded as the excessively wide latitude the Senate had given to this officer in deciding points of order. As he noted in the introduction to his *Manual*:

> The Senate have accordingly formed some rules for its own government: but these going only to few cases, they have referred to the decision of their President, without debate and without appeal, all questions of order arising either under their own rules, or where they have provided none. This places under the discretion of the President a very extensive field of decision, and one which, irregularly exercised, would have a powerful effect on the proceedings and determinations of the House.

In order to promote the orderly conduct of business in the Senate and prevent its presiding officer from acting arbitrarily, Jefferson decided to prepare a body of parliamentary precedents for the upper house to draw upon in transacting its work. To this end he compiled a collection of precedents on fifty-three points of parliamentary procedure from the history of the British Parliament, the "model which we have all studied," as he noted in the *Manual*, and published the resulting work in February 1801 just before he left office as vice president. Although intended for the Senate, Jefferson's *Manual* was later adopted by the House of Representatives as well, and even today it continues to guide the conduct of business in both houses of Congress.

While presiding over the Senate as vice president, Jefferson emerged as the chief Republican Party leader, a role that had hitherto been played by Madison. After an initial effort to cooperate with President Adams, the leader of the moderate wing of the Federalist Party, circumstances compelled Jefferson to act as the leader of the Republican opposition to the second president. Jefferson and his followers favored a more conciliatory policy toward France than the one pursued by Adams, and they viewed the Alien and Sedition Acts of 1798 as a transparent effort to crush them as a legitimate political opposition. In order to energize Republican opposition to Adams and the Federalists, Jefferson formulated legislative strategy with congressional Republicans, formed intersectional alliances with northern Republicans, and encouraged Republican journalists to keep up a drumbeat of criticism of

Federalist policies. In his most dramatic move of all, he secretly drafted the Kentucky Resolutions of 1798, which denounced the Alien and Sedition Acts as unconstitutional and asserted the right of the states to nullify any law they deemed contrary to the Constitution.

Convinced that Federalist centralism imperiled the survival of republican liberty in the United States, Jefferson unhesitatingly stood as the Republican Party's standard bearer in 1800. In deference to his personal temperament and the electoral customs of the age, Jefferson refrained from campaigning openly for the presidency. However, behind the scenes, he encouraged Republican pamphleteers and journalists to articulate the party's position, circulated Republican campaign tracts, coordinated political strategy with Republican Party organizations, and enunciated a party platform emphasizing the virtues of limited government, states' rights, strict construction of the Constitution, and noninvolvement in European political affairs. After a vicious campaign, in which he was denounced as an atheist, an unworldly philosopher, and a Jacobin fanatic, Jefferson defeated Adams by a margin of seventy-three to sixty-five electoral votes. However, because Jefferson and his running mate, Aaron Burr of New York, received the same number of electoral votes, the election was finally decided in the House of Representatives, which, after thirty-six ballots and in the face of determined Federalist efforts to select Burr, at length declared Jefferson the winner.

Jefferson's two terms in office were a crucial stage in the development of the American presidency. As the first party leader to serve as the country's chief executive, Jefferson adopted an activist popular style of governance to reverse the Federalist centralizing policies he regarded as dangerous to republican liberty. Whereas his two predecessors viewed themselves in effect as republican patriots governing above political parties and through cabinet ministers in pursuit of the common good, Jefferson was the first president to govern through a political party in the interests of the people. By combining the roles of chief executive and Republican Party leader, Jefferson significantly enhanced the power of the presidency by uniting the authority granted to the president by the Constitution with the popular support he derived from his party leadership. However, like Washington and Adams, Jefferson ultimately hoped to eliminate political parties, not to function within the framework of a two-party system. He never accepted the Federalists as a legitimate political opposition, and he long sought to rid America of institutionalized conflict between contending political parties by enticing the Federalist rank and file to embrace the Republican cause. It remained for Andrew Jackson, by combining the roles of president and party leader with an acceptance of the legitimacy of the party system, to complete the transition Jefferson began.

Jefferson enjoyed a triumphal first term as president, aided in no small measure by the restoration of peace in Europe in 1801 after nearly a decade of devastating wars between revolutionary France and its antagonists. During this period, Jefferson's overriding domestic priority was to reverse Federalist centralizing policies by reducing the federal government to its proper constitutional limits and paying off the national debt. To this end, he prevailed upon Congress in 1802 to approve Secretary of the Treasury Albert Gallatin's plan to retire the national debt of $82 million in sixteen years, which also entailed eliminating all internal taxes as well as a number of federal offices and sharply reducing the size of the army, the navy, and the diplomatic corps. Whereas Hamiltonians viewed a national debt as an effective instrument for creating a strong nation-state by attaching public creditors to the central government, Jeffersonians regarded it as the source of a corrupt monied interest that encouraged dangerous speculative habits among, and imposed burdensome taxes on, the agrarian majority. Because of a tremendous upsurge in the volume of foreign trade and thus the payment of import duties, by the time he left office in 1809 Jefferson had effected a substantial reduction in the national debt and generated a surplus in the Treasury. But it was not until the time of Andrew Jackson's administration that the Jeffersonian dream of completely eliminating the national debt was briefly realized.

Despite his wish to avoid foreign entanglements, Jefferson was obliged to face two serious international crises during his first administration. In response to news of increasing Tripolitan aggression against American merchant shipping in the Mediterranean, Jefferson in May 1801 dispatched a naval squadron to protect the nation's growing commerce in that area. There ensued four years of naval warfare with Tripoli that ended in 1805 with a peace treaty by which the Tripolitan government exempted the United States from the payment of the customary tribute to protect American shipping from Barbary piracy. Although Jefferson had long opposed this practice as an affront to national honor, the United States continued to pay annual tribute to the other Barbary states of Algiers, Morocco, and Tunis until 1815.

The war with Tripoli was far overshadowed by the Louisiana Purchase, the crowning achievement of Jefferson's presidency. The Spanish retrocession of Louisiana to Napoleonic France in 1800 threatened to create a revived French empire in the New World that would endanger the United States's vitally important right to navigate the Mississippi and halt the westward sweep of American expansion along the eastern bank of this waterway. In the face of this threat to his vision of a continental "empire of liberty" in North America, Jefferson brought diplomatic pressure to bear on France to leave Louisiana in Spanish hands and at the same time sought to purchase New Orleans and the Floridas to guarantee western settlers the right of navigation on the Mississippi. Owing to diplomatic developments in Europe, however, Napoleon agreed in April 1803 to sell all of Louisiana to the United States for $15 million—a deal that doubled the size of the nation and seemingly secured for ages yet to come Jefferson's vision of the United States as a virtuous agrarian republic.

The frustrations of Jefferson's second term stood in sharp contrast to the successes of his first, largely because of his inability to cope successfully with the challenges to U.S. neutrality stemming from the renewal in 1803 of the momentous struggle for mastery in Europe between Great Britain and France. In domestic affairs Jefferson continued his policy of redirecting the flow of power from the federal government to the states. In addition, in 1807 he prevailed upon Congress to pass legislation implementing the constitutionally authorized ban on U.S. participation in the African slave trade after that year, but he failed to win congressional approval for an imaginative plan to use surplus government revenues to finance a system of internal improvements to cement the bonds of union. Moreover, in a matter that had domestic and diplomatic ramifications, he thwarted a plot by his former vice president, Aaron Burr, to detach the West from the Union and invade Mexico.

Jefferson's very success in reducing the powers of the federal government prevented him from responding effectively to the growing British and French violations of United States neutrality that formed the central theme of his second administration. Although both nations tried to prevent American ships from trading with the other, Great Britain, with its enormous naval power, was by far the worse offender, impressing thousands of seamen on American ships, patrolling American harbors to enforce British neutrality policies, and striving to prevent American trade with the British or French West Indies. After failing to achieve a diplomatic settlement of these Anglo-American differences, Jefferson had to face the issue of peace or war in its starkest form in June 1807, when H.M.S. *Leopard* attacked the American warship *Chesapeake* off Norfolk, Virginia, and removed four alleged British deserters. In the end, however, Jefferson chose economic coercion over war. Lacking credible military or naval power, troubled by the thought that war would impede his effort to pay off the national debt, and convinced that Britain was peculiarly vulnerable to economic pressure because of her dependence on American foodstuffs, Jefferson obtained a series of Embargo Acts from Congress that interdicted all U.S. exports to foreign countries. But the Embargo generated widespread economic hardship and popular resistance at home, while failing to obtain any British or French concession on neutrality issues, and on the eve of Jefferson's departure from office in 1809 it was replaced by the Non-Intercourse Act, which allowed the United States to trade with all nations except Britain and France and set the stage for the War of 1812.

Despite widespread Republican pleas that he serve a third term, Jefferson returned to private life in March 1809, determined to follow Washington's example and thereby help to make the two-term limit on presidents a binding precedent. In one sense, the last seventeen years of Jefferson's life were richly rewarding, marked as they were by the resumption of his rich correspondence with John Adams, the sale of his library to the Library of Congress, the foundation of the University of Virginia, and the continuation of his biblical studies. In another sense, however, these were deeply troubling years for Jefferson for, in addition to plunging deeper and deeper into a debt that was to deprive his family of Monticello after his death, he grew more and more concerned about the threats posed to his vision of the United States as a virtuous agrarian republic by increases in urbanization, manufacturing, speculation, and sectional strife after the War of 1812. However, in the end, optimism prevailed over pessimism, and in his last surviving letter, written only ten days before his death on the fiftieth anniversary of the Declaration of Independence, Jefferson proclaimed his faith that this document would "be to the world, what I believe it will be, (to some parts sooner, to others later, but finally to all,) the signal of arousing men to burst the chains under which monkish ignorance and superstition had persuaded them to bind themselves, and to secure the blessings and security of self-government."

In the years since Eugene Sheridan, the author of this biography of Jefferson, was killed in 1996, historical scholarship on Thomas Jefferson has been shaped in new ways, especially by knowledge about his relationship with his slave Sally Hemings. Jefferson was publicly accused of fathering children with Sally by the journalist James Callender in 1802, but Jefferson never commented publicly or privately. Jefferson's descendants later claimed that Jefferson's nephews Peter and Samuel Carr fathered Hemings's light-skinned children, but Sally Hemings's descendants consistently maintained throughout the nineteenth century that they were related to Thomas Jefferson. In 1998, genetic testing confirmed that Hemings's descendants were related to Jefferson, and the test precluded a link between the Hemings and Carr families. While some groups, notably the Thomas Jefferson Heritage Society, continue to resist the conclusion, most historians and the Thomas Jefferson Foundation now believe that Thomas Jefferson likely fathered Sally Hemings's six children.

The drama and conflict over Jefferson's sexual relationship with Sally Hemings reflect the continuing importance of slavery in the lives and reputations of the founders of the United States. Although Jefferson was brilliant writer and a proselytizer for equality, he was still a slaveholder, and the institution shaped his life. Many slaveholders had close family ties to their slaves because sexual relations between white masters and black slaves were widespread and common. In many ways, the labor provided by Sally Hemings and Jefferson's other slaves allowed him the time and leisure to participate in government and to achieve his important place in the pantheon of American historical figures. Even today, however, many people do not want to recognize the close ties and the oppression that slavery created between whites and blacks—ties with legacies in modern U.S. society.

REFERENCES

Noble Cunningham, *In Pursuit of Reason: The Life of Thomas Jefferson* (Baton Rouge, La.: Louisiana State University Press, 1987); Dumas Malone, *Jefferson* and *His Time,* 6 vols. (Boston: Little Brown, 1948–81); Merrill Peterson, *Thomas Jefferson and the New Nation* (New York: Oxford University Press, 1970); Robert M. Johnstone, Jr., *Jefferson and the Presidency: Leadership in the Young Republic* (Ithaca, N.Y.: Cornell University Press, 1978); *The Papers of Thomas Jefferson,* Julian P. Boyd et al., eds., 26 vols. (Princeton, N.J.: Princeton University Press, 1950–   ); *The Writings of Thomas Jefferson,* Paul L. Ford, ed., 10 vols. (New York: Knickerbocker Press, 1892–99); *Jefferson's Parliamentary Writings,* Wilbur S. Howell, ed. (Princeton, N.J.: Princeton University Press, 1988); Roy Swanstrom, *The United States Senate, 1787–1801* (Washington, D.C.: Government Printing Office, 1985); Stanley Elkins and Eric McKitrick, *The Age of Federalism: The American Republic, 1788–1800* (New York: Oxford University Press, 1993); Henry Adams, *History of the United States during the Administrations of Jefferson and Madison,* 9 vols. (New York: Charles Scribner's Sons, 1889–91); Annette Gordon-Reed, *Thomas Jefferson and Sally Hemmings: An American Controversy* (Charlottesville, Va.: University Press of Virginia, 1997); Joseph J. Ellis, *American Sphinx: The Character of Thomas Jefferson* (New York: Vintage, 1998, reprint); R. B. Bernstein, *Thomas Jefferson* (New York: Oxford University Press, 2003); Joseph J. Ellis, *Founding Brothers: The Revolutionary Generation* (New York: Alfred A. Knopf, 2000); Alan Pell Crawford, *Twilight at Monticello: The Final Years of Thomas Jefferson* (New York: Random House, 2008); Kevin J. Hayes, *The Road to Monticello: The Life and Mind of Thomas Jefferson* (New York: Oxford University Press, 2008); Peter S. Onuf, *The Mind of Thomas Jefferson* (Charlottesville, Va.: University Press of Virginia, 2007); Francis D. Cogliano, *Thomas Jefferson: Reputation and Legacy* (Charlottesville, Va.: University Press of Virginia, 2006); "Thomas Jefferson and Sally Hemmings: A Brief Account." Available online. URL: http://www.monticello.org. Accessed September 22, 2009.

EUGENE R. SHERIDAN was senior associate editor of *The Papers of Thomas Jefferson* and a member of the Princeton University History Department. He was killed in an automobile accident in the spring of 1996 as the first edition of this volume was in preparation. Before coming to Princeton, he was an editorial fellow with the *Adams Family Papers* at the Massachusetts Historical Society and associate editor of *Letters of Delegates to Congress* at the Library of Congress. He was the author of *Lewis Morris, 1671–1746: A Study in Early American Politics* (Syracuse, 1981), coeditor with John Murrin of *Congress at Princeton* (Princeton, 1985), and editor of the *Papers of Lewis Morris, 1698–1746,* 3 vols. (Newark, 1991–93).

SARAH J. PURCELL's biography can be found following the entry on ELBRIDGE GERRY.

AARON BURR (1756–1836)

Vice President, 1801–1805

(President Thomas Jefferson)

AARON BURR
(Library of Congress)

By Mary-Jo Kline

Born on February 6, 1736, in a Presbyterian parsonage in Newark, New Jersey, Aaron Burr, Jr., seemed destined for a life of intellectual and moral leadership. His father was not only pastor of the town's First Presbyterian Church but also president of the fledgling College of New Jersey. His mother, Esther Edwards Burr, was the daughter of Jonathan Edwards, the famed new England theologian. Yet, at his death in a rooming house on Staten Island, New York, September 14, 1836, Burr had made his name a symbol for treachery and corruption. Even *Princetonians, 1769–1775*, his alma mater's official alumni biographical directory, describes Burr as "the traditional bête noire of American political history." While modern scholarship has softened many harsh contemporary judgments on Burr, no other American vice president led a more troubled, complicated, tumultuous, and mysterious life.

25

Tragedy came early to Burr. His father died in September 1757 shortly after taking his family to Princeton, where the College of New Jersey had found a permanent home. The college trustees persuaded Jonathan Edwards to succeed his son-in-law, but in March 1758, Edwards died at Princeton of smallpox. Edwards's daughter fell victim to the same disease two weeks later, leaving her son and his older sister Sarah orphaned, hundreds of miles from any members of their immediate family. When their grandmother Edwards journeyed south from Stockbridge, Massachusetts, to put her husband's affairs in order and take her grandchildren home, she too died.

The Burr children lived with friends in Philadelphia until 1760, when their mother's brother Timothy was able to assume his responsibilities as their guardian. Thus Aaron and Sarah grew up in the frontier village of Stockbridge, where their uncle was a successful merchant, respected agent with native tribes, and enthusiastic speculator in western lands. Burr left the Edwards home at the age of thirteen to attend the College of New Jersey. There he displayed two traits that marked the rest of his life: an incredible capacity for hard work and self-discipline, which he displayed in his first college year, and a capacity for what Matthew Davis, his first biographer, termed "idleness, negligence and . . . dissipation," which he showed generously in his later college career.

After graduating from Princeton in 1772, Burr briefly studied for the ministry. Quickly realizing his error in judgment, he traveled to Litchfield, Connecticut, to master the law with Tapping Reeve, his sister's husband. The outbreak of the Revolution cut short Burr's professional studies, and in the spring of 1775, Burr set out for Cambridge, Massachusetts, to join Benedict Arnold's expedition to Canada. Burr remained with Arnold's rapidly shrinking army at Quebec through that winter. In June 1776, he won appointment as Israel Putnam's aide-de-camp in Washington's Army and served in the Battle of Long Island and the American evacuation of Manhattan. The next year, Burr joined William Malcolm's "additional" regiment in the Hudson Valley, wintering at Valley Forge before returning north to guard the American border against the British, their Loyalist allies, and nonpartisan outlaw brigands in the Hudson Valley. In March 1779, after nearly four years of active service, Burr succumbed to ill health and resigned his commission as a lieutenant colonel.

By 1780, Burr was strong enough to resume his legal studies, a process that took him from one mentor to another until the fall of 1781, when he applied for admission to practice in the State of New York. In January 1782, he received that license, and six months later married Theodosia Bartow Prevost, a widow ten years his senior who brought five children to their marriage. Mrs. Prevost's first husband, a Swiss-born British army officer, had died in the West Indies in the fall of 1781, and there was no shortage of gossip about courtship that surely began before that news reached New Jersey and New York. The Burrs ignored wagging tongues and settled in Albany, where he practiced law until the British evacuation of New York City opened the way to move to the more profitable life of a lawyer in Manhattan. In November 1783, Burr took his wife, five stepchildren, and infant daughter Theodosia to the city where he would make his mark as a lawyer and politician.

New York State's anti-Loyalist statutes created a situation described by Alexander Hamilton as "so plentiful a harvest to us lawyers that we have scarcely a moment to spare from the substantial business of reaping" (to Gouverneur Morris, February 21, 1784). Mrs. Burr's many Tory kinsmen and in-laws assured her husband an ample share in this harvest, while their claims under royal land grants introduced Burr to speculating in lands on the New York and Pennsylvania frontiers. Business and legal affairs left Burr little time for public life during the Confederation period, but he did serve one term in the state assembly, 1784–1785. Tradition has it that he spoke on behalf of the abolition of slavery in that forum, but this stand is less well documented than his work as legislative spokesman for his circle of fellow speculators.

In the years following the Revolution, New York's political world was dominated by George Clinton, the state's first and only governor from 1777 to 1795 and leader of the state's Antifederalist wing in the hotly contested 1788 battle over Constitutional ratification. Burr was not counted among Clintonians at this point. His position on the adoption of the proposed federal constitution was ambivalent, and his only recorded contemporary expression of opinion on the subject came when New York finally approved the new frame of government after Virginia's ratification had already made the new government a reality: "I congratulate you on the Adoption of the New Constitution. I think it a fortunate event and the only one which could have preserved peace; after the adoption by ten States, I think it became both politic and necessary that we should also adopt it" (to Richard Oliver, July 29, 1788). To cloud his loyalties further, in early 1789 his name appeared among members of a committee supporting Judge Robert Yates against Clinton in the gubernatorial race.

By the fall of 1789, Burr and Clinton had overcome whatever differences in opinion or principle divided them earlier. Burr accepted appointment from Clinton as state attorney general, a post that made him an *ex-officio* member of the state Land Office Commission. There Burr had a hand in decisions on the construction of the roads and bridges that opened New York's frontier and in the sale of parcels of public lands.

In January 1791, a joint session of the state legislature introduced Burr to national office by naming him Philip Schuyler's successor as one of New York's United States senators in the Second Congress. During Burr's single Senate term, 1791–97, the politics of his state and nation underwent a transformation. On the national level, Alexander Hamilton's controversial Treasury Department policies created an opposition that eventually was formalized as Jefferson's Democratic-Republicans. New York's

intricate partisan patterns were complicated further by the gubernatorial election of 1792. Burr was held up briefly as a candidate in opposition to George Clinton, but his chances were dashed when Chief Justice John Jay, a far more prominent and popular candidate, agreed to run against the incumbent.

When the election returns were in, however, Burr's role became more important. So many votes were challenged that neither candidate had a clear majority. The official committee of canvassers was divided along party lines and persuaded New York's two senators, Burr and Federalist Rufus King, to review a formal "Statement of the Case." Not surprisingly, Burr and King could not agree. Ignoring Burr's suggestion that they remain silent, King insisted on submitting a written opinion in favor of counting the ballots that would give Jay the governorship. Burr had no choice but to provide a written statement of his own position. When the committee of canvassers then voted on party lines to award the prize to Clinton in June 1792, Federalists coupled Burr with the canvassers as instruments of Clintonian fraud and corruption.

This embarrassment was especially irritating to Burr as his national reputation among anti-Hamiltonians had sparked talk of his nomination for vice president. Although this boom soon died, Burr was now sufficiently aware of the need to protect his national standing and published a pamphlet defending his role: *An Impartial Statement of the Controversy, Respecting the Decision of the Late Committee of Canvassers*

Burr's emergence as a national politician within the Senate is harder to document, for the upper house at the time conducted debates in secret. Most of Burr's committee appointments reveal no special pattern of expertise or interest, but one group of deliberations was especially significant—Burr's role in fighting for Albert Gallatin's right to a seat as U.S. senator from Pennsylvania in the Third Congress. The 1792 elections gave the new Republican Party a majority in the Senate and admitting a new and able opponent like Gallatin was unthinkable. Burr and the Republicans lost their fight in early 1794, but as the controversy focused entirely on the date of Gallatin's naturalization, the Swiss-born politician simply waited another year and easily won election to the Senate again for the Fourth Congress, when no challenge to his qualifications could be raised. Gallatin easily assumed a leadership role and did not forget Burr's role in trying to gain him a seat earlier.

As the Third Congress progressed, Burr again balanced national and state ambitions and personal concerns. Sometimes these interests coincided, as in April 1794, when he moved that justices of the Supreme Court be barred from accepting "any other office or employment, emanating from and holden at the pleasure of the Executive"—a resolve that would have prevented Chief Justice John Jay from accepting nomination as special envoy to Britain. Burr himself was mentioned as a candidate for a special mission to France, but that post went to another Republican, James Monroe of Virginia. In May, Burr's wife Theodosia died after an illness of two years, leaving Burr to care for their precocious ten-year-old daughter.

The fall of 1794 found Burr marshaling forces for the state elections the following spring. In January 1795, Clinton announced that he would not seek another term. Jay, the likely Federalist candidate, was still abroad on his diplomatic mission to Britain, and his absence could give rivals a handsome advantage. Burr's hopes to head a coalition ticket were soon dashed. Even thousands of miles away, Jay was far more attractive to Federalists than Burr, and realistic Republicans realized that Burr's role in the 1792 election controversy made him an easy target in a race against Jay.

Even as an absentee campaigner, Jay won election easily in the spring of 1795, but Burr did not let him enjoy victory long. New York's Republican senator played a central role at the special Senate session called that summer to consider the newly negotiated treaty with Britain that bore Jay's name. Ratification of the treaty required a two-thirds majority, and neither side had votes to spare. James Monroe and John Taylor of Virginia, Republican Senate leaders in the Second and Third Congresses, had resigned, and their successors had not had time to establish themselves in the House. Thus Burr played a key role in holding Republican votes together and wooing Federalists to their cause. While Burr and his allies failed to break Federalist control of twenty of the thirty votes, they did force a conditional rather than an unqualified ratification of the treaty, and the issues raised on the Senate floor provided ammunition for Republicans at the state and local level for years to come.

In the Fourth Congress that fall, Burr continued to be a Republican gadfly, attacking the Federalist majority in the Senate on every front, ever mindful of the elections of 1796. Federalists now controlled the New York legislature, and Burr knew that his career in the U.S. Senate would end in March 1797. He knew, too, that Washington was unlikely to seek a third term, and the probable Federalist candidacy of John Adams opened the field for ambitious Republicans. Debate over Tennessee's admission to the Union in the spring of 1796 spotlighted his role. Congressional Federalists opposed immediate admission of the territory, for it was clear that Tennessee voters would align themselves with the South, opposing Adams in his expected race to become the second president. While the House quickly voted for Tennessee's admission, Federalist opposition in the Senate was substantial. Burr led advocates of Tennessee statehood and was a member of the House–Senate conference committee that agreed on a bill for immediate admission.

When Washington issued his formal Farewell Address in September 1796, Burr was recognized as the Republicans' vice presidential nominee, with Jefferson the party's presidential candidate. While Burr failed in this ambition (despite the votes of Tennessee's members of the electoral college), he did contribute to undermining the strategy of Hamiltonian Federalists. Members of the electoral college could not designate which of their votes were for president and which for vice president, and Hamilton hoped to persuade some Federalist electors to withhold enough votes from Adams to give the top prize to Adams's running mate, Thomas Pinckney.

Once it was clear that he himself would fare badly in the college vote, Burr wrote to Federalists and Republicans alike to ensure that Adams, not Pinckney, would win. Jefferson was left to serve as vice president, and Burr returned to New York to rebuild his personal finances and political career.

Land speculations during his years in the Senate were now on the verge of collapse and demanded Burr's attention. In April 1797 he also accepted the Republican nomination for a seat in the New York State assembly. There Burr and allies worked to secure passage of a bill that would allow aliens to buy and hold real estate in the state—a prerequisite to the success of sale of Burr's own lands abroad. In August, he played a more creditable role by resolving a dispute between Alexander Hamilton and James Monroe that had threatened to end in a duel.

It was during these years that Burr seems to have created the urban political machine linked to the Tammany Society that served him later. Republicans in New York City triumphed in the spring 1798 elections, and Burr's position of leadership was recognized when his name appeared first among the list of assembly candidates that year. To be sure, he did not neglect nonpartisan appearances, working effectively with Governor Jay in refurbishing New York's defenses in the Quasi-War with France as well as attending to the interests of his urban constituents and his business associates.

But his success was his undoing. In the spring 1799 assembly campaign, Federalists attacked Burr's assembly record, focusing on his work for legislation favoring land speculators and his role in advancing the fortunes of the Manhattan Company, a municipal water-supply scheme exploited by Burr and the Republicans to give their party its own bank. Burr and the New York City assembly ticket he headed lost badly in the election, and he returned to private business, land speculation, and plans for the 1800 national races.

Rebuilding the Republican Party in Manhattan, Burr focused on retaking the city's assembly seats. This gave the party a majority in that house large enough to counter the Federalist margin in the state senate, thus assuring the 1800 Republican presidential candidate the state's electoral college votes when the two houses met in joint session that December. Persuading Republican celebrities such as George Clinton and Horatio Gates to run for the assembly, Burr saw the ticket win in May 1800. Burr himself was returned to the assembly from upstate Orange County. Over the summer, the party came to agreement on Jefferson as presidential candidate, with Burr as his running mate.

As soon as the November elections were over, it was apparent that there might be a tie in the electoral college between Jefferson and Burr if some Republican electors did not withhold votes from Burr by voting for another candidate. Rumors, bargains, and deals were gossiped about, but no agreements were met. Soon after delegates to the electoral college cast their votes in mid-December, it was known that there was a tie. Some Federalists hoped to make deal with Burr: if he committed himself to Federalist demands, he would receive that party's votes when the electoral deadlock was thrown into the U.S. House. Burr's old enemy Alexander Hamilton fought the bargain and campaigned for Jefferson's approval.

The electoral tie became public when the votes were counted on February 11, 1801. The House met continuously for six days until two Federalist state delegations broke the impasse by casting blank ballots: Jefferson would be president and Burr vice president. Even while Burr traveled to Washington to take his oath, he was confronted with public questions about the position he had taken when the Federalists tried to enlist him in a deal for the presidency.

The question would haunt him through his vice presidency.

In the months following the inauguration of the Jefferson–Burr administration, Burr gave his chief new reasons for distrust. The questions of patronage arose quickly: How many Federalist officeholders would be turned out and which Republicans would be rewarded? Burr's own healthy interest in distributing political favors was exaggerated when Republican politicians throughout the country came to view him as a conduit for their own requests, thus forcing Burr to present the claims of dozens of men whom he had never met and whose good will meant nothing to him.

In New York, affairs were going badly. Burr's old enemy George Clinton was elected to another term as governor in May 1801, and Burr's beloved daughter Theodosia was married to Joseph Alston, a wealthy young planter who took her away to his home in South Carolina. Burr's financial interests were, as usual, troubled, and by November, he was looking for a buyer for Richmond Hill, his Manhattan estate. Burr's personal, financial, and political problems were so pressing that he missed the first weeks of the opening session of the Seventh Congress and his initiation as presiding officer of the Senate.

The New York political drama now had a new player: John Wood, a Scottish pamphleteer who began work on a *History of the Administration of John Adams* in June 1801. Burr and other Republicans helped him with his research that fall, but Wood's book proved to be so scurrilous that not even New York Republicans dared see it published. Burr became entangled in tortuous negotiations to suppress the book, and word of the matter was soon known to James Cheetham, proprietor of New York's Republican *Morning Chronicle* and now Burr's avowed enemy. By the close of the year, New York was involved in a partisan pamphlet war that would continue for two years.

Thus Burr could not join the Senate until January 15, 1802. Eleven days later, he made his first casting vote in a tie, sending the bill for repeal of the Federalist Judiciary Bill of 1801 on to its third reading. Repeal of the statute and removal of the "midnight" judges whom Adams had appointed under the measure were cornerstones of Jeffersonian policy. The next day, however, Burr gave his enemies new ammunition by casting the vote that sent the bill to a select committee—a vote that endeared him to moderates but infuriated Jeffersonian partisans.

Personal considerations led Burr to leave the Senate before the end of the session, and he traveled to South Carolina in April 1802 to be with his daughter when she gave birth to a son, Aaron Burr Alston. His enemies in New York took advantage of Burr's absence to publish the first pamphlets concerning Burr's role in suppressing Wood's *History,* and Burrites replied in kind. Burr returned to New York in June—just in time to see a new round of pamphlets examining his role in the 1801 electoral tie. Burr spent the fall desperately trying to persuade his friends and political allies of his innocence: "You are at liberty to declare from me, that all those charges and insinuations which aver or intimate that I advised or countenanced the opposition made to Mr. Jefferson pending the late election or balloting for President . . . that all such assertions are false and groundless" (to Joseph Bloomfield, September 21, 1802). January 19, 1803, found him back in the Senate in time to witness attempts by William Marbury's attorney to obtain evidence of his client's appointment from Senate records. At the end of the session, Burr traveled south to visit his daughter and men fences among southern politicians.

Jefferson had called the Senate together early in the fall of 1803 to consider the Louisiana Purchase treaty. As usual, Burr missed the session's opening. Indeed, his friend Senator Jonathan Dayton of New Jersey wrote him in mid-November "to loiter on your way." A constitutional amendment reforming presidential balloting procedures had been introduced, and the debates were expected to be embarrassing for Burr. Burr finally made his appearance on December 7—five days after the Senate adopted the Twelfth Amendment. All that was left for him was a flurry of correspondence concerning the etiquette of forwarding the amendment to the states for consideration.

The session was a busy one for Burr. On January 5, 1804, Congressman John Randolph introduced a resolution for the impeachment of the outspokenly partisan Federalist Associate Supreme Court Justice Samuel Chase. Articles of impeachment were not adopted until March 26, so Burr could look forward to these proceedings in the fall. As a dress rehearsal, however, Burr presided over the Senate impeachment trial of another judge, the tragically demented John Pickering. Burr had a fateful conversation with Jefferson on January 26 in which the president made it clear that George Clinton, not Aaron Burr, would be his running mate that year. Burr was given leave to absent himself from the Senate for a few weeks at the end of January, and on his return he was furious to learn that William Duane of the Jeffersonian *Aurora* had been present in the chamber in his absence. Burr's patience with newspaper editors had grown short; it was at this time that he had brought suit against James Cheetham for libel.

The libel suit, of course, was tied to Burr's last desperate political hopes. George Clinton's nomination as vice president meant that the old man could not run in the 1804 gubernatorial race, and Burr was busy restoring his reputation in New York in preparation for that race. Federalists stood aside to let Burr run against a fellow Jeffersonian, Judge Morgan Lewis, who billed himself and his followers as the "Genuine Republicans." Burr suffered a humiliating loss in May despite his flirtation with Federalists— even Federalists with sectionalist leanings.

The aftermath of the May election ended Burr's political career. Even by New York's standards, the campaign had been a bitter one, filled with vilification and innuendo. In mid-June, Burr exploded on hearing rumors of remarks Alexander Hamilton had made at his expense. Through his friend William Van Ness, Burr demanded an explanation—and Hamilton refused. For ten days, Burr's and Hamilton's

friends scurried back and forth with notes and letters. On July 28, it became apparent that nothing but a duel would settle the matter of honor, and those friends then became seconds for the two principals. On June 11, Burr, Hamilton, and their entourages rowed across the Hudson to a dueling ground in Weehawken, New Jersey. Burr's bullet struck Hamilton in the abdomen, and the Federalist died two days later. A week passed, and Burr fled a murder indictment in New York, taking refuge with friends in Philadelphia before sailing to West Florida and South Carolina for the late summer and early fall.

By the time Burr returned North, New Jersey had added a murder indictment to Burr's list. On November 4, Burr was in his chair in the Senate chamber for the opening day of business—the first and only time in his vice presidential term that he had attended so promptly. Federalists were furious at the sight of Hamilton's killer presiding over the upper house, while Burr's friends in Congress busily circulated a petition letter to the governor of New Jersey asking that his state's indictment against Burr be quashed. Burr conducted business with quiet dignity. He was applauded for his conduct of the trial that led to Samuel Chase's acquittal, and no one could fault his manner or manners on February 15 when he formally notified Jefferson of his reelection to a second presidential term. Burr's enemies were less gracious: Federalists in the House blocked a vote to grant him franking privileges for his mail.

On March 2, Burr delivered his Farewell Address to the Senate—his last public appearance as an officeholder. He spoke his regard for the Senate and of his own feelings at "a final separation—a dissolution, perhaps forever, of those associations" with individual lawmakers: "It is here if any where, that our country must ultimately find the anchor of her safety; and if the Constitution is to perish, . . . its dying agonies will be seen on this floor. . . ." Senators wept after Burr walked out of the chamber that day, and New York's Samuel Latham Mitchill, a firm Clintonian, wrote his wife: "Burr is one of the best officers that ever resided over a deliberative assembly. Where he is going or how he is to get through with his difficulties I know not" (letter of March 2, 1805).

One thing Burr could not do was return to his old life. On March 22, he wrote his son-in-law: "In New-York I am to be disfranchised, and in New-Jersey hanged. Having substantial objections to both, I shall not, for the present, hazard either, but shall seek another country." That country was, inevitably, the West. Dueling was unpopular throughout the Northeast, and Burr had no future there. The Southeast tolerated duels, but that region was solidly Jeffersonian. In the West, however, Burr still had friends and a future—or so he thought.

Burr visited Ohio, Kentucky, and Tennessee in the spring and summer of 1805, gathering support for an ill-defined expedition whose objects may not have been entirely clear even to him. He climaxed the trip with a September meeting in St. Louis with his most ill-chosen collaborator, James Wilkinson, the unstable and treacherous commander of the American Army in the West. Returning to the East, Burr spent the next months organizing his supporters and even sounding out Jefferson.

Burr went west again in early August 1806, but suspicious of his motives dogged his every step. In Kentucky, he was arrested. With Henry Clay as his counsel, Burr was acquitted of charges of planning a war on Spain, but his support from prominent men such as Tennessee's Andrew Jackson was slipping away. Worse still, James Wilkinson had embarked on his own, private campaign, sending Jefferson a report of Burr's activities in the West. The report included an incriminating cipher letter that had, in fact, been written to Wilkinson by Jonathan Dayton. Burr moved south to the Mississippi frontier, unaware that Jefferson had issued a proclamation warning "all faithful citizens" of a brewing conspiracy to force war with Spain. By the time Burr saw Jefferson's proclamation in a newspaper in a small town

north of modern Natchez on January 10, Wilkinson had begun to arrest Burr's associates in New Orleans. Burr was arrested again in Mississippi—and again tried and acquitted. Fearing for his safety at Wilkinson's hands, Burr fled, reemerging to be arrested in what is today modern Wakefield County, Alabama, at the end of January.

Burr was taken to Richmond, Virginia, for trial by the U.S. Circuit Court for Virginia, with Chief Justice John Marshall presiding. Proceedings began in May and ended with Burr's acquittal—and the threat of further legal proceedings in the West. For Burr, "another country" now meant a nation an ocean's distance away. After bidding farewell to his daughter and her family, Burr sailed to England in June 1808. He remained abroad for nearly four years, dividing most of his time between England and France. He approached the British Crown and the French Empire with schemes to liberate Spain's American colonies, but to no avail, and he returned to New York City in June 1812 with no prospects, no plans. He ended the year with almost no hope.

In July, Burr learned that his only grandchild, Theodosia's son, Aaron Burr Alston, had died. Grief stricken, Theodosia planned a trip north to be with her father. Her ship sailed north in December 1812—and was never heard from again. Nearly fifty-seven, Burr had no money, no career, few friends, and no immediate family. Yet he went on, rebuilding his law practice from scratch, following the course of New York's courts from Manhattan to Albany to Utica and back. He dabbled in schemes to free Spain's last colonies in America and embarked on a twenty-year campaign to secure his pension as a Revolutionary War veteran.

Eventually Burr found young politicians such as Martin Van Buren willing to become known as his friends. He never again exerted power, but the stain of his old disgrace faded, in part because new scandals replaced it. In 1833, he took a second wife, the notorious and wealthy Eliza Bowen Jumel. The Burrs separated by the end of the year, and Eliza Burr sued for divorce the following summer. By then her husband and had been incapacitated by a stroke, and Burr spent the next two years in a boardinghouse kept by the daughter of an old friend. In 1835, he put the finishing touches to his will, including a rakish codicil that provided a legacy for two little girls whom he acknowledged as his "Two Daughters." When a friend chided him for taking on the responsibility of children whom he knew were not his own, Burr is said to have replied: "Sir, when a lady does me the honor to name me the father of her child, I trust I shall always be too gallant to show myself ungrateful for the favor!" When his health deteriorated in 1836, he was moved to Staten Island, where his Edwards kin could supervise his care. On September 14, 1836, he died. He was buried next to his parents in the Princeton Cemetery.

Burr's legacy to the country was an undisguised relish for partisan warfare and a genius for machine politics, tastes that went unappreciated by such people as Jefferson and Madison and Hamilton. Yet, the vice presidency seemed to bring out the best in Burr: There he put aside partisan interest for impartial statesmanship. Presiding over the Senate while under two indictments for murder, Burr performed with a composure and courage that even his enemies had to admire. Whatever his attitude toward other public offices, Burr held the vice presidency as a trust, one that he discharged with dignity and extraordinary decency.

REFERENCES

Political Correspondence and Public Papers of Aaron Burr, Mary-Jo Kline and Joanne Wood Ryan, eds., 2 vols. (Princeton: Princeton University Press, 1983); Milton Lomask, *Aaron Burr* (New York: Farrar, Straus, and Giroux, 1979 and 1982); Joseph Wheelan, *Jefferson's Vendetta: The Pursuit of Aaron Burr and the Judiciary* (New York: Carroll & Graf, 2004); Nancy Isenberg, *Fallen Founder: The Life of Aaron Burr* (New York: Viking Press, 2007); Peter Charles Hotter, *The Treason: Trials of Aaron Burr* (Lawrence: University Press of Kansas, 2008).

MARY-JO KLINE is the former American history specialist for the John Hay Library at Brown University and is currently a columnist for *History Now,* an online journal. She earned a Ph.D. in American history from Columbia University before embarking on a career in documentary editing. After serving as associate editor of the John Jay papers and the papers of John Adams, she directed the papers of Aaron Burr project at the New-York Historical Society. Her two-volume edition of the *Political Correspondence and Public Papers of Aaron Burr* was published by Princeton University Press in 1983. She is the author of *A Guide to Documentary Editing* (Johns Hopkins University Press), which was originally published in 1987 and appeared in a revised edition in 1997, and *Gouveneur Morris and the New Nation, 1775–1788,* published by Arno Press in 1978.

GEORGE CLINTON (1739–1812)

Vice President, 1805–1812

(Presidents Thomas Jefferson and James Madison)

GEORGE CLINTON
(Library of Congress)

By L. Edward Purcell

George Clinton was elected to the vice presidency when the office still seemed to have significant potential for power—his immediate predecessor had, after all, nearly become president by virtue of a defect in the electoral system—and Clinton was regarded by his contemporaries as one of the first among national political leaders. At the time of his election, it was still not clear just what the vice presidency meant politically: was it a way station for the heir presumptive to the presidency, or was it doomed to become an empty office? Although he definitely played second fiddle to President Thomas Jefferson during the election of 1804 (the first to be conducted under the amended electoral procedures that specified a separate vice-presidential candidate), the following campaign in 1808 found an aged Clinton nominated simultaneously as Madison's running mate *and* as a rival candidate for the presidency itself.

Clinton was elected vice president at the end of his career when he was old and much diminished in his capacities, and he performed indifferently, especially during his second term. In his younger and middle years, however, Clinton had been a larger-than-life figure whose leadership spanned the events of the imperial crisis with Great Britain, the American Revolution, the Confederation period, the struggle over the Constitution and the founding of the new nation, and the development of a working government and party system during the Early Republic.

During the 1780s, Clinton was one of America's most vigorous governors and among the very first during the Revolution to base political power on the democratic mass of freehold voters, repeatedly dealing his aristocratic opponents in New York frustrating and mortifying electoral defeats. He was a dedicated democrat as well as an irod-bound conservative. He was steadfastly practical in his approach never uttered or wrote an inspired thought (at least none that have survived). In part because of his unphilosophical bent and inarticulateness, he has not been much remembered as one of the important figures present at the creation of the American nation. Moreover, his intense focus on his native state as well as his strongly held opinions about the proper scope of government put him among the foremost Antifederalists during the contest for ratification of the new U.S. Constitution, and that was a position that did not play well afterward among makers of historical reputations: it was against George Clinton that Alexander Hamilton, James Madison, and John Jay directed their "Federalist Papers."

Clinton was born in the village of New Britain in Ulster County, New York, to Charles and Elizabeth Clinton, a Scotch-Irish immigrant couple who had landed in America in 1729 after a tragically disastrous voyage during which two of their three children died. They made a new life in America, however, and gained a modest measure of financial success and local prominence. George's siblings—he was the youngest of four children born in the New World—included his brother James, who became an important Revolutionary War general and married into the DeWitt clan of New York, a union that produced George's political heir, DeWitt Clinton.

Ulster County, which for many years formed George's political base, was a region of small freehold farms, populated mostly by Presbyterian Scotch-Irish farmers who gave definition to the classic American stereotype of agrarian virtue: the yeomanry. They owned and worked their own land, with few slaves, and they were not usually tenants or beholden to patroons or powerful families, as was the case in much of the colony of New York east of the Hudson River, where the power of the manor still held sway.

Clinton received a poor education and never really mastered language skills—he was at best a mediocre writer and often called on aides or his nephew DeWitt to draft official messages—although he was competent in mathematics and a good practical surveyor. During the Seven Years War, he served aboard a privateer for a ten-month voyage against the French and then as a lieutenant in his brother's militia company on Lord Jeffery Amherst's expedition against Montreal in 1760.

Late in the same year, Clinton moved to New York City and entered the law office of famous attorney William Smith, the younger. After three years of Smith's legal tutelage, Clinton returned to Ulster County and took up the practice of law with a side occupation of land surveying.

Five years later (1768), George Clinton was elected to a seat in the New York Assembly as a representative of Ulster. He was seldom out of public office for the rest of his life, establishing early on in his career that he could win a majority of the voters in almost any contest. For a man of his modest background, this meant overcoming a big challenge. For decades before the Revolution, officeholding in New York was at the disposal of the big, rich, and quarreling but powerful political families; the Livingstons, for example, were pitted against the De Lanceys during the 1760s. There was also an ongoing political split between New York City with its associated counties to the southeast and the northern counties. To some extent the north–south political polarity also reflected the divisions between merchants and agriculturalists and between urban and rural interests. For all of his life, George Clinton was the champion of rural, west-of-the-Hudson farming constituencies. He was disliked by the aristocratic family politicians and seldom won support in New York City or its surrounding counties.

One of the hallmark's of George Clinton's political life was his long-term, often shifting relationship with other powerful figures of the New York and national scene. He initially was an ally of the immensely wealthy Philip Schuyler, although he eventually came to be on the opposite side from Schuyler and Schuyler's son-in-law, Alexander Hamilton. For years, Clinton was alternately allied with and then opposed to Aaron Burr, whose main political strength was in New York City. Clinton almost always, however, could be found on the opposite side of the fence from the aristocratic John Jay.

In 1770, Clinton married Cornelia Tappen, who brought with her a close alliance with the old-line Dutch interests in New York and a connection to the Livingston family. The couple moved to New Windsor in the Hudson Highlands, and their daughter, Catherine (the first of five Clinton children), was born by the end of the year. Catherine eventually married Pierre Van Cortlandt, which forged another important political link for her father.

George Clinton provided his family a living by legal work and the income from ownership of a local mill, but most of his time and energies were consumed by the New York Provincial Assembly, which sat continuously from 1769 until April 1775, with only a short period of prorogation in 1774. Thus, Clinton was involved in and became a leader of the struggle between the assembly and New York's colonial governor and the British government in general. When the official assembly was dissolved in 1775 and New Yorkers moved to set up an extralegal Provincial Convention, Clinton was named as Ulster's representative. He was selected immediately by the convention as one of New York's delegates to the Second Continental Congress, and he attended sessions of the congress in Philadelphia from May to August. At the end of the year, Clinton was commissioned by the New York Provisional Assembly as a brigadier general of militia.

George Clinton took advantage of the dislocations and changes set loose by the revolutionary movement to transform himself from a small-town lawyer and surveyor into a man with powerful political and military positions. The idea that the American Revolution was a double revolution—one internally of the lower socio-economic colonial classes against the ruling upper classes as well as an external revolution of all the colonies against Great Britain—has been a matter of tiresome historical debate for generations, but the case of George Clinton fits the model quite snugly. While he might have become someone of importance without the Revolution, he certainly would never have attained the heights of office and power that he did, especially in a place like New York, which was dominated by upper-class families. Clinton was a man of ability who was standing on the threshold as the Revolution weakened or swept away the old structures.

From March to May 1776 and again during parts of June and July, Clinton returned to the Continental Congress. During these stints as a legislator (a role he never much took to), Clinton established a firm and lasting friendship with George Washington. Of course, this personal bond, which developed over the years of fighting the British and subsequently as the two men invested together in frontier lands, turned out to be of immense importance to Clinton. Washington genuinely liked Clinton and on more than one occasion swept aside what appeared to be sharp political differences for the sake of friendship. Washington was the most important American alive, and Clinton could always call on him for help and support.

Unfortunately for Clinton's place in history, he left Congress to return to his military duties in New York in the summer of 1776 before signing the Declaration of Independence, so he could never claim membership in the august group of "The Signers."

Clinton was charged with defending the Highlands of the Hudson River against a British offensive. This was one of the key assignments of the war in the north because the British held New York City from 1776 on and if they could gain control of the up river country the northern colonies would be split. Early in 1777, Clinton received a full commission from Congress as a brigadier general in the Continental Army, a rank of much higher standing than his state militia commission, and he set up defenses at Fort Montgomery, just below present-day West Point.

During the same period, Clinton was technically a member, but seldom attended, the drawn-out New York convention called to write a state constitution. Finally, the constitution was proclaimed in April 1777, and the first election for governor was set in motion. Because New York City and much of the southern part of the state were in the hands of the British or Loyalists and because there were no political parties to help organize the election, the entire affair boiled down to the personalities of the many candidates. Philip Schuyler, for example, was the leading candidate of the traditional officeholding New York aristocracy. He was serving as a major general in the Continental Army (a highly unpopular one with his New England troops), had important family ties, and was immensely wealthy, so most observers at the time thought he was a shoo-in and that Clinton would do well to stand only for the lieutenant governor's post.

Schuyler and his friends were shocked when Clinton won the governorship easily, taking 49 percent of the ballots to Schuyler's 32 percent (John Scott Morin and John Jay split the remaining votes).

Schuyler was relatively gracious about Clinton's victory, however. He wrote to Jay that: "Gen. Clinton's having the chair of Government will not cause any divisions amongst the friends of America. Alto' his family and connections do not entitle him to so distinguished predominance; yet he is virtuous and loves his country, has abilities and is brave." Schuyler might have been less magnanimous if he had known that this was only the first in seven gubernatorial elections that Clinton would win in New York and that Schuyler's side of the political division in the state would never unseat the plebeian Clinton. The fact that the election was conducted for the first time by secret ballot, thus freeing tenants and debtors to vote as they wished, probably played an important part in Clinton's win, as did a sizable soldier vote.

Clinton took office in July 1777 and established himself at his in-law's house in Kingston, New York, which was the temporary capital of the new state government. Most of his time, however, was spent at his military post on the Hudson. The British had launched a grand invasion from Canada led by "Gentleman Johnny" Burgoyne and headed toward Albany and point south. The British commander in New York, Sir Henry Clinton (probably a distant relative of the new rebel governor), moved up the Hudson from the south with the goal of linking with Burgoyne. Along the way, Sir Henry attacked Fort Montgomery and easily ousted the American garrison. Governor George Clinton barely escaped capture, and the British took control of the key river position, although with the defeat of Burgoyne at Saratoga, they failed in their grand plan.

In fact, the defeat at Fort Montgomery was the highlight of George Clinton's military career. Washington continued to praise him and express every confidence in his abilities despite his defeat, and for the rest of his life, Clinton was hailed as a Revolutionary War hero, a reputation that bolstered his political potency. As E. Wilder Spaulding, one of his biographers, wrote: "Democracies are lavish in the honors they bestow on their war heroes."

Clinton's service as wartime governor was much more effective than his generalship. He did an excellent job of organizing troops and supplies for a long and difficult period, during which the British held the key port of New York City as their main troop base in the North and the pivot of several key campaigns, including the seizure of Philadelphia and Charleston. When the British raided Kingston, burning many of Clinton's official papers in the process, the state government repaired to Poughkeepsie, where Clinton established a new family home and official residence.

Clinton's energy level during the long, drawn-out final years of the Revolution was extraordinary. He seldom flagged in his efforts to help keep the army intact, and he supported Washington's difficult task of holding on at Newburgh, New York, to an ill-used and unpaid force that seemed often to be on the verge of revolt or dissolution. It was a sweet triumph when Clinton rode side-by-side with Commander-in-Chief Washington into New York in November 1783 to reclaim the city from the British. The state government of New York moved back into that city, and the Clintons took over the spacious home of an ousted Loyalist, remaining in the city until a new state capital was established in Albany in 1801. Clinton purchased a farm in the nearby rural community of Greenwich and spent much of his limited leisure time there.

Although he was intensely patriotic during the Revolution and never for a moment stinted in his support of the war effort, toward the end of the conflict, Clinton began to consider the best balance of powers between the individual states and the central government. In this, he confronted the most fundamental question in American history, one that has proved constantly since the 1780s to be the basis for the essential political division in the country between those who favor a strong, active central government and those who want power dispersed and reserved locally.

At first, Clinton leaned toward a stronger central government because his wartime experiences showed him the defects of the congressional and confederation systems, but soon the practical issues he faced as New York's governor prompted him to change his mind. For example, when struggling to feed and clothe the army during the last years of the war, the idea of a national import tax (known as the impost) seemed like a good way to fund the operations of both the army and Congress. When the great commercial port city of New York was restored to his state, however, Clinton began to see that there would be tremendous local advantages to collecting an impost but keeping the money at home. Also, apart from the financial question, Clinton probably came to believe in the idea that each state should chart its own destiny and decide its own affairs, although abstractions did not often play a big role in George Clinton's political decisions. Whatever the philosophical underpinnings of his position, during the months after the ratification of the peace treaty, Clinton became more and more wedded to the defense of *local* New York State interests and less and less interested in supporting the concerns of a central, national corporate government.

This set of beliefs and attitudes coalesced nationally as what later historians labeled Antifederalism (although Clinton and his contemporaries did not use the term). At the time Antifederalism made great sense to a large number of Americans and many of their political leaders, and it reflected a reasoned position in defense of hard-won democracy and liberty. Many Antifederalists were loath to give up the precious freedoms won from Britain to a new central government, which they feared would be captured by aristocratic, perhaps even monarchical, elements who would not understand or care for local or state concerns. The concept that the states had rights that were more important than the nation as a whole was not on the fringe of American political thought in Clinton's day but rather near the center.

Unfortunately for Clinton's historical reputation, the states' rights, Antifederalist position was coopted by the slaveholding states before the Civil War and by southern racial discriminators for several generations after, and it was thus largely discredited. In Clinton's own time, however, he stood staunchly for what we today fondly call the Jeffersonian tradition of a limited state and rural virtue.

Clinton was easily reelected as governor for a series of three-year terms in 1780, 1783, and 1786. As chief executive of New York State, Clinton confronted a series of issues that only reinforced his adherence to the states' rights, Antifederalist position. The long-festering fight with the renegade Vermonters, who had the effrontery to rebel against New York just as New York had rebelled against Britain, was a hot button for Clinton and many other New Yorkers. The Vermonters nearly succeeded in gaining recognition from Congress in 1778 and 1779, and they came close to statehood in 1781. Only Clinton's most strenuous efforts blocked what he understood to be a dire threat to the well-being of his state, and the pro-Vermont role of Congress in all these episodes helped form his anti-central-government stance.

He also was at odds with the Confederation Congress over the treatment of Loyalists and their property, the renewed question of approving a national impost tax, and claims and rights to western lands. Clinton's fiscal conservatism and rejection of national interests in favor of local interests consolidated New York's natural economic advantages and made him an immensely popular figure in New York: Indeed, there was always a surplus of revenue over expenses and never a general property tax in the state during all of Clinton's administrations, and he financed government from the state impost and land sales. It was ironic, however, that Clinton's chief rivals in New York for local power were also the most vocal and effective advocates of the pronationalist position. By the mid-1780s, it was clear that Alexander Hamilton was going to lead the anti-Clinton forces in the state and was likely to have a major role in resolving the national crisis of government that was building rapidly.

The pressures came to a head in 1787 after Daniel Shays's rebellion, and the proposed new national constitution and the effort to achieve ratification produced some of the defining moments in American history.*

Both opponents and advocates of the proposed constitution knew that ratification by New York would be crucial to the success of the new plan of government. The ratification process called for approval by only eleven of the thirteen states, but without the assent of the large states, such as New York, the chances for failure were good. Clinton had generally opposed the participation of New York's representatives at the constitutional convention, but it was not until the fight over ratification that he came to the forefront of the Antifederalists.

The contest was fought as a war of words in New York. The Antifederalist side was taken in the papers by a series of letters published under the name *Cato* which were perhaps written by Clinton himself. Cato's letters touched on both principles and practical matters, all condemning the proposed constitution and urging delay or rejection. In response, Hamilton, James Madison, and John Jay wrote a series of beautifully articulate and well-reasoned essays that have come to be labeled as the "Federalist Papers" that remain major texts of American political thought.

In June 1788, elected delegates met at Poughkeepsie to debate and vote on ratification. Clinton was chosen as president and presided over an initial forty-six to nineteen Antifederalist majority. Personally, however, he was circumspect and surprisingly did not take the lead against the Constitution, preferring apparently to wait to see what would happen. To the great consternation of the Antifederalist forces, the supposed majority against ratification slipped away and the proratifiers won by a slim margin. The struggle polarized politics in

*Editor's note: See ELBRIDGE GERRY for further explanation of Shays's Rebellion.

the state and became the basis for party organization and faction battles for years to come. The defeat damaged Clinton, and he never quite enjoyed the same state power and reputation again.

"Paradoxically," wrote Clinton biographer Spaulding, "it was Governor Clinton's provincialism and his stubborn championship of the rights of his state that made him a national figure." Even though he had lost at home, his stand against the Constitution made him a logical rallying point for Antifederalists in other states. As the first national election under the new plan of government approached, several influential voices, including Patrick Henry of Virginia and a caucus of the Federal Republican Society, urged that Clinton be a candidate for the vice presidency. Washington was the unanimous choice for president, but the vice presidency might well be contested. In fact, all the Federalist forces, lead by Hamilton, threw their support behind John Adams, who was elected with no serious opposition, and Clinton received no electoral votes. He might have received the approval of at least some of the New York electors, but a dispute of his own making stymied selection of electors, and New York failed to cast any electoral votes at all during the first presidential election.

Historians debate when and where political parties were born in the United States, but it seems clear that the conflicts over the Constitution and the way the new federal government was to be conducted were the catalysts for new forms of political organization and allegiance, especially in places such as Clinton's New York. However, it is misleading (and somewhat bewildering to late twentieth century Americans) to describe the political alliances of the 1790s and early 1800s as parties in the modern sense. Political campaigns revolved much more around individuals than nascent parties, and there was a great deal of crossover and shifting back and forth in ways that seem irrationally undisciplined to anyone accustomed to the two-party system as it eventually developed. There were, for example, few formal party structures that

politicians could rely on year in and year out to assist in election to office. In general, however, the "Clinton Party" was a consistent factor in New York politics throughout George Clinton's career and the career of his nephew, DeWitt Clinton, who became his uncle's secretary in 1788 and eventually took over the direction of the faction. Antifederalists never really became organized as a formal party, but many of Antifederalist bent—such as George Clinton himself—eventually found their way into the fold of the party that formed around Jefferson's and Madison's leadership, a party usually referred to as the Jeffersonian Republicans or the Democratic-Republicans. Clinton was a natural for the Republicans with his history of vocal opposition to a strong central government and his support for a vision—held in common with Jefferson—of a democratic, agrarian society. The Republicans also catered to Clinton as a way to cement the New York–Virginia coalition that was potentially strong enough to control national presidential elections.

Clinton was reelected for a fifth term as governor in 1789, but the opposition of Hamilton and Aaron Burr, a New York City lawyer who was intensely ambitious for high office, made it a much closer race than the four previous. The Hamilton-led Federalists won control of the New York Assembly and Senate, and Hamilton looked forward to exercising considerable power. The former aide to the commander in chief was somewhat chagrined, therefore, that when George Washington arrived in New York City to assume the presidency, the new chief executive chose to dine on his first night privately with his old friend and business partner George Clinton rather than Hamilton or any of the leading Federalists of the city.

The next election for governor proved nearly to be Clinton's undoing. The Federalists selected John Jay as their candidate (Burr was also in the field), and the campaign was particularly bitter and hard fought. Clinton, as head of the state land office, was accused of complicity in a huge recent land-speculating scandal and of misusing his position on the Board of Appointment to dispense patronage too liberally. The race was exceedingly close, and it was only after disputed ballots from three counties were thrown out that Clinton could claim a victory. There was widespread public belief that he had stolen the election and that a more honorable man would have conceded to Jay.

Within months, Clinton's attention turned to the upcoming second national election. It was a foregone conclusion that Washington would be reelected for another term, but it was not so clear that Adams would be supported again for vice president. There was no standard nominating procedure at this stage of U.S. national politics, so the field appeared at times to be wide open. Aaron Burr was the first to have his name put forward, but his support proved to be thinly based. Clinton was a much more popular choice among antigovernment politicos in the important states, based on his prominence as an Antifederalist spokesman. Hamilton, who had emerged as the most influential member of Washington's administration and the leader of the national Federalists, would have been happy to rid himself of Adams, but in the face of a Clinton candidacy, Hamilton had to back the incumbent vice president. Adams reclaimed his office but by a diminished majority in the electoral college, receiving seventy-seven votes to Clinton's fifty.*

During the following year, Clinton was personally involved in the famous episode of Citizen Genêt. The revolution in France had unleashed wild forces in Europe and a flood of reaction in the United States. Federalists were aghast at the excesses of the revolutionaries, but many Jeffersonian Republicans were enthused by the vision of an ancient monarchy following America's revolutionary lead. In 1793, the French revolutionary government sent Edmond Genêt to the United States as an emissary. He intended to galvanize the pro-French forces in the United States, but he managed instead to insult George Washington and to make a complete fool of himself. Worse for him, even as his mission dissolved, a factional change in Paris resulted in a call for his return. Suspecting it was an invitation to his own beheading, Genêt wisely sought asylum in the United States. Meanwhile, during a visit to New York, he had fallen in love with Clinton's daughter Cornelia. Clinton grumbled, but the couple were married in late 1794 and settled on Long Island.**

Clinton himself had begun to slow down a good deal, and he apparently had lost some of his relish for the rough and tumble of New York politics. As the 1795 election for governor approached, he decided to retire from office. The voters of the state had known no one else as governor since the Revolution, but they turned to Clinton's longtime opponent John Jay, electing him to office easily. Clinton withdrew to his Greenwich farm and by all signs appeared to be done with officeholding.

This was misleading. Within five years, Clinton was back in office, first as a member of the assembly and then once again as governor. The circumstances were noticeably different, however, from his previous eighteen-year stretch in the governor's chair. The power structure in New York State had shifted toward younger men such as DeWitt Clinton and Aaron Burr, although Hamilton remained at the head of the Federalists. Burr and his associates (known at the time as the "Martling Men," in honor of their favorite tavern, although officially organized as the Society of Tammany) had succeeded in converting New York City from a Federalist stronghold to the Republican column; however, Burr was never steady in his political allegiances, except to himself, and he was capable of switching sides or making allies of those who had been foes only yesterday.

Burr and the Clinton factions were soon to fall out, but in 1800, Burr convinced George

*Editor's note: See JOHN ADAMS for further explanation of this election.

**Editor's note: See JOHN ADAMS for further explanation of the Genêt Affair.

Clinton to allow himself to be put on the ballot for a Republican seat in the state assembly. The plan was to capture the state for the Republicans and thus assure New York's electoral votes for a national Republican ticket of Jefferson and Burr. Clinton was elected and the Republicans won a majority, but soon thereafter politics in the state and at the national level lost all semblance of order.

The year must have been full of confusion and agitation for Clinton. In March, his wife Cornelia died after a lingering illness, leaving him to rely more and more on the personal support of his daughters. He stood for the assembly in the spring and then was briefly in contention for the national Republican nomination for vice president with Jefferson. The movement to put Clinton on the ticket dissolved, and Burr claimed the prize. In November, however, Clinton was nominated by the Republican caucus of the New York Assembly as a candidate for governor. With the election in the following spring, Clinton became governor for the seventh time.

Meanwhile, Burr and Jefferson had won a great national victory over the Federalists but had tied in the electoral college voting. The major defect of the new Constitution's electoral system was revealed: the provision that the second-place finisher would become vice president did not anticipate nor could it deal with a tie. It would seem a simple step for Burr to have withdrawn in Jefferson's favor, but Burr demurred and allowed the contested election to be thrown into the U.S. House of Representatives, which finally selected Jefferson as president. When the smoke cleared, the Clinton faction and the Burr faction in New York were irretrievably split, and Burr had in effect been pushed out of the fold by Jefferson's national Republican supporters.

Clinton served out his final term as governor but declined to run again, which had momentous consequences for Burr, Hamilton, and the nation. Although serving as vice president, Burr realized he would be ignored in the future by the Republicans, so he ran to replace Clinton as governor of New York. He lost badly to the Clinton-faction candidate, Chief Justice Morgan Lewis, but came to blame Hamilton for his defeat. The result was the infamous duel in Weehawken, New Jersey, in July 1804. With a single exchange of shots, two of the great players in the drama of George Clinton's political life were removed: Hamilton was dead and Burr was banished. This was the curtain raiser on the final act of Clinton's career and his national service as vice president.

As the 1804 election approached, the Republicans looked for strong candidate to replace Burr and bolster Jefferson's electoral total. The old idea of a New York–Virginia power connection was still in play, so even though George Clinton gave more and more the impression of an aging hero, well past his prime, he was still an attractive vote-getter and highly recognizable in other states for his longtime stand on limited government. Moreover, the 1804 election would be conducted for the first time under the provisions of the Twelfth Amendment, which was passed to prevent a recurrence of the Jefferson–Burr electoral tie. The new procedure called for separate balloting for president and vice president, and it began what over the long haul proved to be the diminution of the vice presidency. It is little remembered, however, that the amendment also required electors to cast ballots for presidential and vice-presidential candidate "one of whom, at least, shall not be an inhabitant of the same State with themselves." This provision meant that if Virginia was not to waste some of its electoral votes, then a non-Virginian would have to be nominated as Jefferson's running mate. Clinton seemed the obvious choice, and he was nominated officially at a caucus of the Republican congressional continent.

Jefferson and Clinton easily defeated their Federalist opposition of Charles Cotesworth Pinckney and Rufus King by 162 electoral votes to 14.

In general, George Clinton's time as vice president was not happy. He was sixty-five when elected—ascension to the top office seemed unlikely at his age—and he gave the appearance in public of mental torpor, if not downright deterioration, although on occasion he could be roused to vigor. He lived most of the time in Poughkeepsie, where he had moved after his wife's death, but beginning in December 1805, Clinton traveled to Washington when the Senate was in session with his daughter, Maria, boarding with John Beckley, Thomas Jefferson's political campaign manager. After Beckley's death in 1807, the Clintons lived in a variety of boardinghouses.

Clinton had a hard time with the Senate, which one of his biographers described as "a tiny assemblage of thirty-four mediocrities." He had never been much inclined toward the pace of legislative deliberation, having avoided service as a delegate during most of his career in favor of executive office, and he was apparently too old to learn either the substance or the subtleties of the Senate presiding officer's role. He also suffered by comparison to his immediate predecessor, Burr, who, whatever his defects of character, had been a superb president of the Senate.

The tenor of the complaints about Clinton's shortcomings can be heard in a letter from John Quincy Adams to his father, who had of course been the first presiding officer of the Senate, written in early 1805 during Clinton's first session:

> Mr. Clinton is totally ignorant of all the most common forms of proceeding in the Senate, and yet by the rules he is to decide every question of order without debate and without appeal. His judgement is neither quick nor strong; so there is no more dependence upon the correctness of his determinations from his understanding than from his experience.

Clinton cast tie-breaking votes to pass a bill postponing the abolition of the slave trade and to confirm General John Armstrong as a negotiator with Spain. Otherwise, he bumbled along during the first session and left for New York in March well before adjournment. This was the pattern he followed throughout his vice presi-

dency. As the end of Jefferson's second term approached, however, circumstances allowed George Clinton to take an important political role one last time.

Clinton had been circumspect in general about criticizing Jefferson or the Republican Party, but with the eclipse of the Federalists after Jefferson's election and Hamilton's death, there were fewer reasons to keep peace within the Republicans' own house. Clinton was irritated with Jefferson's failure to take the British military threat to New York seriously, and he especially disagreed with Jefferson's embargo scheme. By 1807, the vice president had become a vocal critic of the administration.

So it was that antiadministration elements within the Republican Party, who wanted to mount a challenge to Secretary of State James Madison's "inheritance" of the presidency, looked to Clinton in 1808. There were sharp divisions within the Virginia section of the party, with many pushing for the candidacy of James Monroe in place of Madison. The lack of an established nomination process lead to a very confused situation. Knowing that they controlled the majority of the members of congress, Republican supporters of Madison called a congressional caucus in January. The caucus was poorly attended, but after a quick endorsement of Madison, the members present nominated Clinton as the party's vice-presidential candidate. They had failed, however, to consult Clinton beforehand and acted without his knowledge or approval. Clinton was offended by the caucus's behavior and refused ever to accept the nomination at its hands.

Many of Clinton's friends and allies proceeded then to put his name forward for the presidency, employing the usual technique of ballyhooing him in the papers and writing letters to leading politicians in the states. The hope was to make Clinton the fountainhead of anti-Madison Republicanism. The Federalists, meeting in what some historians consider the first political convention, came within a whisker of nominating Clinton as their candidate as well!

The result of all this maneuvering was that Clinton ran as both the Republican vice-presidential candidate hitched to Madison *and* as a presidential candidate in opposition to Madison. Not many appeared to take Clinton's chance for election as president too seriously, but he was a bona fide candidate by the standards of the time.

The tally of electoral votes gave Madison an easy victory of 122 to 47 over the Federalist Charles Cotesworth Pinckney, but George Clinton received 6 electoral votes for president. Of the vice-presidential votes, cast separately, he won in ten states with 113 electoral votes in total to 47 for Rufus King, the Federalist vice-presidential candidate.

Clinton's second vice-presidential term began with his calculated snub to the new president—Clinton delayed his arrival in Washington City until after Madison's inauguration in March 1809. In fact, he didn't arrive in the capital to take the oath of office until May.

In general, Clinton's second term was plagued by misfortune and increasing illness. His daughter Cornelia Genêt died in 1810, a significant blow to Clinton, and he himself suffered from a variety of ailments. His one important act, however, was to cast a deciding vote in 1811 defeating the attempt to recharter the National Bank. President Madison and Secretary of the Treasury Albert Gallatin supported the bank, but a significant number of Republicans were against it. Clinton's speech explaining his vote (apparently drafted by Henry Clay) condemned the prevailing broad interpretation of the Constitution that justified chartering a National Bank. Clinton, thus, remained loyal to the narrow Antifederalist position he had held for so long, and it must have been an additional measure of satisfaction to give a blow to the pet project of his old nemesis, Alexander Hamilton.

Clinton attended his last session of the Senate in the spring of 1812, but he was repeatedly ill and often unable to preside. He died on April 20 and was buried in the Congressional Cemetery—the first president or vice president to die in office—with great ceremony. In 1908, his coffin was removed from Washington, and George Clinton was laid to rest at Kingston, New York. The inscription on his tomb says in part: "While he lived, his virtue, wisdom, and valor were the pride, the ornament and the security of his country. . . ."

REFERENCES

E. Wilder Spaulding, *His Excellency George Clinton: Critic of the Constitution* (New York: Macmillan, 1938); John P. Kaminski, *George Clinton: Yeoman Politician of the New Republic* (Madison, Wisc.: Madison House, 1993); Gilbert D. B. Hasbrouck, "Governor George Clinton," *Quarterly Journal of the New York State Historical Association*, 1 (July 1920), 143–164; *Public Papers of George Clinton*, Harold Hastings, ed. (New York and Albany, 1899–1911); John K. Lee, *George Clinton: Master Builder of the Empire State* (Syracuse, N.Y.: Syracuse University Press, 2009).

L. EDWARD PURCELL is the author, coauthor, or editor of 17 books, including Facts On File's *Who Was Who in the American Revolution* and *Encyclopedia of Battles in North America*. Purcell holds history degrees from Simpson College and the University of Iowa. He was previously editor in chief of publications at the Iowa State Historical Society. He has taught history at several colleges and universities.

ELBRIDGE GERRY (1744–1814)

Vice President, 1813–1814

(President James Madison)

ELBRIDGE GERRY
(Library of Congress)

By Sarah J. Purcell

Elbridge Gerry was a public-minded "Founding Father" whose term as vice president capped a long and illusions political career spent fighting for the security of the new American nation. Gerry's involvement in nearly every major political event between 1775 and 1812 is little remembered, and his main public legacy remains the dubious political practice of "gerrymandering," which is named after him. Contemporaries, as well as some historians since, characterized Elbridge Gerry as a man of contradictions, but he was consistently motivated by a desire to do what he thought was right to create the most virtuous, moral, and stable American nation possible.

Gerry spent the last two years of his life as James Madison's vice president. His election as vice president was ironic, given his vocal opposition during the 1787 Constitutional Convention to creating such an office. At the convention,

Gerry had spoken against establishing the office of vice president as a violation of the separation of powers, stating: "We might as well put the President himself at the head of the Legislature."

Although a renowned antiparty politician for most of his career, Gerry had become an ardent Jeffersonian Republican by the 1810s, when he became convinced that the Federalists increasingly represented a threat to the new nation. By the time he was elected vice president in 1812, Gerry had lost most of the tremendous political influence he had once possessed, yet he proved to be a strong presiding officer in the Senate. Gerry's own term as vice president demonstrated his trademark adaptability when faced with an opportunity to help his country.

Elbridge Gerry was born January 17, 1744, in Marblehead, Massachusetts, to Thomas and Elizabeth Gerry. Elbridge's parents participated in the economic expansion that began in the 1730s and that turned Marblehead into one of the most important ports in New England, vital to both the fishing industry and to colonial trade with Britain and the West Indies. Thomas Gerry was a merchant seaman from Devonshire, England, who married Elizabeth Greenleaf, the daughter of a Boston merchant, before moving to Marblehead to raise twelve children and build a thriving merchant house and retail business. By the 1770s, Thomas Gerry ranked as one of the wealthiest men in the region.

Befitting his station as son of a wealthy, prominent family, Elbridge was educated by tutors in Marblehead and then sent to Harvard College in 1758 at the age of fourteen. He was ranked twenty-ninth in a class of fifty-two on entrance, a standing determined by the student's social prominence, not his academic merit. Gerry received a thorough education in classical political theory, and he graduated from Harvard in 1762, staying to study for an M.A. until 1765. Gerry exited Harvard in the year the Stamp Act inaugurated the full-scale British-American crisis in Massachusetts, ready to take up his role as a gentleman dedicated to public service.

Elbridge returned to Marblehead, entered the family mercantile business with his brothers Thomas and John, and set about becoming a prominent citizen of the town in his own right. Although he had no formal legal training, Gerry performed legal duties for the business. A handsome man, Elbridge Gerry became a popular guest at social occasions. As Gerry sought to become more cosmopolitan and refined, he joined a prestigious Marblehead political club and made the acquaintance of prominent men from other colonies on his business travels.

Gerry entered politics when he was appointed with his brother to the Marblehead patriot Committee of Inspection following the Boston Massacre in January 1770. The committee was charged to pressure local merchants and inhabitants to observe the American boycott against specified British goods. Gerry was committed to political opposition to Britain's unfair taxation, but he was obviously also concerned about the economic effects of harsh British legislation on his merchant community. He expressed a desire to fight what he viewed as corrupt governmental power on a local and colonial level, a desire that shaped much of his subsequent career.

As the crisis with Great Britain worsened, Gerry joined the extensive network of correspondents and committees who formed the backbone of American Revolutionary politics. This marked the beginning of Gerry's lifelong career as an ardent letter writer who debated theories of politics, society, and diplomacy with a wide variety of other public figures. Gerry's most faithful prominent correspondents included Samuel Adams, Rufus King, John Adams, Abigail Adams, Thomas Jefferson, Mercy Otis Warren, and James Warren. Gerry eventually served on both the Marblehead and Massachusetts Committees of Correspondence.

One of Marblehead's strongest patriots, Gerry headed a town-meeting committee that strongly assented to the Boston Town Meeting's 1772 circular letter that roundly condemned parliamentary action against the colonies.

Over the objection of some Marblehead moderates who found Gerry's Revolutionary politics too radical, Elbridge Gerry was elected to the Massachusetts General Court in 1773. In the Massachusetts legislature, Gerry advocated stronger boycotts and the formation of a colonial militia. Thus began Gerry's lifelong advocacy for state militias to hedge against what he considered the frightening prospect of a standing army.

The year 1773 brought smallpox to Massachusetts, and Elbridge Gerry was tangled up in the social and political ramifications of the epidemic. His brother John was one of a group of Marbleheaders who constructed Essex Hospital, a private hospital on Cat Island to provide inoculation, and Elbridge Gerry became one of the proprietors when the hospital opened. Because of uncertainty about how smallpox was spread, the public was fearful and opposed the hospital. In January 1774, rioters attacked the island and burned down the hospital, an incident subsequently referred to as the "Smallpox War." The violence shocked Gerry and reinforced his belief that the passions of the common man had to be controlled and channeled for the public good. Gerry resigned from the Marblehead Committee of Correspondence in protest.

Gerry reentered public affairs later in 1774 when he spearheaded Marbleheaders' resistance to the closing of the Port of Boston by the British and took over local relief efforts. He was unanimously nominated as a potential local Marblehead representative to the first meeting of the Continental Congress in September, but when only colonywide representatives were sent to Congress he attended the Essex County convention instead. Gerry was publicly hailed as a leading member of the convention, which resolved the most strenuous resistance to British punishments of Boston, and after the convention he began to consult with local leaders from around Massachusetts to coordinate anti-British actions.

After General Thomas Gage dissolved the Massachusetts legislature in October, Gerry helped to form the alternative Provincial Congress and was elected as a Marblehead representative. The Provincial Congress was an extralegal body that would evolve into the new Revolutionary legislature of the state of Massachusetts. As a member of the Provincial Congress, Gerry served on many important committees, but he particularly concerned himself with encouraging statewide military preparations. Gerry began to coordinate the collection of weapons and ammunition and soon began to organize military supplies of all kinds. As he became more prominent throughout Massachusetts, Gerry continued to be concerned with issues in Marblehead, including the formation of a corps of minutemen and local protests against British curtailing of fishing rights.

As the leader of the Provincial committee in control of military supplies, Elbridge Gerry played a role in the dramatic events at Lexington and Concord on April 19, 1775, that marked the beginning of the Revolutionary War. Gerry's committee was in charge of the weapons stored in Concord, the seizure of which was one of the British soldiers' primary objectives in their foray out of Boston. Gerry and several of his fellow committee members narrowly escaped capture by the British on their march to Concord by fleeing from the Black Horse Tavern in Menotomy in their nightclothes to hide in a cornfield. After the battles of Lexington and Concord, Gerry collected, from minutemen and witness, depositions for the Provincial Congress that were published in pamphlets and in newspapers around the country.

Although he despised arbitrary military power, Gerry was quickly convinced by his involvement at Lexington and Concord that the Revolutionary War was a necessary defense against tyranny. As a politician and as a merchant, Gerry continued to coordinate military supplies and funding, and he continued to be interested in the workings of militia and Continental army and navy forces.

Gerry soon came to realize that reconciliation with Britain would be impossible, and late in 1775 he became an early and strong proponent of American independence. In January 1776, after a fight against a more conservative Provincial Massachusetts faction lead by John Hancock (whom he despised for playing on popular passions), Gerry was elected to the Continental Congress, and he immediately helped the Massachusetts delegation take the lead on the question of independence. Gerry felt that independence was the only way for Americans to guard their virtue and morality from contamination by the corrupt British Empire. Gerry's leadership paid off, and on July 2, Congress voted for independence. Gerry was proud to sign the Declaration of Independence.

Gerry continued his interest in military matters a a member of Congress. He chaired a committee that oversaw supply of the Continental Army and investigated the quartermaster department, and he traveled with a committee to inspect several of Washington's encampments. Gerry also directed his brother to use the family's merchant fleets to trade with the army's commissary agents and with Joseph Gardoqui and Sons, a company of Spanish traders who were secretly sending funds to help the American cause. Enlistments were a constant problem for the army, and Gerry advocated extending the term of service for the entire war (a much more extreme position than Congress would ever endorse).

Gerry's name was linked with the Conway Cabal, a movement by some members of Congress in 1777 to replace George Washington as commander of the Continental Army with Horatio Gates, the hero of Saratoga. While Gerry was a great supporter of Gates's victory, there is no conclusive evidence that Gerry actually conspired to oust Washington.

Alongside military matters, Gerry became interested in finance. He openly advocated price controls after 1777 and was constantly concerned with bolstering the stability of paper currency. Much of Gerry's considerable personal fortune was invested in paper money and government securities during the war; yet he was in favor of limits on profiteering and attended several price-fixing conventions around the country. He also pushed to have fishing rights included in the economic demands placed on the British in peace negotiations.

Although Gerry was in favor of a central government to coordinate financial and military actions and was a proponent of the Articles of Confederation, he remained a strong advocate in Congress for the interests of Massachusetts. In 1780, Gerry objected to a committee recommendation for the requisitioning of supplies from the states because he felt the bill particularly hurt Massachusetts. When Gerry called for reconsideration of part of the bill, he became incensed when he was ruled out of order. He returned to Massachusetts and vacated his Congressional seat until 1783, despite the fact that he was frequently reelected. Under the current election system, which allowed candidates to run for more than one office at a time, he had also been elected to both houses of the Massachusetts legislature, and he served as a member of the state house of representatives, where he continued to oppose John Hancock.

Once the Revolutionary War was over, Gerry's support for a national military force ended. He strenuously opposed the maintenance of any peacetime standing army (such as the one proposed by Alexander Hamilton) as the potential tool of arbitrary governmental power, and he continued to be a supporter of the state militias' right to keep the peace once he reentered Congress in 1783. Another institution that Gerry despised was the Society of Cincinnati, founded in 1783 as an hereditary honorary association of officers of the Continental Army. Gerry contended that members of the society, including George Washington, were susceptible to becoming military dictators and represented a dangerous aristocratic element that was detrimental to society.

Gerry opposed the Impost of 1783, a national tariff designed to grant more independent revenue to the federal government, which was financially dependent upon the states under the Articles of Confederation. In

Gerry's mind, the states needed to be able to check any power held by a few individuals in the central government, and he was even wary of letting the Confederation government regulate foreign commerce, although in one of his many seeming contradictions, Gerry did favor federal assumption of each state's war debts.

When the question of where to locate the newly planned national capital arose in 1783, Gerry led two congressional committees to review proposed locations. Gerry balanced sectional and economic conflicts to favor a location on the Potomac River.

Ineligible for reelection to Congress in 1785 according to the Articles of Confederation, Gerry returned to the Massachusetts house of representatives. During 1785, Gerry opposed the efforts of Governor James Bowdoin and others in the state who began to call for a stronger national government. In 1786, he refused to attend the Annapolis Convention, a meeting called to discuss measures for bolstering national power.

Gerry's years as an unmarried ladies' man came to an end in 1786. He had courted Katherine Hunt of Watertown, Massachusetts, during his early years in Congress, but her illiteracy had stood in the way of his continuing their romance through correspondence, and he never proposed to her. Instead, Gerry married the intelligent and beautiful Ann Thompson, daughter of a prominent New York merchant family who was twenty-one years his junior.

Gerry had always cultivated good taste and public approval as a learned gentleman; in 1781 he had been elected to membership in the American Academy of Arts and Sciences. Marriage marked the beginning of his effort to be even more gentlemanly and refined as Gerry became an Anglican, shifted his investments into land and farming, bought a large estate in Cambridge (which he named Elmwood), and settled into polite society. Elbridge and Ann never again lived in the provincial fishing town of Marblehead.

Gerry was an extremely devoted husband and father. Ann bore ten children, nine of whom survived. Elbridge encouraged the education of both his sons and daughters, and he carried on tender correspondences with them when his political commitments took him away from home. Once he was married, Gerry expressed a constant desire for a comfortable home life, and he never ceased worrying about how his public commitments affected his family. Although Elbridge frequently worried about Ann's poor health, she was to live until 1849, making her the last surviving widow of a signer of the Declaration of Independence.

The year 1786 brought not only marriage for Gerry but also the signal event that frightened him into support for a stronger national government: Shays's Rebellion. In September, Daniel Shays, a poor Revolutionary war veteran, led a group of disgruntled debtors from western Massachusetts in a mob action to close down the county courts that were foreclosing on their mortgages. Though they were put down by the Massachusetts militia under Benjamin Lincoln (whom Gerry supported), the rebels shocked elitists like Gerry and caused even more consternation the following year when they began to be elected to offices in state government. Gerry saw the democratic threat he had been aware of since the Smallpox War horribly realized as the "rabble" became successful in the newly opened field of electoral politics.*

Convinced that an excess of either aristocracy, as embodied in the Society of Cincinnati, or of democracy, as in Shays's Rebellion, would lead to the downfall of the republic, Gerry now became persuaded that a stronger national government would help ensure stability. Gerry began his stint as a delegate to the Constitutional Convention in May 1787 still committed to states' rights but willing to consider more centralization of power in the interest of preserving a republican nation. Gerry's middling opinions shaped the ideas about separation of

*Editor's note: See GEORGE CLINTON for further explanation of Shays's Rebellion.

powers and checks and balances that he put forth throughout the convention.

Gerry was bothered by several points in the initial Virginia Plan offered by Edmund Randolph early in the convention. The plan called for a "National legislature" based on population, with a popularly elected lower house that would elect the upper house, a chief executive elected by the legislature, and a federal court system. Gerry thought the term "National legislature" to be too sweeping, opposed direct election of the lower house, and wanted the executive to have a council. One of Gerry's greatest concerns was about how the chief executive should be elected, and his constant efforts to oppose direct election in order to assure the merit of the candidates eventually led to a compromise between direct and legislative election and the creation of the electoral college.

After William Paterson introduced the New Jersey Plan, a scheme much closer to the Articles of Confederation and more favorable to small states and to the South than the Virginia Plan, Gerry was appointed head of a committee to work out a compromise. The "Great Compromise" that Gerry's committee produced became the new working plan for the convention, but as he worked on the document, Gerry's personal apprehension about the entire project began to increase, as did his old worries about militarism and aristocracy. By late July, when a draft of the document was drawn up, Gerry had become skeptical of the prospects of working out any satisfactory national government. Gerry could not accept a modern definition of federalism under which ultimate sovereignty resides in the people but where the federal and state governments share the power to govern.

Gerry particularly thought the Senate was being given too many powers. He opposed the creation of the vice presidency, and he thought having the vice president preside over the Senate was a direct violation of the separation of powers so necessary to the health of any republican government. Gerry felt it would be too easy for the president to impose the will of the executive branch on Congress through the vice president, and he feared that such corruption might unalterably weaken the republic.

By the end of the convention, in a highly controversial and exceptional move, Gerry decided not to sign the Constitution. A month later, Gerry wrote a public letter explaining his Antifederalism; his reason included the lack of a bill of rights and the possible damage to the independence of the states. The letter brought public scorn from the staunch Federalists in Massachusetts, but the state ratifying convention invited Gerry to appear and explain his position. Gerry was angered by the conduct of the convention, however, and when he left the proceedings he forever severed ties with some of his closest political friends, including Rufus King and Francis Dana. In the end, the Federalists prevailed.

Once the Constitution was ratified in 1789, Gerry decided to support the new federal government in the interest of national unity and stability. He reluctantly stood for election to Congress. Gerry was committed to no party but was sympathetic to many national Federalist positions, although he was never overly fond of George Washington and feared that some, such as Alexander Hamilton, still harbored monarchical tendencies.

Though he still clung to the ideas of states' rights, Gerry supported the Bank of the United States and invested his personal funds in the bank. He continued to advocate federal repayment of all war debts, but he opposed the creation of strong Treasury Department. Separation of powers continued to interest Gerry, who demanded particularly strict limits between the executive and the legislative branches, as in 1789 when he voted in Congress to oppose the presidential removal of Theodore Sedgwick as secretary of state. When the Bill of Rights was adopted, Gerry especially advocated the independence of the state militias, and he continued to object to centralized military force.

Gerry left the Congress in 1793. He was mentioned by several political backers as a candidate for governor of Massachusetts in

1794, but his middling politics satisfied those on neither side of the increasingly well-defined political split between Federalists and Jeffersonian Republicans. In 1796, Gerry became a presidential elector, and he supported John Adams for president despite Adams's strong Federalism.

Gerry had maintained his close personal ties to John Adams during Adams's vice presidency, and he continued the relationship after Adams became president. As an antiparty politician, Gerry particularly felt that Jefferson's "opposition" vice presidency during the Federalist administration could be a successful test of party cooperation. Gerry probably also hoped that having a president and vice president of different parties would provide another check on the potential growth in the power of the presidency that he so feared. Gerry corresponded with both Jefferson and Adams about his hopes that the president and vice president would rise above party spirit, and he even told Adams that he should try to garner Jefferson's cooperation as vice president by assuring him that he would someday become president. In reality, the party split between president and vice president during the Adams–Jefferson administration drove the parties farther apart.

Gerry faced his own political test during the XYZ affair, a major diplomatic crisis between the United States and France in which he played a prominent role. In 1797, President John Adams, over the objections of his own Federalist cabinet members, appointed Gerry to accompany Charles Coatsworth Pinckney and John Marshall to France to try to negotiate a peaceful solution to the increasing friction with France. France had stepped up harassment of American shipping in the wake of the Jay Treaty, which abrogated the Franco-American alliance and which France considered to be far too pro-British.

Gerry arrived in France after Pinckney and Marshall firmly resolved to uphold U.S. neutrality toward France and to prevent a full-scale war. French Foreign Minister Charles Maurice de Talleyrand-Périgord, whom Gerry had met in America during the Revolutionary War, sent four associates to make demands upon the American negotiators. Talleyrand's representatives, three of whom were identified in America only as X, Y, and Z, insisted that in order to avoid a war, the Americans would have to pay bribes and loans to the French. For several months, the Americans resisted the demands for payment, and eventually negotiations broke down.

Pinckney and Marshall left Paris in April 1798, but Gerry stayed behind at the demand of Talleyrand. When the XYZ "dispatches" were published to great public outcry in the United States, Gerry smoothed over the controversy in France by substantiating Talleyrand's claim that the agents had acted independently, while at the same time Gerry assured John Adams that Talleyrand was at fault. Gerry's frequent requests for a passport to leave France were not granted until August. France never declared full-scale war on the United States, but its harassment increased after the breakdown of the negotiations.*

Gerry acquired a bad reputation from the affair, based largely on the hostile impressions of him recorded by John Marshall in a journal that he later made public. Gerry argued, counter to Marshall's charges and to attacks on him by Timothy Pickering, that he had not taken advantage of his personal relationship with Talleyrand, but rather that he had always sought to include the other two Americans in their talks and to defend American neutrality. Contrary to the picture of Gerry painted by the Federalists upon his return, the evidence bears out his claim that he sought no personal advantage by remaining in France, but rather saw his remaining there as the only chance to preserve peace. Upon his return to Boston, Gerry was snubbed by the Federalists, who became increasingly militant toward France. Particularly bothersome to Gerry were vicious personal attacks on his family that included threats and burnt

---

*Editor's note: See JOHN ADAMS for further explanation of the XYZ Affair.

effigies on the front lawn of Elmwood. Gerry was not publicly vindicated until his correspondence with Talleyrand was published in 1799.

While Gerry remained personally loyal to John Adams in the aftermath of the affair, he was slowly drawn toward the Jeffersonians. In the wake of the XYZ affair, the Federalists became even more publicly identified as pro-British and the Jeffersonian Republicans as pro-French. Gerry did not embrace France, but he did want peace, and he thought the British were dangerous. Jefferson personally urged Gerry to be the Republican candidate for the Massachusetts governorship in 1800, on a platform of peace with France. Gerry lost the election, but he received a record number of votes against the Federalists and even won a majority of votes in Boston.

Still hoping that neutrality would dull the political forces that threatened to rip the country apart, Gerry supported Adams's presidential race in 1800 hoping that Jefferson would again come in second and be reelected as vice president. When Jefferson beat Adams for the presidency in the election, the Federalist Party was taken over by the Hamiltonian Federalists, whom Gerry viewed as dangerous militants and possible monarchists.

Elbridge Gerry then abandoned his anti-party status and became a Jeffersonian Republican because he thought it the only way left to protect America's virtue. Gerry ran as the Republican candidate for Massachusetts governor from 1801 to 1803. Each race was unsuccessful but showed an increase in Republican votes.

For a time, it seemed Gerry was finally to have the tranquil private life away from demanding public service that he had craved for so long. Not yet ready to embrace all the machinations of modern party politics, Gerry left the governing to others during Jefferson's first administration. Elbridge and Ann raised their children at Elmwood, and Elbridge sought to straighten out financial troubles caused by the shoddy handling of the family businesses by his brother Samuel.

During the Embargo Crisis in 1809, when the Jeffersonian blocked all exports to protest foreign interference with American trade, Gerry became more convinced than even that the Federalists were plotting with the British to undo the republic. The danger he perceived convinced Gerry to reenter public life. He agreed to stand for governor in 1809 after the Republican candidate died. When Gerry ran again in 1810, he won. Although he had embraced party politics, Gerry still sought political middle ground during his first administration as governor.

Gerry's second term as governor of Massachusetts in 1811 was far more partisan. Gerry lost patience with the Federalists, who were viciously attacking President Madison, and he purged Federalists from public office in Massachusetts wherever possible. Gerry appointed a particularly high number of Republicans to the state judiciary and ended the Federalist hold on the Corporation of Harvard University. Gerry also investigated and prosecuted a record number of Federalist newspapers for libel.

It was during Gerry's second term early in 1812 when the term "gerrymander" was born. The Republican state legislature redistricted the state along heavily Republican lines, and the Federalists were none too pleased. Although Gerry himself always claimed that he protested the redistricting, he was targeted by the Federalists as the culprit. A Federalist cartoonist, Elkanah Tisdale, drew Gerry's head atop a map of the new district of Essex County. The caption drew attention to the cartoon district's resemblance to a salamander, and the name "gerrymander" stuck to the practice of partisan redistricting.

Gerry was nominated as the Republican candidate for vice president in 1812 after John Langdon of New Hampshire declined the nomination. The election was fought mainly over the War of 1812, and supporters hoped that Gerry's reputation as a supporter of Madison and of the Revolutionary military would counteract some antiwar Republicans. Although he had always opposed arbitrary military power, Gerry viewed the War of 1812 as a fight necessary to save the American republic. Republican handlers also supported Gerry's nomination because his age (sixty-eight) would prevent him from threatening James Monroe as Madison's presidential heir apparent and because they hoped he would draw support away from the Federalists in New England. Madison and Gerry defeated the Federalist ticket led by DeWitt Clinton, and Gerry was inaugurated as vice president on March 4, 1813.

The war added new fuel to Gerry's partisan fire during his vice presidency. In his first inaugural address, Gerry claimed that the war would decide "whether the republican system adopted by the people is imbecile and transient, or whether it has force and duration worthy of the enterprise." Gerry was not alone in considering the War of 1812 a test of the strength of the American Revolution.

Gerry did not perform many important political functions as vice president, but he did take his role as presiding officer of the Senate very seriously. Gerry shaped the office by refusing to abide by the tradition that the vice president would allow another presiding officer to be named in case both the president and vice president both died while Congress was not in session over the summer. In June 1813, Gerry was unwell and President Madison was gravely ill, yet Gerry would not resign his senatorial leadership for fear that if he died, William B. Giles, a political enemy, might become presiding officer and hurt the war effort.

Gerry was concerned with preserving the integrity of the Republican Party and of the office of vice president. During the 1814 session of the Senate, Gerry discovered that a stenographer whom the Senate had appointed to record its debates was publishing antiadministration articles in Washington, D.C., newspapers. After suspecting that the entire affair consisted of a plot just to embarrass him, Gerry avoided scandal and refused to dismiss the man.

During his vice presidency, Elbridge Gerry took an active part in the Washington, D.C., social scene. While his wife remained at home in Massachusetts, he accompanied the famous and fashionable Madame Bonaparte, the daughter of a Maryland merchant family and the wife of Jerome Bonaparte, to many public functions. Gerry spent much of the remainder of his time in office trying to secure patronage positions for members of his family who were beginning to suffer financially.

Gerry became ill, probably from a stroke, during the summer of 1813. He recovered from the initial attack, but at the age of seventy he did not regain his full strength. On November 23, 1814, Gerry was afflicted again in the Senate chamber, and he died later that day. Gerry was buried in the Congressional Cemetery in Washington, D.C., where a monument to his vice-presidential years marks his grave. Senator Christopher Gore proposed that Gerry's wife be paid his full vice-presidential salary for life, but the proposal was rejected by Republicans who feared setting a precedent for Federalist pensions.

Elbridge Gerry was in many ways an important Founding Father of the United States—revolutionary, signer of the Declaration of Independence, member of the Constitutional Convention, diplomat, congressman, and governor. Although he was accused of vacillating over the course of his political career, he worked tirelessly on behalf of measures he thought would be best for the nation. It was fitting that Gerry died still in the service of his country as vice president. Abigail Adams provided a just eulogy for Gerry in a letter to her sister Elizabeth Peabody on December 12, 1814:

> Alas, the last compatriot is gone . . . A Friend who was neither warped nor shaken by change of time or fortune . . . Faction may rave & Party spirit slander, but an honester man he has not left behind nor a more sincere disinterested Friend of his Country.

REFERENCES

George Billias, *Elbridge Gerry: Founding Father and Republican Statesman* (New York: McGraw-Hill, 1976); James T. Austin, *The Life of Elbridge Gerry,* 2 vols. (Boston: Wells and Lilly, 1828–29); Samuel Eliot Morison, "Elbridge Gerry, Gentleman-Democrat," *New England Quarterly,* II (1929), 6–33; *A Study in Dissent: The Warren-Gerry Correspondence, 1776–1792,* C. Harvey Gardiner, ed. (Carbondale, Ill.: Southern Illinois University Press, 1968); *Elbridge Gerry's Letterbook, Paris 1797–1798,* Russell W. Knight, ed. (Salem, Mass.: The Essex Institute, 1966); James Austin, *The Life of Elbridge Gerry* (Applewood Books, 2009).

SARAH J. PURCELL teaches American history at Grinnell College in Iowa, where she earned her bachelor's degree and is director of the Rosenfield Program in Public Affairs, International Relations and Human Rights. She received both the master's and Ph.D. degrees in history from Brown University, where she was also a fellow at the John Carter Brown Library. She is the author of *Sealed in Blood: War, Sacrifice, and Memory in Revolutionary America* (University of Pennsylvania Press, 2002) and *The Early National Period* (Facts On File, Inc., 2004) and is coauthor of *Encyclopedia of Battles in North America* (Facts On File, Inc., 2000). In addition, she has written several articles in historical journals and regularly gives papers at historical conferences in the United States and abroad. Purcell is coauthor of a biography of Eleanor Roosevelt and has written articles for the *American National Biography* and *The Encyclopedia of New England Culture.* She also has served as a consultant on the Bunker Hill Monument for the National Park Service.

DANIEL D. TOMPKINS (1774–1825)

Vice President, 1817–1825

(President James Monroe)

DANIEL D. TOMPKINS
(Library of Congress)

By Gaspare J. Saladino

Daniel D. Tompkins was the sixth vice president. At about age twenty-six, Tompkins entered public life, and before his thirtieth birthday he became a New York State supreme court justice, a remarkable achievement for a farmer's son. In 1807, "The Farmer's Boy" was elected governor of New York, holding that position for ten years. A democrat, republican, humanitarian, and patriot, Tompkins achieved unparalleled popularity, especially during the War of 1812 when he was America's finest war governor. His splendid war record brought him national attention, and he was considered for the presidency. An ambitious man, Tompkins took his presidential candidacy seriously, but astute politicians recognized that he lacked widespread support.

Therefore, Tompkins settled for the vice presidency, a dead-end office in which his reputation suffered badly. His financial problems and related intemperance caused him to neglect his duty as president of the Senate and made his vice-presidential years the unhappiest of his life. Notwithstanding, he was courted by presidential candidates who recognized his enormous popularity in the important state of New York. They took his presidential aspirations in earnest, or at least did not openly disparage them. His enemies—often wealthy aristocrats with personal grudges—mercilessly belittled him, however. Tompkins ended his vice presidency aware that his political career was over, even though he was but fifty years old.

Tompkins was born on June 21, 1774, in Scarsdale, Westchester County, New York, the son of Jonathan Griffin Tompkins and Sarah Ann Hyatt. His father was descended from English settlers, his mother from Scottish. The elder Tompkins, a farmer and Revolutionary patriot, became a county judge and state assemblyman. Daniel Tompkins entered Columbia College as a sophomore in 1792, and three years later he was valedictorian. In his senior year, he entered the New York City office of attorney Peter Jay Munro and in 1797 was admitted to the bar. That same year he married Hannah Minthorne, daughter of Mangle Minthorne, a wealthy New York City merchant from the city's Seventh Ward. The Tompkinses had seven children.

Tompkins was part of "The Little Band," young intellectuals who met at the home of New York City lawyer Aaron Burr, a powerful Republican leader. In the spring 1800 state elections, Burr controlled the city's General Republican Committee and turned his "Little Band" into campaign workers. Tompkins operated in the Seventh Ward. The Republicans elected their entire slate of candidates to the state assembly, giving them a majority in that body. Later that year, the assembly and the senate gave the state's twelve electoral votes to Thomas Jefferson and Burr for president and vice president, respectively. New York's electoral votes were critical to Jefferson's ultimate election.

The election brought Tompkins to the attention of President Jefferson, who appointed him a commissioner of bankruptcy under the Bankruptcy Act of 1800. Burr engineered Tompkins's election to the state constitutional convention of 1801, Tompkins's first elective office, where he distinguished himself by his independence. In 1802, Tompkins was elected a New York City assembly delegate, serving for several months the next year; he resigned in 1804 to become an associate justice of the state Supreme Court and in the same year was elected to (but resigned from) the U.S. House of Representatives. In 1805, he declined appointment as judge of the U.S. District Court for New York because he earned more as a state judge. These were the first of several federal positions that Tompkins turned down in favor of a state office, a not uncommon practice among New York politicians. In these years, Tompkins also became a Mason, a founder of the New York Academy of Fine Arts, an organizer of the New-York Historical Society, a member of the New York Manumission Society, and a founder of a free school for poor children.

His judicial position boosted Tompkins's public career. As he rode circuit, he became acquainted with voters and developed a statewide reputation as an honest judge who rendered accurate judicial decisions and delivered eloquent charges and addresses. According to Jabez Hammond, a Republican politician and a New York historian, Tompkins (as a judge) was "extremely prepossessing, his manners highly popular, and his address . . . every way pleasing." Mordecai Noah, a Republican newspaper editor, asserted that Tompkins also had "the faculty of attaching every person to him who once knew him."

In 1807, DeWitt Clinton, leader of the Clintonian wing of the Republican Party and a nephew of U.S. vice president George Clinton, wanted to unseat Governor Morgan Lewis, a leader of the party's Livingston wing who was also favored by Federalists. DeWitt Clinton wanted to be governor (as his uncle had been), but his aristocratic background made that difficult. Therefore, he convinced the Republicans in the state legislature to nominate Tompkins, thinking that he could "mould" him. Tompkins won by more than 4,000 votes in an election that was described as a Tompkins crusade to frustrate "a combination of rich families."

Tompkins was inaugurated governor in July 1807 and moved his family to Albany, the state capital, a few months later. He was reelected in 1810, 1813, and 1816. During his first administration (1807–10), he diligently enforced the embargo against Great Britain levied by Congress, although he was reluctant, despite President Jefferson's entreaties, to use force to do so. Nevertheless, Tompkins's support was "highly consolatory" to Jefferson. His actions marked the beginning of an alliance with the Virginia Dynasty, to which he was drawn both by political philosophy and expediency. He also began to distance himself from DeWitt Clinton, an opponent of the embargo. His breach with Clinton widened during the presidential election of 1808 when he backed James Madison against George Clinton. With little aid from the federal government or state legislature, Tompkins prepared for war with Great Britain by raising and equipping the militia and constructing arsenals and fortifications.

His war preparations did not diminish his Jeffersonian humanitarianism. In his state papers—praised for their brevity, vigor, and eloquence—Tompkins stressed the pivotal role of education in a democracy, advocated the improved treatment of the insane, sought to restrict capital punishment, pardoned criminals to relieve overcrowding in prisons, and opposed whipping and other humiliating punishments. He developed most of these ideas, as his college essays attest, when he was young.

In 1810, the Republicans again nominated Tompkins for governor. He defeated Federalist Jonas Platt of Herkimer by more than 6,000 votes. DeWitt Clinton was elected lieutenant governor despite the opposition of Tompkins and the "Martling-Men" of Tammany. ("Martling" was the name of the New York City tavern where they met.) The Tammany faction had recently become a significant political force, one that would back Tompkins for his entire

political career and would try to drive the aristocratic and despised Clinton from power.

Harshly critical of Great Britain, Tompkins continued his war preparations and was so effective that in 1811 it was rumored that he would become secretary of war in Madison's administration "with a reversion of the presidency, when Monroe and Madison have done with it."

In 1811, Congress failed to renew the charter of the Bank of the United States, and to fill the void New York investors, mostly Federalists, sought to incorporate the Bank of America. In January 1812, Federalists, aided by some Republicans, introduced and pushed for an incorporation bill in the New York legislature. Tompkins told the legislature that the state already had too many banks; too much wealth was amassed and concentrated in bank stock, and bankers were not accountable to the public. Nevertheless, the assembly adopted the bank bill, and in March Tompkins prorogued the legislature to prevent the senate from acting. Seeking Federalist support for the presidency, DeWitt Clinton equivocated on the bank bill. His brother-in-law remarked: "Our Governor has prorogued our Assembly. Farmer's boys are apt to use power when in power as perhaps Gentlemen's sons." Some Clintonians charged the prorogation was really an attempt to prevent the legislature from endorsing Clinton for the presidency before a congressional caucus could nominate Madison.

About a week after the legislature convened on May 21, 1812, Republicans nominated Clinton to run for president against Madison, who had been unanimously nominated by congressional Republicans on May 18. (The legislature also incorporated the Bank of America.) Tompkins supported Madison. In June, war was declared against Great Britain. Tompkins called out the militia, ordered men and equipment to New York's northern and western frontiers, helped to defend New York City, erected more arsenals and magazines, made inspection tours, and tried to rouse a deeply divided public. However, he was hampered by the Federalist-dominated assembly which, for example, refused to vote funds for the militia.

In November 1812, Madison was reelected president, although New York's electoral votes went to DeWitt Clinton, the favorite of peace Republicans and Federalists. In February 1813, Republicans in the New York legislature unanimously nominated Tompkins for governor and refused, to Tompkins's delight, to renominate Clinton for lieutenant governor. State Senator Martin Van Buren led the fight against Clinton and joined Tompkins as a leader of the state's Republican party. Clinton's courting of Federalists was anathema to these two loyal party men. Federalists nominated "The Great Patroon," the wealthy Stephen Van Rensselaer, for governor.

Described as Madison's "tool," Tompkins was attacked for calling out the militia and proroguing the legislature, but the bitter campaign's main theme was support for the war, and a vote for Tompkins was a vote for the war. In the spring elections, Tompkins defeated Van Rensselaer by more than 3,600 votes. His greatest support came from the militarily vulnerable southern and western districts. The Madison administration rejoiced in Tompkins's victory because it destroyed the prospects of a northern confederacy; New York was not likely now to join violently antiwar New England. By late 1813 and early 1814, Tompkins was being boosted for the presidency, but most knowledgeable politicians dismissed him.

In August 1814, Washington, D.C., was burned, and a British invasion of New York City seemed imminent. Although the city's defenses needed improvement, its banks refused to lend money for that purpose solely on the security of U.S. Treasury notes. Encouraged by prominent New Yorkers, including U.S. Senator Rufus King (a Federalist), Tompkins personally endorsed these notes. In September, he called a special session of the legislature, which, under the leadership of Van Buren (a loyal ally of Tompkins), hiked the militia's pay, raised twenty companies to protect New York City,

and provided for fortifications in the area of the city. In later years, King praised Tompkins for "performing the duties of almost every Department" in prosecuting the war.

On September 28, 1814, Madison offered Tompkins the position of secretary of state, "then regarded as the stepping stone to the Presidency." Tompkins declined, stating that he could serve the war effort better as governor of New York. Moreover, he believed it was unwise to leave New York because, in his absence, his unauthorized defense expenditures might be used against him by his political enemies. According to Van Buren, who praised Tompkins's genuine patriotism, his declining the office and "the subsequent selection of Mr. Monroe, in all probability controuled the question of succession to Mr. Madison." Tammany leader Matthew L. Davis disagreed; if Tompkins wanted the nomination, he needed some "warm, open, and active friends" in Washington or else he would "be *led off the course as a distanced poney; or not in a condition to run the heats.*"

Madison was disappointed and angry, but in October 1814 he gave Tompkins command of the Third Military District, embracing southern New York and much of New Jersey. Colonel Washington Irving, a recent addition to Tompkins's staff, was overjoyed; the governor was "absolutely one of the worthiest men" he ever knew. He had "good sense and ready talent" and "nerve to put into immediate execution any measure that he is satisfied is correct." Taking command immediately, Tompkins made inspection tours, improved the city's and district's defenses, and organized and disciplined 25,000 troops. In December the United States and Great Britain signed the Treaty of Ghent, and in February 1815 the U.S. Senate ratified it. Tompkins relinquished his command in April. Jabez Hammond wrote:

> The popularity and influence of Gov. Tompkins may be said now to have been at its zenith. In New-York he was all but idolized by a formidable and well organized political party,

who held strong majorities in both branches of the legislature; abroad he was esteemed and respected, and at Washington the national cabinet had virtually declared him their candidate for the next national executive vacancy.

A confident Tompkins moved against DeWitt Clinton in 1815. Although he refused to break a tie in the five-member Council of Appointment, he convinced the two Clinton supporters to oust Clinton as New York City mayor. He wanted to maintain party harmony so that his presidential chances would not be hurt. One politician noted: "The Governor is every man's friend & he is so ardent in his pursuit of popularity, that he will not venture to lose an atom of it." Tompkins also attacked Clinton's campaign to build the popular Erie Canal. Because the anglophobic Tompkins believed that the Treaty of Ghent (1815) was only a truce, he wanted state money to be spent in preparing for another war, not on the canal.

In February 1816, the Republicans in the state legislature nominated Tompkins for the presidency and instructed the state's congressional delegates to support him. The delegates were already working for him, even though they were not optimistic. Tompkins had no support in the South. The same month, the Republican legislative caucus also backed him for governor. Tompkins did not want the nomination, but ever loyal to the party, he accepted. He preferred a presidential nomination, being among those politicians who thought that the next president should come from a state other than Virginia. When he realized he could not be nominated, Tompkins agreed to accept a vice-presidential nomination on a ticket with either Secretary of the Treasury William Crawford of Georgia or Secretary of State James Monroe of Virginia. In March, the Republican congressional caucus gave Monroe sixty-five votes to fifty-four for Crawford for the presidential nomination and Tompkins eighty-five votes to thirty for Pennsylvanian Simon Snyder for the vice-presidential nomination. The vice presidency, however, was not a path to the presidency. The Virginia Dynasty used it to obtain support outside the South.

In the spring 1816 gubernatorial election, Tompkins defeated Federalist Rufus King by almost 7,000 votes after a bruising campaign in which the war and Tompkins's conduct of it were the main issues. His greatest support came from western New York, whose protection had been one of his wartime concerns. Monroe and Tompkins were elected in November 1816, each receiving 183 of 217 electoral votes. In January 1817, Tompkins—reiterating a plea that he made to the state legislature in 1812—recommended (in a special message) that the state legislature expunge "the reproach of slavery" from the statute book by 1827. The legislature responded on March 31 by emancipating all African Americans born before July 4, 1779, as of July 4, 1827. On February 12, 1817, Congress counted the electoral votes and declared Monroe and Tompkins elected Tompkins resigned as governor on February 24.

Monroe and Tompkins were inaugurated on March 4, 1817. As president of the U.S. Senate, Tompkins had a poor attendance record. In his two vice-presidential terms, he never presided over an entire session of the Senate, and he missed two of eight sessions (plus a brief special session). The two missed sessions were the last ones in each of his terms. Sometimes Tompkins did not even leave his Washington boardinghouse to preside, once lamenting that "there is nothing for him to do here, and any other man may preside in the Senate as well as he." As presiding officer, he was cordial and conciliatory, although Delaware Congressman Louis McLane found him awkward in the chair.

Tompkins's profound financial problems (personal and official) and his related intemperance prompted his poor attendance. During the war and after, the "Farmer's Boy" purchased land on Staten Island, built a mansion, and developed Tompkinsville on the island's northeastern end directly opposite lower Manhattan. With others, he undertook projects that connected Tompkinsville by steam ferry with Manhattan and joined the northern and southern ends of Staten Island by turnpike. These grandiose schemes, common to America's budding entrepreneurs, ran him into debt.

As war governor, Tompkins expended about $4 million of state and federal money, as well as money he raised. Unfortunately, according to Jabez Hammond, Tompkins "was irregular and unmethodical in business; not systematical in keeping his accounts; employed too many agents; mingled his own private funds with those of the public; was naturally careless about money, and sometimes profuse in his expenses." The accounts of the New York comptroller showed in 1816 that Tompkins had not legally accounted for $120,000 in state funds. In 1819, a legislatively appointed commission recommended that Tompkins be paid a premium of $120,000 on money he had raised, thereby offsetting what he owed. The legislature passed a bill approving the premium. But Tompkins claimed the state owed him $130,000. Clintonian comptroller Archibald McIntyre rejected this claim, and the issue became a political football before it was resolved. Although Tompkins tried repeatedly to settle his federal accounts, the government's system of accountability for many years after the war was in a chaotic condition. It was several years before he was even told whether or not he owed or was owed money.

An embittered and disillusioned Tompkins probably started to drink heavily at this time. Van Buren visited him early in 1820 and discovered that Tompkins's "habit of intemperance" had started. He explained that Tompkins's "feelings had not been callous or his resolution strong enough to enable him to bear up against the injustice, the ingratitude and the calumny of which he was now made the victim." Hammond speculated that Tompkins drank "in order to allay nervous irritability and excitement." A less sympathetic Clintonian described Tompkins as "a degraded sot."

In his first vice-presidential term, Tompkins cast two of his five tie-breaking votes as the Senate's president. On January 21, 1819, he voted against an amendment to strike out a clause in a military appropriations bill, requiring the army to give extra pay to noncommissioned officers and soldiers employed in military road construction and repair. In a message (the only extant one for his casting votes), he defended the clause's constitutionality, declaring that Congress continuously gave the president the power to build and repair military roads, a power that he had exercised for years. "When they give to the Executive plenary powers to effect any certain and legal public object, the right to employ all lawful means to accomplish that object is necessarily implied and conferred." On February 10, 1819, Tompkins voted negatively on a motion to postpone a bill providing for an equestrian statue of George Washington.

On January 24, 1820, Tompkins wrote his wife that he was much occupied in the Senate: "The question of slavery in Missouri has been debated for 12 days past with great animation and at great length." During the history-making debate, the "gallant" Tompkins permitted some women to sit on the floor in seats usually reserved for dignitaries. To the dismay of the senators, others followed them to the floor. The next day Tompkins affixed a note to the Senate's door "excluding all ladies" not introduced by a senator. Senator Rufus King was unhappy with Tompkins for another reason; he thought Tompkins questioned whether Congress could exclude slavery from Missouri as a condition for statehood. King apparently believed that Tompkins's hankering for the presidency made him curry favor with the South. A Clintonian was more candid, describing Tompkins as "that miserable Sycophant who betrayed us to the Lords of the South, to enable him to subserve his own purposes."

Led by Van Buren, the Republican Party's "Bucktails" (named for a Tammany insignia, a deer tail worn in a hat; formerly the Martling-Men) nominated Tompkins on January 16, 1820 to run for governor against Governor DeWitt Clinton, who had won a special election in 1817 after Tompkins resigned. Upon Tompkins's return to Albany in February, he hesitantly accepted the nomination because he realized that the campaign, centering on his wartime accounts, would be vicious. The election drew national attention because politicians believed that Tompkins and Clinton would be presidential candidates in 1824.

Beginning in February 1820 the Bucktails sought an alliance with Federalist Rufus King, who was indebted to them. Led by Van Buren and Tompkins, the Bucktails had engineered King's reelection as U.S. senator the previous month, against Clinton's opposition, but King was disturbed by the state of Tompkins's wartime accounts and his alleged attitude on Missouri statehood. Tompkins wrote King's son in March that Congress possessed the constitutional authority to require the exclusion of slavery as a condition for Missouri statehood. This reply satisfied King, but he still did not openly favor Tompkins. Clinton was elected narrowly—47,447 to 45,990. Most Federalists voted against Tompkins, who had long been their chief foe. The most damaging vote against Tompkins came from western New York, which repaid Clinton for supporting the Erie Canal. Tammany got an astonishing 59 percent of Federalist New York City's vote for Tompkins. Later in the year the Bucktail-controlled legislature, led by Van Buren, passed an act balancing the wartime accounts of Tompkins, who had released his claims against the state.

In 1820, the congressional caucus did not even bother to renominate Monroe and Tompkins. In mid-November, after the presidential election, Massachusetts Congressman Daniel Webster hatched a plot whereby he and others would cast their electoral votes for Secretary of State John Quincy Adams of Massachusetts instead of Tompkins. Their purpose was not to defeat Tompkins, but only to lay groundwork for Adams's run for the presidency in 1824. Adams rejected the scheme, urging his adherents to vote for Tompkins. Adams refused to antagonize Tompkins, who was so popular in New York; moreover, Tompkins was an enemy of Clinton, a man whose presidential aspirations Adams feared more.

Congress counted the electoral votes in February 1821 and declared Monroe and Tompkins elected. The former received 231 of 232 votes cast, the latter 218 votes. William Plumer, Sr., a New Hampshire elector who cast the only vote against Monroe in December 1820 and who also voted against Tompkins, explained that Tompkins

whose duty consists in presiding over the senate—for which he receives annually a salary of five thousand dollars; during the last three years he was absent from the senate during their session nearly three fourths of the time, & thereby occasioned an extra-expense to the nation of nearly twenty five hundred dollars. He has not that weight of character which his office requires—the fact is he is grossly intemperate. I cannot vote for him to be again Vice President.

Because Tompkins failed to attend the previous congressional session, Monroe sent a messenger to New York to inform him of his reelection. Tompkins took the oath of office on March 3, 1821, and again on March 5, upon learning that Monroe would take the oath that day.

Before Tompkins was on hand for the first session of his second term in December, he was Staten Island's sole delegate to the New York constitutional convention, called to revise the state constitution of 1777. The calling of the convention by popular referendum was a manifestation of the democratic fervor sweeping the state. The Bucktails, the Republican Party's more democratic wing, elected 110 of the 126 delegates. On August 28, Tompkins was elected president. He excused himself once for ill health, but apparently attended the convention almost every day until it adjourned on November 20, demonstrating his keen interest in democratic reform and state government. He was delighted to see the abolition of the "aristocratic" and "partisan" Council of Revision, a body composed of the governor, the chancellor, and supreme court judges, that could veto laws.

But he opposed the convention's decision to give the governor sole veto power. Tompkins successfully argued for the abolition of the Council of Appointment and the placing of its power in the hands of the executive and legislature. He supported universal manhood suffrage, which the convention did not accept, although it extended the suffrage to more men. Early the next year the voters overwhelmingly accepted the new constitution.

On December 28, 1821, Tompkins began to preside over the U.S. Senate, remaining until about February 1, 1822. Upon arriving in Washington, he was refused admittance into the congressional mess at Strother's boardinghouse, according to Louis McLane, because "he bears the most evident and conclusive marks of a sot." A friend of General Andrew Jackson of Tennessee, a candidate for the presidency in 1824, wrote him that Tompkins was "several times so drunk in the chair that he could with difficulty put the question." In mid-January 1822, Tompkins, hounded by his creditors, placed in trust for their benefit all his real and personal property. His Washington stay was enlivened by a dispute over the appointment of a new Albany postmaster. The postmaster general wanted to appoint a Clintonian Federalist but was opposed by Tompkins and New York senators Van Buren and King, all political enemies of DeWitt Clinton. Monroe refused to interfere, and the postmaster general prevailed. Tompkins was once so angry that he used "violent language" against the president. On January 30, he cast a vote (his third) to keep the revenue officer at Natchez, Mississippi, who a propose bill sought to remove. Two days later Tompkins informed King officially that his poor health forced him to leave Washington.

The longtime failure of the federal government, despite Tompkins's many efforts, to settle his wartime accounts compounded his problems. His plight became more desperate in April 1822 when Congress placed a rider on an appropriations bill stating that any person in arrears would have his salary withheld until his accounts were settled. Such a person, however, could demand prompt action from the Treasury. By this time, the Treasury had finally certified that he owed the government about $11,000. In June 1822, Tompkins went to the federal district court in New York, claiming that the government owed him money. Rufus King and many others testified for him. Tompkins spoke of ten years of "fears, anxieties, perplexities, sorrows, sicknesses, blighted prospects, and wounded feelings." The jury concluded that the government owed him about $137,000.

Tompkins returned to the Senate in December 1822 in such good spirits and health that, for the first and perhaps only time, he brought along his wife. A correspondent of Kentucky Congressman Henry Clay thought Tompkins still wanted to be president. Tompkins pursued the settlement of his accounts. In January 1823, a select committee of the House of Representatives backed most of his claims. The House and Senate adopted a bill in February, authorizing the Treasury and the president to adjust and settle his accounts and claims. The bill also repealed the rider to an earlier law that had cut off his salary. In late November 1823, Monroe informed Congress that the Treasury had certified that Tompkins was owed $35,190. Before year's end, both houses adopted a bill appropriating that sum. In the House one of the bill's sponsors was Henry Clay, a candidate for the presidential nomination in 1824, who well understood Tompkins's "controuling influence" in New York. Earlier in the year Clay wrote a New York correspondent that he "cherished the greatest respect" for Tompkins. Secretary of War John C. Calhoun of South Carolina, another presidential candidate, also considered Tompkins's backing critical; in October 1823 he told a New York supporter that it was necessary Tompkins should "heartily acquiesce" in Calhoun's choice of a New York vice-presidential candidate. Calhoun hoped that Tompkins would not depart from "the 8 year rule" and seek a third term. Calhoun need not have worried because, according to New Hampshire congressman William Plumer, Jr., no one wanted Tompkins, "much fallen both in fortune & in fame," to serve again.

On January 21, 1824, Tompkins began to preside over the Senate for the last time, remaining in the chair until May 20, his longest continuous service. John Quincy Adams visited Tompkins on January 25 and recorded in his diary that the vice president

> told me that he had recovered his health, with the exception of sleepless nights, and that he was relieved from all his embarrassments; that he had no intention of being a candidate for election to the Presidency or for re-election as Vice-President. All he wanted was justice . . . quiet and retirement.

In April, Monroe recommended that Tompkins be awarded more money on his accounts, and in May the two houses approved an appropriation of $60,239, bringing the amount due Tompkins to over $95,000. During these same months, Tompkins cast his fourth and fifth votes. On April 22, he approved a motion to adjourn rather than to consider further a bill for surveying roads and canals.

On May 17, he accepted a Senate amendment to a tariff bill that provided for a 25 percent ad valorem duty on woolen manufactures.

On May 20, 1824, the last day Tompkins presided, his public career ended. He retired to Tompkinsville and took no part in the presidential election of 1824. Before long, he began to drink heavily again, and he died on June 11, 1825, still in debt. With much ceremony, "The Farmer's Boy" was buried in his wife's family vault in lower Manhattan's fashionable St. Mark's-in-the-Bowery.

REFERENCES

Ray W. Irwin, *Daniel D. Tompkins: Governor of New York and Vice President of the United States* (New York: New-York Historical Society, 1968); Ray W. Irwin and Edna L. Jacobsen, eds., *A Columbia College Student in the Eighteenth Century: Essays by Daniel D. Tompkins, Class of 1795 . . .* (New York: Columbia University Press, 1940); Jabez Hammond, *A History of Political Parties in the State of New-York . . .*, 4th ed., 3 vols. (Syracuse, N.Y.: Hall, Mills, and Company, 1852); John Niven, *Martin Van Buren: The Romantic Age of American Politics* (New York: Oxford University Press, 1983); Alvin Kass, *Politics in New York State, 1800–1830* (Syracuse, N.Y.: Syracuse University Press, 1965); Jerome Mushkat, *Tammany: The Evolution of a Political Machine, 1789–1865* (Syracuse, N.Y.: Syracuse University Press, 1971); and J.C.A. Stagg, *Mr. Madison's War: Politics, Diplomacy, Warfare in the Early Republic, 1783–1830* (Princeton, N.J.: Princeton University Press, 1983).

GASPARE J. SALADINO is coeditor of *The Documentary History of the Ratification of the Constitution* (twenty-two volumes to date) at the University of Wisconsin-Madison. He earned his B.A. at Brooklyn College and his M.A. and Ph.D. degrees at the University of Wisconsin–Madison. He has taught at the State University of New York at Albany and has been a fellow at the Adams Papers at the Massachusetts Historical Society. His publications include several articles on the ratification of the Constitution in New York and Delaware, the evolution of liberties in Delaware, and the historiography of the Bill of Rights and the era of the founding of the republic.

JOHN CALDWELL CALHOUN (1782–1850)

Vice President, 1825–1832

(President John Quincy Adams and Andrew Jackson)

JOHN CALDWELL CALHOUN
(Library of Congress)

By Mark G. Malvasi

The 1820s and 1830s marked a transition in American political history from the patrician republic of the eighteenth century to the spirited, disorderly, turbulent, and volatile democratic republic of the nineteenth. With the election of 1800, the so-called First American Party System, composed of Federalists and Democratic-Republicans, began to disintegrate. By 1820, the Federalist Party of Alexander Hamilton and John Adams had all but withered away and presented no opposition at the national level to the Democratic-Republican Party of Thomas Jefferson and James Madison.

Yet, having eliminated the Federalists as a force in national politics, the Democratic-Republican Party itself began to dissolve into factions. No opponent contested James Monroe's reelection in the perfunctory campaign of 1820. But four years later, in 1824, no fewer than five candidates sought the presidency: William H. Crawford of Georgia, John Quincy Adams of Massachusetts, Henry Clay of Kentucky, and Andrew Jackson of Tennessee.

The fifth candidate for president in 1824 was John Caldwell Calhoun of South Carolina. Calhoun was born at Long Canes settlement, near Abbeville, South Carolina, on March 18, 1782. His father, Patrick Calhoun, rose to prominence as a planter, slaveholder, and Indian fighter, and later represented the Abbeville district in the state legislature. Although he died in 1795 when John was but a boy of thirteen, Patrick Calhoun exercised a remarkable influence on the formation of his son's temperament and world view.

A stern Scotch-Irish Presbyterian, Patrick Calhoun taught his son that life was a perpetual struggle against evil. To do God's will on earth required discipline, strength, perseverance, and courage. He also instilled in young John an abiding love of liberty and an unqualified hatred of tyranny. For Patrick Calhoun, the obligations to God, family, neighborhood, and country defined the parameters of private and public life. Calhoun fully absorbed his father's convictions.

Although only forty-two years old in 1824, Calhoun had already enjoyed a distinguished political career. He entered public life with his election to the South Carolina House of Representatives in 1808. He then served as a member of the United States House of Representatives from 1811 until 1817. There Calhoun became one of the leaders of the "War Hawks," who supported James Madison in his fight to defend the republic against British commercial restrictions and political insults.

The War of 1812 was unpopular among the maritime and mercantile interests of the Northeast and proved a near catastrophe for the United States. But by the time it ended in 1815, Calhoun, "the young Hercules who carried the war on his shoulders," had emerged as one of the dominant figures in the Democratic-Republican Party and in Congress.

The American experiment in republican government faltered badly during the years 1812 to 1815. After the war, Calhoun advanced a strategy of national development to revitalize it. He proposed that the federal government, operating within the strict limits imposed on it by the Constitution, moderately expand the army and the navy, restore the national bank, and undertake a vigorous program of internal improvements. By these means, Calhoun hoped to rectify the glaring inadequacies he saw in the organization of the military; the condition of U.S. roads, bridges, and waterways; and the financial structure of the nation. Most important, he sought to strengthen and preserve the Union.

These activities earned Calhoun a reputation as a nationalist. This view has remained powerful enough among historians to make it conventional practice to divide Calhoun's career broadly into "nationalist" and "sectionalist" phases that seem to contradict one another, but Calhoun's principles changed little, if at all, over the course of his long career. If sentiment made Calhoun a nationalist, circumstances soon made him a sectionalist.

Against the advice of political friends and colleagues who believed that he was damaging his future prospects, Calhoun resigned his seat in the House of Representatives to become the secretary of war, a post he occupied from 1817 until 1825, throughout the eight years of Monroe's presidency. During Calhoun's tenure, the War Department was the largest and most diverse federal agency. The secretary of war not only supervised the military, but administered Indian affairs as well. Calhoun was an efficient and scrupulous executive, eliminating bureaucratic confusion in the War Department and fashioning a system of management that won him acclaim at home and abroad.

Confident of his abilities and his principles, Calhoun entered the race to succeed Monroe, but when it became apparent that he did not have extensive support in the North and that he had to compete with Crawford and Jackson in the South, Calhoun withdrew and agreed to accept the vice presidency.

As it happened, no candidate in the presidential election of 1824 won the required majority of electoral votes. Of the 261 electoral votes cast, Jackson won 99, Adams 84, Crawford 41, and Clay 37. Jackson prevailed in a contest with Adams for the popular vote, accumulating 153,544 votes to 108,740 for Adams. By this reckoning, Andrew Jackson should have become president, but because no candidate had garnered a numerical majority of electoral votes, the House of Representatives, with one vote for each delegation, had to choose the president from among the three leading candidates: Jackson, Adams, and Crawford.

Thus eliminated, Clay could broker a deal that would bring victory to one candidate in return for certain considerations. After long deliberation, Clay awarded his support to Adams. His decision was logical because both he and Adams favored a similar domestic policy, including a vigorous federal program to promote internal improvements and economic growth.

On February 9, 1825, Adams, who had carried just seven states in the election, received thirteen of the twenty-four votes cast in the House and won the presidency by a bare electoral majority. To Jackson and his supporters, the outcome reflected not only the extent of Clay's sinister influence on American politics but an audacious veto of the popular will. When Adams imprudently appointed Clay as his secretary of state, the Jacksonians clamored that their man had been robbed of the presidency by a "corrupt bargain."

There is no hard evidence to confirm that Adams entered into any sort of formal arrangement with Clay. The charge, nevertheless, gained credence among many voters who, as a consequence, expressed their sympathy for Jackson and their suspicion of Adams. Calhoun, meanwhile, had easily been elected vice president. The editor of Calhoun's papers, Clyde N. Wilson, has maintained that ". . . Calhoun was Vice-President because of his importance, not important because he was Vice-President." Indeed, Calhoun received more electoral votes than any of the presidential candidates. He was an independent agent who rose to the vice presidency of his own accord, not as the representative of a political party or the ally of a presidential nominee.

Owing nothing personally or politically to Adams, Calhoun thus felt no obligation to embrace his policies. Even before he took office on March 4, 1825, Calhoun began to disengage himself from the administration and to associate more intimately with the Jacksonian opposition. Nearly a month before the inauguration, President-elect Adams already sensed what he erroneously characterized as Calhoun's betrayal. Writing in his diary on February 11, 1825, Adams noted that Calhoun's sinister purpose was ". . . to bring in General Jackson as the next President. . . . To this end, the Administration must be rendered unpopular and odious; whatever its acts and measures may be. . . ."

During the first year of Adams's term, a lively debate about the nature and extent of the powers and duties of the vice president as the presiding officer of the Senate illustrated the growing estrangement between Calhoun and Adams. Under the leadership of John Randolph of Virginia, Adams's opponents in the Senate tried to embarrass him and to undermine his ability to govern. For hours at a time, Randolph lectured his fellow senators on the subtleties of the Constitution and denounced Adams and Clay for the chicanery they had perpetrated in the recent election. Calhoun refused to call Randolph to order. Adams's supporters accused Calhoun, by his willful inaction, of harming the government.

In a speech that he delivered on April 15, 1826, Calhoun defended himself against these charges, arguing that under the rules of the Senate, "the right to call to order, on questions touching the latitude or freedom of debate" belonged to the senators themselves and not to the presiding officer. A few weeks later, on May 1, a correspondent to the *Washington National Journal,* an administration newspaper, writing under the name "Patrick Henry," assailed Calhoun's judgment and demeanor. He characterized Calhoun's conduct as unseemly, insulting, and malicious.

On May 20, Calhoun replied using the pseudonym "Onslow," after a celebrated Speaker of the British House of Commons. He thereby inaugurated an exchange that continued for six months and revealed not merely a disagreement about an arcane question of parliamentary order, but also a conflict about the fundamental principles of republican government and the very nature of political power.

Contemporaries and scholars have long disputed the identity of Calhoun's antagonist. Duff Green, a political associate of Calhoun and the editor of the Jacksonian *United States' Telegraph,* believed that the author of the "Patrick Henry" letters was none other than President Adams himself. In his biography of Calhoun, Charles M. Wiltse arrived at the same conclusion, but Calhoun's most recent biographer, Irving H. Bartlett, revived an older argument, dating from at least 1888, that identifies "Patrick Henry" as Philip Ricard Fendall, a clerk in the State Department who sought to vindicate Adams.

Clyde N. Wilson, the editor of *The Papers of John C. Calhoun,* has also been reluctant to ascribe the "Patrick Henry" letters definitively to Adams's pen, asserting the impossibility of establishing the author's identity with confidence. Nevertheless, he deduced that, like Adams, "Patrick Henry" was learned, sympathetic to the Federalist heritage of New England, and "personally involved in the issues" under review. The letters, according to Wilson, represent Adams's opinions and beliefs, whether he composed them himself, supervised their composition, or had no involvement with them at all.

Apart from partisan bickering and personal recrimination, the debate between "Patrick Henry" and "Onslow" offered a sophisticated exposition of two conflicting definitions of power in a republic. For "Patrick Henry," Calhoun had erred by not exercising the full prerogatives of his office. It was a dereliction of duty, "Patrick Henry" charged, for the vice president to refuse to control the proceedings of the Senate, to discipline unruly members, to

silence critics of the administration, and to organize committees friendly to the president. The principal at stake, beyond the immediate occasion of the dispute, was the conviction that government officials not only had the authority but the obligation to use the powers inherent in their office.

Calhoun demurred. He embraced the Jeffersonian suspicion of power and feared political consolidation and governmental initiative. If "Patrick Henry" urged the fullest discharge of the powers of office, Calhoun alternately warned that their application in all cases must be undertaken with prudence and caution. In his view, political power flowed from the sovereignty of the people, and legitimate authority rested on the consent of the governed. Except in extraordinary circumstances, virtuous representatives of the people would thus not evade or ignore the customary limitations imposed on their actions. They would instead hesitate to use even the powers vested in their office and would never assume additional powers that remained equivocal or dubious.

The exchange between "Patrick Henry" and "Onslow" represented another chapter in the continuing debate that had originated in the 1790s about the tenets of republican government. Calhoun remained convinced that, like the Founding Fathers, he defended the cherished liberty of the people against the encroaching power of the state—an enterprise that guided and sustained his political career from beginning to end.

On June 4, 1826, Calhoun wrote to Andrew Jackson that

an issue has been fairly made ... between *power* and *liberty;* and it must be determined in the next three years, whether the real governing principle in our political system be the power and patronage of the Executive, or the voice of the people. For it can scarcely be doubted, that ... those now in power act on a scheme resting on the supposition, that such is the force of Executive influence, that they, who wield it, can mould [sic] the publick [sic] voice at pleasure by an artful management of the patronage of office.

In this estimation, events proved Calhoun incorrect. Whatever patronage Adams may have disbursed, it was not enough to save his presidency, which was doomed to frustration and failure from the outset. By 1825, an opposition party was rapidly coalescing around the figure of his arch rival, Andrew Jackson, whose supporters openly defied the administration and bided their time, awaiting the election of 1828. In the process, they began to assemble one of the most enduring popular organizations in modern U.S. political history: the Democratic Party.

Policies and issues were not very important in the bitter campaign of 1828. The race was largely a personal contest between Adams and Jackson. When the returns came in, Jackson, who portrayed himself as a "man of the people," had won by a comfortable margin. The electoral vote was 178 for Jackson to 83 for Adams, and the popular vote was approximately 647,276 to 508,064. Adams carried New England and had some support in Illinois, New York, New Jersey, Delaware, and Maryland. The rest of the country belonged to Jackson. With his rise to power, the age of democracy was born.

Principle more than expedience inspired Calhoun to attach himself to Jackson. He believed, naively as it turned out, that Jackson would prove a better friend of liberty than Adams. Adams's election by the House of Representatives in 1824 seemed to Calhoun a terrible affront to the integrity of republican institutions and a callous disregard for the will of the people. He feared above all the substitution of rule by political parties for government according to constitutional regulation. Apprehensive about the manifest indifference to the Constitution and the growing consolidation of political power, Calhoun, quite sensibly from his perspective, rallied to Andrew Jackson.

Once again, Calhoun's nomination and reelection to the vice presidency were virtually uncontested. He brought a distinguished record of statesmanship and public service to the Democratic ticket, for even in 1828 Jackson's fame rested on his military exploits, not on his political accomplishments. Calhoun knew that to satisfy his political ambitions he needed Jackson, but Jackson, if only for the moment, also needed Calhoun.

The Jacksonian coalition was composed of diverse elements that had no common purpose except the attainment of political victory. Only after coming to power did this coalition acquire a program, an ideology, and an identity. Throughout the eight years of Jackson's tenure, however, the Democratic Party remained largely his personal organization. He seldom forgot a friend or forgave an enemy. The compass and nature of personal dominion was especially apparent in his choice of advisors. He pieced together his cabinet from among old friends, political cronies, and men to whom he owed favors. With a few notable exceptions they were impotent and weak, and Jackson knew it.

Except for Secretary of State Martin Van Buren, Jackson relied not on his cabinet but on an influential though informal coterie of politicians and journalists known as the Kitchen Cabinet. One member of the official cabinet who, besides Van Buren, stood close to Jackson's inner circle was Secretary of War John H. Eaton. Eaton was at the center of a scandal that aroused Jackson's intense loyalty and intense scorn, divided his cabinet, and at last destroyed his cordial relations with Calhoun.

Peggy O'Neill Timberlake was the daughter of an Irish innkeeper in Washington. Her first husband had allegedly committed suicide, evidently distraught over his wife's love affair with John Eaton, then a senator from Tennessee. Eaton's marriage to her, which took place at Jackson's insistence on January 1, 1829, scarcely made an honest woman of Peggy in the eyes of the proper ladies of Washington society. Floride Calhoun, the wife of the vice president, was particularly adamant, publicly snubbing Mrs. Eaton. The wives of most of the other cabinet members followed suit.

But Jackson sympathized with the Eatons, for their plight reminded him of the accusations of adultery and bigamy that had tormented his beloved wife Rachel, who had died shortly before the inauguration. Jackson pronounced Peggy as "chaste as a virgin." Among the members of Jackson's cabinet, only Van Buren, a widower, was free to lavish on Peggy the attention that Jackson thought she merited. Van Buren's graciousness endeared him to Jackson, who now took him ever more fully into his confidence.

Van Buren had quickly surmised that Jackson, as a matter of honor, would never abandon Peggy Eaton. Initially, Jackson believed that the "Eaton Affair" was the work of Henry Clay, but when the wives of his cabinet members disclaimed any knowledge of Clay, Jackson began the search for other villains. Eventually, following a bizarre exchange of accusations, Jackson settled on the vice president and his wife as the principal culprits.

Floride Calhoun was the most outspoken critic of Mrs. Eaton, but Calhoun himself neither instigated nor participated in any plot to embarrass her or to discredit Jackson. Nevertheless, Jackson was outraged with Calhoun, who suffered most from what Van Buren dubbed "the Eaton Malaria." Calhoun had already aroused Jackson's ire, and from Jackson's point of view, the "Eaton Affair" presented yet another reason to distrust him.

On May 13, 1830, in the midst of the controversy over Peggy Eaton, Jackson challenged Calhoun to explain whether, while secretary of war, he had favored an investigation of Jackson's attack on the Spanish government of Florida in 1818 and Jackson's subsequent execution of two British subjects. Calhoun, like President Monroe, believed that on the occasion in question Jackson had exceeded his orders and his authority. Only John Quincy Adams, who was secretary of state at the time and who sought to annex Florida, exonerated Jackson.

Rumors had circulated for years that Calhoun had opposed Jackson, but because the political fortunes of the two men seemed for a time to be intimately intertwined, Jackson chose to ignore them. The dispute resumed when a letter that William H. Crawford had written to Major William Lewis, an old friend of Jackson and a member of the Kitchen Cabinet, came to Jackson's attention. In this letter, Crawford, a fierce political rival of Calhoun, maintained that Calhoun was duplicitous. In cabinet he had been adamant not only to probe Jackson's conduct but to punish him. In public, however, Calhoun had long taken credit for defending Jackson and had implied that Crawford was Jackson's main adversary.

At Crawford's revelations, Jackson's anger exploded. He convinced himself that Calhoun was intent on destroying his administration and positioning himself to win the presidency in 1832. He demanded an explanation and an apology. Calhoun declared that his conduct was above reproach and, in turn, defied Jackson to do the "impossible" and prove that he had not disobeyed orders during the Florida campaign.

Behind the scheme to implicate and discredit Calhoun lay Martin Van Buren. Van Buren had first suggested to Jackson the possibility that Calhoun and his wife were responsible for the insults leveled against Peggy Eaton. He had also encouraged Major Lewis to solicit the letter from Crawford that identified Calhoun as the most stubborn and ruthless critic of Jackson in Monroe's cabinet. Van Buren, of course, intended to provoke a confrontation between the president and the vice president that would prompt Jackson to dismiss Calhoun and exalt Van Buren. "Van Buren glides along as smoothly as oil and as silently s a cat," wrote Amos Kendall, one of Jackson's closest advisers. "He has the entire confidence of the President and all his personal friends while Calhoun is fast losing it."

Van Buren had little difficulty in persuading Jackson that Calhoun had masterminded a conspiracy to disgrace his presidency. Jackson's administration, and, indeed, the emerging Democratic Party, thus became divided between the partisans of Van Buren and of Calhoun.

Much of United States political history during the early 1830s turned on the growing rivalry between these two men as each jockeyed for position as Jackson's successor.

In this contest, Van Buren had most of the advantages, foremost among which was his skill at political manipulation and maneuvering. Calhoun bested him in acuity of intellect but operated from an increasingly obsolete set of assumptions about the character of American politics. Never at ease with mass politics, Calhoun found it impossible, as his most recent biographer, Irving Bartlett, concluded, "to speak to the democratic spirit of the age." No such inhibitions troubled Van Buren. By the end of 1832, Jackson had designated Van Buren as his heir apparent.

But it was not political ambition alone that motivated Van Buren. It was also the deepening antagonism between the North and the South. Van Buren represented the progressive, commercial, democratic, and capitalist interests of the North. Calhoun stood for the more traditional, agrarian, republican, and slaveholding South. Once more, the very meaning and prospects of the United States were in dispute.

As his political isolation deepened and as his apprehension about the future of the republic escalated, Calhoun became more completely the spokesman for southern interests and states' rights. The final drama of his vice presidency, and one of the most critical episodes of his political career, began to unfold in 1828 with the passage of another tariff that once again, as in 1824, raised duties on imports.

In 1816, Calhoun, then a member of the House of Representatives, had voted in favor of a tariff as a temporary measure to protect domestic industry from foreign competition, even though it artificially raised the price of manufactured products for southerners. In the spirit of compromise and reconciliation, Calhoun had argued that justice demanded concessions be made to the manufacturing and commercial communities of the Northeast that had suffered under the burdens of a trade embargo in the years before the War of 1812.

But, by 1828, Calhoun feared that the tariff had become a permanent means for the government to subsidize industrialists indirectly at the expense of farmers and consumers. This development he found intolerable.

While still vice president, Calhoun anonymously drafted a pamphlet entitled the "South Carolina Exposition and Protest," in which he argued that the tariff was unconstitutional and pernicious. Legally, Congress could impose a tariff to raise revenue but not to promote one interest, in this case domestic manufacturing, at the expense of any other. The Tariff of 1828, the so-called Tariff of Abominations, was, therefore, "unconstitutional, unequal, and oppressive." Such legislation, Calhoun warned, would divide citizens into two antagonistic classes with interests as distinct and hostile as those of two separate nations. The tariff made southerners "the serfs of the system—out of whose labor is raised, not only the money paid into the Treasury, but funds out of which are drawn the rich rewards of the manufacturer and his associates in interest." The results of such policies were wholly predictable: the appearance of political envy, the development of class conflict, and the end of national unity.

In the 3:33 "Exposition and Protest," Calhoun did not merely identify the problem but also proposed a remedy. He preferred to call his doctrine interposition, although it became more commonly known as nullification. Before the adoption of the Constitution, Calhoun explained, the states were independent and sovereign. They had created the federal government and had endowed it with strictly limited powers. The federal government possessed only the authority that the sovereign states had consented to surrender. A state, therefore, had the right to "interpose" its original sovereignty against the "despotism of the many." The citizens of a state could summon a state convention and nullify any act of Congress that exceeded the authority granted the federal government under the Constitution.

Calhoun believed that when conventional politics failed to redress the grievances of a minority, some relief had to be found. The doctrine of interposition provided it. In propounding this theory, Calhoun argued that the ability to check federal power was essential to preserving constitutional government. On October 30, 1830, he had written to his friend Samuel D. Ingham of Pennsylvania that: "To protect the subject against the Government is in fact the only object & value of the Constitution. The government needs no constitution. It is the governed, that needs its protection."

In Calhoun's view, the purpose of a constitution was to restrain government, as it was the purpose of the law to restrain individuals. He assessed the merit of any constitution according to the degree to which it incorporated this principle of restraint. The ultimate recourse, he maintained, was the state veto of a federal law. That action, Calhoun thought, was much less dangerous than the power of an unrestrained federal government. Nor could the states, in his estimation, rely on the Supreme Court to protect them or to resolve constitutional conflicts. For "it is not possible to distinguish, practically, between a government having all power," he wrote, "and one having the right to take what power it pleases."

The doctrine of interposition, as Calhoun proposed it, offered a peaceful remedy to constitutional disputes that superseded the resort to coercion, violence, revolution, and bloodshed on the one hand and despotic government on the other. Interposition was one more qualification on majority rule and one more defense of the ideal that government rested on the consent of the governed, which, Calhoun affirmed, had been the founding principle of the American republic.

After Congress not only failed to enact significant tariff reform but passed a new tariff bill in 1832 that contained no significant reduction in rates, evens in South Carolina moved quickly. On November 24, 1832, a special convention met in the state capital, Columbia, and enacted an Ordinance of Nullification that declared the Tariffs of 1828 and 1832 unconstitutional and, therefore, null and void in South Carolina. The federal collection of duties was forbidden after February 1, 1833, unless Congress lowered the tariff rate to 12 percent. Any attempt on the part of federal authorities to coerce the state into obedience would be "inconsistent with the longer continuance of South Carolina in the Union."

At the same time, Calhoun resigned the vice presidency to accept a seat in the Senate, to which the South Carolina legislature elected him on December 12, 1832. Amid rumors of his imminent arrest, he hastened to Washington not only to defend the interests of his state but also to moderate public opinion and, if possible, to defuse the crisis. By the time Calhoun arrived, Jackson had already declared the actions of South Carolina to be treasonous. Jackson's "Nullification Proclamation" of December 10, 1832, repudiated nullification as "endangering the integrity of the Union." The power to nullify a law of Congress was, Jackson declared, "incompatible with the existence of the Union, contradicted expressly by the letter of the Constitution, unauthorized by its spirit, inconsistent with every principle on which it was founded and destructive of the great object for which it was formed."

Although he admonished the South Carolina nullifiers, Jackson also urged Congress to lower the tariff and to limit protection to articles essential to national defense. However, he did secure passage of the "Force Bill" early in 1833, which authorized the collection of import duties in cash from all ships entering American harbors and the use of the state militia and the federal armed services to enforce the ordinance.

Infuriated by the arrogance of the Force Bill, many South Carolinians were eager for secession, but Calhoun opposed what he called that "most fatal of steps." Writing to leading advocates of nullification in late January 1833, Calhoun urged that "we must not think of secession but in the last extremity. . . . A year would make an immense difference in our fortunes. . . . I feel confident, we want only time to ensure victory." Some nullifiers thought that Calhoun had surrendered. They believed that the choice of nullification rather than submission implied secession in the event of failure. Having taken their state to the brink of secession, and perhaps of civil war, they were not prepared to give up the fight.

To Calhoun, suspension of the Ordinance of Nullification represented a strategic retreat designed to prevent secession and civil war, rather than an abandonment of the principle of interposition itself. He always considered nullification as a way to protect the South and to preserve the Union. To leave the Union because nullification had failed—and perhaps only for the moment—was to sacrifice the reason for having waged the struggle in the first place: the assertion of the right of a state to protect itself against the unlawful encroachment of the federal government.

Calhoun was one of the most ardent and determined southern sectionalists, but throughout his career, his love of the Union almost balanced his fear for the South. He proposed the doctrine of nullification because he wished to save his nation and his section and because he understood the dangers that threatened to destroy both.

In this instance, Calhoun's wisdom, prudence, and moderation prevailed. As the "fatal first" of February approached, he delayed the enforcement of the Ordinance of Nullification at least until Congress had completed its deliberations. In early February, Calhoun agreed to cooperate with Henry Clay on a compromise tariff. On February 13, 1833, Clay introduced his tariff bill into the Senate, and Calhoun spoke in favor of it. On February 26, Clay's measure passed the House of Representatives, and on March 1 the Senate concurred.

Although the new rates were considerably higher than those demanded in the Ordinance of Nullification, South Carolinians welcomed the compromise tariff with a mixture of relief and disappointment. When the South Carolina legislature reconvened on March 11, 1833, it repealed the ordinance and accepted the compromise tariff. In a symbolic gesture of defiance, the legislature nullified the Force Bill,

thus demonstrating that nullification remained a legal and viable option.

In a speech delivered against the Force Bill on February 15 and 16, 1833, Calhoun was careful to distinguish between a majority of consenting citizens and a powerful coalition of interests backed by force. He concluded that "the government of the absolute majority, instead of the government of the people, is but the government of the strongest interests, and when not efficiently checked, is the most tyrannical and oppressive that can be devised." South Carolinians, he maintained, had merely invoked the reserved powers of a state to effect a temporary suspension of a law widely agreed to be unconstitutional and to prevent so unprecedented an assertion of federal power as the Force Bill.

He continued, asking his colleagues in the Senate: "Does any man in his sense believe, that this beautiful structure—this harmonious aggregate of states, produced by the joint consent of all can be preserved by force?" He answered his own question, saying that the mere introduction of force ". . . will be certain destruction to this Federal Union. . . . Force may, indeed, hold the parts together, but such a union would be the bond between master and slave: a union of exaction on one side, and of unqualified *obedience* on the other." Calhoun argued that the Force Bill defied the principles of republican government. It implied despotism instead of consent. The Force Bill, as he understood it, imposed unquestioning obedience at the expense of enlightened self-government.

Nullification never became the kind of constitutional remedy that Calhoun hoped it would be. It was a theoretical, but not yet a very practical, alternative to the consolidation of federal power that he recognized was embodied in legislation like the Force Bill. Calhoun nevertheless always regarded the episode as the finest moment of his political career. Sacrificing ambition, status, and his immediate prospects for presidency, he had cast his lot with a small but gallant state that unflinchingly defended the cause of republican self-government. Their actions had proved, he later wrote, that nullification was a principled, conservative, peaceful, constitutional, and efficient means to preserve the legitimate rights of a free people.

After 1832, save for a brief period from 1843 to 1845, Calhoun remained in the Senate. There, for the most part, he operated independently of either the Democratic or the Whig parties that constituted the "Second American Party System." He condemned the Democrats as unscrupulous and unprincipled but at the same time denounced the Whigs as self-seeking and shortsighted. Having regained some of the national esteem that he had lost as a result of his defense of nullification, Calhoun launched his last serious effort to attain the presidency in March 1843, but in February 1844 he withdrew his name from consideration.

In March 1844, President John Tyler appointed Calhoun secretary of state to succeed Abel P. Upshur, who had been killed on February 28 when a gun exploded aboard the USS *Princeton* during an inspection tour. Although his tenure at the State Department was brief, Calhoun initiated negotiations that led to the acquisition of the Oregon Territory from the British. He also fashioned a treaty for the annexation of Texas, but the Senate did not ratify it.

In 1845, when James K. Polk failed to reappoint him to his post in the State Department, Calhoun returned to the Senate and retained his seat until his death on March 31, 1850, becoming an outspoken and eloquent critic of the war with Mexico that began in 1846. Drawing on his long experience in public life and relying on the principles that had sustained him in many partisan battles, Calhoun asserted that Polk had illegally brought the United States into war, for he had not first received the consent of the Senate to sanction his course of action. He detected in Polk's declaration of war the same sort of execution usurpation of power that he had combated in Adams and Jackson. Calhoun lamented that "Mexico is to us forbidden fruit; the penalty of eating it [is] to subject our institutions to political death."

Calhoun devoted the last years of his life to encouraging southern unity against the mounting northern hostility to slavery. He believed that a unified South could operate as a restraint on federal power and thus hold at bay the forces of national dissolution. Although disappointed in this quest, Calhoun explored its ramifications in his most systematic and theoretical work on politics, *A Disquisition on Government.*

Elaborating on ideas that he had articulated in the "Onslow Letters," the "South Carolina Exposition and Protest," many of his major speeches, and his public and private correspondence, especially the "Fort Hill Address" of 1831, Calhoun formulated the theory of the concurrent majority. According to this concept, the majority was prevented from undertaking certain actions or implementing certain policies without the willing agreement of the minority. To Calhoun, the concurrent majority did not represent an impediment to the operation of majority rule or weaken the power of the general government; instead, he regarded it as the logical fulfillment of the democratic ideal of government by consent, in which the vital interests of a minority group or section remained inviolate.

Most of Calhoun's political aspirations ended in frustration. He never attained the presidency, which he ardently desired, but he was no political opportunist. He repeatedly declined to advance his career at the expense of the country and thus sacrificed ambition in defense of all that he cherished.

Events also ruined Calhoun's hopes for the future of the republic. During his lifetime, he never effected southern unity. When national division at last came a decade after his death, his doctrine of state interposition could not prevent secession and civil war, which rent asunder the Union that he loved and desired above all else to save.

Yet, his private disappointments and public defeats notwithstanding, Calhoun identified the enduring dilemma of American politics: the tension between centralized power and republican self-government, between unbounded majority rule and ordered political liberty. Interpretations of Calhoun's character and accomplishments have ranged from enmity to misunderstanding to admiration, but in the end, Calhoun can neither be evaded nor ignored. Indeed, Vernon L. Parrington long ago recognized as much when he wrote in *Main Currents in American Thought:* "Whatever road one travels one comes at last upon the austere figure of Calhoun, commanding every highway of the southern mind." However scholars may judge him, American political history offers few examples of statesmen whose legacy has continued to generate such vital interest or to excite such passionate controversy as that of John C. Calhoun.

REFERENCES

Irving H. Bartlett, *John C. Calhoun: A Biography* (New York: W.W. Norton & Company, 1993); John C. Calhoun, *A Disquisition on Government* (Indianapolis, Ind.: Bobbs-Merrill, 1953); *John C. Calhoun,* Margaret Coit, ed. (Englewood Cliffs, N.J.: Prentice-Hall, 1970); *John C. Calhoun: A Profile,* John L. Thomas, ed. (New York: Hill & Wang, 1968); Margaret L. Coit, *John C. Calhoun: American Portrait* (Boston: Houghton Mifflin, 1950); *Correspondence of John C. Calhoun,* J. Franklin Jameson, ed., *American Historical Association Annual Report for 1899* (Washington, D.C.: Government Printing Office, 1900); Richard N. Current, *John C. Calhoun* (New York: Washington Square Press, 1963); Richard Hofstader, "John C. Calhoun: The Marx of the Master Class," *The American Political Tradition and the Men Who Made It* (New York: Alfred A. Knopf, 1948); John S. Jenkins, *The Life of John C. Calhoun* (Auburn, N.Y.: James M. Alden, 1850); Ralph Lerner, "Calhoun's New Science of Politics," *American Political Science Review,* 57 (December 1963), 918–932; William M. Meigs, *The Life of John C. Calhoun* (New York: Neale, 1917); John Niven, *John C. Calhoun and the Price of Union* (Baton Rouge: Louisiana State University Press, 1988); Vernon L. Parrington, *Main Currents in American Thought* (New York: Harcourt, Brace and Company, 1927), 2: 69–82; Merrill D. Peterson, *The Great Triumvirate: Webster, Clay, and Calhoun* (New York: Oxford University Press, 1987); James H. Read, *Majority Rule versus Consensus: The Political Thought of John C. Calhoun* (Lawrence: University of Kansas Press, 2009); August O. Spain, *The Political Theory of John C. Calhoun* (New York: Octagon Books, 1951); Arthur Styron, *The Cast-Iron Man: John C. Calhoun and American Democracy* (New York: Longmans, Green, 1935); *The Essential Calhoun: Selections from Writing, Speeches, and Letters,* Clyde N. Wilson, ed. (New Brunswick, N.J.: Transaction Publishers 1992); *The Papers of John C. Calhoun,* Robert I. Meriwether, W. Edwin Hemphill, and Clyde N. Wilson, eds. 22 vols. to date (Columbia: University of South Carolina Press, 1959–); *The Works of John C. Calhoun,* Richard K. Cralle, ed., 6 vols. (Columbia, S.C.: A.S. Johnston, 1851; New York: A. Appleton, 1853, 1857); Charles M. Wiltse, *John C. Calhoun,* 3 vols., *Nationalist, 1782–1828; Nullifier, 1829–1839; Sectionalist, 1840–1850* (Indianapolis, Ind.: Bobbs-Merrill, 1944–1951).

MARK G. MALVASI received his B.A. from Hiram College in 1980, his M.A. in history from the University of Chicago in 1981, and his Ph.D. from the University of Rochester in 1991. He has taught history at the University of Rochester, the University of Puget Sound, and the University of Alabama. He joined the faculty of Randolph-Macon College in Ashland, Virginia, in 1992 where he is now Vaughan Professor of History. He is the author of *Slavery in the Western Hemisphere, 1500–1888* (St. James Press, 2003), the coeditor of *History in Dispute: Slavery in the Western Hemisphere* (St. James Press, 2003), and coeditor of *The Remembered Past: John Lukacs on History, Historians, and Historical Knowledge.* His book, *The Unregenerate South: The Agrarian Thought of John Crowe Ransom, Allen Tate, and Donald Davidson,* was published by Louisiana State University Press in 1997. He has written for such journals as *Chronicles: A Magazine of American Culture; Crisis: A Journal of Catholic Lay Opinion; Southern Partisan;* and *The Journal of the Early Republic.* And he has contributed articles in several historical encyclopedias.

MARTIN VAN BUREN (1782–1862)

Vice President, 1833–1837

(Second Term of President Andrew Jackson)

MARTIN VAN BUREN
(Library of Congress)

By Charles H. Schoenleber

Martin Van Buren is often viewed as a political manipulator or intriguer, as "The Little Magician" or "The Red Fox of Kinderhook." Such stereotyping, however, does severe injustice to Van Buren's political skill. He was an excellent judge of people and was a political innovator throughout his career. He carefully brought together an able group of New Yorkers to form the Albany Regency that dominated state politics for more than two decades. Van Buren plotted strategy, expertly timed political moves, and adroitly employed patronage. He was in large part responsible for reinvigorating the Virginia–New York coalition that put Andrew Jackson into the White House in 1828. He provided Jackson with cogent political advice and then served one term as president.

Politics to Van Buren was much more than just organization and campaigning. He believed that an active and competitive two-party system was essential to the nation's future. He saw the United States perpetually divided between the competing interest groups that originally backed Thomas Jefferson and Alexander Hamilton. The sharp contest over these differing political visions had to be maintained. Hence the two parties had to maintain their distinctiveness and ideological purity. Party loyalty and regularity were very important for Van Buren.

Van Buren himself was always a Jeffersonian Republican. He advocated states' rights and a limited federal government, but he also firmly believed in a strong Union. He supported the interests of the farmers and workers but was no agrarian or urban radical. Government had to encourage business, commerce, and manufacturing because they were essential to national economic growth, but all Americans—all regions of the country—must share in this increased prosperity.

Van Buren's lack of formal education gave him a feeling of inadequacy. To compensate, he always worked harder and was better prepared than his opponents. He was a stylist dresser, in part to show his importance. Van Buren did not let politics lead to personal hatreds. Differences were based on principle and issues and did not preclude civil social relations with his opponents.

From the mid-1820s onward, Van Buren had his eyes on the presidency. He swung his political forces into the Jacksonian camp, served as Jackson's secretary of state, and isolated his rival, John C. Calhoun. Being eighth vice president was the last step before the presidency. When Jackson selected him for the job, the Old Hero anointed his heir—a first for the vice presidency in American politics. Van Buren's role as one of Jackson's key political advisers and second in command in the Democratic Party was another first for that office. In what was often considered a dead-end job, Van Buren wielded substantial political power and crucial influence in Jackson's administration.

Van Buren was born in Kinderhook, New York, on December 5, 1782. His parents, of Dutch ancestry, operated a farm and tavern that provided a modest living for their large family. Van Buren attended the local one-room school until age fifteen and then read law with the respected Kinderhook lawyer Francis Sylvester. While clerking in the law office and working in a store for his board, the seventeen-year-old Van Buren attended the Jeffersonian Republican congressional district convention in Troy in 1800. So far, Van Buren had benefited significantly from the encouragement of the leading Federalist gentlemen in Columbia County; yet he became increasingly active in the Republican Party organization.

With a loan from Republican Congressman John P. Van Ness, Van Buren moved to New York City in 1802 and clerked for Van Ness's lawyer brother. He observed firsthand the Aaron Burr–DeWitt Clinton infighting in the Republican Party as he completed his legal studies. Admitted to the bar in November 1803, he returned to Kinderhook and began a law partnership with his half-brother James Van Alen. In April 1804, in his first chance to vote, Van Buren broke with the Federalist elite in Columbia County and the Burrite Van Nesses to vote for the Clintonian candidate for governor. In the courtroom, he also challenged the elite by often representing small farmers and tenants in cases involving the Livingston family's claims under old British grants to much of the land in Columbia County.

On February 21, 1807, Van Buren married Hannah Hoes in a private and small (to save money) ceremony. The next year their first of four sons was born. As an increasingly popular and prosperous lawyer who was active in the Republican Party, he was appointed county surrogate (replacing his half-brother and partner) on March 20, 1808. The office provided Van Buren with a small income, but of more importance, it increased his prestige in the country and offered him increased opportunities to meet the voters.

In 1808, Van Buren supported New York's George Clinton for the presidency over James Madison. Recognizing his mistake, Van Buren retreated temporarily from politics to practice law. In 1812, he reluctantly agreed to run for the state senate and then vigorously campaigned and defeated Edward P. Livingston by 200 votes of the 40,000 cast. As victor over a Livingston-Federalist coalition, Van Buren became the defender of the party and Republican leader in the Middle Senate District. He, nevertheless, supported New York's favorite son, DeWitt Clinton, over Madison in 1812. Soon disillusioned with Clinton's willingness to sacrifice party principles and loyalty for personal gain, Van Buren joined Governor Daniel D. Tompkins and state Supreme Court Justice Ambrose Spencer in working to overthrow Clinton.

Van Buren promoted a vigorous military policy in the state senate and ably aided Governor Tompkins's efforts to ensure that New York could defend itself during the War of 1812. Because Van Buren refused to support Spencer's candidate for the U.S. Senate, the justice tried to block Van Buren's appointment as state attorney general. Governor Tompkins, however, broke a tie vote in the Council of Appointment by voting for Van Buren on February 17, 1815.

Van Buren now moved his lucrative practice to Albany and supplemented his income by speculating in land and lending small amounts of money. Reelected to the state senate in April 1816, Van Buren struggled against a reunited Spencer-Clinton coalition. Heading the opposition to Clinton known as the Bucktails, Van Buren nevertheless supported Clinton's cherished project, the Erie Canal. He made an impassioned speech in the senate on behalf of the project, underscoring the canal's economic benefits to the state. While he was in the midst of building a powerful political machine known as the Albany Regency, Van Buren's wife died on February 5, 1819. He was distraught and ill but soon plunged back into the political maelstrom. Joining with the Rufus King Federalists, the Bucktails elected one of their members to the canal board. Governor Clinton retaliated by using his control of the Council of Appointment to remove Van Buren from the attorney generalship. The Council of Appointment then considered putting Van Buren on the supreme court, but Clinton blocked "that prince of villains" from being shunted aside to the high court. In 1820, Van Buren lacked the strength to block Clinton's reelection, but the Bucktails gained control of both houses of the legislature. Van Buren and his supporters pushed for a state constitutional convention in 1820 and 1821 against Clintonian opposition. In the latter year, they used their control of the Council of Appointment to remove all Clintonians from office. On February 6, 1821, the Bucktails also elected their leader to the U.S. Senate. Before heading off to Washington, Van Buren—a convention delegate from Otsego County, where he owned land—smoothed over the differences between the radicals among the Bucktails and the more conservative King supporters in the state constitutional convention by guiding the delegates in crafting a moderate constitution for New York.

In going to Washington, Van Buren was determined to make New York once again central in national politics. He hoped to revitalize the New York–Virginia coalition that had propelled Jefferson to the presidency. With control of New York assured by the Bucktail sweep of the state elections in April 1821, Van Buren arrived in Washington in November. He immediately worked to defeat the incumbent Speaker of the House of Representatives, John W. Taylor, a New Yorker too closely associated with Clinton. Van Buren also succeeded in putting Philip P. Barbour of Virginia in the chair and in the process established a working friendship with Thomas Ritchie, the editor of the Richmond *Enquirer* and one of the leaders of the conservative and states' rights Old Republican Richmond Junto political faction. However, he was unable to block the appointment of Federalist Solomon Van Rensselaer as postmaster of Albany.

When Van Buren returned to the nation's capital from New York in November 1822, he came with a secure base of support. His choice for governor had easily won, and the Albany Regency controlled both houses of the legislature. Now Van Buren turned his attention to presidential politics. He had already decided privately to support William H. Crawford of Georgia for the Republican nomination. Crawford was attractive to Van Buren as a conservative, an advocate of states' rights, and a loyal party member. But Crawford was a southerner and had to be carefully sold to New Yorkers. Once Congress adjourned in March 1823, Van Buren returned to New York and immediately faced newspaper attacks on nominations made in party caucuses that they stated were undemocratic. Soon a People's Party coalesced out of the opponents of the Albany Regency. The party carried New York County in the November legislative elections. Faced with revolt in New York, Van Buren attended the Republican congressional caucus on February 14, 1824. Half of the attendees were New Yorkers and Virginians.

Crawford received the nomination as Van Buren planned, but the nomination was tainted by the scant turnout. Crawford was also seriously ill. Back in New York, the Regency blundered by firing Clinton from his job as unpaid president of the canal board. When the People's Party nominated Clinton for governor, he won easily, and the People's Party captured the New York House of Representatives. Van Buren and the Regency were able to capture only four of New York's thirty-six electoral votes for Crawford. Van Buren learned that even the best party organization was ineffective against an aroused public. He had to find a new presidential candidate who possessed traditional Republican views, was acceptable to the New York–Virginia coalition, and had broad popularity.

Crawford had no chance for victory once the presidential election of 1824 was thrown into the House of Representatives. Van Buren excelled in putting together majority coalitions in caucuses or legislative bodies, but he remained on the sidelines in the struggle between John Quincy Adams and Andrew Jackson. He still supported Crawford and had not as yet decided whom next to support.

In November 1825, the Regency overwhelmed its opposition in the state elections.

Adams's first annual message supporting a grand system of federally financed internal improvements gave Van Buren the issue to begin to swing the New York Republicans into the Jacksonian camp. New York had built its Erie Canal and consequently opposed federal funding of competing ventures in other states. Van Buren and the Regency also advocated a limited national government, which made opposition to Adams also a matter of remaining true to Republican ideals. Van Buren, however, faced a major problem. In New York the Clintonians had been the original supporters of Jackson. Van Buren decided that he needed a rapprochement with Clinton. He maneuvered the nomination of a weak Regency gubernatorial candidate, which gave Clinton a narrow victory in November 1826. The legislature, remaining solidly in Regency hands, reelected Van Buren to the Senate on February 6, 1827.

Van Buren toured the seaboard south after the Senate adjourned in March 1827. He met with Crawford, and both men agreed that Jackson was the logical choice to support for the presidency. Crawford also shared his fierce hatred of Vice President John C. Calhoun with the visiting New Yorker. Now a comparatively wealthy man, Van Buren sold his house in Albany; Washington henceforth would be his stage. His position, however, was precarious: Jackson was intensely suspicious of Van Buren, whom he believed to be overly ambitious and an intriguer. Jackson also admired Clinton. In New York, Van Buren's Regency was being vigorously challenged by a growing Anti-Masonic movement. Van Buren also was being forced to finesse the tariff issue by taking a position that would neither alienate protectionist sentiment in New York nor his Richmond Junto allies who were free traders.

Van Buren skillfully managed to win Jackson's favor and maintain intact the New York–Virginia coalition. In 1827, Van Buren saw to it that most of the Republican newspapers in New York simultaneously came out in favor of the Old Hero. When Congress met, Van Buren used his persuasive powers to get Andrew Stevenson of Virginia elected speaker: Stevenson, Van Buren believed, would bind together all the opponents of Adams in the House into an effective opposition. Next, Van Buren worked for passage of a tariff bill that would both strengthen the Regency and elect Jackson. As Van Buren shrewdly calculated, the South would be dissatisfied with higher rates but, because of its dislike of Adams, would have to support Jackson's candidacy. The bill, therefore, was designed primarily to win northern support for Jackson without unduly offending the South. Van Buren's maneuvering on the tariff bill turned Calhoun against the New Yorker. With the death of Clinton, Calhoun realized that Van Buren was his chief rival to succeed Jackson as president. Calhoun now began to calculate how he could thwart his rival.

Van Buren's actions in Congress had helped Jackson defeat Adams. In New York, Jackson's margin of victory was slim, winning by some 5,000 votes, translating into 20 of the Empire State's 36 electoral votes. To bolster Jackson's victory and extend his influence, Van Buren ran for governor. Although he faced both National Republican and Anti-Masonic candidates, Van Buren won by 30,000 votes, and the Regency carried both houses of the legislature. In his message to the legislature, the new governor recommended a progressive program that included establishing a safety fund to regulate the banks within the state, election reform, and reform of the corrupt auction system for goods imported into New York City.

In early January 1829, President-elect Jackson offered Van Buren the cabinet position of secretary of state. Van Buren accepted but remained in New York to wind up his gubernatorial responsibilities. He resigned on March 12, serving a mere forty-three days as New York's chief executive. Jackson, who had hoped for Van Buren's able counsel, expected the New Yorker in Washington by inauguration day, but he was not able to leave Albany until March 17.

When Van Buren arrived in Washington, he had to be concerned over how much input he would have in the new administration. In his absence, the president had appointed ministers to England and France without even notifying his secretary of state. Jackson's close Tennessee friend John H. Eaton was in the cabinet as secretary of war. The other cabinet members were undistinguished, but Tennessean William B. Lewis was a powerful adviser to Jackson.

Van Buren was also immediately forced to wage an unsuccessful battle to prevent Jackson from appointing Samuel Swartwout, a man abhorrent to Van Buren's Tammany Hall allies, to the important patronage position of customs collector of the Port of New York. In the midst of this uncertainty, Van Buren came to see his role in the administration as a steadying influence on the president. By giving Jackson careful and cautious advice, he could curb some of the president's impulsiveness. Van Buren was also alert to Vice President Calhoun's power and influence in Washington. Calhoun had a hand in Swartwout's appointment, and his newspaper voice, DuffGreen's *United States Telegraph,* was hard at work promoting the vice president.

Van Buren quickly eclipsed Calhoun. The secretary and the president became warm friends, sharing evening rides into the country. The two men agreed on public policy, and the president incorporated Van Buren's suggestions into his first annual message. Calhoun even attributed Jackson's new opposition to federally financed internal improvements to the secretary of state's influence. Both Van Buren and Jackson were looking for ways to isolate the vice president. Jackson disliked Calhoun's blatant attempt to anoint himself Jackson's heir; Van Buren, of course, hoped to be the next president.

A series of interrelated events in 1830 undid Calhoun and assured Van Buren of the succession. One involved Peggy O'Neal Eaton, the wife of the secretary of war. Most of social Washington, including the vice president's wife and all of the cabinet except Van Buren, snubbed Peggy. Van Buren, a widower, went out of his way to greet Peggy and thereby endeared himself to the president, who championed the unjustly abused Peggy.* Jackson, Van Buren, and the circle of advisers around the president, known as the Kitchen Cabinet, forced Calhoun to respond to the president's toast supporting the Union at the Jefferson Day Dinner on April 13. Jackson also took a slap at Calhoun and Kentucky Senator Henry Clay by vetoing the Maysville Road Bill. Van Buren had helped draft the veto message that put the administration firmly in the camp of the Old Republicans. The secretary of state thereby solidified his support with conservative and states' rights southerners such as the Richmond Junto, while painting the vice president as an extremist whose views threatened the Union and pure Republican principles.

To end the controversy over Peggy Eaton and to purge the cabinet of Calhoun's influence, Van Buren convinced Jackson to accept his resignation as secretary of state and to demand that of the other members. The cabinet reorganization occurred in April 1831. Van Buren virtually selected the new secretary of state and was rewarded by being named minister to Great Britain. He sailed for the Court of St. James on August 16.

Van Buren was well qualified for his diplomatic post. Although he had spent much of his time as secretary of state advising Jackson on political matters, he had not neglected his foreign policy duties. He skillfully directed negotiations with Britain that allowed the United States its first unrestricted trade with the West Indies since independence. In London, Van Buren was on the most cordial terms with Lord Palmerston, the British foreign minister. On December 17, 1831, Jackson wrote Van Buren that he could not close his letter, although it was getting late, without confiding a subject that was constantly on his mind. The president continued:

> If I am reelected, and you are not called to the vice presidency, I wish you to return to this country in two years from now, if it comports with your views & your wishes. I think your presence here about that time will be necessary. The opposition would if they durst try to reject your nomination as minister, but they dare not, they begin to know if they did, that the people in mass would take you up & elect you vice president without a nomination; was it not for this, it is said Clay, Calhoun & Co would try it.

On February 20, 1832, Van Buren received the news that his nomination as ambassador to Great Britain had been rejected by the Senate, with Vice President Calhoun breaking a contrived tie vote. Jackson wanted Van Buren to return immediately to help him battle Calhoun and Clay. The rejected minister, however, decided to stay in London until after the Democratic convention. A quick return, Van Buren reasoned, would make it appear that he was grasping for the vice presidency. In his absence, the Regency and the Kitchen Cabinet directed his campaign for that office. He won the Democratic Party nomination on the first ballot, with 208 votes to 75 for two opponents.

When Van Buren arrived in New York City from Britain, he was met with an urgent letter from Jackson stating that the president was working on a veto message to the bill rechartering the Bank of the United States and wanted Van Buren's advice on it as soon as possible. Van Buren arrived in Washington on the evening of July 8. He had always believed that banks were essential to the growth of the United States economy, but also that their abuses had to be restrained. He read the veto message and heartily approved. The next day, Jackson drove Van Buren to the Capitol, where the New Yorker lobbied Congress to sustain the veto and to pass a compromise tariff bill. Congress was unable to muster the votes needed to override, and it soon passed the tariff bill. Once Congress adjourned, Van Buren returned to New York to campaign. He personally canvassed the state and adroitly stated his political

---

*See JOHN CALDWELL CALHOUN for further explanation of the Peggy Eaton affair.

views in reply to a series of antitariff resolutions adopted by a public meeting in Shocco Springs, North Carolina. Van Buren asserted that Congress had the power to regulate commerce, that a tariff should not benefit one part of the Union at the expense of the others, and that with the rapid repayment of the national debt, tariff rates could soon go down. He opposed federally funded internal improvements of a local nature and stated that even national projects must be postponed until the debt was liquidated. He also defended the bank veto and denounced nullification as a threat to the Union. The Jackson–Van Buren ticket carried all of New York's thirty-six electoral votes.

Between the election and the inauguration, Congress met and the crisis caused by South Carolina's attempt to nullify the tariff simmered. Van Buren remained in New York to solidify the Regency's control over the state. He attended a mass meeting in Albany on January 24, 1833, called to debate the tariff. In the next few days, he drafted a report that argued that nullification threatened the Union and was just as dangerous as Federalist extremism had been at the Hartford Convention; that Jackson as president had to stand firm against disunion in his Nullification Proclamation; but also that tariff rates should be reduced to bring about reconciliation. Circulation of Van Buren's views did much to calm the fears among Old Republican states' righters in the South. Van Buren also worked through New York Senator (and Regency stalwart) Silas Wright to push through Congress a compromise tariff acceptable to southerners. He also hoped that Jackson's Force Bill would quietly die in Congress. Both measures, however, became law on March 2, and Van Buren's political enemies—Calhoun and Clay—used them to attack the vice president-elect.

On March 4, 1833, Van Buren was sworn in as the eighth vice president of the United States, the first vice president to be elected into the office as the anointed heir of the current president. He was also the first vice president to be a close and very important adviser to the president. Essentially, Van Buren continued to serve Jackson as he had done as secretary of state, replacing the conducting of foreign affairs with presiding over the Senate. Van Buren also continued to head the Albany Regency.

Van Buren, nevertheless, was in an awkward position: While advising the president, he had to avoid alienating Jackson without being reduced to being a mere yes-man because he needed Jackson's support to be elected the next president but could be hurt politically by any rash measures adopted by the current administration. Van Buren also had to avoid the appearance of orchestrating administration policy in such a way as to secure his election to the presidency or to benefit his home state.

The first test of Van Buren's political skill as vice president involved the future of government funds in the Bank of the United States. Jackson and his Kitchen Cabinet advisers Amos Kendall, Roger B. Taney, and Francis Preston Blair favored the immediate removal of government deposits from the "monster" bank. Van Buren was more cautious: He supported removal but only if the public had been prepared for such a move. He also clearly realized the power held by the bank and the economic chaos that removal of the deposits might cause. He hoped to delay removal until the next Congress met. Jackson had not made a final decision when Van Buren left Washington for New York. The president planned a northern tour and consequently the two men would soon meet again in New York City.

Jackson's reception in the city was a triumph, and Van Buren accompanied him on his tour of New England; while together they discussed removal of the deposits. Van Buren eventually supported removal as early as September when convinced that Kendall's plan of gradually withdrawing government funds from the Bank of the United States and then depositing them in state, banks contained the safeguards necessary to protect the government's money. Still the vice president preferred a cautious approach. He did not want to alienate Congress or to panic the banking community with precipitous action. Jackson almost misread Van Buren's caution as disloyalty, prompting careful fence-mending on the part of the vice president. The president wanted Van Buren back in Washington by October, when the removals would begin; instead Van Buren remained in New York, traveling throughout the state with author Washington Irving. The vice president had convinced Jackson that his absence would hinder the opposition's attempts to paint removal as a grab by New York banks for supremacy.

Van Buren's tour was cut short when Jackson—faced with a cabinet crisis—summoned his vice president to Washington. Van Buren, nevertheless, remained in New York City, where he could easily give timely advice without providing the opposition with the opportunity to picture Jackson as the hapless tool of the Little Magician. He also served the president by persuading his former law partner Benjamin F. Butler to fill the vacant post of attorney general.

Jackson looked to Van Buren for more than advice. The two men were also close friends. When the vice president arrived in Washington, Jackson was heartened. Following precedent, Van Buren was absent from the capital when Congress convened on December 2, 1833. Although as presiding officer of the Senate the vice president had the power to appoint the committees, vice presidents in the past had remained absent until the president pro tempore had made the appointments. The current president pro tempore, Hugh Lawson White of Tennessee, was reluctant to appoint the committees, hoping to avoid alienating either the administration or its opponents. Tennessee Senator Felix Grundy then struck a deal with Senator Daniel Webster of Massachusetts to delay the appointments until Van Buren arrived. Webster offered to join the Jacksonians in opposing the Clay–Calhoun coalition in the Senate. Van Buren arrived in Washington late on December 14. The next morning he discussed with the president Webster's offer. Van Buren totally rejected amalgamation. He had

long believed that the nation needed two parties opposed to each other on key issues of public policy. Amalgamation with Webster would undermine what had been his life's work. Not lost on Van Buren were the implications that a Webster–Jackson alliance might have on his own chance to be president. Jackson agreed with Van Buren, and Webster rejoined the opposition.

Van Buren took his seat in the Senate chair on December 16. In a short speech, he asked that body's indulgence as he reacquainted himself with the Senate's procedures. As presiding officer he had to listen to Whig attacks on the administration's policy of removing the deposits from the Bank of the United States. Clay denounced Van Buren for destroying the bank for the benefit of New York bankers.

The bank began to call in loans, causing a tremendous disruption in the U.S. economy. Petitions flooded Congress demanding reversal of the administration policy. Van Buren drafted resolutions for the New York legislature to adopt the support of removal.

On March 7, 1834, Webster read a petition from the mechanics of Philadelphia, castigating removal. Clay then rose and asked Van Buren to intercede personally with the president to end the nation's anguish. Van Buren carefully vacated the chair, walked up to Clay, and upstaged the Kentuckian by asking for a pinch of snuff.

On the March 17, Van Buren presented a petition from a public meeting in York County, Pennsylvania, opposing recharter of the bank and supporting removal of the deposits. After some debate, Clay moved that the petition should not be received. The vice president then addressed the Senate at length. Van Buren defended his practice of presenting all petitions sent to him to the Senate, withholding only those few that were blatantly disrespectful to that body. He did not consider the York County plea to be such and submitted it because the subject was already before the Senate. Clay's motion not to receive the petition was carried 24 to 21 and, continuing the assault on the administration, the Kentuckian soon pushed through the Senate a measure to censure Jackson for unconstitutionally removing the deposits. The censure passed Van Buren helped Jackson draft a protest, but Clay kept the protest from being entered into the journal.

Presiding over the "Panic Session" of the Senate exhausted Van Buren, but the vice president continued to entertain as was expected of his office. He also provided timely advice to prevent any rash or politically embarrassing administration action in the crisis that arose over settlement of spoliation claims against the French. Van Buren also selected John Forsyth of Georgia to replace Louis McLane, who had left the State Department.

In November 1834, the Albany Regency won a landslide victory in the state elections. With his home-state political base secure, Van Buren was virtually assured of being the Democratic presidential nominee in 1836, but he continued to need Jackson's support. The crisis with France over its refusal to pay spoliation claims due Americans still festered. Jackson was determined to act decisively, even threatening to use force. Seeing the political damage that the crisis could do to the administration, Van Buren urged caution. He eventually found a formula to diffuse the crisis, but it took the vice president's considerable persuasive powers to convince Jackson, Forsyth, and the Kitchen Cabinet to risk a compromise solution.

In contrast, presiding over the Senate during the second session of the Twenty-third Congress was uneventful. Van Buren was in the chair on the opening day, December 1, 1834, and left the evening of March 3, 1835, the last day in the session.

The 1836 presidential campaign began early for Van Buren. The Whigs attacked the vice president as an eastern political schemer who was unfit to be president. Van Buren had to struggle to hold together the New York–Virginia alliance that had propelled Jackson to the presidency in 1828. The Democratic Party convention met in Baltimore in May 1835 and nominated Van Buren. In replying to the com-

mittee informing him of his nomination, Van Buren promised to follow "generally in the footsteps of President Jackson" if elected.

While directing his presidential campaign, Van Buren presided over the Senate at its 1835–1836 session. He was in the chair as the Twenty-fourth Congress opened on December 7, 1835. On February 13, 1836, Van Buren ruled that Thomas Hart Benton, a Democratic senator from Missouri, was not out of order in what the Whigs believed was a personal attack on Senator Calhoun. Voting 24 to 21, the Senate rebuked the vice president by affirming that the ruling was incorrect. On May 21, Van Buren broke a tie by voting against a bill to extend the charters of certain banks in the District of Columbia. However, he faced a potentially embarrassing decision on June 2. The Senate tied 18 to 18 on whether to order the engrossing and third reading of a bill designed to prevent abolitionist literature from being sent through the mails into the southern states. The vice president voted yes, but the Senate rejected the bill 25 to 19 six days later. This issue could easily split the North–South Democratic coalition that Van Buren had labored for years to build.

Although Van Buren remained in the senate chair until June 30, the fifth to last day of the session, he was actively directing his presidential campaign throughout this period. He publicized his opposition to the distribution of surplus federal revenue to the states and his support of Jackson's Specie Circular of July 1836 that ordered federal land offices to accept only gold and silver coin in payment for public lands. His political skill yielded a narrow 28,000-vote victory over four regional Whig candidates. Van Buren had 170 electoral votes to 124 for his combined opposition.

The president-elect was still vice president and presiding officer over the Senate for the short session of the Twenty-fourth Congress. He was in the chair as the session opened on December 5, 1836. Van Buren cast another tie-breaking vote on December 21. This time the issue was procedural: Van Buren voted to refer

Calhoun's bill on extending an 1836 act regulating deposits of money in the Treasury to the Finance Committee, rather than making it the order of the day the following Monday. On January 28, 1837, Van Buren made a short farewell speech and retired from the chair. Senator Benton asked for unanimous consent to a resolution thanking the vice president for the "impartiality, dignity, and ability" with which he presided over the Senate. Calhoun objected in another swipe at his arch rival but withdrew his objection, allowing Benton's resolution to pass.

On March 4, 1837, Van Buren became president. His administration was mostly a continuation of Jackson's presidency. Van Buren had been a key adviser during Jackson's eight-year tenure; now Van Buren was his own chief adviser. The new president kept Jackson's cabinet, only filling the vacant position of secretary of war with Joel Poinsett. He inherited a costly and politically embarrassing war with the Seminole Indians in Florida that would not end. Likewise, Jackson's Indian policy finally culminated with the removal of the Cherokee under Van Buren. His opponents seized the issue to condemn the mistreatment of the tribes, which cost the administration political support, especially in the Northeast.

As one of his last acts in office, Jackson had recognized Texas independence. Van Buren faced strong protests from Mexico as a result. United States annexation of Texas would not only eventually cause war with Mexico, but it was also a sectional issue that could tear asunder the Democratic coalition. Van Buren handled the explosive Texas issue by ignoring it until it disappeared, at least for the time being.

In other areas of foreign policy, the administration had remarkable success. The president skillfully resolved crises with Britain over Americans aiding Canadian rebels and over the disputed Maine–New Brunswick border. Eventually Van Buren also replaced members of his cabinet as resignations occurred.

Foreign policy, Indian affairs, and cabinet appointments turned out to be minor concerns for the administration. The economy came to dominate Van Buren's presidency and eventually brought it down. On March 17, 1837, an economic panic began with the failure of a New York City commercial house. Economic misery would last for the rest of Van Buren's term. The president decided to retain the Specie Circular to prevent banks from paying debts in depreciated paper money. On May 16, Van Buren called a special session of Congress for September. Van Buren decided to ask Congress to establish an Independent Treasury so that the government would not have to entrust its funds to private banks. He also needed congressional permission to withdraw government funds from the deposit banks and issue short-term treasury notes to cover the deficit in the Treasury.

The Independent Treasury proposal split the Democrats. Conservative and probusiness Democrats refused to support it. Van Buren stubbornly clung to his proposal. It failed in Congress during three sessions before the economy rebounded slightly in May 1838 when New York banks resumed specie payments. In the summer of 1838 Van Buren toured the North, breaking all precedent by making campaign speeches. The president and Senator Calhoun also made peace, allowing the South Carolinian to bring his supporters back into the Democratic fold. When Congress met in December 1839, Van Buren again pushed the Independent Treasury. With Calhoun's help, the bill passed and Van Buren signed it into law on the Fourth of July 1840. By then the Whigs were campaigning furiously to put William Henry Harrison into the White House. Van Buren valiantly fought back, but he could not overcome the burden that depression placed on his administration. Harrison had 234 electoral votes to the incumbent's 60.

Before retiring from office, Van Buren entertained president-elect Harrison; then he moved back to Kinderhook, taking up residence at Lindenwald, the first permanent home that he owned. He immediately contemplated a run for the presidency in 1844. Between February and July 1842, he toured the South and West in a private journey that soon became a campaign swing. With Harrison dead and President John Tyler feuding with the Whigs in Congress, Van Buren quickly built an organization to win back the presidency. His principal rival Calhoun blundered himself out of contention for the Democratic nomination, so Van Buren expected to face his Whig rival Henry Clay in 1844. On April 27, Van Buren published his "Hammet Letter," in which he opposed the annexation of Texas. (Clay published his opposition on the same day.) Van Buren's stance on Texas cost him the Democratic nomination. Unable to obtain the necessary two-thirds majority needed for the nomination, he withdrew in favor of James K. Polk, who defeated Clay for the presidency.

Polk soon alienated Van Buren and much of the Democratic Party in New York. Disagreements over cabinet appointments and patronage joined with opposition to the extension of slavery into the territory conquered from Mexico propelled Van Buren to leadership of the "Barnburner" faction within the New York Democratic Party. They wanted Van Buren as the Democratic presidential candidate in 1848; instead they ran Van Buren as the unsuccessful Free-Soil Party candidate. In 1852, Van Buren returned to the Democratic fold and supported Franklin Pierce for the presidency. As the nation drifted toward secession and civil war, Van Buren became increasingly disillusioned. At seventy-nine, he died at Lindenwald on July 24, 1862.

REFERENCES

Joel H. Silbey, *Martin Van Buren* (Lanham, Md.: Rowman and Littlefield, 2005); John Niven, *Martin Van Buren: The Romantic Age of American Politics* (New York and Oxford, England: Oxford University Press, 1983); Robert V. Remini, *Martin Van Buren and the Making of the Democratic Party* (New York: Columbia University Press, 1959); Ted Widmer, *Martin Van Buren* (New York: Times Books, 2005); Major L. Wilson, *The Presidency of Martin Van Buren* (Lawrence, Kans.: University Press of Kansas, 1984); *The Autobiography of Martin Van Buren*, John C. Fitzpatrick, ed., *Annual Report of the American Historical Association for the Year 1918* (Washington, D.C.: Government Printing Office, 1920); Joel H. Silbey, *Martin Van Buren and the Emergence of American Popular Politics* (Lanham, Md.: Rowman and Littlefield, 2005).

CHARLES H. SCHOENLEBER holds a Ph.D. from the University of Wisconsin, Madison. After teaching at the University of Wyoming, he joined the Documentary History of the Ratification of the Constitution project in Madison in 1987. His research interest is the politics of Indian removal, especially in the southern states.

RICHARD MENTOR JOHNSON (1781–1850)

Vice President, 1837–1841

(President Martin Van Buren)

RICHARD MENTOR JOHNSON
(Library of Congress)

By Lindsey Apple

Richard Mentor Johnson, the ninth vice president of the United States, was certainly one of the most colorful men to serve in that position. A frontier entrepreneur, Indian fighter, and military hero, he shared many of the personal characteristics that made Andrew Jackson so popular with Americans and assured his own intimate friendship with General Jackson. Plainspoken, of a democratic manner, loyal to friends, and disinterested in dress or genteel manners, Richard Mentor Johnson embodied the frontier politician. Because he championed causes popular with the common man he also became the candidate of the northeastern worker, including the radical "locofoco" faction. He also encouraged the development of educational institutions of many types across the nation and on a personal level sought to educate disenfranchised elements of the American people—the American Indian, women, and even African American slaves.

Like many vice presidents, however, Johnson's election to the office marked the end of his political career rather than a stepping stone to the presidency. Noted as a potential presidential candidate throughout the 1830s, he was nearly forgotten, or dismissed, soon after his term as vice president. That says as much about the United States and its people as it does about Johnson. His political career reflects the rapidly changing nature of American political life; the homespun frontiersmen became a caricature as the country became more complex. Johnson's historical reputation says a great deal about American social values and attitudes, particularly those regarding race.

Richard Mentor Johnson was born in a hastily constructed fortress near Louisville, Kentucky, when that region was the American West. In the fall of 1779 his parents, Robert and Jemima Suggett Johnson, moved their growing family from Orange County, Virginia, to the Beargrass Creek settlement. While Robert Johnson was off fighting Indians with George Rogers Clark, Jemima awaited the birth of their fifth child, the future vice president. The family then moved to Bryan Station in the Bluegrass region, where the entire family became involved in the Indian wars. At the siege of Bryan Station, Richard's older brother James, at the age of eight, dashed across the roofs of the cabins dousing fire arrows launched by the attacking Indians. On the frontier, women also played an active role. His mother led a group of women to get water for the fort, and older sister Betsy pulled a flaming arrow from the cradle where Richard slept. Such stories may have been embellished over time or for political purposes, but they are the means by which families shape an identity and politicians create careers.

The Johnson family quickly developed that identity. Robert Johnson built a fortified homestead on a 2,000-acre tract of land purchased from Virginia patriot Patrick Henry. The tract was located at the Great Crossings, a buffalo trace on North Elkhorn Creek. The family farmed the land, but they also created commercial and manufacturing ventures as diverse as hemp factories, general stores, stage lines, and steamboat construction. Richard Johnson later operated a tavern and a spa where wealthy southerners came to spend their summers.

Like many frontier families, the Johnsons had journeyed west to prosper economically, and they pursued that goal relentlessly, seeing no contradiction in mixing economic gain with their political, cultural, and even religious activities. Quite common among frontier folk, such mixing of goals gave Johnson's political rivals, and later historians, significant ammunition to use against him.

Johnson's father was an influential member of the legislature that created the first Kentucky state constitution. Family members were also leaders in the affairs of the Baptist Church, served on the boards of Transylvania College and Georgetown College, and became leaders in the judicial, legislative, and cultural affairs of the region. Some have argued that Scott County was created by the state legislature virtually as a Johnson fiefdom. Their political and economic empire became the base from which three of Robert Johnson's sons won election to national office.

The education of Richard Mentor Johnson is shrouded in the mystery of the frontier. After attending a local common school, he is believed to have attended Transylvania College briefly. He then studied law with George Nicholas and James Brown, men who trained a generation of Kentucky leadership. Admitted to the bar in 1802, he practiced law at Great Crossings. Johnson was not well read, nor could he be considered an intellectual. His abilities were of a more practical nature. He saw business opportunities everywhere, enjoyed politics, and was said to have a "natural aptitude" for military affairs. Throughout his career he combined the three areas, usually to his advantage.

Johnson served in the United States House of Representatives from 1807 to 1819, except for two years when he fought in the War of 1812 and recovered from wounds received at the Battle of the Thames. In 1819, the Kentucky legislature named him to the U.S. Senate, where he remained until defeated ten years later. He then returned to the House of Representatives, where he served until chosen as vice president in 1837. Thus, he had significant experience in the legislative branch of government before he became the presiding officer of the Senate.

Johnson's rise to political prominence rested on a number of factors. Modern historians have been inclined to dismiss his importance by questioning aspects of his political power and his personal life. There is certainly evidence to support such attacks, but the issues are far more complex. Some argue that his fame rested on an undeserved military reputation. Johnson was, before the War of 1812, one of the War Hawks, a group of congressmen who believed that the United States should stand up to the British. Once war was declared, Richard M. Johnson left Congress to raise a regiment from Kentucky, which he led north to join the army of General William Henry Harrison. At the Battle of the Thames, Johnson, with help from others, devised a plan to expel British General Henry Proctor and his Indian ally Tecumseh from a strategic position along the Thames River. James Johnson, Richard's brother, attacked the British forces of General Proctor. Richard Johnson led twenty men in a suicide mission, called the "forlorn hope," to discover the position of Tecumseh and his warriors. Fifteen of the twenty were killed immediately, and four others were wounded. Johnson, shot through the hip and thigh, managed to remain on his horse to direct the force that then attacked the warriors. Though receiving several additional wounds and having his horse shot out from under him, Johnson was able to kill an Indian who charged at him. Later, he claimed that his dead adversary resembled Tecumseh. Political supporters proclaimed Richard Johnson the "hero of the Thames" and the slayer of Tecumseh. He would later campaign under the slogan "Rumpsey, Dumpsey, who shot Tecumseh!"

Political detractors and historians have argued that he probably did not kill the Indian chief. Historians also argued that his actions were foolhardy. Whether he killed Tecumseh is a mute point, the chieftain was killed in the battle. Moreover, foolhardy or no, such actions were seen as signs of manliness, and Richard M. Johnson was a legitimate hero in his day. Even the Congress presented him with a ceremonial sword when, recovered from five separate wounds, he returned to Washington. A severe limp spoke to his patriotism thereafter wherever he campaigned.

In addition to military heroism, Johnson's political success rested on his family's economic power and his ability to use his political position to enhance the region in which he lived. In Kentucky there was no secret ballot after 1799. The "voice vote" meant that few men could afford to vote against the Johnsons. Conversely, the Johnsons were also the subject of local admiration. They had accomplished what most people came west hoping to achieve. Richard Johnson also brought national attention to the area. Famous visitors frequently journeyed through Kentucky to pay their respects to Johnson and to Henry Clay, 15 miles away in Lexington: In 1819, President James Monroe visited Johnson's farm; in 1825, the Revolutionary War hero Lafayette was entertained by Johnson, who invited most of Central Kentucky to participate. Johnson also used his political position to create government spending in the West and to secure contracts for western businessmen.

One such venture nearly bankrupted the Johnson family and damaged the reputations of President Monroe and Secretary of War John C. Calhoun. It might be argued that the affair permanently shaped Johnson's reputation. In 1818, Calhoun sought to establish a line of fortresses up the Missouri River to the Yellowstone, thereby strengthening control of a vast new frontier. Johnson, the chairman of the House Committee on Military Affairs and a friend of Calhoun, used his influence to secure contracts to supply the materials for the new fortresses. The Johnsons began to collect the supplies and built four steamboats to carry them, drawing frequent advances from the government. The project was a disaster. The Johnsons sensed the commercial value of steam transportation but knew too little about the technology and made bad decisions. The steamboats could not navigate the shallow water. They were also confronted by the financial panic that began in 1819. Creditors began to call in notes owed by the Johnsons or guaranteed by them. The venture cost the United States government approximately $266,000. Richard Remini calls the Yellowstone affair a "colossal boondoggle." "Honest men," he argues, "shook their heads in disbelief when they heard about it."

In fact, there was nothing illegal by nineteenth-century standards about the venture, and the courts later accepted James Johnson's financial accounting of the incident. The War Department also continued to award the Johnsons contracts to provision military bases at New Orleans, Natchitoches, St. Louis, and elsewhere. Moreover, the Johnsons hardly profited from the venture: Local court records indicate that they sold large parcels of land to meet their obligations. Historians have been inclined to evaluate the incident by twentieth-century standards, but the *Argus of Western America,* a major western newspaper of the time, praised the Johnsons for bringing so much currency into the specie-starved West.

Johnson also won the support of many individuals and communities by his consistent support of pensions for veterans and their widows and orphans. He seemed to have the interests of the common man uppermost in his thought. He fought against imprisonment for debt on both the state and national level and opposed an effort to stop the transportation of mail on Sunday because, in a nation as mobile as the United States, citizens needed to maintain contact with their relatives. Johnson also opposed the National Bank, believing it, erroneously or otherwise, to be a tool of the wealthy, and encouraged internal improvements as a means to develop the western territories.

Richard Johnson's political prominence also rested on his intimate friendship with Andrew Jackson. Jackson held virtually all veterans in high esteem, but Johnson had exhibited the kind of courage the general most admired: he had been wounded in defense of his country. Johnson also had been the sole member of the committee on military affairs to support Jackson when charges were brought in 1819 regarding Jackson's conduct in the Seminole Wars. Again in 1824, Johnson argued that Henry Clay's "corrupt bargain" with John Quincy Adams was no way to treat a true patriot.

Johnson was also led into the Democratic Party by events in Kentucky. The economic Panic of 1819 created great suffering in Kentucky. One of the main causes for the failure of the Yellowstone expedition, the panic nearly destroyed the Johnson family. Like many Kentuckians, the Johnsons were inclined to blame the Bank of the United States. Richard Johnson voluntarily left Congress in 1819 to run for election to the state legislature, where he supported government relief for those who were losing their property because of the financial collapse. Known as the Relief/Antirelief controversy in Kentucky, the struggle colored Kentucky politics for years. Jasper B. Shannon and Ruth McQuown note in their study of Kentucky elections that areas that supported the Relief candidates became Jacksonian Democrats and those who opposed relief to debtors became Whigs. Richard Johnson joined fellow Kentuckians Amos Kendall, Francis Preston Blair, and others in the Democratic Party. The fact that Johnson controlled the party in Kentucky, a very important state at the time, no doubt endeared him to Jackson and his political supporters as well.

When Jackson was elected president in 1828, Johnson exhibited the loyalty that characterized his political life: He signed a report condemning the Bank of the United States, an issue central to Jackson's thinking; supported the president's tariff policies despite his long friendship and political alliance with John C. Calhoun; and even supported the president's opposition to internal improvements, though he felt them essential to economic development in his home state.

Jackson had stated his intention to serve only one term. Johnson was mentioned as a possible presidential candidate of the Democratic Party because of his party loyalty and his popularity. He had the misfortune, however, to be pitted against one of the shrewdest politicians in antebellum America. Martin Van Buren, the political boss of New York, was known as the Little Magician because of his ability to manipulate people and conditions to his advantage. Moreover, conditions favored the magician. The United States was no longer a frontier republic. The number of states had more than doubled by 1832, and the population was growing even faster. Seven out of ten Americans were still farmers, but commerce and manufacturing were growing, spurred by population growth and the building of canals and railroads. The role government should play was being questioned, and the issue began to divide the commercial North from the rural South. The issue of slavery also led to sharp differences. It was a difficult time for any politician. Caucuses, party conventions, and outright manipulation became the means to build an electoral majority in an age when support of principles was almost a guarantee of the animosity of half the nation.

During Jackson's first term, Martin Van Buren used his charm and his manipulative abilities to endear himself to Andrew Jackson. Calhoun, Johnson, and other presidential hopefuls were no match for the wily New Yorker. Johnson was described by his contemporaries as mild mannered and pleasant, open and honest in his dealings. One prominent Washington hostess described him as "the most tender-hearted, mild, affectionate and benevolent of men." Intensely loyal to friends and political allies, he was more inclined to compromise, to seek consensus. Fair minded and lacking strong prejudices, he often sacrificed his own interests to secure harmony and the interests of his region for that of the nation. A border-state politician, he seemed, perhaps like his rival and fellow Kentuckian Henry Clay, to recognize that the issues that increasingly separated North from South were more complex than either region admitted. Such qualities had served him well in the past; they were handicaps in the new politics of Martin Van Buren.

Johnson played the role of mediator in Jackson's administration. When a group of western congressmen urged Johnson to speak to the president in favor of internal improvements, he agreed; however, he confronted not only Jackson but a whispering Van Buren, who had carefully nurtured Jackson's opposition to internal improvements. Johnson also became involved in the Peggy Eaton affair when he tried to serve as mediator. Mrs. Eaton was married to one of Jackson's cabinet members, but her life before that marriage had been somewhat scandalous.

When the other ladies of the cabinet snubbed her, President Jackson was furious. He blamed his vice president, John C. Calhoun. Johnson, a friend of Jackson and Calhoun, attempted to mediate. Van Buren championed Mrs. Eaton, thereby increasing his standing with Jackson.*

Such conduct won Van Buren the support of Jackson and the distrust of many others. Some have argued that Jackson chose to accept a second term because he realized the nation would not accept Van Buren as his successor. Johnson was mentioned as a presidential candidate for the 1832 campaign until Jackson decided to run again, and as a vice-presidential candidate until Jackson handpicked Van Buren as his running mate. Johnson supported the ticket, stumping the country on its behalf, but

*Editor's note: See JOHN CALHOUN for further explanation of the Peggy Eaton affair.

his position with the president waned as Van Buren's influence grew.

In 1836, Jackson chose Van Buren to run for president. To assuage Johnson's disappointment at not getting the nomination for the presidency and, to a degree, Jackson's sense of guilt for his own disloyalty, Johnson was offered the position of vice president. Jackson's support proved sufficient for Van Buren but less so for Johnson. By 1836, the issues of slavery and race were hardening attitudes across the United States. Within the Democratic Party, the Virginians wanted their own native son, William Cabell Rives, to be chosen as the candidate, and they were willing to play the race card to defeat Johnson.

Richard Johnson never married, but he maintained a long-term relationship with Julia Chinn, one of his slaves. She lived in his house, ran his farm in his absence, and even accompanied him to Washington. She was, in short, his wife in every way but the legal sense. When apart they corresponded regularly, his letters suggesting that he held her opinions in high regard. They also had two, daughters, Adeline and Imogene, whom Johnson educated and, if his correspondence is any indication, adored and respected. Rev. Thomas Henderson, the girls' tutor, claimed Johnson insisted that they were to be educated as well as any woman of the time. Adeline, for example, played the piano for General Lafayette when he visited Colonel Johnson in 1825. Johnson also arranged marriages for his daughters to white men and provided them with substantial farms.

In the 1820s, little of this seemed to matter. John Niven, Van Buren's biographer, notes that Johnson's family was accepted by "the easygoing society of the West." Even the good folk of the Great Crossings Baptist Church accepted them, and only an occasional comment on their octoroon mother called attention to Johnson's domestic life. President Jackson knew of it. Henry Clay was aware of it. In 1836, however, it became a major issue. The South declared Johnson unacceptable as a candidate, and even within his own party, the attacks were cruel,

scurrilous assaults. The Whigs continued the assault when, with Jackson's support, Johnson prevailed at the convention. Johnson refused to respond to the charges. Julia Chinn had died in 1833, the victim of a cholera epidemic, and Johnson refused to deny their relationship. The attacks were so harsh that some have argued that Adeline grew ill because of them. She died just prior to her father's election. Johnson proclaimed her a "lovely and innocent child . . . a source of inexhaustible happiness and comfort to me. She was a firm and great prop to my happiness here—but she is gone where sorrow and sighing can never disturb her peaceful and quiet bosom." Johnson won the nomination and the vice presidency, but his family and his chance for higher elective office had been destroyed.

Ironically, it was not miscegenation that bothered southerners. Indeed, the mixing of the races was quite common on southern plantations. George Prentice, the Whig editor of the Louisville (Kentucky) *Journal,* and, according to one author, no stranger to "blood pollution" himself, captured the real issue and the hypocrisy when he wrote:

> If Col. Johnson had the decency and decorum to seek to hide his ignominy from the world, we would refrain from lifting the curtain. His chief sin against society is the publicity and barefacedness of his conduct, he scorns all secrecy, all concealment, all disguise.

Even for political gain Johnson would not deny his "wife" and daughters. Future generations of the family and society in general did seek to conceal his relationships, however. Members of his white family tried to forget, perhaps even destroying some of his papers. The local newspapers cooperated in hiding such a "blight" upon the community, and Johnson's biographer, Leland Meyer, handled the matter very discreetly. Historians relegated Johnson to a footnote that usually referred to his domestic arrangement. In the late nineteenth century, the United States, not just the South, wished to conceal its hypocrisy on racial issues.

Johnson won 147 electoral votes in the election of 1836, just short of the required majority, and the election was thrown into the Senate. Johnson became the only vice president to be elected by the Senate. The vote was 33 to 16.

Like many who held the office, Johnson found the vice presidency frustrating. As presiding officer in the Senate, the major issues of the day passed before him, but he was not at liberty to speak on them. For men who actively participated in the affairs of state, the inactivity was difficult. Perhaps the harshness of campaign rhetoric and the human cost sapped his energies. A biographer of Franklin Pierce claimed that Johnson presided over the Senate in a careless and inefficient manner. He was more inclined to leave the chair "to lounge around" or to stand and chat near one of the four fireplaces that warmed the Senate chambers. Johnson spent a lot of his time seeking support for his Choctaw academy and actually left the chair for an entire summer, apparently preferring to operate his tavern and spa at the Blue Springs.

Despite their rivalry during the Jackson years, Johnson and President Van Buren remained on cordial terms. Though never one of his major advisers, Johnson supported the president's legislative program as the presiding officer of the Senate. Historians have made much of his role as a compromiser or peacemaker. One implied that his tolerance of differing views may have resulted from "a fuzzy timidity" rather than from any liberal spirit. That seems too harsh for one who exhibited a personal tolerance in so many areas. It should also be noted that another famous Kentuckian of the era made a reputation as a compromiser and "pacificator" too.

Johnson's moderating skills and his easy, gregarious manner made him an excellent choice for the presiding officer of the Senate. The nation faced a number of divisive issues during Johnson's term of office. A financial panic brought on in part by the debates over national monetary policy and the government's efforts to shape it accompanied Van Buren's inauguration. The Senate debated the issues of responsibility for economic collapse and the solutions. Disassociation from private banks and the development of an independent treasury highlighted the discussions of nearly the entire four years, and the debates became quite heated at times. There was also the issue of federal land policy and also the annexation of Texas, issues on the periphery of a larger one that would dominate political debate for more than a quarter of a century—slavery and its place in American life.

Such issues created party and personal divisions. Senatorial privileges were demanded and the rulings of the chair carefully assessed. As presiding officer, Johnson recognized senators seeking the right to address the body. A perusal of the *Congressional Globe* suggests that it was more than perfunctory courtesy when, at the end of his term, several senators, including Clay, spoke to his impartiality and fairness. Though most vice presidents extol the virtues of the Senate, Johnson's service in that body made him particularly respectful of its function. He claimed to have attempted to give to each senator the respect due "the representative of a sovereign and independent state."

The presiding officer of the Senate also has the duty to break the deadlock when votes on an issue are evenly divided. Johnson cast fourteen tie-breaking votes, the fourth highest in U.S. history. On March 25, 1840, he cast three deciding votes that secured the passage of a treaty. It was fitting, given his interest in Native Americans, that the treaty was one signed between the government and the Six Nations, a confederation of tribes. It was equally appropriate that several of his deciding votes were for the relief of individuals.

The role of Richard M. Johnson was, however, far more important in the politics that led to office than in the exercising of it. By 1840, Johnson was considered a major liability to the Democratic Party. He had cost the party the support of the South. He had even failed to carry his own state, proving far less effective in the West, supposedly the area where he could add most to the ticket. Party leaders encouraged the selection of another candidate: Andrew Jackson urged Van Buren to drop Johnson and run with James K. Polk of Tennessee. Amos Kendall, a former ally, accused Johnson of having taken a second slave mistress. Ironically, he had also lost his appeal in the North. The locofocos announced their opposition to any slaveholder.

Van Buren remained neutral, at least in public, and the Democratic convention decided to let the states support their own candidate for vice president. As the campaign progressed, however, Johnson became the major candidate when James K. Polk withdrew. Whether an asset or a detriment to the campaign, it mattered little. Feelings ran high against Van Buren, and the Whigs, who had argued that Johnson's military record did not mean political ability, nominated their own military hero, William Henry Harrison. The Democrats lost the election.

Defeated for national office, Johnson returned to his home in Kentucky, where he took an interest in local affairs. He represented Scott County in the Kentucky legislature from 1841 to 1843. He then retired from politics for a few years but traveled throughout the country as if he intended to be a candidate for national office again. Mentioned briefly for office in 1844, Johnson played only a spoiler's role in politics. In 1848, he again served in the state legislature and was briefly a candidate for state governor before his death in 1850.

Most of his energies after 1841 involved his life long interest, education. Except for the Choctaw Academy, historians have virtually ignored his support of education. Johnson served for many years as a trustee of Georgetown College and encouraged other Baptist efforts to establish academies and schools. After the War of 1812, he also encouraged the government to create military academies throughout the nation, and he was an organizer of Columbian College, the predecessor to George Washington University.

Some of Johnson's ideas about education were decidedly progressive, albeit limited. As early as 1819 he had attempted to establish a school for Indian youths. His Choctaw Academy educated hundreds of young men from a variety of tribes. Ella Drake criticizes him in an article in the *Register of the Kentucky Historical Society* for seeking a profit and saving money at the expense of education at the academy. As noted earlier, frontiersmen sought economic gain through political, cultural, and religious offices far too openly for modern taste. Though the educational opportunities seemed limited at the academy, they were limited in most Kentucky schools. Johnson's nephews and other local white youth attended the Choctaw Academy, which would suggest that it was not considered substandard at the time. Moreover, most people in the 1820s and 1830s were far more interested in removing the tribes to the west than in educating them.

Johnson also insisted that the school superintendent educate Adeline and Imogene, as well as several promising slaves. In an uncharacteristically quiet way, Johnson spoke to his neighbors about the abilities of Native Americans, women, and African Americans. At the Choctaw Academy, red, white, and black Americans were educated together, and even gender was overlooked.

Richard Mentor Johnson died on November 19, 1850, in Frankfort, Kentucky, where he was serving in the state legislature. Though his term as vice president lacks distinction, Johnson's life should stand as an indication of the dangers of generalization in the study of history. It also speaks to the speed of change in American life.

REFERENCES

Leland Winfield Meyer, *The Life and Times of Colonel Richard M. Johnson of Kentucky* (New York: Columbia University Press, 1932); Lindsey Apple, Frederick A. Johnson, Ann Bolton Bevins, eds., *Scott County Kentucky: A History* (Georgetown, Ky.: Scott County Historical Society, 1993); Robert Bolt, "Vice President Richard M. Johnson of Kentucky: Hero of the Thames—Or the Great Amalgamator?"

The Register of the Kentucky Historical Society, 75 (July 1977), 191–203; Ella Wells Drake, "Choctaw Academy: Richard M. Johnson and the Business of Indian Education," *The Register of the Kentucky Historical Society,* 91 (Summer 1993), 260–297.

———————————

LINDSEY APPLE retired as professor of history at Georgetown College, Georgetown, Kentucky, in 2004. He is an editor and an author of *Scott County Kentucky: A History* (Georgetown, 1993) and a biography of Susan Clay Sawitzky, a great-granddaughter of Henry Clay, entitled *Never Excelled: Tradition and Modernity in the Life of a Southern Lady* (Kent State University Press, 1997). He has written articles for the *Register of the Kentucky Historical Society, The Filson Club Quarterly, Border States, The Kentucky Encyclopedia,* and a sketch on James Johnson for the *American National Biography.*

JOHN TYLER (1790–1842)
Vice President, March 4–April 4, 1841
(President William Henry Harrison)

JOHN TYLER
(Library of Congress)

By M. Boyd Coyner, Jr.

With the death of William Henry Harrison on April 4, 1841, John Tyler became not only the first vice president to succeed to the presidency, but also the vice president with the shortest tenure in that office and, only six days past his fifty-first birthday, the youngest chief executive up to that date. As the first accidental president, he set the precedent for his successors by his insistence that he was no mere acting president but fully president, by title as well as in privilege and function. Unfortunately for Tyler, he also set a pattern for his three nineteenth-century successors as accidental presidents by failing to win renomination to succeed himself.

It is highly unlikely that Tyler, because of the political dogmas to which he so strictly adhered, would have come to the presidency by any route other than that which brought him to the White House. His early political successes came quickly enough; he inherited position and sufficient fortune to place him among the plantation elite of the James River bottoms in Virginia. Born in Charles City County, in Virginia's Tidewater, less than a year after George Washington's first inauguration, with the exception of a dozen years in nearby Gloucester County and the colonial capital of Williamsburg, his permanent residence for the other six decades of his life was in his native Charles City, one of the oldest counties in that oldest section of that Oldest Dominion. He became both exemplar of and spokesman for the dominant rural squirearchy, representing and embodying the strictest sect of Old-School Republicanism. His father, Judge John Tyler, had served in the Virginia legislature, was elected to a maximum-possible three terms as governor, served for many years as judge of the general court of Virginia, and at his death was judge of the federal district court of eastern Virginia. Through both his parents and by an early marriage to Letitia Christian of a neighboring county, Tyler was well connected with the plantation elite of the James–York Peninsula.

Tyler himself possessed talents that would enable him to translate the advantages of birth and position into political leadership very early in life. Discounting the partisan vitriol of his enemies, by general accounts this six-foot Virginian was thought to be attractive in appearance, even handsome to some, amiable and cordial in manner, endowed with a good mind, and an able speaker. Charles Dickens, not inclined to be overly kind to things American, met Tyler during his presidency and wrote of him that "the expression on his face was mild and pleasant, and his manner was remarkably unaffected, gentlemanly, and agreeable. I thought that, in his carriage and demeanor, he became his position singularly well."

A graduate of William and Mary College at the age of seventeen, admitted to the bar at twenty, he was barely twenty-one when he won a seat in the Virginia House of Delegates in 1811. He served five successive terms in that body, during which time he was elected to the executive council of state. From the Virginia House he was elevated in 1816 to the U.S. House of Representatives at the age of twenty-six. He resigned from the federal House in 1821, was returned to Virginia's lower house in 1823, and resigned in 1825 to assume the governorship of the state. He resigned from the governorship to take a seat in the U.S. Senate, where he remained until his resignation in 1836.

During this first quarter-century of his political career, Tyler was a thoroughgoing and consistent champion of Old Republicanism of the very starched variety. His convictions well illustrate the minds of those popular and legislative majorities who chose him to be their spokesman. Tyler would have nothing of an "American system" and spoke and voted against those chief agencies of economic nationalism: the National Bank, protective tariffs, and federal subsidies for roads and canals. In the Missouri Crisis of 1819–20, he insisted that the federal government had no right to exclude slavery from the territories. In Virginia he opposed reformers' efforts to bring a greater degree of democracy to the commonwealth.

In 1811, when only twenty-one, the young legislator introduced resolutions of censure directed against Virginia's two senators for defying legislative instructions to vote against recharter of the First National Bank. He served on a committee to investigate the Second Bank in 1818., concurred with the committee report denouncing the bank's practice, and in a lengthy speech declared that the bank had been unconstitutional in the first place, and because it had so grossly violated its charter, the charter should be annulled. He voted against recharter of the Second Bank as a senator in 1832, and joined the successful effort to sustain Andrew Jackson's veto of the recharter bill.

In 1816, a month after taking his seat in the House of Representatives, Tyler joined a majority of Virginians east of the Blue Ridge in opposing John C. Calhoun's Bonus Bill, by which the federal government was to provide a fixed annual subsidy to construct roads and canals. The federal government had no authority for such endeavors, Tyler maintained, and the Richmond *Enquirer* published a letter from the congressman to his constituents in which he said that the state of Virginia was not "in so poor a condition as to require a *charitable* donation from Congress." In his first speech as a senator, he denounced a proposed appropriation to extend the Cumberland Road; it was unconstitutional, and bad policy to boot, according to Tyler. Among many objections, he deplored the federal patronage that would be created. As governor, he had denounced such appropriations as bribes. In opposing the Maysville Road Bill in 1830, he warned of a dangerous expansion of a national authority, and expressed the concept of "federal republicanism" so characteristic of gentlemen of his stripe:

I have no such word (as national) in my political vocabulary. A nation of twenty-four nations is an idea which I cannot realize. A confederacy may embrace many nations; but by what process twenty-four can be converted into one, I am still to learn.

This doctrine was the basis for Tyler's Senate denunciation of Jackson's Force Bill on February 6, 1833.

With all the invective hurled against bank and federal subsidies, it was the protective tariff that most excited—and unified—southerners of the middle and lower regions (those that later would join the Confederacy, that is) during the 1820s and early 1830s. Protectionism was indeed a levy on exporters of southern staples to benefit a manufacturing interest concentrated in the free states, and demands for higher levies came with the depression that followed the Panic of 1819. Tyler was in the House of Representatives in 1820 when the first depression-era demands reached the Congress, and he became a major spokesman of the antitariff forces. Not only was a protective tariff clearly unconstitutional, but it was also an unjust levy by one section of the Union on another. Tyler warned of a cyclical pattern of tariff hikes as one set of manufacturers after another, who could not compete in the free marketplace, were "protected" into being; as Jefferson before him, Tyler believed that the seemingly endless supply of land in the United States destined the country to be primarily agricultural; the artificial encouragement of manufacturing "would subvert the order of Heaven itself." The iniquitous Tariff of Abominations of 1828 was "a curse on the whole South." Even the Tariff of 1832 that, by lowering a number of nonprotective duties, won the support of a majority of Virginia's house delegation, was unacceptable to Tyler. He delivered a three-day assault on the bill, denouncing it, among many reasons, for raising consumers' prices. "It cripples the farming interest of the Union," he charged, not without justice for those who exported their produce, with no concurrent benefits from the growth of towns and cities as home markets for their foodstuffs. It was this tariff that South Carolina was to nullify in November 1832.

The Missouri Crisis erupted during Tyler's second term in the House, and he became a spokesman for the more intransigent segment of southerners. He took an unyielding stand on the right of slaveholders to take their slaves into federal territories; this was to characterize him for the rest of his life. He was among those southerners who professed slavery to be an evil, a profession shared by virtually all who spoke during the Missouri debates, as well as by the Virginians of the notable antislavery debates in the legislature a dozen years later. Tyler and a great majority of his fellow southerners were adamantly hostile, however, to what seemed to them as dangerous outside meddling with the institution. Tyler's speech of February 17, 1820, was as clear an exposition as the House would hear of the widely held southern argument by which they could profess hostility to the institution at the same time that they urged its expansion into new territories. This was the "diffusion" argument, whereby it was maintained that by spreading slaves more thinly over the territories, the concentration of bondsmen and bonds-women in the older slave states would be alleviated, thus allowing them to think more readily of some form of emancipation. With the importation of slaves made illegal, there would be no new slaves; they would simply be "diffused."

Tyler correctly pointed to the fact that gradual emancipation had been begun where there were the fewest slaves. "What enabled New York, Pennsylvania, and other states to adopt the language of universal emancipation?" Tyler questioned rhetorically. "Rely on it, nothing but the paucity of the number of their slaves. That which would have been criminal in these states not to have done would be an act of political suicide in Georgia or South Carolina." When the Missouri Compromise was presented to the House in segments, Tyler joined a unanimous southern delegation to remove the anti-slave restriction on Missouri. He was, however, with a majority of his fellow Virginians, and roughly half the slave-state delegation, in rejecting the ban on slavery in the remainder of the Louisiana Purchase territory above the 36°30′ parallel. It was an unconstitutional restriction, Tyler believed, and in later years he was to write that the South, by yielding on this point in 1820, had brought upon itself much of its subsequent difficulties.

Tyler also, as spokesman for the plantation elite, opposed efforts to push Virginia in the direction of white male democracy. As a member of the legislature in 1825 he had opposed demands for a convention to reform the constitution of 1776. During his years as senator, he rather reluctantly served in that "assembly of notables" that was the constitutional convention of 1829–30; he did not care to antagonize western reformers or eastern conservatives lest he lose support in his struggle against federal encroachment. He took little part in the proceeding but voted with the conservatives to retain a property qualification for suffrage, against making white population the sole basis for representation in the legislature, and against popular election of the governors. Tyler had, in the federal House in 1818, taken a procreditor stand in opposing a federal bankruptcy law.

Tyler's legislative elections to both the governorship and the Senate demonstrated quite clearly the political direction in which the state seemed to be moving. When first elected to the U.S. House in 1816, his Old Republicanism had put him in a rather small minority within the Virginia delegation, let alone in the rest of the country. Missouri and the depression-born tariffs had pushed Virginia and much of the middle and lower South in the direction of strict construction and states' rights, on many issues at least. Reconciling such views within the nation at large was to become increasingly difficult, however. With the development of a national two-party system—Andrew Jackson versus his opposition, more or less—the dilemma for ambitious political leaders was to choose that party most congenial to their principles and to their desire for political preferment. What proved to be Tyler's wrong choice of national party led, after his accidental election to the White House, to his sixteen-year elimination from the political scene, both in the state and in the nation.

Tyler was born when Virginia was by far the most populous state, and during his first thirty-five years he would only have had a boyhood memory of the only four years in which a Virginian did not occupy the presidency. "The Virginia Dynasty" came to an abrupt end, however, with the completion of James Monroe's second term in 1825. Tyler, with a large majority of Virginians, supported that most logical heir of The Dynasty, William H. Crawford of Georgia. When Crawford came in third in a field of four candidates and a second Adams from Massachusetts was chosen president in the House, it was indeed the end of an era—not only so, but President Adams's expansive nationalism created a virtually one-party region in presidential balloting among the states that would one day join the Confederacy. The only question was the most propitious means of sending the president back to his native state. Adams suffered dearly at the hands of southerners. He was to have ample opportunities for vengeance, not least of which was his memorable diary. On the day of Harrison's death, attempting to absorb the idea of a Tyler presidency, he said of the new chief executive that he was "a political sectarian of the slave-driving, Virginia, Jeffersonian school . . ." and other such niceties.

Tyler was a rather reluctant latecomer to the coalition that put Jackson in the White House in 1828; it was a choice of evils for that Virginian. Tyler was most definitely not among those Virginians, led by Thomas Ritchie, editor of the Richmond *Enquirer,* who forged an alliance with Martin Van Buren of New York, an alliance that did much to secure Jackson's victory. Tyler was, rather, friendly to the interest of Calhoun, Jackson's vice president, erstwhile nationalist; Calhoun had, in fact, suggested Tyler's name to Jackson as secretary of state. When Calhoun fell from the president's favor and Van Buren emerged as heir apparent, Tyler was in a faction of very restless Jacksonians in his state. The Hero of New Orleans was enormously popular among Virginia voters; he won staggering majorities in Virginia and in the other states of the middle and lower South in both 1828 and 1832—with the exception of South Carolina in 1832. Tyler could not quarrel with Jackson's vetoes of the bank and the Maysville Road. What the cryptic Calhounites needed was an issue that would arouse the voters, and Jackson obliged them with his Nullification Proclamation.

It is difficult to find a political leader in Virginia who openly espoused the doctrine of nullification, and not many more to justify fully South Carolina's use of it in late 1832. Certainly Tyler did not endorse the doctrine, although he thought South Carolina and the rest of the South to be much injured by the tariffs. But Jackson's proclamation was another matter. The president denied the right of peaceful secession, that sword in the attic for many a southerner, and his Force Bill threatened military coercion to enforce federal law in South Carolina. For a time it looked as if east Virginia would desert the president *en masse.* Tyler talked of the imminence of civil war and urged Vir-

ginians to stand fast in the defense of their principles. In his speech denouncing the Force Bill delivered in the Senate in February 1833, Tyler scoffed at the idea of an American "nation." Each individual state was a nation and, acting together, they had created a confederacy, the United States of America. A state convention had taken Virginia into the union, and a state convention called for that purpose could take her out. Southerners would defend themselves against such a "consolidated despotism" as Jackson threatened.

It was in the midst of this crisis that Tyler was reelected to the Senate. His first election, in 1827, had been made possible by the support of a solid base of the National Republican minority, plus those states' righters who thought the Ritchie faction's candidate, the irascible John Randolph, was a bit too much. In his second elections, Tyler's support came from National Republicans (Henry Clay himself urged a supporter in the Virginia legislature to cast his vote for Tyler) and the extreme states' righters. It was a coalition of opposites—they had little in common save opposition to President Jackson—but it was an alliance Tyler worked to maintain until it proved, in his presidency, impossible to hold together. Tyler later claimed that it was he who suggested the Compromise Tariff of 1833 to Clay, a law that lowered the tariff significantly over a period of nine years. Whoever suggested it, the crisis was resolved; whatever threat of civil war there might have been was defused.

Following the crisis, Ritchie and a large number of east Virginians returned to Jackson's Democratic Party. Another group, which might be loosely called the extreme states' righters, possibly rivaling in numbers the Jacksonians in east Virginia—at first—left the Democratic Party. Jackson once again obliged them with an issue, the issue through which southerners such as Tyler could cement a political union with National Republicanism, arguably the least logical alliance in the history of American parties.

It was in Tyler's second term in the Senate that President Jackson, in an effort to weaken the dying Second Bank, determined to make no further deposits of federal money in the institution. To Tyler and others of his faction, this was executive usurpation. In a long and vigorous speech in the Senate delivered in February 1834, Tyler denounced the president's action as a violation of the bank's charter; it was a "flagrant assumption of power" by the chief executive. Tyler joined Clay and Calhoun in passing senate resolutions of censure: the president had assumed an "authority and power not conferred by the Constitution and laws." So was born the Whig Party, with a common purpose of curbing executive usurpation.

In the meanwhile, in Richmond, a Whig majority in the legislature celebrated its success by instructing Virginia's two senators to vote for the censure, as if they needed such instruction. Unfortunately for Tyler and the Whigs, Democrats won control of the legislature in 1835, and that body instructed the Virginia senators to expunge the censure from the record. Much to the chagrin of many Whigs, and particularly distressing to the other Whig senator who kept his seat, Tyler resigned from the Senate rather than obey the instructions. His decision was in keeping with previously expressed opinions as to the right of instruction. It was a decision also in keeping with his theories of state sovereignty; by right of legislative instruction, it was almost as if senators were ambassadors from sovereign entities. However consistent he may have been, Tyler's resignation from the Senate in February 1836 was the worst political defeat he had suffered. He was a casualty of the two-party system that now embraced Virginia, the South, and indeed the nation at large. There was, however, consolation for the Virginian when, later in 1836, he was nominated for the vice presidency to run with Hugh Lawson White on a Southern Whig ticket.

White carried only two states, but Jackson's astonishing majorities in the middle and lower South in 1828 and 1832 shrank to a bare popular majority for Van Buren, Jackson's handpicked successor. Virginia and other states of the future Confederacy had for the first time given a majority of their popular and electoral votes to a northern candidate, but the region had also for the first time been almost evenly split in its political allegiance. Tyler had, in fact, run better than White. Maryland chose electors for the northern and western Whig candidate, William Henry Harrison, but those electors cast votes for John Tyler as vice president. South Carolina went its independent way, choosing electors for Willie P. Magnum as an expression of gratitude for support in its crisis, and the same electors voted for Tyler as vice president, for services he had rendered.

Even historians most inclined to give Tyler a sympathetic hearing have been known to fault him for not following Calhoun and other states' rights Whigs back to the Democratic Party in the late 1830s. On the other hand, *if* he had not been catapulted into the presidency in 1841, one can well imagine Tyler finding reasons to support Whig candidates so long as they supported him in return. He was elected as a Whig to the Virginia House in 1838, and that amorphous party chose their ex-senator as Speaker. Tyler spoke well of Clay—they were friends of long standing—and of Clay's distribution bill, then being debated in Congress. Clay himself contributed to Tyler's decision not to switch parties. In the 1830s, the Kentuckian was positioning himself to win Whigs of both North and South in his run for the presidency in 1840. Without repudiating any of his economic nationalism, he declared himself ready to postpone its chief measures: state activity lessened the demand for federal aid to transportation systems. The Compromise Tariff of 1833, his own work, had put that issue at rest for at least nine years; the voters were evidently not ready to support a bank recharter at that time. Not only that, Clay professed to see the greatest threat to the Union in the abolition movement.

It was hardly surprising that southern Whigs flocked to his support and Tyler was in the forefront. So great was Tyler's commitment to Clay that it was said that he wept when the Whigs rejected the Kentuckian in their nominating convention, passing him over in favor of their military hero, William Henry Harrison of Indiana. Under those circumstances, as it turned out, John Tyler was as "available" a vice-presidential candidate as there had ever been: he was both a prime supporter of the defeated candidate, and his nomination would be a gesture to the southern states' righters who had not deserted to the Democrats.

It was a measure of the hype and buncombe of the presidential election of 1840 that the Whigs, with great acumen, did not present a platform to the voters. It was all "Log Cabin and Hard Cider," "Tippecanoe and Tyler Too," while the issues that so often bedeviled the politicians were laid to rest for the duration. It had some of the stuff of modern politics, and indeed something of modern political organization was emerging, encouraging, and responding to the popular excitement. The number of Americans who went to the polls in 1840 represented a two-thirds increase over the number of voters in 1836; in the middle and lower South, the increase was a whopping 80 percent. With a presidential candidate known to the general public as a slaughterer of Indians, and for the alleged simplicity of his lifestyle, and with southerners such as Tyler not only still in the party but recognized on the ticket, the middle and lower South gave "Tip and Tyler" the largest popular and electoral majorities any Whig presidential candidate ever received.

Tyler's services as vice president, with the possible exception of Andrew Johnson, were the least eventful in a long succession of uneventful vice presidencies. After being sworn in, in the presence of the accustomed dignitaries assembled in the senate chamber, Tyler delivered a brief homily containing a reference to the senators assembled before him as "the immediate representatives of the States, by whose sovereign will the Government has been spoken into existence." The gathering adjourned shortly thereafter to accompany Harrison to the east portico of the Capitol, where he took his oath of office and delivered his lengthy inaugural address. As vice president, Tyler then chaired a session of the Senate that approved with unanimity President Harrison's choice of cabinet officers. The Virginian was now free to return to his home in Williamsburg; with the paucity of vice-presidential functions, he had every right to anticipate four years of relative independence, couched in obscurity. Within weeks, loud knocks on his door at 5:30 of a Monday morning introduced messengers from Washington informing Tyler that the president was dead. Geographical propinquity and the railroad made it possible that only a fifty-three-hour interval separated the death of one president and the accession of another.

If George Washington was called upon to set all manner of precedents in the conduct of the presidency, John Tyler was called upon by fate to blaze a path for subsequent vice presidents succeeding to the presidency. Fifty-two years had elapsed under the federal constitution with no death or other removal of a president. However, since Tyler's accidental accession in 1841, four assassinations, three deaths by natural causes (wild fancy has supposed that two of them were by assassinations), and one resignation have meant that at no time since 1841 has there been an interval of uninterrupted presidential administrations half so long as that first half-century.

Tyler's presidency is, of course, the period of his life most familiar to historians and to the general reader; naturally enough, these years have been most subjected to scholarly scrutiny. He managed to become "the President without a Party"; his tiny "Corporal's Guard" of loyal supporters in Congress constitute a sort of record for minimal allegiance. The generality of historians of the United States, it would be fair to say, have assigned to his role as president a ranking of below average at best. A few specialized studies of his presidency have reminded us that, despite Tyler's failure to generate a coalition to support his reelection in 1844, third party or otherwise, his vetoes, like Jackson's before him, sustained by Congress, helped set the course of American political life. Certainly, if Jackson's veto killed the Second

National Bank, Tyler's vetoes aborted the birth of a third. Likewise in diplomatic matters of foreign policy, where the chief executive has more freedom to initiate policy, very significant and positive achievements resulted, and, for weal or woe, Tyler himself and his administrators did much to initiate the process by which Texas was annexed during the closing days of his administration.

First of all, as indicated earlier, there was the question as to whether he were a mere acting president. After Harrison's death, the Harrison cabinet first addressed Tyler as vice president. Some in both parties considered him as caretaker, a regent, officially the Acting President, "His Accidency" in scorn. Some among modern historians have questioned the soundness of Tyler's argument, but Tyler insisted upon the title and full function as president, equal to any other president, and it was accorded to him and to his successors. In the words of one modern historian, it was "a constitutional coup."

As to the possibility of chartering a Third National Bank or some reasonable facsimile thereof, it is certainly possible the gridlock between president and Congress could be attributed to either or both of the parties to the conflict. Tyler has been said to have planned from the beginning of his administration to use the bank or anything else to gain renomination in 1844. Senator Clay, most assuredly embittered by Harrison's nomination in 1840, at first consoled himself with Harrison's pledge to serve but a single term. Clay was the unquestioned leader of the Whig majorities in Congress, and a majority of Harrison's cabinet were active in his interest. Harrison, in fact, had felt called upon to remind the Kentuckian that it was he, Harrison, who was president. The accession of Tyler meant the replacement of the oldest president before Ronald Reagan by the youngest in the first half-century under the Constitution. Something, at any rate, led the Kentuckian to conclude that his earlier talk of no popular demand for a bank was untrue as of 1841. There was no difficulty in persuading the Whig Congress to ratify Clay's decision.

Tyler most probably decided early on to veto this would-be Third Bank, although ten days elapsed between the time Tyler received the bill and the submission of his veto. Everything in Tyler's career justified his claim that his opposition to a national bank on constitutional grounds "has been uniformly proclaimed." Tyler's veto brought such jubilation among Democrats that the president here, and afterwards, entertained the forlorn hope that they might accept him as their leader; Democrats might contribute mightily to sustaining his vetoes and afterward rejoice at the defeat of the bank, but they had their own chieftains who would profit from the issue. From Whigs came a storm of protest, although many of their leaders were conciliatory, hoping to tailor a new bill to satisfy the president's constitutional scruples. In the Senate they had been able to muster only a one-vote majority to override Tyler's veto.

The second bank fight presents more ambiguities. The Whigs did construct a proposal—a Fiscal Corporation—more in keeping with the president's sensitivities; the president gave evidence of vacillating before making his final decision. The sincerity of Clay's overtures has been questioned, as has the degree of Tyler's approval on first being presented the outlines of the Fiscal Corporation. Of many accommodations in the new bill, perhaps the most striking example was the claim that this "Corporation was to be established by Congress in its duly recognized authority as the legislature of the District of Columbia." Just as state governments were chartering a great multitude of state banks, so might Congress establish a bank in the district. In Tyler's veto was the rejoinder that because Congress was creating a bank designed to do business in all of the states, it was acting in its capacity as a national legislature. However much he may have vacillated, the president did finally veto the Fiscal Corporation, and it was this veto that brought down the full fury of Whig vituperation upon Tyler, a venom scarcely matched in American political history. The Lexington *Kentucky Intelligencer* caught the savagery of it: "If a God-directed thunderbolt were to strike and annihilate the traitor, all would say that 'Heaven is just.'" Four days after the House received Tyler's veto, a caucus of fifty or so Whig members met and formally drummed the president out of their party.

To be sure, Tyler's "victory" was a negative one, and it cost him the party that had brought him to the presidency, but a National Bank similar to the first or second, or of either of the two Whig proposals, rather quickly left the center stage of American political debate. The Whig platform of 1844 made no mention of a national bank. It was not only that Tyler had aborted the birth of a Third National Bank, but the erosion of interest in such an institution suggests that, on this one issue, at least, Tyler spoke with the voice of the people. How much happier would he have been as a Democrat.

Tyler's six vetoes were two more than those of Andrew Jackson. Counting pocket vetoes, Jackson in his two terms had the advantage. Between the two of them, they submitted more than two-thirds of all presidential vetoes from the beginning of the Republic through Tyler's administration. Tyler was the first president to have a veto overridden—that of a naval appropriation bill—but on the larger issues, Democratic minorities plus the minuscule Corporal's Guard were numerous enough to sustain him.

Another significant issue on which Tyler used his veto to influence the course of political history was to intertwined issues of the tariffs and Clay's pet project of distribution. The two issues meshed nicely in Clay's arsenal of economic nationalism. By distributing to the states federal money derived from the sale of public lands, not only were many states happy to receive federal subsidies, but by giving money to the states the federal government could more readily justify higher tariffs to meet its expenses. Tyler had kind words to say of distribution in the late 1830s, but times were hard in the early 1840s. The federal government was spending more money than it was taking in, and President Tyler did abhor a national debt; frugality

was an essence of Old Republicanism. This arch antiprotectionist did agree that the tariff needed to be raised above levels set by the Compromise Tariff of 1833, but that was a tariff for revenue only. Tyler would not hear of raising the tariff while at the same time giving money to the states. Twice he vetoed Whig bills that combined distribution with and increase in the tariff. This did nothing to alleviate Whig hostility, especially as Democrats were able to sustain the vetoes. Tyler signed into law a tariff bill in 1842, one that raised duties above the Compromise Tariff level, and for that he was denounced by some Democrats, for whom any rise in the level of protection was anathema.

On one significant issue Tyler could agree with the Whig leadership in Congress, one that came up before Tyler was drummed out of the party. Harrison's predecessor in the White House, the Democrat Van Buren and his party, had ceased depositing money in state banks because political favoritism was too likely to affect the choice of state banks as repositories. Federal money was then put in what amounted to a government vault, the Subtreasury, the system itself being known as the Independent Treasury. Tyler, by contrast, and the Whig majorities preferred to keep federal money in state banks. It seeded their capital, thus making credit more available, and in general strengthened the state institutions. The Whig majorities readily produced a bill to repeal the Subtreasury, and Tyler signed it into law at almost the same moment he vetoed the first bank bill. Democratic dismay over the former was tempered by their jubilation over the latter, a mirror opposite of the Whig reaction. On neither the tariff nor the Subtreasury did Tyler's approval have any permanent effect: Democrats returned to power after Tyler's single term, and they lowered the tariff and reinstituted the Independent Treasury. Tariffs stayed low until southern secession, and the Independent Treasury survived the Civil War by some decades.

It was in the realm of foreign affairs that the achievements of the Tyler administration were positive—in the sense that they were not accomplished by the veto, and, in significant areas, in the sense that the achievements have rated general applause from the community of historians.

When Harrison's cabinet resigned after Tyler's bank vetoes, one stayed on: Secretary of State Daniel Webster. Webster was engaged in delicate negotiations with the British concerning a number of issues, the most dangerous of which was the disputed boundary between Maine and New Brunswick. War had been threatened in the disputed area in 1839, and there was fear of renewed violence at any time. Frederick Merk, in a volume cited below, has credited Tyler himself and other members of his administration with an innovative use of propaganda to persuade the residents of Maine to abandon an obstinate resistance to compromise and to accept the treaty settlement, which was, in effect, splitting the difference. The Webster-Ashburton Treaty of 1842 settled more than the Maine boundary, but the resolution of that dispute was its most signal accomplishment. President Tyler also dispatched Caleb Cushing of Massachusetts to China to negotiate a commercial treaty. The resulting Treat of Wanghia (1844) gained for the United States access to ports already opened to the British, most-favored-nation privileges, and rights of extraterritoriality. Cushing's treaty, as Webster's before it, won approval in the Senate.

Tyler's efforts to annex Texas were manifestly a part of his effort to win a presidential nomination in 1844, and that resulted in part from a desire to see the addition of new slave territory to the United States. He defended the expansion of slavery with the "diffusion" argument he had expounded in the Missouri Crisis two decades earlier. Unquestionably Tyler deserves much credit for bringing Texas annexation to the center stage of national politics. In so doing he helped break the sectional equilibrium that made possible the national two-party system of Whig versus Democrat, which in so many ways transcended sectional boundaries. As late as the votes in Congress on Texas annexation in early 1845, members of Congress voted

in great degrees as party members, not as southerners or northerners. It was the right to take slaves to federal territories versus the right to exclude slavery from the territories that brought the sections to the brink of disunion. Agitating the Texas question in the 1840s was a huge step in the process by which parties were ultimately sectionalized.

James Knox Polk, the Democratic nominee in 1844, temporarily nationalized the annexation issue by promising Oregon to the free states and Texas to the slave. Tyler also had interests in Oregon. Webster and Ashburton had wrestled with the border question. Tyler insisted on the forty-ninth parallel as the line of division between the United States and Canada, as did Polk in 1846, but the British were not ready to deal in 1842 as they were with the bellicose Polk in 1846. Tyler also favored the construction of U.S. forts to protect settlers on the way to Oregon, the U.S. portion of which was to be organized as free territory in 1846, but what Tyler might have wanted to do does not justify what he did: push for Texas annexation with no compensating territory for the free states.

The chief difficulty for Tyler and his lieutenants—and some of his nominal lieutenants acted as if they were the generals—was to win the support of enough northern senators to give the two-thirds majority necessary to ratify a treaty of annexation. Other than elaborations of the diffusion argument, the principal tactic was to play the British card. Once again the engines of propaganda rolled: without Texas annexation, the United States might awaken one fine day and find John Bull ensconced on its southwestern frontier. For southern audiences, the British threat had a more sinister element: John Bull was plotting to abolish slavery in Texas. Tyler himself refused to endorse the charge that Britain was plotting to emancipate the Texas slaves—refused, in fact, until British Foreign Secretary Lord Aberdeen declared in the House of Lords in August 1843 that Her Majesty's government hoped to persuade Mexico to recognize the independence of the Republic of

Texas in exchange for the abolition of slavery in the latter. The aging Democratic chieftain Andrew Jackson was enlisted in the cause of annexation; on the other hand, Tyler's appointment of Calhoun as secretary of state did nothing to win northern support for the project. Calhoun, far more than Tyler, pursued southern ends, with less concern for parties and sectional adjustment. For the secretary of state, if the South were united, the North would have to accommodate it—or else. With Tyler there was always the hope that Texas might be his guarantee of a presidential nomination in 1844.

With Calhoun managing the State Department, a treaty of annexation was agreed to by representatives of two republics, Texas and the United States, and submitted to the Senate in April 1844. It was a disaster for the annexationists: more than two-thirds of the senators voted *against* the treaty. It was a vote both partisan and sectional, but more partisan than sectional. Of twelve northern Democrats, five joined all the southern Democrats in favor; a Mississippian was the only Whig to vote for annexation. With the hindsight of so many votes during the Tyler administration, it was demonstrated with great clarity to which party the president should have adhered. In Tyler's mind, those same figures might have illustrated the possibilities of his political advancement, as well as the possibilities for Texas annexation.

Any hope that Texas might further the president's ambitions rested on the assumption that the major party nominees would continue the eight-year practice of excluding Texas annexation from partisan controversy, and as candidates began to jockey for position in early 1844, the exclusion of Texas seemed a strong likelihood. The strongest candidates for each party, Clay for the Whigs and Van Buren for the Democrats, gave every indication that Texas would not be an issue, and what an opportunity that would be for President Tyler! That enthusiastic unanimity among southern Democratic senators! That near-half of northern Democrats voting for a Tyler treaty! Perhaps even southern Whigs might be persuaded

to see their true sectional interest. With a solid southern base and a strong northern minority—James Buchanan's winning combination in 1856—the presidency itself was a possibility. But it was to be others who reaped where Tyler had sown.

The principal results of Tyler's Texas policy among southern Democrats, as it turned out, were, first, to rouse their enthusiasm for, and excite their hopes that, Texas might be had. It was not long before that translated itself into a determination not to support a Democratic candidate who would not declare himself for Texas annexation.

It is perhaps idle to speculate on what might have been—for Tyler *and* the nation—if the majority of delegates to the Democratic convention, a majority Van Buren possessed, had been sufficient to nominate. Then there would indeed have been a third-party, pro-Texas Tyler candidacy that might well have drawn large numbers of southern defectors from the Democratic candidate—large enough numbers to throw the election to Tyler's nemesis, Whig candidate Henry Clay, but enough defectors to pull the Democratic Party southward in the near future. But a majority of the delegates was not enough; Van Buren needed two-thirds, and that he could not get. The convention finally turned to Polk of Tennessee, whose broad-scale annexationism reduced a Tyler candidacy to irrelevancy. Tyler's friends had engineered a convention in Baltimore in late May 1844, timed to coincide with the Democratic convention. That meant that Tyler was informed of his nomination exactly one day before the exhausted Democrats turned unanimously to Polk. Even so, the Tyler candidacy worried the Democrats to the extent that considerable effort was expended to persuade Tyler to withdraw. Tyler did finally bow out, but not until August 20 was his decision made public.

With all the correct stands on major issues, Polk rolled up the largest Democratic majority of popular votes in the middle and lower South in the twenty years between Jackson and Franklin Pierce. His support elsewhere was thin enough to make him, by a gnat's eyelash, a plurality winner in the nation at large.

Through forces over which Tyler had little control but which received his eager support, Texas annexation was accomplished in the last days of his presidency. Winning a two-thirds majority for a treaty of annexation in the Whig-controlled Senate was an impossibility, so the measure was achieved through joint resolutions of the houses, requiring only a majority in each. It was a party triumph. Every Democratic senator, North and South, voted for annexation; their narrow victory in the face of a slim Whig majority was made possible by the support of annexation by three of fifteen southern Whigs. The Democratic-controlled House concurred by a heavily partisan vote. Those majorities were the sort of figures of which Tyler might once have dreamed. In the meantime, Tyler had made a belated return to the Democratic Party. He voted for Polk in 1844 and thereafter supported Democratic candidates for as long as he lived—which meant Southern Democrat John C. Breckinridge in 1860.

Some among modern historians of the South have given Tyler an eminence in history scarcely imagined by either his contemporaries or previous historians. A recent two-volume history of the South by William J. Cooper, Jr., and Thomas E. Terrill contains this startling assessment: "Usually dismissed as an unimportant president, John Tyler was in fact of enormous importance. Between 1815 and 1860 only Andrew Jackson and John C. Calhoun had more influence on southern politics, and a legitimate argument can be made that Tyler ranked with the other two." Tyler is granted this extraordinary ranking because he deliberately used the issue to stir southern passions on slavery: "Texas could cause such a thunderous reaction because it touched the raw nerve of southern politics." And again, "Texas obliterated economics. The Texas issue proved again that in the South nothing could withstand the force of a political issue closely connected with slavery and liberty." Thus can yesterday's image of a hapless and beleaguered president, with no claim to any major significant, be transformed, not into a great president, but one of the greatest significance in stirring up the worst in the southern psyche.

In an entirely different vein, several recent studies of Tyler's presidency, concerned more with conventional "successes" and "failures," have rather balanced the two concerning both Tyler and his administration. Norma Lois Peterson, in a volume listed below, wrote of Tyler's presidency that it "was flawed as, to a greater or lesser extent, all presidencies are, but it was not a failure. On numerous occasions he demonstrated exemplary executive skill and common sense." One wonders if Peterson and professors Cooper and Terrill are describing the same human being.

Tyler left the White House to take up permanent residence in his new home, called Sherwood Forest, located in his native county of Charles City. In the years of his involuntary political exile, he did have the leisure to enjoy his many children and his young second wife, to whom he had been married for less than a year when he retired from the presidency. Tyler was a genuinely good husband and a good father; there is much to suggest it and nothing to suggest otherwise. He had married his first wife, Letitia Christian, on his twenty-third birthday. She bore him several children who survived infancy, including two sons who would become officials of the Confederate government. She was admirably suited by nature and social custom to fulfill the role of hostess in the governor's mansion when her husband was its occupant. She suffered a stroke before Tyler entered the White House, was paralyzed, and died less than a year and a half after the beginning of Tyler's presidency. Within two years, President Tyler was married for the second time—to Julia Gardiner whose father had been killed by the same tragic *Princeton* explosion that had also killed two members of Tyler's cabinet.

Tyler was fifty-four and Julia twenty-four when they were married less than a year before leaving the White House. Despite the difference in their ages, they obviously cared much for each other; they richly deserved that cliché, "they had a happy marriage." Robert Seager, by an intelligent and resourceful use of correspondence and other sources, leaves us little room to doubt. In a recent doctoral dissertation, Julia is portrayed as an independent figure in her own right, especially in the years after her husband's death. Julia bore her husband seven children, the youngest born when the father was seventy. Julia's oldest son, David Gardiner, named for her father, served, like his father, in the House of Representatives and as a judge of a Virginia circuit court. Another of Julia's sons, Lyon G. Tyler, became a historian and was for many years president of the College of William and Mary. He edited and published a great number of family manuscripts, most of them relating to his father, and conducted during his lifetime a spirited defense of his father's career.

Ex-president Tyler was returned to public life during the secession crisis. At the age of seventy, Tyler was sent by his native state as a delegate to the Washington Peace Conference in January 1861 when the lower South was in the process of withdrawing from Union. Tyler had no great hopes for this last-gasp search for some form of compromise that might prevent secession and civil war. As the attendant ex-president, Tyler was made president of the conference. He and the Virginia delegation voted against the recommendation of the conference—they proposed the revival of that 36°30′ line—and he returned to Virginia ready for secession.

REFERENCES

Edward P. Crapol, *John Tyler: Accidental President* (Chapel Hill: University of North Carolina Press, 2006); Gary May, *John Tyler* (New York: Times Books/Henry Holt and Co., 2008); *The Letters and Times of John Tyler*, Lyon G. Tyler, ed., 3 vols. (1884–96: reprint, New York: DaCapo Press, 1970); Oliver P. Chitwood, *John Tyler, Champion of the Old South* (New York: Appleton-Century, 1939); Robert Seager II, *And Tyler Too: A Biography of John and Julia Gardiner Tyler* (New York: McGraw-Hill, 1963); Norma Lois Peterson, *The Presidencies of William Henry Harrison and John Tyler* (Lawrence, Kans.: University Press of Kansas, 1989); Frederick Merk, *Fruits of Propaganda in the Tyler Administration* (Cambridge, Mass.: Harvard University Press, 1971); Robert J. Morgan, *A Whig Embattled: The Presidency Under John Tyler* (Lincoln: University of Nebraska Press, 1954); Theodore Delaney, "Julia Gardiner Tyler" Ph.D. diss., College of William and Mary, 1995); Harold D. Moser, *John Tyler: A Bibliography* (Westport, Conn.: Greenwood Press, 2001).

M. BOYD COYNER, JR., a native of Lynchburg, Virginia, received his B.A., M.A., and Ph.D. degrees from the University of Virginia. He taught history at Southwestern at Memphis (now Rhodes College), Hampden-Sydney College, and the College of William and Mary. He taught many advanced undergraduate and graduate courses in various aspects of the Old South and slavery.

GEORGE MIFFLIN DALLAS (1792–1864)
Vice President, 1845–1849
(President James K. Polk)

GEORGE MIFFLIN DALLAS
(Library of Congress)

By John M. Belohlavek

George Mifflin Dallas, the scion of a powerful Philadelphia family, pursued Jeffersonian politics with a Federalist mindset. Born of patrician cultural tastes and political values, he would seem to have been more comfortable as a Whig rather than a Jacksonian. Yet, Dallas hoisted the banner of "Old Hickory" and became a force in Pennsylvania politics for over a generation as United States senator, minister to two countries, and vice president under James K. Polk. Controversy marked his tenure in the Polk administration, including a heated tariff debate, the question of slavery in the territories, and the explosive expansionism of the Mexican War. Although he played an outspoken and some-times courageous role as vice president, the coyly ambitious Dallas received neither the recognition he desired nor the party's nomination he awaited.

Dallas benefited greatly from the mentoring of his father, Alexander. The elder Dallas, a lawyer-politician, achieved social prominence and political stature that culminated in his appointment as secretary of the treasury under James Madison. Alexander named his second son, George Mifflin, born July 10, 1792, after Democratic-Republican friend and ally, Governor Thomas Mifflin. The Dallas family enjoyed an elegant lifestyle, with a mansion on Fourth Street and a country house ("Devon") on the Schuykill River. Young George received an appropriate education—Quaker preparatory schools and Princeton University, where he became valedictorian of the class of 1810. He began his legal studies soon thereafter, but they were fortuitously interrupted by the War of 1812.

Early in 1813, Albert Gallatin received an appointment to travel to Russia to seek the czar's mediation to end a conflict with Great Britain over international shipping rights. George Dallas prevailed upon the old family friend to take him along as his private secretary. The two-year sojourn in Russia, England, and the Netherlands matured Dallas and prepared him to take on new responsibilities at home. Upon his return in October 1814, he began a brief stint in Washington in a minor treasury post before moving on to private legal practice in Philadelphia with Charles J. Ingersoll. His marriage to Sophia Chew Nicklin, the daughter of a prominent businessman, in 1817 boosted the career of the aspiring young barrister. Happily united for almost fifty years, George was a devoted husband and father of eight children.

The vacuum in the Era of Good Feelings created by the death and retirement of a number of leading figures—including his father—allowed Dallas to move quickly into a position of leadership in the chaotic world of Keystone State politics. In 1817, Dallas played a pivotal role in forming a cadre of economic nationalists dubbed the "family party" because of their marital connections. These "New School" Republicans included Samuel Ingham, William Wilkins, Richard Bache, and Thomas Sergeant. They pro-

vided a leadership core from Philadelphia but relied heavily upon the Scotch-Irish vote of the West. The family party successfully elected two governors and then transferred its energies to the presidential campaign of John C. Calhoun in 1824. When this effort foundered badly, Dallas salvaged the situation by leading the family party in an eleventh-hour endorsement of frontier hero Andrew Jackson. Calhoun no doubt felt abandoned, but Dallas had changed direction at a propitious moment: in November Jackson overwhelmed all opponents in the Keystone state.

The election of 1824 indicated clearly that Dallas was not a prisoner of ideology. A member of the silk-stocking gentry and a spokesman for eastern Pennsylvania economic interests, Dallas had virtually nothing in common with the mechanics, small farmers, and coonskin-clad pioneers who comprised the bulk of the surging movement for Old Hickory. Personal relationships and private ambitions, not party principles, determined the Philadelphian's allegiances. On issues such as slavery, Dallas could fall back upon his genuine devotion to the permanence of the Union and the inviolability of the Constitution. With such matters as the national bank, protective tariffs, and internal improvements, however, he appeared hopelessly out of step with his Jacksonian compatriots.

During the next four years, Dallas and the family party battled the "Amalgamators," led by former Federalist James Buchanan, for control of the nascent Democratic Party. When Jackson soared to victory over John Quincy Adams in 1828, family-party favorite John C. Calhoun continued in the vice presidency. Such alliances boded well for Dallas—at least temporarily. Deserting his post as mayor of Philadelphia, Dallas accepted the position of district attorney for the eastern district of Pennsylvania and then was elected to the U.S. Senate in 1831. Meanwhile, Ingham received a cabinet slot as secretary of the treasury, and Dallas's brother-in-law, William Wilkins, was chosen by the legislature as the other U.S. senator. The family party had reached the zenith of its power and influence.

After almost a decade of dominating state politics, the family party then fell victim to greed, ambition, and internecine struggles. When Calhoun embraced nullification, Dallas could not distance himself quickly enough from the Carolinian. Although the Philadelphian hoped somehow to weather the political gales, the forces of Jackson, Calhoun, and National Republican aspirant Henry Clay formed a whirlwind that enveloped and blew away the once-powerful family party.

If Dallas envisioned reaching a new accord with President Jackson, the recharter of the Bank of the United States in 1832 doomed those prospects. The freshman senator had been chosen—against his will—to champion the Philadelphia-based institution in Congress. Dallas understood that the bank was being used as an issue in the upcoming presidential campaign, and his advocacy of the bill would be seen as a decidedly anti-Jackson move. As a promoter of the interests of his state, however, he felt he had no choice but to sponsor the bank. Although the recharter passed through both houses of a Democratically controlled Congress, Jackson registered his famous veto on July 10. Dallas's endorsement of the bank, combined with his support in the Senate for federally funded internal improvements and a protective tariff, marked him as a true Pennsylvanian—but such allegiances seemed too often incompatible with the program of the president. The disillusioned and discredited senator decided not to seek reelection and returned to private life in 1833.

Dallas's retirement was brief. Appointed attorney general for the commonwealth in October, he remained there for the next three years, battling for penal reform and opposing the anti-Masonic with hunt that enveloped the state. When New Yorker Martin Van Buren captured the White House in 1836 (and the votes of Pennsylvania as well), he sought to end Jacksonian factionalism. Accordingly, he offered the post of minister to Russia to Dallas in February 1837. The Philadelphian agreed to this self-exile, following his likewise errant relative, Wilkins, to St. Petersburg.

For the next two and-a-half years, Dallas struggled to survive at the Court of Nicholas I as underpaid diplomat representing a second-rate power. Because he was paid only $9,000 a year and had taken his family with him, poverty compounded his rapidly rising disaffection with the mission. Dallas bemoaned the constant round of parties and balls, which he found unexciting, and the society, which he found oppressive. Dallas did develop, however, a personal fondness for Czar Nicholas I, a man he respected, admired, and warmly compared to Peter the Great.

Tedious diplomatic disputes did little to relieve Dallas's boredom, although at times they threatened Russo-American tranquility. For example, American violations of Russian fishing and trade restrictions off the Alaskan coast resulted in a reaffirmation of czarist sovereignty but no change in the activities of Yankee sea captains.

Dallas realized, however, that he could accomplish little personally or professionally by remaining in St. Petersburg. He departed Russia in July 1839, following an undistinguished stint in which he did penance for his sins against the national party.

In the autumn of 1839, Dallas returned to Philadelphia to practice law. For the next four years, he held no elective or appointive public office but remained an active and eager—if not powerful—force in the national and state Democratic Party. Dallas supported energetically a variety of candidates for the 1844 presidential contest. He also commented on a number of issues, including the independent treasury, the national bank, and Texas annexation. His views of this last problem of widespread concern would be a primary factor in catapulting him into the vice presidency.

The Dallas faction of the Pennsylvania Democratic Party now constituted a narrow, isolated clique and was, outside the confines of Philadelphia, politically ineffectual. The blows the old family party had sustained at the hands of Jackson, combined with the successive exiles of Wilkins and Dallas to Russia, severely wounded the organization. For the next two decades Dallas attempted to recapture the political magic of the 1820s and failed because he burdened himself by a tendency to commit on too many pressing state and national issues. James Buchanan, ever evasive and thus increasingly acceptable to the electorate, emerged in sharp contrast; from his lofty perch as U.S. senator, he controlled the state party.

Despite Dallas's minority status in the state party, he retained influence in Washington. Van Buren offered him the attorney generalship in 1839, but the Philadelphian declined. (Van Buren, of course, failed in his reelection bid in 1840, losing Pennsylvania and the nation to William Henry Harrison.) When the ambitious Buchanan threw his hat in the ring in an ill-timed bid for the 1844 nomination, Dallas remained loyal to Van Buren. He hoped to parlay his support for the Little Magician's comeback into a resurgence of control of the state Democracy.

Unfortunately for Van Buren, Texas stood in his path. The Lone Star Republic, independent since 1836, desired to become a state. A sizable body of congressmen, mostly expansionist-minded southerners, but also many Yankees like Dallas—wanted immediate annexation. This group became increasingly skeptical about Van Buren's position on Texas and flirted with a variety of alternative candidates in the winter of 1843–44. When Van Buren opposed the Tyler–Calhoun annexation treaty in April 1844, the pro-Texas cadre began its search in earnest. Led by Senator Robert John Walker of Mississippi, the group first blocked Van Buren's candidacy in the May convention by passing a two-thirds rule for nomination. They then proceeded to weigh the merits of Senators Lewis Cass of Michigan, Richard Johnson of Kentucky, James Buchanan, and President John Tyler. Nine ballots produced a compromise choice on May 28 in Texas annexationist and former Speaker of the House James K. Polk.

In an effort to assuage the Van Buren forces, Walker placed loyal New Yorker Silas Wright in nomination as vice president. The selection carried easily on the first ballot, but an offended Wright would not be co-opted and refused a spot on the ticket. On May 30, the disappointed convention returned to its task with the goal of attempting to balance the team with the choice of a northeastern candidate. The Maine delegation offered Buchanan's name but withdrew it under his own instructions. Levi Woodbury of New Hampshire, Marcus Morton of Massachusetts, and Governor John Fairfield of Maine comprised a band of nominated New Englanders, while westerners pushed Lewis Cass and Richard Johnson. Fairfield emerged as the solid leader (106 votes) on the first ballot but fell short of a majority.

George M. Dallas lurked in the shadows. He had the support of some Pennsylvania delegates and had garnered thirteen votes. Walker, Dallas's nephew by marriage, immediately gained the floor and argued that his uncle's views were in accord with Polk's in opposition to the recharter of the national bank and in favor of Texas annexation. Additionally, Dallas had the respect of northern commercial interests and could influence a significant portion of Pennsylvania. The speech was magic. On the second ballot the delegates stampeded to Dallas, who won with a resounding 220–30 margin over Fairfield.

The selection of Dallas received widespread—though hardly uniform—support among Democrats. Many argued that he was more acceptable than Silas Wright, seemed solid on Texas, and insured Pennsylvania for the Jacksonians. Buchanan backers voiced predictably less enthusiasm. The Whigs, countering with the venerable Henry Clay of Kentucky and Theodore Frelinghuysen of New Jersey, seemed genuinely delighted over a seemingly lacklustre Democratic team. Philadelphia Whig aristocrat Sidney George Fisher offered a hyperbolic analysis of the ticket:

> Polk is a fourth rate partizan politician, of ordinary abilities, no eminence or reputation and chiefly distinguished for being a successful stump orator in Tennessee. . . . Mr. Dallas

is a gentleman by birth and education (but) . . . a reckless partizan totally devoid of principle and capable of upholding or relinquishing opinions whenever his own or his party's interests require it. His talents are very moderate, his acquirements scanty, he has an inferior position at the bar, and no one would give a dollar for his opinion. . . .

Dallas reacted to his nomination with amazement and some indifference. He realized that he was being used by his party, not having been chosen for his political record or his abilities, but because he happened to agree with Polk on the major national issue of the day—Texas—and because he came from Pennsylvania. Dallas also recognized the political feebleness of the vice presidency but would endure it for the good of the party and his country. He described his position to Polk as "a bobtail annexed to the great kite."

The campaign of 1844 focused upon both issues and personalities. While the party press of the nineteenth century commonly employed character assassination, Texas, the bank, and the tariff presented problems that had to be discussed or properly evaded Dallas, in trying to capture Pennsylvania for the Democrats, had to deal with all three. He had made his position on Texas clear long before the convention and, while annexation certainly became an issue in some quarters, it received considerably less attention in Pennsylvania. The bank and the tariff constituted different matters, however. Dallas's support for recharter in 1832 haunted him, but he blamed his position at that time on instructions from the legislature. The Democrats opposed the bank in the 1844 platform as unconstitutional and inexpedient. Dallas agreed, declaring: "The principles and policies of Andrew Jackson are of more value to the United States than the Bank in its purest form." Dallas spoke aggressively about the tariff, but had to convince many doubting Pennsylvanians about Polk's reliability on the issue. In July, Dallas wrangled a document from the reluctant Polk (the Kane letter) and then offered a middle position between tariffing for protection and revenue. Polk proffered a half loaf, but it satisfied many skeptical Democrats.

Dallas also feared the divisiveness of the immigrant issue and abolitionism on the party. He personally was a fellow traveler of nativists in his anti-Catholicism, and he viewed abolitionists as fanatics and threats to the Constitution. He recognized, however, that any opinions on these issues would damage the Democrats in both Pennsylvania and the nation. His concern was justified.

Polk and Dallas triumphed, albeit with a popular vote margin of just 37,000 out of 2.7 million ballots cast across the country. The decision in Pennsylvania was just as narrow; a 6,382 vote plurality out of a total of 328,000 votes. Even the 170–105 electoral majority was misleading: the switch of either New York or Pennsylvania from the Democratic to Whig column would have given the election to Clay. Dallas had apparently justified his place on the ticket.

The first two years of the Polk administration were significant for the nation and the political career of Vice President George M. Dallas. During this period, Dallas displayed unusual ambition and made conscious efforts toward reaching the White House. In his way stood the personage of James Buchanan and a host of dangerous issues. A wrong vote, for example, on the tariff would alienate a substantial portion of his Pennsylvania base. Ultimately, Dallas failed to win control of the state Democratic Party or to rally the support of the general populace to his side. The events of 1845–46 forever doomed Dallas's chances of attaining the presidency.

Although Polk was an unknown quantity to Dallas, the Philadelphian hoped to be a powerful influence in the new administration. Dallas told Robert J. Walker:

I have become Vice President willy-nilly, and anticipate the necessity of enduring heavy and painful and protracted sacrifices, as the consequence. Well!—I am not, in the bargain, disposed to be considered a cypher! Contrary, I am resolved that no one shall be taken from Pennsylvania in a cabinet office who is notoriously hostile to the Vice President. If such a choice be made, my relations with the administration are at once at an end.

Dallas's intentions received a prompt challenge in February 1845 with the appointment of Buchanan as secretary of state. The vice president deemed this "a most dangerous choice." Instead of sulking, however, or breaking the bond with Polk, Dallas redoubled his efforts. Polk selected Walker as his secretary of the treasury in March as a balm to the wounded Dallas men. Fearful of factionalism, the president warned his administration that he expected cooperation with his principles and policies and would promptly accept the resignation of anyone who demonstrated White House ambitions for 1848. While the choice of Buchanan was a transparent effort to balance the factions in Pennsylvania and placate both sides, it only served to heighten existing tensions and frictions. Unfortunately, too, Keystone factionalism represented the plight of the party throughout much of the nation.

After the inauguration on March 4, 1845, the battle for power began in earnest between Dallas and Buchanan. The struggle revealed itself most immediately in patronage contests: When Polk attempted to compromise or adopt a neutral course, he angered everyone. The embattled chief executive could do nothing right. Polk tried to mollify Dallas in August, writing that he would be gratified to confer with him on policy matters and benefit from his sage counsel. The president promised additional patronage but delivered little. By the end of the summer, Dallas had been defeated. His loss resulted from a combination of intertwined factors: he commanded a small faction with a narrow geographical base, he was not influential with the state administration in Harrisburg, his efforts to become a confidant of Polk had failed, and he was typically unaggressive in demanding patronage posts for his compatri-

ots. By October 1846, Polk confessed that he had given too many appointments to Buchanan and that severe damage resulted. The admission came too late; the wounds inflicted in the patronage wars in Pennsylvania never totally healed.

While Dallas's political future suffered a setback in 1845, he remained eager to fulfill his role as presiding officer of the Senate. An avowed expansionist on the Oregon issue, Dallas played a key role in selecting fellow extremists to the Foreign Relations Committee in the March session of Congress. The "All Oregon" men held their positions when the regular session met in December in spite of a rebellion by the Whigs and a handful of moderate Democrats. Nevertheless, an angry Dallas lamented:

Parties are in a wretched condition in both houses of Congress and are likely to get worse and worse. It can hardly be said that the administration has a majority in the Representative chamber. In the Senate on all measures beyond mere form, it is in a decided minority. The Triumverate of [Thomas H.] Benton, [John C.] Calhoun, and [Daniel] Webster—of men whose greatness has been achieved by hostility to each other—is too powerful to be resisted by [Lewis] Cass, [William] Allen and [John] Dix.

The party had been prostrated by factional patronage disputes and the Oregon issue; yet, Dallas served the administration well in the Senate, and the vice president had taken advantage of every opportunity to ingratiate himself with the president. When Buchanan and Polk fell out over a Supreme Court nomination in late 1845, Dallas's stock rose appreciably. The vice president told Richard Rush in December:

My relations with the President are just now of the kindest and most confidential nature. How long to continue so I cannot venture to guess as the foible of instability on some matters is, I fear radical.

Dallas realized, however, that his relationship with Polk was tenuous at best and might be sundered by the slightest incident. He never became a true confidant of the Tennesseean. Sometimes, Dallas believed the president sought his exclusive advice on important matters of state (he did not), while at other times Polk irritated him by "making mountains out of mole hills." Nevertheless, Dallas demonstrated unswerving loyalty to his chief and to the party.

Dallas was an important man in the plans of the Polk administration. Senators loyal to the president formed a minority and the deciding vote of the vice president in the Senate could be crucial on a number of issues. Therefore, in late 1846 and early 1847, Polk carefully cultivated Dallas and won his support but without deliberately placing him in a position of power or authority within the administration.

The tariff loomed in 1846 as an issue where the vice president's vote might be crucial. Polk considered the reduction of tariff duties as the most important domestic measure of his administration, but home industry—for example, Pennsylvania coal and iron interests—feared the collapse of all American production. In Harrisburg, panicky legislators urged national representatives and senators to oppose any tariff reduction. Meanwhile, Democratic committees and conventions throughout the state denounced this attempt to destroy the protective system. On April 14, James McKay reported the tariff bill out of committee to the House of Representatives. During the last two weeks of June, the committee of the whole intensely debated the measure. Pennsylvania congressmen spoke loudly against the bill, but to no avail. The House approved the revisions (114–95) on July 3. David Wilmot, the only Pennsylvania representative to vote for the reductions, represented a northern agricultural district. He viewed the Tariff of 1842 as oppressive to American industry. On July 6, the Senate received the bill and promptly began two weeks of debate. While Pennsylvania broadly opposed revision, the Baltimore convention

(at which Dallas had been nominated) and the Polk administration had pledged alteration. If Dallas remained loyal to his party and sacrificed his state's interests, he would be committing political suicide.

Fully aware of the situation in which he might be placed, the vice president thought out his position carefully. He believed that the convention's resolutions committed him to represent the whole of the American people as well as the executive branch of government. He would study the situation daily, and if he judged that the nation and the party would benefit from a lower tariff, then this state would have to suffer. Dallas worked mightily through mid-July in a futile effort to arrange a compromise and avoid personal disaster. He failed. The pressure mounted as Senator William Haywood of North Carolina resigned on July 25 rather than vote for the bill, as instructed by his legislature. Whig Senator Spencer Jarnagin of Tennessee refused to cast his ballot, leaving the chamber deadlocked in a 27–27 tie (twenty-seven Democrats in favor, twenty-four Whigs and three Democrats opposed). Dallas had prepared carefully for this dreaded moment. He told the senators that he had analyzed the vote and determined it was not on a sectional basis. The will of the House had expressed a desire to change the system as well. Certain provisions clearly offended him, but this tariff provided greater equality and justice than the Tariff of 1842. Because of the obvious sentiments of his native state, Dallas's decision was more difficult and painful. But as a representative of all the people, he was obliged to vote for the tariff. Before he could cast his ballot, however, Jarnagin changed his mind, and following the wishes of his Democratic legislature, voted for the measure. The Tariff of 1846—the so-called Walker Tariff—become law on July 30.

Dallas knew full well that his stand placed him in an unenviable position in Pennsylvania. Fearful of violence against his family, he told his wife Sophy to "pack up and bring the whole brood to Washington" if rioting commenced. The predictions of reaction were all too real. A crowd hanged Dallas in effigy from the telegraph wires of a main street in Philadelphia, and Whig newspapers branded Dallas "a scourge of mankind," "treacherous," and an "assassin." Democratic editors in Pennsylvania had difficulty defending the vice president, but those outside the state praised his self-sacrifice for placing the value of the nation over his local interests.

The tariff evinced strong political and economic feelings, however, in the commonwealth. Even though unbiased sources noted that the teal reduction on coal and iron was 25 percent (from 40 percent to 30 percent duty rate—maintaining a strong protectionist level), anger flowed unabated. Dallas had taken an active part in convincing Pennsylvanians that "Polk, Dallas, and the Tariff of '42" would provide a safeguard for their industries. Since he knew that the Baltimore convention had promised reductions, Dallas engaged knowingly in deceiving his state during the campaign. Democrats trumpeted tariff reform in the South and West and played it down in the North. The vice president had been instrumental in this campaign, which was at best equivocal and at worst fraudulent.

Dallas realized that Pennsylvania industry would not be destroyed by his tariff vote. Yet, he engaged in a political trade-off: the sacrifice of support in his native state for that of southern and western Democrats. Dallas believed in the Union and the Democratic Party and could vote in good conscience for a measure he deemed to be for the betterment of both. The vice president would rely on his stand on the tariff as well as views on foreign affairs to carry him to the White House in 1848. However, just as his tariff vote ruined him in Pennsylvania, so did his extreme views on Oregon and the Mexican War blunt his campaign efforts in the rest of the nation. He clung to a precarious position in 1846.

As an expansionist and exponent of American Manifest Destiny, Dallas espoused an aggressive foreign policy. He viewed the Monroe Doctrine with favor and the Western Hemisphere as a U.S. preserve. Great Britain posed a particular obstacle to United States goals, especially in Oregon, Texas, and Cuba, Perennially anxious about the "pearl of the Antilles," he feared that Britain would pluck Cuba before the "pear would ripen and fall into our lap." The vice president judged that $100 million was not too great a price to pay Spain for the island.

Oregon had been an Anglo–American problem since the 1790s. Although other European powers had been squeezed out and Britain and the United States now jointly occupied the territory, the two nations could not agree on a boundary. In 1845, British Minister Richard Packenham rejected an American offer to set the boundary between Oregon and Canada at 49° north latitude, which had given the United States control of the vital Columbia River. The threat of war with Great Britain loomed large, and Dallas did not recoil from it. His fears rested less with the damage that the British navy would likely inflict on the eastern seaboard and more to the danger caused by a division of effort if the United States engaged Mexico simultaneously at the Rio Grande. Nonetheless, for Dallas, settlement at 49° would be a national disgrace. An even worse fate—disunion—would befall the country, however, if the administration sacrificed the Columbia River.

By April 1846, a less-jingoistic Dallas counseled diplomacy. Although his private position had not changed on the justice of claiming the boundary as far north as 54°40', he recognized that negotiation must be allowed to take its course before more extreme measures could be adopted. Dallas believed that Prime Minister Robert Peel's experiment with free trade would force an English compromise. He was correct. London offered to settle the boundary at 49° and Polk accepted. Although Oregon "ultras" screamed foul, the Senate approved the agreement on June 15. A realistic Dallas concurred with the treaty—war with Mexico had been declared on May 13. Throughout the Oregon crisis of 1845–46, Dallas shared his views with the president, but there is no evidence that he affected policy in any meaningful way.

The caution that Dallas displayed toward Britain evaporated in regard to Mexico. He respected and feared English power but viewed the Mexicans with racist contempt and disdain. He envisioned a war with Mexico as an opportunity to gain territory, as well as to unify the nation and the Democratic Party. Just as his early extreme views on Oregon had endeared him to westerners, he combined his advocacy of the annexation of California and New Mexico with the demand for the cession of a strip of land across the Isthmus of Tehuantepec for a U.S. canal or railroad. By February 1848, the vice president had moved to the land-hungry position of the "All Mexico movement" and conceded that the United States "might be assigned to it by the resistless force of events—guardianship of a crowded and confederated continent."

Once again, Dallas's extremism collided with Polk's realism. In February 1848, the president accepted a treaty negotiated by diplomat Nicholas Trist that gave the United States *only* California and the Southwest. Dallas lamented the signing but continued to hope for further territorial concessions, noting in 1855, "the door of peaceful annexation ought never to be shut."

Dallas's presidential hopes expired with the demise of radical expansionism. The vice president, however, challenged his more powerful rivals—especially Cass and Buchanan—for the nomination. Dallas clubs, formed as early as 1845, held a series of dinners and rallies for the vice president. Five thousand people appeared at a fete on December 1, 1847, at the Chinese Museum in Philadelphia. The campaign established the *Daily Keystone* to promote the candidate properly.

Dallas also found an issue—slavery in the territories—to assist in defining his philosophy of government. The debate over the ill-fated Wilmot Proviso of 1846, which demanded no slavery in the territories gained from the Mexican War, ripped the Democratic Party asunder. On September 18, 1847, in Pittsburgh, Dallas promulgated the doctrine of *popular sovereignty*—an ambiguous posture that allowed each territory to decide its own fate on slavery at some undetermined time in the future. While the vice president intended his sentiments to appeal to radicals on both sides of the issue, the concept received a weak response in the press.

In March 1848, the Buchanan forces captured the majority of the delegates at the Pennsylvania state convention. With the May national gathering in Baltimore only weeks away, Dallas's candidacy seemed at an end. His own state had committed for "Old Buck." The Northeast seemed alienated by his opposition to the protective tariff, his stand against the Wilmot Proviso, and his alignment with the South. The West was not opposed to him, but it backed sectional favorite Lewis Cass of Michigan, and the South factionalized over a number of candidates.

Dallas's only hope was a repeat of 1844: a failure of the front-runners to achieve the two-thirds necessary for nomination. The possibility evaporated as Cass, who had embraced Dallas's popular sovereignty position in January, moved to an easy fourth-ballot victory. November, however, brought despair for the Democrats as Cass lost both Pennsylvania and the national election to Mexican War hero Zachary Taylor.

Dallas, more disappointed over the fate of the party than his personal failures, now turned his attentions to Congress, the Wilmot Proviso, and his future in the Democratic Party. As a lame duck, the vice president could now be more outspoken and corrosive in his comments on events and personalities. Dallas feared the passage of the Wilmot Proviso, a measure he was convinced the great but misguided Calhoun would use to promote disunion. A firm believer in the sanctity of the nation, Dallas balanced his concerns about the proviso with a naive optimism that president-elect "Old Rough and Ready" had the tools to hold the country together. This view quickly disappeared in March 1849 after Dallas met with the general.

Meanwhile, relations between the vice president and Polk virtually collapsed. Tardy presidential dinner invitations angered the sensitive Philadelphian, and when Polk invited Dallas to visit Nashville in the fall, he refused. "Bah!" he commented pointedly in a letter to his wife. Dallas took simple pleasure in presidential embarrassment. He appeared almost gleeful when the first attempted use of gaslights in the White House in January 1849 resulted in powerful odors and a mass exodus to the front lawn. Dallas also confided to his diary the devious similarities in character between Polk and English King Charles I, who was deposed and executed in the seventeenth century. Unless he had an eleventh-hour rehabilitation, it is unlikely that Dallas shed, any tears over Polk's untimely death in June 1849.

The experiences and disappointments of the campaign and the election of 1848 removed the excitement and enjoyment from many of Dallas's official duties. He now wanted to escape Washington for the pleasures of family and career in Philadelphia. Sophy disliked the capital and chose not to stay there, although she visited often. Consequently, Dallas lived a rather Spartan life in Washington, first residing with Lewis Cass and then taking rooms on Capitol Hill. He dined out frequently with Secretary Robert John Walker. In an effort to support his family comfortably, he continued his law practice, taking on sometimes controversial cases (such as high-profile divorces) for lucrative fees. Although his name was already bantered about for the 1852 nomination, a bitter Dallas embraced the idea of retirement. He autobiographically confided to his diary: "Truth, courage, candour, wisdom, firmness, honor, and religion. Many by accident now and then [may] be serviceable, but a steady perseverance in them leads invariably to private life."

Between 1849 and 1856 George Dallas experienced the private life that he clearly viewed as a mixed blessing. He rebuilt his law practice with such profitable business cases as railroad mergers and argued before both state and national courts. Never far from politics, however, the Philadelphian offered his views oh the leading issues of the day. The Compromise of 1850, for example, angered Dallas because it allowed Congress to legislate on slavery in the territories. This topic, he determined, presented a Pandora's box of problems. Once opened, the lid could never be closed on the antislavery forces. For Dallas, constitutional guarantees protected the institution, and legislative directives would lead to disunion. An amendment should be passed that would guarantee the rights of the stages to slavery and thus forever end the divisive debates.

Undoubtedly, Dallas's position in defense of southern rights, the Fugitive Slave Law of 1850, and the purchase of Cuba are what marked him as a "Doughface Democrat"—a Yankee sympathetic to the cause of the South. In 1852, the nation elected a man of exactly such principles in Franklin Pierce of New Hampshire. As a loyal Democrat, Dallas campaigned for Pierce, but he grew disillusioned as the administration blundered badly in both foreign and domestic affairs. That much-abused president sought to eliminate potential rivals for the 1856 nomination, and Dallas marginally fell into this camp. Consequently, in January 1856, Pierce named Dallas minister to Great Britain to replace the retiring James Buchanan.

Dallas accepted the British mission, abandoning all fleeting hope of becoming president, but commencing the most active and exciting segment of his long public career. Dallas arrived with his family in London in mid-March 1856 to face several festering Anglo-American problems. Prime Minister Palmerston and Foreign Secretary Clarendon demanded redress for the so-called Crampton Affair.

In December 1855, Washington had asked for the recall of British Minister John Crampton for recruiting Americans for the British army in the Crimea. When Clarendon refused to do so, Crampton and several English consuls were dismissed in May 1856.

Much to Dallas's amazement, Palmerston and Parliament acted with restraint. Crampton would be sacrificed in the interests of promoting the resolution of a larger issue—Anglo–American accord in Central America. Both nations had been competing for influence in the area since the 1820s. Economic and military power had given the British the edge; they held British Honduras, the Bay Islands off the coast of Honduras, and the Mosquito Coast of Nicaragua. An American bid for canal or railroad transit increased, however, in 1855 when adventurer William Walker gained control of Nicaragua. The Clayton-Bulwer Treaty of 1850 had promised that neither Britain nor the United States would further colonize Central America, but members of Congress remained angry over tile strong preexisting English presence.

Dallas attempted to negotiate the British out of Central America, and he partially succeeded. The Dallas-Clarendon Convention of October 1856 ended British ownership of the Bay Islands and protection of the Mosquito Coast and provided restrictions on the borders of British Honduras. Unfortunately, southern senators reacted strongly to a provision that prohibited slavery in the Bay Islands. Senate amendments that dealt with slavery and other issues doomed the convention. Clarendon refused to compromise on such points and allowed the treaty to die a quiet death in April 1857.

A frustrated Dallas continued his ministry, however, under newly inaugurated President James Buchanan. With an old enemy now in the White House and his ineffectual former roommate Lewis Cass as secretary of state, Dallas had little influence on policy. Nonetheless, he performed well in a crisis. Most notably, Dallas helped resolve to U.S. satisfaction a nettlesome point of law that allowed the English to visit and search United States vessels on the high seas—often slavers flying the U.S. flag.

In 1860, a disconsolate Dallas observed from afar as "Black Republican" Abraham Lincoln triumphed in November and South Carolina seceded in December. With relief, Dallas turned over the legation to Charles Francis Adams in May 1861 and sailed for Philadelphia. Although now withdrawn from public life, he staunchly defended the republic and leveled blistering attacks on secessionist agitators. The next three years would be spent practicing law

and holding a sinecure appointment as president of the Atlantic and Great Western Railroad. He quietly cast his ballot for George B. McClellan for president in 1864. Until his death of a heart attack on December 31, George M. Dallas remained loyal—as he always had been—to the Democratic Party, the Union, and the Constitution.

REFERENCES

John M. Belohlavek, *George Mifflin Dallas: Jacksonian Patrician* (University Park, Pa.: Penn State University Press, 1977); Bruce Ambacher, "George M. Dallas and the Family Party" (Ph.D. diss., Temple University, 1970); Philip S. Klein, *Pennsylvania Politics, 1817–1832: A Game Without Rules* (Philadelphia: Historical Society of Pennsylvania, 1940); Charles M. Snyder, *The Jacksonian Heritage: Pennsylvania Politics, 1833–1848* (Harrisburg: Pennsylvania Historical and Museum Commission, 1958); John F. Coleman, *The Disruption of the Pennsylvania Democracy, 1848–1860* (Harrisburg: Pennsylvania Historical and Museum Commission, 1975); Philip S. Klein, *President James Buchanan* (University Park, Pa.: Penn State University Press, 1962); Paul Bergeron, *The Presidency of James K. Polk* (Lawrence: University of Kansas Press, 1987); Charles Sellers, *James K. Polk: Continentalist, 1843–1846* (Princeton, N.J.: Princeton University Press, 1966); Norman Saul, *Distant Friends: The United States and Russia, 1763–1867* (Lawrence: University of Kansas Press, 1991); Mary Williams, *Anglo-American Isthmian Diplomacy, 1815–1915* (New York: Russell and Russell, 1914).

JOHN M. BELOHLAVEK is a professor of history at the University of South Florida. He is the author of a number of works on Jacksonian diplomacy, including *George Mifflin Dallas: Jacksonian Patrician* and *"Let the Eagle Soar!": The Foreign Policy of Andrew Jackson*. His biography of nineteenth-century politician and diplomat Caleb Cushing, *Broken Glass: Caleb Cushing and the Shattering of the Union*, was published in 2005.

MILLARD FILLMORE (1800–1874)
Vice President, 1849–1850
(President Zachary Taylor)

MILLARD FILLMORE
(Library of Congress)

By Dieter C. Ullrich

Millard Fillmore has become somewhat of an enigma in the history of American politics. Prolific critics and political enemies of his generation labeled him as an ineffective, self-serving politician who lacked insight and political finesse. Modern historians, on the other hand, have characterized Fillmore as an energetic and modest individual whose perseverance and self-sacrifice lifted him into the forefront of antebellum politics. In recent years, with the added discovery of unpublished personal correspondence, Fillmore's role has been reevaluated and his impact on American history more fully recognized.

The vice presidency of Millard Fillmore lasted a mere fifteen months, but his brief term was both eventful and controversial. Two major, related issues troubled Fillmore as vice president and during his later role as successor to

President Zachary Taylor: the chronic controversy over slavery and the territorial expansion in the American West. The dilemma over slavery had plagued the United States since the Constitutional Convention of 1787, but the new territories acquired following the war with Mexico threatened the equilibrium of antislave and proslave representation in the Senate. Fillmore's role as vice president was decisive, particularly in the debates that devised the Compromise of 1850. President Zachary Taylor's untimely death on July 9, 1850, ended Fillmore's brief reign as vice president and placed him in the seat of chief executive. He became the second vice president to attain America's highest office due to a presiding president's death.

Millard Fillmore was born in a wilderness cabin on January 7, 1800, in the township of Locke (now Summerhill), Cayuga County, in the Finger Lakes region of New York State. He was the first son born to Nathaniel and Phoebe Fillmore and was given his mother's maiden name of Millard. His parents were originally from Bennington, Vermont, and were among many of the recent migrants to settle in central New York. Millard's father and his uncle Calvin purchased the land, sight unseen, in 1799 and moved there soon afterward. Their expectations of finding fertile lands for farming proved to be unfulfilled. What awaited the Fillmore family were clay fields, poor crops, and bitter weather. Eventually, poverty and a defective land tide caused the family to relocate to a tenant farm in Sempronius (now Niles), New York.

Millard spent most of his youth working on his father's farm in Sempronius. As a boy, he experienced the hard and tedious labors of a frontier farmer. By the time he was a teenager, he had matured enough to manage his father's farm effectively. Millard's father had higher expectations for and him, and he encouraged his son to pursue a more profitable trade than farming. Lacking the funds to educate Millard in a learned profession, his father decided to apprentice him to a cloth dresser in 1814. After four months, Millard returned home disheartened and confused. His father

encouraged him to try again and apprenticed Millard the following year to a cloth dresser and wool carder in nearby New Hope, New York. During his apprenticeship Millard recognized his limited education. Unable to read or write well, he found his ignorance to be a great handicap. At age seventeen, Millard bought membership in a circulating library in New Hope, purchased a dictionary, and diligently studied while working the carding machine at the mill. In 1818, when times at the mill were slow, he enrolled in an academy in New Hope, where he continued to enhance his education while he apprenticed.

The next year brought many surprises and changes for Millard. While attending the academy in New Hope he met a young lady named Abigail Powers, the daughter of a minister, Reverend Lemuel Powers, and the younger sister of a local judge. Millard began to court Abigail by winter 1819, but, recognizing that he was not of the proper stature to marry, he chose to wait before asking for her hand. During that period, Millard's father sold his tenancy in Locke and relocated to Montville, New York, where he became a tenant to a distinguished county judge, Walter Wood. Seeing an opportunity to advance his son's career, Nathaniel persuaded the judge to try Millard for a couple of months as a clerk in his law office. Millard was overjoyed by the opportunity and worked hard during those two months. After his trial period ended, the judge offered him advice and assistance: He told Millard to study law and offered to employ him as a clerk while he did so. Millard found the opportunity irresistible and so began his career in the field of law.

In 1820, after a disagreement with the judge, Fillmore moved to his father's new farm in Aurora, New York, with hopes of revitalizing his plans to become an attorney. In nearby Buffalo, he continued working as a law clerk and taught school on a seasonal basis. Teaching paid his expenses and clerking allowed him to acquaint himself with prominent attorneys in the region. Although he had not completed the several years of course study usually required, he was admitted to the Erie County bar in 1823. His cultivation of key members of the bar and his upstanding image in the Buffalo community hurried along his admittance. He was offered a position at one of the more prestigious firms where he had studied and clerked, but he chose instead to open a small law office in East Aurora.

Fillmore's law office became successful in a few short years, as his practice rapidly grew with western New York's agricultural and industrial development. His early professional labors focused on local land titles, mortgages, and debt collections in the East Aurora and Buffalo region. By late 1825, he was confident about his future and decided that it was now the proper time to marry the woman he had courted for more than five years. On February 5, 1826, in Moravia, Abigail Powers and Millard Fillmore were joined in matrimony.

Fillmore became actively involved in local and state politics soon after his marriage. Prior to 1826, Fillmore had been affiliated with the National Republicans, though he was never motivated to participate in the leadership of the party, but his desire to seek political reform in New York State drew him into the Anti-Masonic movement of the late 1820s and early 1830s. After the mysterious abduction and disappearance of William Morgan, a Mason known to be publishing a book criticizing the order, Fillmore joined the reform movement. He was further influenced by the writings of Thurlow Weed, who was then the editor of an Anti-Masonic paper in Rochester and the chief promoter of the Anti-Masonic movement.

In spring 1828, he served as an Anti-Masonic delegate during the Erie County National Republican convention and supported John Quincy Adams for the presidency. As the months progressed toward the elections, Fillmore became more and more entwined in both the Anti-Masonic movement's political leadership and Weed's plans for a third political party. When the Anti-Masonic Party materialized, the leaders of the new party declared Fillmore a candidate for the state assembly in September.

He had his doubts about his success as a candidate: He was considered an underdog to the Democrat contenders, who were riding on the popularity of the Andrew Jackson–Martin Van Buren presidential ticket. On election day, Fillmore was surprised to find that he had won, receiving more votes in Erie County than any other candidate. His election to the state assembly was the beginning of his long career in politics.

Fillmore's first term as a state assemblyman was unimpressive as he lacked confidence and experience for the position. In his succeeding terms, however, he began to show more conviction and a growing desire to engage in political discussions and debates. Between 1830 and 1831, he supported the building of branch canals to extend the Erie Canal's waterways, fought against statewide banking monopolies, and made efforts to secure the abolition of imprisonment for debt in New York State. He also began to make significant strides toward organizing the Anti-Masonic Party's leadership within the state. In a short amount of time, Fillmore had become a major force in the New York political arena.

He and Abigail moved to the village of Buffalo in 1830, where Fillmore accepted a partnership in Joseph Cleary's prestigious law firm. Though their partnership would dissolve within a few years, Fillmore gained a sure foothold for his legal practice. To become better community members and to increase his popularity, he and Abigail joined various village social and religious groups. The most significant group in which he and his wife became active was the new Unitarian Church, where they would be lifelong members and faithful supporters. Fillmore was now more socially active, attending formal dinners, dances, and other events. His integrity and growing popularity marked him as a likely candidate for the United States Congress.

Withholding his name from nomination for a fourth term in the state legislature, he decided to run as his district's Anti-Masonic Party candidate for the United States House of Representatives. His allegiance to the Anti-Masonic movement faded during the campaign as Fillmore foresaw the party's eventual demise. Nonetheless, he was elected to the Twenty-third Congress in 1832, receiving a solid majority of his district's vote. He arrived in Washington in 1833, supporting the concept of forming a new political party that would unite the fractured National Republicans and Anti-Masons.

In his first congressional year, Fillmore acquainted himself with the federal structure of government and the key politicians in both the House and the Senate. His activities on the House floor were minimal as he focused his concerns on the birth of a new party. Fillmore had supported his Anti-Masonic colleagues on major issues brought before the Congress but was tactfully disengaging himself from the party. By his second year in office, he decided not to resolve the vast differences between the National Republicans and Anti-Masons but to cross party lines, so in August 1834, he withdrew his name from the Anti-Masonic ticket and threw in his lot with the upstart Whig Party. The Whigs offered him the nomination to run for his current congressional seat, but Fillmore declined. Recognizing that the Anti-Masonic Party still controlled his congressional district, he decided to retire temporarily from politics and wait for a more opportune moment.

The opportunity to reclaim his congressional seat came in fall 1836, when Fillmore was offered and accepted the Whig nomination. He was highly optimistic about his chances for victory, and after a well-prepared campaign he regained his old House seat. The Whig Party, however, did not fare as well as Fillmore. The party's popularity continued to increase in 1835 and early 1836, but after a series of setbacks and internal disputes the Whigs popularity began to wane. The Whigs lost the presidential election of 1836 and suffered their worst defeat in New York State in sixteen years. Being one of the few Whig stars in New York, Fillmore was thrust into the forefront of his adopted party.

Fillmore served three consecutive terms in the House of Representatives between 1836 and 1842. While in Congress he quickly acquired recognition as an influential leader within the Whig Party and gained his colleagues' respect. Fillmore became a key player in the National Bank's demise and in the protectionist movement that designed the Whig tariff of 1842. When the Whig Party won control of the House of Representatives in 1840, Fillmore ran second in votes behind Henry Clay to receive the coveted Speakership. As was House custom, the runner-up was offered the powerful Ways and Means Committee chairmanship. Fillmore gladly accepted the appointment and effectively governed the committee from 1840 to 1842. In July 1842, he declined his district's renomination as representative and publicly announced that he would retire to "family and fireside."

In reality, Fillmore stepped down to seek other opportunities that would further enhance his political career, much as he had done in 1835. While still in the House of Representatives, he had had thoughts of seeking a U.S. Senate seat, but the two incumbent New York senators were well entrenched in their positions. A year after his departure from Congress, he was called upon by the Whigs to consider a nomination as Henry Clay's running mate for the presidency. In the spring of 1844, Fillmore met with other prominent Whigs in New York and agreed to take part in the Whig convention to be held in Baltimore. Just prior to the convention, the leading Whig candidate for governor of New York, Willis Hall, fell ill and became physically unable to run an effective campaign. The Whig Party's elite, particularly Thurlow Weed, realized that the party's best hope lay with Millard Fillmore for governor. Weed asked him to ran for the governorship, but Fillmore declined the offer and continued to press for the vice presidential nomination. Weed and other members of the party elite withdrew their support, and Fillmore lost the nomination to Theodore Frelinghuysen on the third ballot.

Distraught over the loss, Fillmore returned to Buffalo and quietly withdrew from the presidential campaign of 1844. He continued to support the Whig ticket of Clay-Frelinghuysen, but his pride was deeply hurt by the loss of the nomination. Meanwhile, Weed and his supporters continued to encourage Fillmore to run for the New York governorship. Fillmore resisted the offer for a while longer, but after prolonged encouragement he reluctantly agreed to run for office. His spirits began to rise as he launched a gubernatorial campaign that concentrated on the growing abolitionist and nativist movements in western New York. His campaign focused on uniting the antislavery and antiforeigner vote within the Whig Party. The immigrant and Catholic vote in New York's urban areas led to his slim defeat to Silas Wright. By the end of 1844, he had lost two major campaigns and was bitterly disappointed in the Whigs' inability to embody nativist and abolitionist interests within the party's platform.

For the next three years, Fillmore withdrew from the political scene and concentrated on the home life he had promised himself in 1842. His retirement from politics, however, was at most partial; he continued to be involved in the Whig Party's reunification and restructuring in the mid-1840s. In 1846, he was appointed to the chancellorship of the University of Buffalo, a college he helped to found earlier in the same year. During the Mexican War, Fillmore publicly spoke out against the conflict as a southern conspiracy to encourage the spread of slavery. He also became more outspoken on the controversial issue of immigrants and Catholics infiltrating the American political system. Fillmore patiently waited in the wings for a challenge that would stimulate his aspirations to reenter politics.

That challenge came by fall 1847 when he was approached by friends in the Whig Party to run for state comptroller. Without much hesitation, he decided to forsake retirement and campaigned for the office. On election day Fillmore won with astonishing numbers, beating his opponent by the largest plurality ever recorded by a Whig candidate against a Democrat.

Fillmore took office as comptroller on January 1, 1848. His term was productive but short lived. In a little more than a year, he developed successful programs that fostered internal improvement projects, revised state banking methods, and devised a currency program that would later be adopted in the National Banking Act of 1863. With renewed confidence in himself and in the Whig Party, Fillmore sought to reassert his efforts to claim the coveted vice presidency.

By early 1848, he had patched up old quarrels with the still influential Thurlow Weed and had become an active participant in the Whig presidential nomination process. The Whig national convention in Philadelphia began with serious divisions between northern abolitionists, southern slaveholders, and western expansionists. The party's leading contenders for the presidential nomination were the aging Henry Clay and Mexican War hero Zachary Taylor. Northern abolitionists promoted Clay's nomination; southern and western segments preferred Taylor, who was a slaveholder from Louisiana. To appease the abolitionists and prevent a fatal breach in the party, an antislavery candidate for the vice presidency had to be selected. Southern and western contingencies favored the nomination of Abbot Lawrence, who was a Massachusetts cotton manufacturer. Clay opposed Lawrence's nomination by declaring that the Whig Party would not "have cotton on both ends of the ticket." The convention was in a deadlock when John A. Collier, the New York delegation's most prominent member, put Fillmore's name in contention. The peace offering worked, and on June 9, Fillmore was nominated on the second ballot. He had finally attained the nomination he was denied four years earlier.

The ensuing presidential election, like most in the years preceding the Civil War, focused on slavery and the new territories. The presidential campaign was intensely fought and was at times dirty. The Democrats openly attacked Fillmore in the southern states as being a hard-line abolitionist, though his stance regarding antislavery was at most middle ground. Fillmore agreed that slavery was an evil but that the slave states had the "constitutional right to enjoy it." Throughout the campaign, Fillmore wisely refused to address the controversial issues of slavery and nativism, fearing it might hinder the Whig Party at the polls. His passive and impartial approach during the campaign succeeded as the Whigs claimed a narrow victory on November 7, 1848.

Fillmore resigned as New York State comptroller on January 1 but continued to perform his official duties until February 20. As inauguration day grew near, the many perplexities over the western territories became more profound and complex. Gold had been discovered in California, and thousands of Americans began to migrate to the West Coast. Tensions had reached a boiling point in Texas as residents in the state's western region sought sovereignty as a territory free from slavery, and reports of anarchy and lawlessness in the West caused great concern and demands for a strong civil government. Congress balked at the issues in the western territories and continued to divide itself into pro- and antislavery movements. The seemingly perpetual argument over slavery in the territories and the proposals for statehood plagued the Thirtieth Congress until its final days in March. The stage had been set for the newly elected Taylor administration, with Vice President Fillmore playing a major role in forthcoming debates.

On May 5, 1849, Millard Fillmore was sworn in by Chief Justice Roger B. Taney as the vice president of the United States. Soon after, he addressed the Senate as their presiding officer, briefly explaining the administration's plans and his personal hopes that "the glorious Union may endure forever." Fillmore's aspirations of unity were dashed, however, when Congress reassembled in December.

The inherited dilemma over California and the other western territories created a division among congressional members who either supported or opposed the spread of slavery. A huge gulf separated the two groups that led to dissension within the ranks of both the Democratic and the Whig parties. Southern legislators had passed resolutions defending the constitutional rights of the slave states and voiced a strong resistance to plans that might restrict the growth of slavery in the territories. Some pro-slavery extremists went as far as to threaten to hold a convention in Mississippi to discuss alternatives to an unfavorable administration decision. Exacerbating hostilities between camps, President Taylor chose unpopular cabinet members and supported a plan that called for free homesteads and the nonextension of slavery into the territories. By the end of 1849, there appeared to be no end to the bitter stalemate that existed in both houses of Congress.

Besides the numerous distractions in the Senate, Fillmore was confronted by a climactic change of power in his home state. Weed had once again turned on Fillmore and allied himself with William Henry Seward, the former governor and newly elected senator from New York. Conspiring against Fillmore, Weed and Seward strove to obtain control of the Whig Party in New York State. Seward gained the confidence of President Taylor, and his political advisers encouraged the administration to secure key appointments in New York State, which in turn greatly enhanced Weed and Seward's position. A determined struggled between Seward and Fillmore to control the New York Whig Party ensued, turning into a political battle that occupied Fillmore throughout his vice presidency and, later, his presidency.

In early 1850, the national issues were again joined when California sought statehood by approving a state constitution that prohibited slavery. President Taylor urged Congress to admit California as a free state and organize New Mexico and Utah as free territories apart from slaveholding Texas. The issues were thrown onto the floor of Congress, where they met with violent opposition from both southern Democrats and Whigs. The evenly split Senate could not agree on admitting California and the new territories as free. The southern legislators declared that if a free California was permitted to enter the Union and new free territories were created, the historical balance of pro-slave and antislave representatives in the Senate would tip toward the northern faction. Various alternative plans were placed before the House and the Senate, but "the great compromiser," Henry Clay, introduced a plan he hoped would ease sectional differences and retain the balance.

Much as he had done during the Missouri Compromise, Clay envisioned a scheme that would extinguish the flames of disunion by accommodating both the antislavery and pro-slavery factions. With the assistance of Stephen Douglas and Alexander Stephens, Clay devised a compromise that would prohibit the slave trade in the District of Columbia, create a stricter fugitive slave law, and incorporate a far-reaching "Omnibus Bill" that would resolved the complicated issues of the new territories. The "Omnibus Bill" proposed the admittance of California as a free state, addressed the Texas debt and boundary issue, and deferred the decision of slavery to the territories prior to their applying for statehood. In effect, the compromise pleased the abolitionists by admitting California as a free state and forbidding slave trade in the nation's capital. It also attempted to satisfy southern demands for an enforceable slave law and the premise that slavery could be expanded into the new territories by self-determination.

Throughout the vigorous and heated debates, Vice President Fillmore maintained order in the rambunctious Senate, a difficult task because fierce rivalries led to personal attacks and confrontations upon the Senate floor. In an effort to curtail the contention and defamation, Fillmore threatened to exercise his power to call members to order. On April 17, Fillmore had an opportunity to use this authority when Senator Henry S. Foote tried to intimidate fellow Democrat Thomas H. Benton by

brandishing a pistol on the Senate floor, but Fillmore merely acknowledged the event and did not exercise his power to punish Foote. The press criticized the vice president for not preventing the incident or disciplining Foote. Fillmore, recognizing the adverse publicity of enforcing discipline on the outlandish Foote, prudently chose to ignore the senator's absurd act. His reasoning proved correct as the debates over compromise continued at a more respectable tone, and Foote's reputation was considerably damaged.

During spring and early summer 1850, Vice President Fillmore remained indecisive and publicly voiced no commitment to either the president's plan nor the solution proposed by Clay and Douglas. Fillmore initially told the president that he favored the administration's plans to admit California as a free state. However, the influence of Senators Daniel Webster and Henry Clay converted the vice president to the practicality of compromise. Aiding in Fillmore's conversion was his distress over Taylor's political appointments in New York and the president's failure to grant him an active role in his administration. By early July, Fillmore formally reversed his stance by informing Taylor that if he were called upon to give a deciding vote in the Senate, he would favor the bill embodying compromise. Fate intervened and the opportunity to cast the deciding vote never came.

On the evening of July 9, Fillmore learned that President Taylor had succumbed to a sudden illness and had passed away. By noon the next day, Fillmore was sworn into office by Circuit Court justice William Cranch in a simple ceremony in the Hall of Representatives. Almost immediately after taking office, Fillmore began to restructure the executive branch by accepting the resignations of Taylor's cabinet and appointing pro-compromise leaders. He chose Webster as his secretary of state and fellow compromise proponent John J. Crittenden as attorney general. In a message to Congress on August 6, Fillmore urged the indemnification of Texas for the surrender of her claim to New Mexico and encouraged compromise. The message persuaded the middle of the road southern Whigs and northern Democrats that compromise was to be supported by the new administration.

By the end of summer, both houses of Congress voted upon and passed all the acts that constituted the Compromise of 1850. On September 9, Fillmore signed acts that admitted California as the thirty-first state and established the territories of New Mexico and Utah. Nine days later, he signed the Fugitive Slave Act, and on September 20, he abolished the slave trade in the District of Columbia. The Fillmore administration had helped break the stalemate in Congress, and so disunion was temporarily averted.

The subsequent presidential years of Millard Fillmore focused upon the implementation of the acts of the Compromise of 1850, the containing of overzealous expansionists, and the promotion of economic development. His actions to enforce strictly the Compromise of 1850 isolated him from both pro-slavery and antislavery factions. In early 1851, Fillmore issued a proclamation that defended the Fugitive Slave Act's provisions by calling for the capture and return of a runaway slave. Northern Whigs and abolitionists were astounded by the proclamation and began a public campaign to criticize his administration. The president separated himself from pro-slavery expansionists by issuing proclamations against U.S. citizens' participation in military expeditions to Cuba and Mexico. By issuing these proclamations, Fillmore helped stifle southern hopes for expanding slavery into other militarily acquired territories. In an effort to promote economic development, the Fillmore administration arranged federal grants for railroad construction, expanded international trade, and advocated internal improvements to both roadways and waterways. It was under Fillmore's authority that Commodore Matthew C. Perry voyaged to Japan to open an American trade route to the Pacific rim.

Fillmore's diligence and determination to keep the peace and preserve the Union were successful but at the cost of his political career. The contest for the Whig nomination for the presidency in 1852 brought forth two contenders for Fillmore's job: New England favorite Daniel Webster and General Winfield Scott, the choice of extreme abolitionists. Fillmore had considerable support from the southern Whigs and received the endorsement of Henry Clay. He sought the nomination on a platform supporting the Compromise of 1850 as a final settlement on the slavery issue. Webster and Fillmore could not find a common ground and after a tight battle, which took fifty-three ballots to decide, Scott won the party's nomination. The controversy over slavery eventually tore the Whig Party apart, and the Democratic candidate, Franklin Pierce, won the presidential election in a landslide victory.

Fillmore's final months as president were politically uneventful. He concluded his presidency by appropriating funds for the repair and maintenance of the Library of Congress, which had been damaged by fire in December of 1851. He signed an act to establish the Territory of Washington on March 2. And on his last day as president, possibly recalling the financial hardships he had as vice president, he signed an act raising the salary of the vice president from $5,000 to $8,000. On March 4, 1853, Fillmore's presidential term ended after thirty-two months.

Fillmore returned to Buffalo alone and anguished. His beloved spouse, Abigail, had died in Washington from complications related to a severe cold she contracted while participating in Pierce's inauguration. Fillmore sought retirement from politics, but after a few brief months loneliness and political aspirations drove him to begin a series of speaking engagements. During the spring and summer of 1854, he toured southern and midwestern states, hoping to resurrect the Whig Party. His efforts failed hopelessly as the Whigs splintered into different sectional groups, including the upstart Republican Party and the Know-Nothing (or American) Party. Fillmore was favored by the pro-Protestant, nativist Know-Nothings, who sought to unite former Whigs with a xenophobia directed against Catholic immigrants. In early 1856, while visiting Europe, Fillmore was surprised to learn that he had received the Know-Nothing nomination for the presidency. He reluctantly accepted the nomination and began a campaign that stressed the significance of the Union and the necessity of compromise. The election was an embarrassing defeat; he collected only 8 electoral votes and ran a distant third behind Democrat James Buchanan and Republican John C. Frémont.

Following the elections, Fillmore finally recognized the inevitable and retired from national politics. In February 1858, he married Catherine C. McIntosh, the childless widow of an affluent merchant from Troy, New York. He and his wife continued to reside in Buffalo, where they became very active in community projects and organizations.

Former President Fillmore became the founder of the Buffalo and Erie County Historical Society, Buffalo General Hospital, and the Buffalo Club. He was a major supporter of the local Society for the Prevention of Cruelty to Animals and was later named the vice president of the society. He contributed large endowments to the local library and created a fund on which the Buffalo Fine Arts Academy was founded. He also donated his personal time to speak at numerous charities and events promoting needy causes.

During the Civil War, Fillmore organized pro-Union demonstrations in Buffalo, encouraged the enlistment of men, created a fund to assist local families of volunteers, and was elected the chairman of the Buffalo Committee for Public Defense. Though Fillmore never approved the Republican Party's conduct of the war, he unselfishly supported the Union cause throughout. When the war concluded, he was given the solemn honor of escorting Abraham Lincoln's body from Batavia to Buffalo following the president's assassination. After the war, Fillmore chaired an organization to erect a monument to the soldiers and sailors of Erie County.

On February 13, 1874, Fillmore suffered a stroke that left the left side of his body paralyzed. Two weeks later, he had a second stroke, and his health deteriorated rapidly. On March 8, at the age of seventy-four, Fillmore died. He was buried two days later at Forest Lawn Cemetery in Buffalo, New York.

The vice presidency of Millard Fillmore proved to be the prologue of his presidency. His quiet restraint during the debates over compromise and his tactful methods of guiding the Senate displayed remarkable insight and prudence. When he ascended to the presidency on Zachary Taylor's death, he totally committed his administration to endorsing and implementing the acts that embodied the Compromise of 1850. Unfortunately, the vast differences between pro- and antislave powers proved to be irreconcilable. Fillmore's efforts to promote compromise and preserve the Union isolated him from both his party and the political mainstream. His determined unwillingness to alter his stance on compromise, slavery, and nativism doomed his later presidential candidacy in 1856. The overwhelming defeat and his inability to conform to popular political ideologies led him into retirement, where he demonstrated his generosity, kindness and devotion to the community.

REFERENCES

Elbert B. Smith, *The Presidencies of Zachary Taylor and Millard Fillmore* (Lawrence: University Press of Kansas, 1988); Robert J. Rayback, *Millard Fillmore: Biography of a President* (Buffalo, N.Y.: Publications of the Buffalo Historical Society, 1959); primary source information can be found in the "Millard Fillmore Papers," Vols. I and II, ed. by Frank H. Severance, in the *Buffalo Historical Society Publications,* Vols. X and XI (1907); collections of manuscript letters are located at the Buffalo Historical Society and the State University of New York at Oswego.

DIETER ULLRICH is head of university archives at Central Washington University. He was previously an archivist at Millersville University and Auburn University and was a special collections librarian and archivist at the University of Tennessee at Martin. He holds graduate degrees in both history and library science and worked with the Millard Fillmore papers while an assistant special collections librarian at the State University of New York at Oswego.

William Rufus de Vane King (1786–1853)

Vice President, 1853

(President Franklin Pierce)

WILLIAM RUFUS DE VANE KING
(Library of Congress)

By Daniel Fate Brooks

William Rufus de Vane King, the second son of William King and Margaret de Vane, was born April 7, 1786, on his family's plantation near Craddock Creek in Sampson County, North Carolina. His father, a planter of Irish descent, was listed in 1790 as owning thirty-one slaves and substantial lands in both North Carolina and Tennessee. The elder King was a justice of the peace, a North Carolina state legislator, and a delegate to the convention that ratified the U.S. Constitution. His son, William R. King, attended the Grove Academy near Kenansville and Fayetteville Academy, and at age thirteen became a student in the Preparatory School of the University of North Carolina. He enrolled in the university in 1801 and later became a member of the Philanthropic Society, a distinguished campus literary club. In 1804, at the end of his junior year, he left Chapel Hill and moved to Fayetteville, where he read law in William

129

Duffy's office. After admission to the bar in 1805, King relocated to Clinton, the county seat of his home county, and opened a law office.

In 1808, King, then age twenty-two, was elected to the North Carolina House of Commons as a Jeffersonian Republican from Sampson County. He was chosen the fifth circuit's solicitor in 1809 and was elected to Congress from the Wilmington District in 1810. Once in Washington, he quickly became a defender of the Madison administration and aligned himself with John C. Calhoun and Henry Clay and the young War Hawks' cause. He firmly believed in the use of tariffs to promote American manufacturing and favored involvement in the War of 1812. Reelected without opposition in 1813 and 1815, he continued to support nationalistic programs.

In spring 1816, King resigned his congressional seat to become secretary of the legation to William Pinckney of Maryland, the newly appointed minister to the Court of Naples and the two Sicilies, and the Court of Russia. During his tenure first in Naples and later in St. Petersburg, King recorded that he traveled extensively and observed social customs, "a desire fostered from the very early period of my life." No doubt the young diplomat greatly profited from this experience. Later in his public career, this mission was cited by the *Illustrated News* of New York as one that "amply improved those abilities that have since been so well tested."

King returned to North Carolina in fall 1817 and was soon persuaded to follow his older brother, Thomas, to the newly opened Alabama Territory. "Alabama Fever" had swept the seaboard states, beckoning planters and plainfolk alike to the newly tamed wilderness. By early 1818, King had relocated on the Alabama River in a fertile region known as the Alabama Black Belt. In a short time he amassed vast acreage, built his home "Chestnut Hill," and by 1820 had assembled the second-largest slave force in Dallas County. In addition to planting interests, he purchased lands in and around the river port of Moore's Bluff and became a partner in the land company that founded the city of Selma. King is credited with naming the city in honor of Ossian's poem, "Songs of Selma."

Recognized by Alabama settlers as a proven leader, King was elected to represent Dallas County in Alabama's Constitutional Convention in 1819 and was named to the subcommittee that drafted the state constitution. During convention debates, King constantly supported a conservative constitution instead of one characterized by lenient democracy. When the first general assembly convened in the fall of 1819, he and John Williams Walker of Madison County were almost unanimously elected as Alabama's first two United States senators. As the representative of south Alabama, King drew a short term but was reelected in 1822 to a full six-year term after defeating U.S. District Attorney William Crawford of Mobile by a vote of 38 to 35. In both the elections of 1828 and 1834, King, then a Democrat, won his Senate seat without opposition and in 1840 was victorious over Whig candidate former Governor John Gayle.

By the third of his first four terms as senator King emerged as a leader in the causes of generous land legislation, tariff reform, and banking. On land questions he supported Jeffersonian principles by declaring that without more reasonable prices and better purchasing terms, the country would be controlled by the monied aristocracy. As chairman of the Public Land committee and a long-time proponent of policies that favored settlers, King led the efforts to oppose Henry Clay's distribution bill, which would allow states to receive proceeds from public-land sales.

On tariff issues, King remained a moderate, even though he rejected the tariffs of 1816, 1824, and 1828. He was a foe of nullification as well as of Jackson's Force Bill, but as a Unionist, he limited his criticism of South Carolina to "most unfortunate" and "an embarrassment to the country." Considering first the good of the Union, King finally accepted the Tariff of 1832 and even supported Clay's tariff bill of 1833 as a restoration of peace.

In 1832, King opposed a bill that would allow the Bank of the United States to be rechartered, which he viewed as partisan legislation and an action that provided no measures to correct abuses. He remained a strong advocate and a leader in the Democratic Party and, with few exceptions, a supporter of Jackson. During the Democratic Convention in Baltimore in 1832, King reported for the Committee on Rules and proposed the rule that provided for a two-thirds vote to nominate a candidate. This rule was used by the party until its repeal in 1936.

Throughout his career, King was respectfully addressed as Colonel King, a title given him by endearing admirers from whom he commanded confidence. He was described as about "six feet high, remarkably erect in figure, well proportioned and impressive even to strangers." One surviving image of King portrays the secretary of legation as a Byronic youth, while later portraits show him as a handsome statesman whose aquiline nose and high cheekbones suggest the Huguenot blood of his mother's family. Seen as "brave and chivalrous" in character, King was remembered by his contemporaries as possessing "manners as courtly as Chesterfield's." He was described as "lavishly hospitable" and "courteous to the humblest," qualities that "marked a finished gentleman."

About 1834, King met and developed a friendship with James Buchanan of Pennsylvania. The two men shared most political sentiments, and both remained lifelong bachelors. In time their relationship became more intimate, and by 1836 the two senators shared a residence in Washington. Soon the usual talk about King's traits as a "southern gentleman" generated amusement from northerners and caused others to joke about the two and refer to them as "the Siamese Twins."

Despite the gossip, King continued to focus his attention on governmental affairs. Concerned about the personal suffering resulting from the panic of 1837 and its threat to the Democratic Party's future, he became a proponent of the Independent Treasury System. During the discussions on the distribution of abolitionist material in the southern states, King remained a moderate, taking a position supporting the view that petitions from distributors should be received by the Senate and rejected.

By 1838, interest was already focused on the Democratic Convention of 1840. While Martin Van Buren was almost certain to be the presidential nominee, there were several likely contenders for the vice-presidential nomination. Included in the list were John Forsyth of Georgia, Richard Mentor Johnson of Kentucky, James K. Polk of Tennessee, and William Rufus King. While the Democratic press in Alabama pushed King's name at home, Buchanan was active in gaining support for him in Pennsylvania. These efforts proved to be popular among Buchanan partisans because the advancement of King would likely deprive Polk of the nomination and eliminate him as a threat to Buchanan's candidacy in 1844. King had previously assured his roommate that should he become vice president, he would not seek the presidency and would endorse Buchanan's nomination.

Using campaign material furnished by Buchanan, some Pennsylvania newspapers praised the Alabama senator for his proven leadership and his "unwavering devotion to the pure and patriotic principles of the Democratic creed." Although King received scattered support in New Hampshire, Indiana, and Virginia, he failed to get North Carolina's endorsement. Disappointed by his native state's rejection, King withdrew from the race, gave his support to Johnson, and eventually endorsed the Democratic ticket.

Interest in the Democratic nomination for 1844 began almost immediately. As early as 1842, newspapers in Alabama and other states advocated a Buchanan-King ticket, but as time passed, optimism about its success waned. Party leaders considered Polk and King to be the leading vice-presidential contenders, but only as long as Van Buren was the presidential nominee. In December 1843, King wrote his niece

Catherine Ellis that even though Buchanan was no longer a contender, he remained optimistic about his own success.

By early January 1844, defaming comments about the intimacy of King and Buchanan again circulated around Washington. Andrew Jackson, who favored his fellow Tennessean, James K. Polk, spoke of King as "Miss Nancy," while the Tennessean Aaron V. Brown, a former law partner of Polk, referred to King as "Mrs. B." and "Buchanan's wife." In a scathing letter to Polk's wife, Sarah, dated January 14, 1844, Brown wrote:

> Mr. Buchanan looks gloomy and dissatisfied & so did his better half until a private flattery and a certain newspaper puff which you doubtless noticed, excited hopes that by getting a *divorce* she might set up again in the world to some tolerable advantage.

Referring to King as "Aunt Nancy," Brown went on to say that he "may now be seen everyday, triged [sic] out in her best clothes & smirking about in hopes of securing better terms than with her former companion."

Once again King's chances of receiving the nomination began to fade. In a letter to his niece, he wrote that he was resigned to surrender the vice presidency "without one feeling of regret." However, by April 1844, King was asked by President John Tyler to accept an appointment as minister to France. Tyler instructed him to strengthen "subsisting relations" but left the method for accomplishment entirely up to King. After King resigned his Senate seat and accepted the post, he wrote a letter in May to Buchanan expressing his reluctance on leaving him:

> I am selfish enough to hope you will not be able to procure an associate who will cause you to feel no regret at our separation. For myself, I shall feel lonely in the midst of Paris, for there I shall have no friend with whom I can commune as with my own thoughts.

As King developed plans to go abroad, he made sure that he surrounded himself with family. Together with his widowed niece Catherine Ellis, two nephews, William T. King and Alfred Beck, and his trusted body servant, John Bell, he sailed from New York to Havre in June 1844. Arriving in Paris, he quickly received an audience with King Louis Philippe and began tedious negotiations regarding U.S.–French relations over the annexation of Texas, the settlement of the Oregon boundary, and problems, with Mexico. Despite several diplomatic differences with French foreign minister François Guizot, King ably expressed the U.S. position and assured the monarch that a French alliance with England in Lord Aberdeen's proposed plan of intervention in the Texas annexation was unwise. Through the "lavish entertaining" hosted by his niece and his own diplomatic skills, King was successful in permitting the United States to annex Texas without fear of foreign interference and gained French neutrality in the Oregon question and the Mexican War.

Completing his mission, King resigned his diplomatic post and returned to Alabama in November 1846. After being virtually cut off from politics for more than two years, he quickly began a campaign to regain his Senate seat. In his absence, Dixon Hall Lewis, states' rights advocate and former House member, had been appointed by his brother-in-law, Governor Benjamin Fitzpatrick, to fill the vacancy. In 1847, Lewis ran for a full term with King as his challenger. Contrary to early expectations, King soon found the almost 500-pound Lewis to be no easy opponent. The race, described by the press as "a meeting of the giants," created a deadlock in the Alabama legislature. With Whigs remaining loyal to their candidate, Arthur F. Hopkins, King's constituency refused to accept Lewis. After two days of balloting, King, unable to secure a majority of votes, withdrew from the race, and Lewis was elected. The loss marked King's only defeat in a state election.

Disappointed and concerned about the division that now existed in the state party,

King focused his attention on the 1848 vice-presidential nomination. While Lewis and other Calhoun supporters failed to endorse him because of his moderate views, Unionists in the North and South once again looked to a Buchanan-King ticket. In February 1848, the Alabama Convention unanimously nominated King for vice president, but only after states' rights leader William Lowndes Yancey attached some extreme resolutions regarding slavery. King supporters reluctantly accepted the resolutions without knowing that Yancey had planned an unsuccessful walkout to ruin their candidate.

During the Democratic national convention of 1848, Lewis Cass was nominated for the presidency. Vice-presidential nominees included William O. Butler, John A. Quitman, John Y. Mason, Jefferson Davis, J. J. McKay, and William Rufus King. When the first vote was counted, King was in third place, with only twenty-six scattered votes, the majority of which came from Alabama and Pennsylvania. General Butler won the nomination, and King received fewer Alabama votes because Yancey had defected from the state delegation and cast his ballot for Quitman. This action signaled an even more decisive split in the Alabama party.

Despite his defeat by Dixon Hall Lewis, King soon found himself back in Washington. In June 1848, Arthur P. Bagby resigned from the Senate to become minister to Russia, and King was appointed by Governor Reuben Chapman to Bagby's seat. The following year, King was reelected to a full term but only after making some concessions to Yancey and his supporters.

With the sudden death of President Zachary Taylor in the summer of 1850, King was again selected president pro tempore of the Senate. He had held this position from 1836 to 1841 and was recognized as the leading authority on senate rules. King readily accepted the duties of presiding officer and acknowledged this as his opportunity to calm the emotions of both North and South and hopefully bring about some compromise to save the Union.

Sectional controversy and the problems with slavery and westward expansion dominated King's last years as a statesman. Realizing that the best hope of the South lay in unity, King wrote that he pleaded with "the patriotic men of every section to meet on grounds of compromise." However, in the following months, lack of cooperation among the southern representation gave more encouragement to the abolitionists and made it increasingly difficult for King to remain a moderate. When California sought admission to the Union, William R. King served as a member of the select committee of thirteen that drafted the Compromise of 1850. He is credited not only with aiding its passage but also with bringing about its acceptance by southern rights enthusiasts. Although he acknowledged that southerners had legitimate complaints about some provisions, he remained an ardent defender of any measure that threatened the good of the Union.

During the next year, King served on various Senate committees, chairing the Committee on Foreign Relations and being credited with responsibility for the passage of the Clayton–Bulwer Treaty. However, most of his energies were spent working to reunite Alabama Democrats, settling dissension in the national party, and steering younger U.S. politicians on a more moderate course. By 1852, King was the last of the Senate leaders of his generation. Calhoun, Clay, and Webster were dead, and Thomas Hart Benton had been defeated. At times it seemed that only he and Buchanan shared a devotion to the Union.

In January 1852, the Alabama Democratic convention endorsed King for vice president, with a resolution proclaiming him "the distinguished, long tried, and ever faithful Senator." At the national Democratic convention in Baltimore the following June, King was the leading contended for the second office, while Buchanan, Lewis Cass of Michigan, William Learned Marcy of New York, and "the little giant," Stephen A. Douglas of Illinois, vied for the presidential nomination. After a grueling battle, Buchanan's name jumped to the top with 104 votes. Needing a majority, Buchanan supporters begged Marcy's New York delegation for their votes, but to no avail. Finally, Buchanan's poll declined, and his bid failed. Two votes later, on the forty-sixth ballot, Marcy's score began to rise, and New York came to Buchanan begging for his support. Pennsylvania partisans, however, had already decided their next move: Buchanan would back General Franklin Pierce of New Hampshire, a dark-horse candidate who was satisfactory to both North and South.

To reward Buchanan and his friends for their endorsement, Pierce supporters allowed them to select William Rufus King as the vice-presidential candidate. On the second ballot, the sixty-six year old Alabamian received the nomination with 282 votes. In a letter to Pierce, one supporter wrote: "I think we did right putting King on the ticket. You know he is Buchanan's bosom friend, and [therefore] a great powerful interest is consolidated."

King had at last reached his ambition and triumphed with a landslide victory. He was pleased with the nomination, but in a letter to Buchanan dated June 12, 1852, King confided disappointment that his friend was not the presidential nominee. Two days later, Buchanan wrote a clergyman and expressed little regret in his own defeat but pledged his "cordial support to Pierce & King; because they are the nominees of the convention & to the latter because I love and respect the man."

In regard to Pierce, King now felt that, next to Buchanan, he was more acceptable to the South than the other candidates. During the campaign, King, who complained of a "distressing cough," rarely gave speeches but spent most of his time writing letters, assuring southerners that the forty-eight-year-old Pierce was indeed a leader they could count on.

In two earlier elections, the Whigs were successful in electing an aging war hero as president. The party elected Harrison in 1840 and Taylor in 1848; therefore General Winfield Scott of Mexican War fame appeared to be a hopeful choice for the Whigs. With "Old Fuss and Feathers" as the presidential nominee, the Whigs looked to balance their ticket with a younger man, William A. Graham of North Carolina.

The Democrats now had the task of maintaining party unity and guarding against dissension and outside intrusion. In fall 1852, the Free-Soil Party, under the slogan "Free Soil, Free Speech, Free Labor, and Free Men," threatened to split Buchanan's supporters with the nomination of John P. Hale for president. Building their platform on the belief that "slavery is a sin against God and a crime against man," the Free Soilers cited Harriet Beecher Stowe's newly published novel, *Uncle Tom's Cabin* which threatened to upset Pennsylvanian's solid Democratic vote. Determined to settle the challenge, Buchanan defended the Democrats and the Compromise of 1850 by offering the question of who would maintain the security of the Compromise of 1850, Pierce and King or the Whigs.

In the weeks before the election, King's cough had turned into a more serious problem. Throughout the fall, he had to decline invitations to events held in his honor. However, when election results were announced, he was elated to learn that the Democrats had carried all but four states with 85.8 percent of the electoral vote. For King the election of Pierce was important "for the protection of southern rights and the preservation of the Union." In a letter dated November 17, 1852, King wrote from Selma: "I am satisfied that the triumphant success of the Democrats has not prostrated the Whig Party but has to a great extent annihilated freesoilism, so that in the future we shall only have to contend against the insane movements of the Abolitionists." Plagued by his bad health and considering a resignation, King continued: "My health is not good. I am troubled by a distressing cough, and if I consulted my own wishes I would not hesitate to resign my senate seat and spend the next winter in Alabama."

Disregarding his health, King left home and returned to Washington. By December

1852, the *Congressional Globe* reported that he had found it necessary to resign as president pro tempore and as senator from Alabama. King had been diagnosed with consumption. Earlier in the year, he had written that he wanted to "seek some quiet watering place in the mountains" where he could find "pure air and rest." However, because it was winter and his doctors had prescribed a warm climate, it was even more difficult to locate ideal conditions in the United States.

Following the advice of his physician, King left Washington on January 15, 1853, bound for Cuba. After stopping in Key West, he arrived in Havana on January 30. Sixteen days later, he moved east into Matanzas to Ariadne, a sugar plantation near the town of Limonar. There he took advantage of the heat in the sugar mill, which he hoped would provide relief from his respiratory ailments.

As weeks passed, however, King's health did not improve, and it became evident that he would be unable to return to Washington for the inauguration. If he was to be sworn in as vice president, Congress would need to work quickly and make a provision for him to be inaugurated in Cuba. On March 2, 1853, a special act was passed that permitted the U.S. Consul General William Sharkey to administer to King the oath of office in "Havana or another place on the Island."

Cuba in the early spring was an exotic place in comparison to cold and windy Washington. On March 24, 1853, the day of King's ceremony, one witness described the elements of the setting: "The clear sky of the tropics over our heads, the emerald carpet of Cuba at our feet, and the delicious breeze of coolness over us." The 300-foot peak overlooking the sea of Ariadne Plantation was indeed an impressive backdrop for this unusual inauguration. As King was sworn in as vice president, he could view a valley with a winding stream, colorful fields, and brown mountain peaks. Following the ceremony, a large open carriage accompanied by more than a dozen Americans on horseback, took the ailing vice president back to his quarters. William Rufus King had gained the distinction of being the first and only United States executive official to take the oath of office on foreign soil.

In the days that followed, King's health steadily worsened. No longer did he resemble the handsome statesman of his earlier likenesses. He was now the subject of his completed inaugural portrait: a sickly old gentleman prophetically holding his Book of Common Prayer. Realizing that death was near, he wanted to go home to his plantation. In a letter to Secretary of State William Marcy dated March 26, 1853, Consul General Sharkey wrote of King's condition: "He is very feeble and thus would seem to be but little ground to hope for a recovery. He proposes to leave the Island on the 6th of April for Mobile on the U.S. Steamer *Fulton*." King departed Cuba on April 7, his sixty-seventh birthday. As he crossed the Gulf of Mexico, he confessed to an Episcopal priest his desire to die among his family.

After a five-day voyage of some 500 miles, the Fulton arrived in Mobile. *The Mobile Register* reported that "an immense assemblage of citizens" waited at the Government Street wharf to greet their beloved leader, but instead of cheers, sadness hung over the crowd as two ship's officers helped the "feeble and attenuated" vice president from the ship and into his carriage. King was not quite home. He remained in Mobile for a few days' rest before he boarded a river packet for his final trip. Running full steam from Mobile to King's landing, the boat broke all previous records for speed on the Alabama River.

As King traveled from the river to Chestnut Hill, he reportedly remarked that his fields never looked greener. At 6:00 P.M. the following afternoon of April 18, 1853, William R. King died in the front room of his one-story house, surrounded by his family and faithful servants. He had been an elected official for forty-five years and vice president for less than a month.

In the days and years that followed the death of Vice President William Rufus de Vane

King, his countrymen recognized that here was no ordinary man. With a colorful life and political views distinctively different from some of his more distinguished contemporaries, King significantly contributed to his state's development and his nation's preservation. Although he never formally served as vice president, he had served his country well.

REFERENCES

Walter Jackson, *Alabama's First United States Vice President, William Rufus King* (Decatur, Ala.: Decatur Printing Co., 1952); Daniel Fate Brooks, "The Faces of William Rufus King," *Alabama Heritage* 69 (2003) 14–23; Henry Poellnitz Johnston, Sr., *William R. King and His Kin* (Birmingham, Ala.: Featon Press, 1975); William Rufus de Vane King Papers (Alabama Department of Archives and History, Montgomery); William Rufus de Vane King Papers (Southern Historical Collection, University of North Carolina Library, Chapel Hill); "Lives of General Franklin Pierce and William R. King, Democratic Candidates for President and Vice President" (Boston, Mass.: George Roberts, 1852); John M. Martin, "William Rufus King and the Compromise of 1850," *The North Carolina Historical Review*, 39, 4 (Autumn 1962), 500–518; John M. Martin, "William R. King and the Vice-Presidency," *The Alabama Review*, 16, 1 (January 1963), 35–54; John M. Martin, "William R. King: Jacksonian Senator," *The Alabama Review*, 18, 4 (October 1965), 243–267; John M. Martin, "William Rufus King, Southern Moderate and Champion of the Southern Cause" (Ph.D. diss., University of North Carolina, Chapel Hill, 1956); Lewy Dorman, *Party Politics in Alabama from 1850 through 1860* (Wetumpka, Ala.: Wetumpka Printing Company, 1935); William Garrett, *Reminiscences of Public Men in Alabama* (Atlanta, Ga.: Plantation Publishing, 1872); *Gleason's Pictorial*, 3, 23 (December 4, 1852); *Illustrated News*, 1, 12 (March 19, 1853); Philip Shriver Klein, *President James Buchanan* (University Park, Pa.: Pennsylvania State University Press, 1962).

DANIEL FATE BROOKS, a native of the Alabama Black Belt, is a past president of the Alabama Historical Association and the author of several articles on William Rufus King. He now lives in Birmingham, where he is director of Arlington, an historic house museum, and he has been an adjunct instructor at Samford University.

JOHN CABELL BRECKINRIDGE (1821–1875)

Vice President, 1857–1861

(President James Buchanan)

JOHN CABELL BRECKINRIDGE
(Library of Congress)

By John Marshall Prewitt

If Hollywood ever decided to make an action film of the life of a vice president of the United States (among those who never became president), the choice might likely fall on John C. Breckinridge. It is difficult to imagine the public buying tickets to see any other vice president's story, with the possible exception of Aaron Burr.

The various periods of Breckinridge's life are each worthy of a tale to be told, except for one—the period of his vice presidency. For three-and-a-half years of his term of office, President Buchanan ignored him, other than to ask advice on a handful of appointments to offices that might affect Kentucky. There is really nothing very unusual about a president ignoring a vice president. Many vice presidents have had no duties or functions but to preside over the Senate and to keep informed of the president's state of health.

Finally, near the end of his vice presidential term, a summons to the White House came to Breckinridge. The great political and national crisis of 1860 was in full bloom, with the country starting to pull asunder in preparation for civil war. Buchanan could not solve the problem. Breckinridge's biographer, William C. Davis, has described Breckinridge's expectations when the interview began. Buchanan told his staff to leave them undisturbed and then, with great ceremony, unlocked a desk drawer and pulled out a manuscript. The president looked gravely at Breckinridge and asked his opinion about issuing a proclamation for a day of humiliation and prayer.

According to Davis:

> The vice president sat in mute shock, fighting with his facial muscles to conceal the anger and frustration that he felt. He listened quietly, respectfully, made a few complimentary remarks, and then smiled and bowed his way out. In time he would be able to laugh over the incident, repeating it to friends with "inimitable narration," but now it was one more example of the stupidity and disarranged priorities on all sides that led the country into its difficulty, and a hallmark of Buchanan's singular incapacity for his office.

To a man as active as Breckinridge, of all the periods of his life, his term as vice president must have been the most restricting and unrewarding.

John C. Breckinridge was born into a political family. His paternal grandfather, John Breckinridge, was a Virginia lawyer who moved near Lexington, Kentucky, in 1793, was appointed Kentucky's attorney general, but preferred the legislative branch, where he became speaker of the Kentucky House of Representatives. In 1800, the grandfather was elected U.S. Senator. His consistent backing of friend President Thomas Jefferson's policies brought him appointment as Jefferson's attorney general. His career was cut short by his death in 1806 at the age of forty-six. He left a substantial estate, mostly in the form of his Fayette County, Kentucky farm, which was called "Cabell's Dale."

John Breckinridge's widow was Mary Hopkins Cabell, known to her descendants as "Grandma Blackcap" for her ever-present head covering. One of the prominent Cabells of Virginia, she survived her husband by fifty-two years to become the dowager empress of the Breckinridge family.

John and Mary Breckinridge's son (John C. Breckinridge's father) was Joseph Cabell Breckinridge. He graduated from Princeton in 1810 and a year later married Mary Clay Smith, daughter of the college president, Dr. Samuel Stanhope Smith (whose own father-in-law was the illustrious Rev. John Witherspoon, a signer of the Declaration of Independence and previous president of Princeton, known in his day as the College of New Jersey). Cabell Breckinridge, as he was known, served in the War of 1812 and then returned to Lexington to practice law. In due course, he, too, was elected to the Kentucky legislature and became speaker of its house, followed by an appointment as Kentucky's secretary of state. At age thirty-four he, like his father, was cut off in his prime by death.

The future vice president, John Cabell Breckinridge, was born January 16, 1821, in Lexington. He was only two years old when his father died, and there was apparently an overwhelming influence of women in Breckinridge's early childhood. His father had not had time to build an estate and left a considerable debt; consequently, the widow and children had to go live with Grandma Blackcap at Cabell's Dale.

Breckinridge found himself living with six women: his grandmother, his mother, and four sisters. The grandmother and mother were both demanding women. The difficulty of two aristocratic and haughty women, used to running their own houses and trying to occupy one together, is obvious. Eventually, after a domestic uproar in 1832 when Breckinridge was nine years old, his mother and family left Cabell's Dale and went to live with her daughter Frances, now married to John Clarke Young, a Presbyterian clergyman and president of Centre College in Danville, Kentucky.

Breckinridge was sent to Pisgah Academy in Woodford County, Kentucky, and later enrolled at Centre College. He continued to live with his sister and her husband when his mother departed to Lexington in 1835 when her daughter Mary Satterwhite died; she spent the next ten years rearing the Satterwhite children.

Presbyterian religious influence appears to have been strong on Breckinridge. His great grandfather, John Witherspoon, was not only the president of Princeton but also the first moderator of the Presbyterian national assembly. His uncles included a chaplain of the U.S. House of Representatives, a nationally known Presbyterian minister, and the Presbyterian president of Centre College.

One of Breckinridge's biographers, Frank H. Heck, points out that although he joined the Presbyterian Church in Danville, he requested that his membership be suspended in 1840 on the grounds that he no longer felt worthy to be a communicant. He was never after an active churchman. Breckinridge followed this incident by joining the Masons, which some considered a religious organization with teachings adverse to Presbyterian Calvinism. The present generation of Americans can scarcely conceive of the church's influence in the times of which we write. Today, a Presbyterian would most likely just quit going to church without feeling any necessity for justification, but in Breckinridge's youth, to be blackballed by your church—any church—was to risk disapproval, even shunning, by the entire community.

Being sent away to school freed Breckinridge from feminine influences, and he was universally popular with his schoolmates. He became a capable athlete and a believer in a daily exercise program. Going further, he adopted "daily regularity in a particular habit," which he applied to all of his activities. It may be that this foreshadowed his later successful adaptation to the routine of military life.

After graduating from Centre, Breckinridge studied law at Princeton and Transylvania University in Lexington, and then under Judge William Owsley. He was admitted to the bar in 1841.

Then an unusual event occurred. This recent graduate, only twenty years old, was asked to deliver the main address at the state Fourth of July celebration at the capitol in Frankfort. Breckinridge's natural flare for oratory was apparently recognized by his schools, classmates, and Judge Owsley, who may have influenced the choice of Breckinridge as the speaker for the occasion. The speech was successful and gained him a considerable measure of favorable notice.

In his oration, Breckinridge mentioned "unlawful dominion over the bodies of men," which seemed to hint at his abhorrence of slavery. His attitudes were probably influenced by his uncle, Rev. Robert J. Breckinridge, an emancipationist of whom he was very fond. His uncle was associated with the American Colonization Society; a group that promoted the founding of the African nation of Liberia as a haven for freed American slaves. Breckinridge's family also all approved the Kentucky slave law of 1833 that prohibited further import of slaves into the state. There was a distinct limit, however, to the range of Breckinridge's thinking on the slavery issue: Although he used the word "unlawful" in his July Fourth speech, for him abolition was the confiscation of property by the government and was constitutionally out of the question, even though he might have viewed slavery as intrinsically evil.

Despite his notable beginnings as a Kentucky lawyer, Breckinridge and his cousin Thomas Bullock soon departed for what they hoped would be greener pastures when they set up a law office in the developing frontier town of Burlington, Iowa. He dabbled there in local politics, abandoning his early Whig sympathies and becoming a Jackson-style Democrat. There does not appear to be any reason of principle behind this change, perhaps only expediency. Two years later, he returned to Kentucky for a visit and met and married Mary Cyrene Burch, which ended the Iowa venture. The new family settled in Georgetown, Kentucky, and Breckinridge formed a few law partnership with another cousin, Samuel R. Bullock. Breckinridge handled the Georgetown office, and Bullock saw to Lexington.

In the 1844 presidential election campaign, Breckinridge made speeches for Democrat James K. Polk, developing such a reputation that he was asked to address a Polk rally in Nashville (he was unable to attend). The speeches had the effect of making him well known in the Bluegrass section of the state.

In 1846, Breckinridge moved to Lexington and the firm's Georgetown office was closed. By this time two sons had been born to the family.

In the same year, war was declared against Mexico. When the battle of Buena Vista produced a number of casualties among Kentuckians, the legislature ordered that the bodies be brought home for reburial, and Breckinridge was chosen to be the main speaker at the ceremony. To 15,000 or 20,000 people, a crowd of unusual size for the time, at Frankfort Cemetery, Breckinridge delivered the address that established his statewide reputation and eventually led him to the vice presidency.

Soon after the memorial ceremony, Breckinridge received a commission and within months was on his way to Vera Cruz and a march to Mexico City as a major of the Third Kentucky Volunteers. Not a shot was fired on the Third during the balance of the war, and eight and a half months after they left home, the peace treaty had been signed and Breckinridge and his men were back home.

In 1849, Breckinridge was elected to the Kentucky House of Representatives on the Democratic ticket. (About this time in Lexington, he met Abraham Lincoln, the husband of Breckinridge's childhood playmate, Mary Todd.) Most members of the Kentucky legislature went to the capital and were seldom heard from again. Fearing to offend even one voter, they introduced no legislation and tried to

avoid voting on anything controversial. Not so with John C. Breckinridge: His legislative record is too voluminous to detail, but it covered a vast number of subjects, particularly so-called internal improvements such as railroads. State financing of public works was a controversial subject at a time when many advocated a laissez-faire state wherein improvements, if any, should be paid for by private enterprise or at the local government level. Breckinridge also spoke out for states' rights and the Union, two principles that were soon proved in actual practice to be mutually exclusive.

Because of his financial situation, Breckinridge turned down a second term in the Kentucky legislature, but in 1851, he was elected to the U.S. Congress in a hard-fought campaign against an elderly Whig candidate, war hero and elder statesman General Leslie Combs. The election was lost in other counties until the final vote from Owen County was received, giving Breckinridge a majority. Thus, his newly born son John Witherspoon Breckinridge acquired from his father the nickname "Owen," which stayed with him all his life.

Breckinridge's first biographer, Lucille Stillwell, reported that prior to the election, a committee came to Breckinridge from Owen County, asking how great a majority in that county would certainly elect him. He named a thousand. Owen County gave him 1,500 votes out of a voting population of less than 2,000. This was typical of Kentucky politics, and county political machines of this type exist to this day. The trick is to control all the voting-booth officials, if necessary by having some of your supporters register as members of the opposing party. They then report whatever voting result is required. If a voter does not come to the polls, an official will cast his vote. Kentuckians took the attitude that if a candidate could not protect himself against fraud, he proved a lack of political acumen and should lose. Few, except the loser, became upset over a stolen election.

In 1852, Henry Clay, the "Great Pacificator" and elder statesman from Kentucky, died.

Although of opposite political parties, he and Breckinridge admired each other, and Breckinridge was selected to deliver a eulogy for Clay. While his speeches in Congress had gained him some national reputation, this speech pushed him toward the forefront of national politics.

Breckinridge was again elected to Congress in 1853 after a hard fought campaign. He soon became involved in the presidential election and strongly supported and spoke for Franklin Pierce, thereafter forming a close alliance with the president.

What were perhaps the defining moments of Breckinridge's subsequent political career came during this second term as Congressman. In 1854, Breckinridge's friend Stephen A. Douglas of Illinois introduced a bill to organize the territories of Kansas and Nebraska on the basis of "popular sovereignty"—that is, letting the residents themselves decide the question of whether slavery would be allowed. The proposal would also in effect have repealed the Missouri Compromise, dating from the early 1820s, which had put the question of slavery in the territories in Congress's hands and ruled out slavery north of Missouri's border. Breckinridge played a key role in helping to broker the bill's final form and securing its passage in the House. Breckinridge's position in the debate (he nearly came to a duel with a representative from New York during consideration of the bill) caused him to be branded as a southern slavery sympathizer and destroyed any chance that he would be considered a moderate who might possibly be acceptable to both sections of a divided country.

Meanwhile, the Kentucky legislature had gerrymandered Breckinridge's district so as to expand the Whig vote. It appeared that he would be defeated if he ran again. He returned to Lexington, and though he decided not to seek office again—he turned down an appointment by President Pierce as minister to Spain—he did not leave politics. He launched a vigorous opposition to the antiforeign, anti-Catholic Know-Nothing (American) Party, which had

scored a sweeping victory in Kentucky, electing a governor and many other officers.

Breckinridge was appalled not only at the Know-Nothings, but also at a party calling itself Republican that had developed in the Midwest and the North out of the Kansas-Nebraska Bill uproar. Breckinridge considered the new party to be purely sectional and a divisive threat to the Union.

As the Democratic Party approached its presidential nominating convention of 1856 in Cincinnati, it was clear that Breckinridge would be likely to play an important role. His prestige nationally had grown during his terms in Congress, despite his image among many as a proslavery southerner, and he had a major influence because Kentucky's votes were thought to be crucial to both the nominating process and the election to follow.

Breckinridge went to Cincinnati as a supporter of Franklin Pierce's renomination, but Pennsylvania Democrat James Buchanan and his strong organization seemed to have the upper hand. The sectional splits that threatened almost all aspects of the Union were at work also within the Democratic Party, so Buchanan could not swing a majority of the delegates immediately, and he calculated that he would need the support of Kentucky in order to win the White House in the Fall. Attention focused on the Kentucky delegation, from which two vice-presidential possibilities emerged: Breckinridge and Lynn Boyd. During the first fourteen ballots, Breckinridge at first supported Pierce but switched to Douglas when it became apparent that Pierce had no chance for renomination. At the end of the first day, Buchanan lead in the voting but without the majority needed. During that evening, Buchanan organizers came to Breckinridge and offered him the vice presidency in return for his support, but he declined.

On the following day, Douglas withdrew from contention after the sixteenth ballot, giving the presidential nomination to Buchanan. A delegate from Louisiana then nominated Breckinridge for the vice president's slot. The

Kentuckian at first declined, but when he received the nomination by acclamation on the second vote, he graciously accepted his party's call to fill out the ticket.

The contest for the presidency reflected the growing fragmentation of American politics. Buchanan and Breckinridge represented the old Democratic Party, which would hold a majority if they could avoid too much splitting over the issues of slavery and sectionalism. The new Republican Party nominated John C. Frémont and William L. Dayton. The Know-Nothings recruited former President Millard Fillmore to head their anti-immigrant ticket. Breckinridge, along with other Democrats, feared that the Know-Nothings would again run strongly in Kentucky, which might siphon enough electoral votes from the Buchanan ticket to throw the election into Congress, where anything could happen.

Finally, Kentucky went Democratic and helped Buchanan and Breckinridge pile up a healthy win, polling nearly a half-million more votes than Frémont and a million more than the Know-Nothings. The Democrats coasted into office with a total of 174 electoral votes.

For Breckinridge, however, the move into the vice presidency proved to be a massive step downward. He hoped to influence Buchanan's cabinet appointments and secure places for Kentuckians among the diplomatic nominees, but the president pointedly ignored him. Worse yet, within a month of the inauguration, Buchanan not only denied a request from Breckinridge for a private audience but insultingly told the new vice president to call instead on the president's niece. Breckinridge was outraged at this treatment—resulting, apparently, from Buchanan's smoldering resentment that Breckinridge had originally supported Pierce and Douglas at the nominating convention—but could do nothing.

The vice presidency completely sidetracked Breckinridge. From that office he had little opportunity to exercise leadership and had no Control or influence over the momentous events of the day. The *Dred Scott* decision came during Buchanan and Breckinridge's first year in office and poured new fuel on the national fires when the Supreme Court ruled that slaves had no rights and that Congress did not have the authority to restrict or interfere with slavery in the western territories. Breckinridge approved the decision. When Kansas burst into open warfare over the question of slavery and the Buchanan administration and Congress were faced with dire circumstances, Breckinridge could do or say virtually nothing. His only opportunities to cast deciding votes in the Senate during most of his term were on inconsequential issues such as a proposed tariff on codfishing.

As he neared the end of his vice-presidential term, Breckinridge moved to reestablish himself as a national leader. One of the senate seats from Kentucky was coming open, and Breckinridge wanted it. As a senator from an important swing state, he would likely wield considerable power and perhaps find a chance to play a key role in the divisive troubles that everyone knew lay ahead. In December 1859, while still vice president, Breckinridge was selected as Kentucky's new senator, but he was not scheduled to take office for more than a year—until after the new presidential election and inauguration.

Given the splintered condition of both the nation and the Democratic Party, when the time came for the 1860 Democratic national convention in Charleston, South Carolina, the heart of the southern opposition, there were candidates from all parts of the spectrum and much political maneuvering. Breckinridge was a serious contender for the Democratic nomination but carried the burden of a prosouthern label.

The Charleston convention was a disaster. The Deep South delegates demanded a proslavery plank in the platform and, failing to get it, walked out. The delegates remaining were divided, many preferring Stephen A. Douglas of Illinois over Breckinridge, but a final vote was not taken. On May 3, the convention voted to recess and to reconvene in Baltimore on June 18.

Between those dates, the Republicans nominated Abraham Lincoln.

At Baltimore, the Douglas faction brought in new delegates from Alabama and Louisiana to replace those who had walked out at Charleston. That provoked a second secession, and the "bolters" reconvened at the Maryland Institute, where they adopted the slave plank and, without his consent, nominated Breckinridge for president. On the same day, the original convention nominated Stephen A. Douglas.

Movements were made to get each man to withdraw in favor of the other. Douglas, from Illinois, was entirely correct in refusing, on the grounds that his northern supporters would shift to vote for Lincoln.

Breckinridge, knowing that his candidacy was a "forlorn hope" and calling it that, considered declining the nomination, which would in effect throw his support to Douglas. His reasons for deciding not to do so are hazy. William C. Davis, one of Breckinridge's biographers, credits the persuasiveness of Senator Robert Toombs of Georgia, who played on Breckinridge's, ambition and insisted that Douglas would find so little support in the South that he would withdraw on his own accord within forty days. This did not occur. John W. Forney may have touched on the truth in his remark about Breckinridge's conduct during this period: "Having taken one step, he was too proud to retract."

Election results were predictable, given the complete disintegration of the Democratic Party and the potential strength of the Republicans' alliance. Lincoln won the popular vote easily with a 400,000-vote plurality over Douglas. Breckinridge finished third, nearly a million votes behind Lincoln. Lincoln had 180 electoral votes, even though he won only 40 percent of the popular vote. Because of the peculiarities of the electoral system, Breckinridge received seventy-two electoral college votes to Douglas's twelve, even though the "Little Giant" from Illinois had greatly outpolled the Kentuckian. John Bell of Tennessee had been the candidate of the "Constitutional Union" Party, largely made up of old Whigs, Know-Nothings, and what might today be called Independents. They appeared to be living in—or wanting to return to—a dream world where the sectional issue of slavery would just go away. Bell received thirty-nine electoral votes. Breckinridge, a man who never lost an election, must have been galled that Kentucky, including his native Payette County, voted for Bell.

Though Lincoln's election caused panic in the South, it was reasonably pointed out that the Senate and the Supreme Court were Democrat in the majority and that Lincoln could not hope to carry out any radical programs. However, on December 20, South Carolina seceded from the Union.

Congress struggled with proposals to preserve the Union, including the famous Crittenden Compromise, which was rejected by the Republicans. Breckinridge looked on it as the last hope. He accused the Republicans of "rejecting everything, proposing nothing," while the Southern states seceded one by one.

In March, no longer vice president but now a senator, Breckinridge was able to take an active part in the Senate's proceedings. He urged that federal armed forces be withdrawn from seceded states "where their presence can accomplish no good, but will certainly produce incalculable mischief"

Breckinridge and the Senate struggled for compromise of the slavery problem as one Southern state after another seceded. In one speech he warned of "what I think Kentucky will do," which was to secede if all else failed. Immediately, the Republicans classified him as a potential rebel, and so did the Southerners. Both sides exaggerated his remarks to suit their own views.

After Fort Sumter was fired on, Kentucky was swept by the impractical idea of declaring itself neutral. This idea arose from the grassroots, and politicians of all parties had to reckon with it for a time, Breckinridge, too, was driven to support this position. However, events were now driving him; he no longer had control.

He returned to Washington and the Senate, where every Democrat was now suspected of treasonous inclinations.

As a war measure, Lincoln suspended the writ of *habeas corpus*. Many persons who simply disagreed with Lincoln's policies were jailed without recourse. Stories of such abuses are innumerable. Breckinridge called this "despotism" in a speech to the Senate, and he was more than correct, but the administration would not allow a wire service to telegraph the speech.

After the battle of Bull Run (also called First Manassas) in July 1861, Breckinridge was still in the Senate, a lonely figure, futilely denouncing the policies of Lincoln at a time when to express such views was considered treason. It was plain that he no longer represented the official views of Kentucky. Many of her legislators, public officials, and influential citizens had "gone South," leaving the pro-Lincoln faction to take charge. Breckinridge spent his time attacking Lincoln while ignoring the Confederacy. He was still for Kentucky neutrality, but now he had no following, and he knew it. In the Senate he said:

> We are making our record here; I, my humble one, amid the snares and aversions of nearly all who surround me, giving my votes, and uttering my utterances according to my convictions, but with few approving voices, and surrounded by scowls.

Then, Breckinridge's sixteen-year-old son Cabell ran off to Tennessee and joined the Second Kentucky Infantry, a part of the Confederate Army.

Breckinridge returned to Kentucky and made a round of speeches, but the legislature, now pro-Union, abandoned the state's official neutral stance on September 8 in favor of adherence to the Union, Arrests began immediately, including that of former Governor Morehead. The prosouthern *Louisville Courier* was suppressed. The heads of both houses of the legislature requested that Union General George Thomas arrest Breckinridge, and Thomas issued the orders. Hearing of this, Breckinridge fled to the Confederacy. Ulysses S. Grant was to say of him: "He was among the last to go over to the south, and was rather dragged into that position."

Jefferson Davis and others thought Breckinridge could help bring Kentucky into the Confederacy. Accordingly, Breckinridge was made a brigadier general and commander of the First Kentucky Brigade. As in most wars, there was a dearth both North and South of professional officers, and many political generals were appointed on both side. Some of them turned out to be natural soldiers and displayed great competence; others did not. Surprisingly, Breckinridge demonstrated undoubted ability as a general. He commanded the reserve at Shiloh and was heavily engaged; subsequently, he was promoted to major general. His attempt to capture Baton Rouge was a failure because of insufficient numbers, and from there his command was moved east and participated in the bloody battle at Murfreesboro (Stones River). Had Braxton Bragg taken Breckinridge's advice, the Confederate Army might have avoided what became a costly near-disaster. Breckinridge's brigade suffered terrible casualties at Stones River, and forever after bore the name he gave it then, the Orphan Brigade. Both his sons, Cabell and Clifton, fought in this battle.

Next, in 1863, his command contributed greatly to the Confederate victory at Chickamauga and participated in the defeat at Chattanooga, a battle during which Cabell was captured (he was later exchanged).

On February 15, 1864, Breckinridge was called to the Confederate capital and given command of the Western Department of Virginia. For a nonprofessional officer to receive command of the area that had been defended by the already immortal Stonewall Jackson was a compliment to Breckinridge's now proven military ability. In May 1864, Breckinridge's forces started north up the Shenandoah Valley, collided with Franz Siegel's much larger Union army at New Market, and, with the help of the Virginia Military Institute Corps of Cadets, routed the Union forces completely. The necessity of putting the cadets into line greatly grieved the general.

Because Grant's army was in motion toward Richmond, Breckinridge was ordered to join the opposing forces of General Robert E. Lee. In the battle of Cold Harbor, Breckinridge's horse was killed and fell on him, causing an injury that temporarily disabled him and that would plague him for years and eventually lead to his premature death. Breckinridge and his troops were ordered back to western Virginia and were later joined by General Jubal Early, to whom Breckinridge became second in command. Their combined forces moved north and without serious opposition proceeded into Maryland and within sight of the Capitol in Washington.

There followed defeats in the Shenandoah at the hands of overwhelming Union forces, with Breckinridge constantly in the thick of battle. Chided by Early for taking risks, he replied: "Well, general, there is little left for me if our cause is to fall."

Few Confederate generals fought over so great an area, from Baton Rouge in the west to the gates of Washington in the east.

On February 6, 1865, Jefferson Davis nominated Breckinridge for secretary of war. Within a month of taking office, Breckinridge found the South to be without resources to continue the war and urged "surrender as a government," opposing proposals for continuing the war as a guerilla operation. He said: "This has been a magnificent epic; in God's name let it not terminate in a farce."

On April 2, Richmond was evacuated, and the Confederate government fled south. Breckinridge made his way to Greensboro, North Carolina. Lee surrendered his army on April 9. On April 18, Breckinridge and Confederate General Joseph E. Johnston met with Union General William T. Sherman and arranged the surrender of the remaining Confederate army. Breckinridge was a wanted man and fled south through the Florida swamps. He then embarked for Cuba in a small boat.

Breckinridge remained in exile in England and Canada for four years, with side trips to Europe, the Near East, and the Holy Land. Two of his five children were sent home to school at Washington College, then presided over by General Lee and now called Washington and Lee College.

At Christmas 1868, President Andrew Johnson issued an amnesty proclamation, and the following February, Breckinridge returned home to Lexington and a warm welcome. In August, he resumed the practice of law and was besieged by offers of corporate office, thus lending his name to the enterprises. His main interest was in railroads, and he became the equivalent of executive vice president of the Elizabeth, Lexington, and Big Sandy Railroad, personally supervising its construction east from Lexington to Mt. Sterling, where progress came to an eight-year halt due to the Panic of 1873. While he was inspecting a proposed right-of-way east of Mt. Sterling, Breckinridge became ill. His health declined over the following months, and although he rallied often, his lungs filled with fluid. Surgery to relieve the pressure revealed a badly damaged liver, probably the result of his wounding at Cold Harbor. He died on May 17, 1875.

What had raised Breckinridge to high positions in life? Foremost was a charisma projected by his physical appearance. He had blue eyes and black hair, with deeply sunk eye sockets. Basil W. Duke said of Breckinridge: "Often a glance over a crowd, while he remained seated and silent, would elicit wild cheers and a tumult. . . ." Champ Clark called him "the handsomest man, the most majestic human being I ever clapped eyes on." Percy Walker, a Washington friend, agreed: "There was a wonderful magnetism about him. You felt instinctively drawn to him. Meet him where you might . . . , there was the same rare power of attraction."

His wife Mary's remark reveals a lot: "I never saw him come without being glad, or leave without being sorry."

REFERENCES

William C. Davis, *Breckinridge: Statesman, Soldier, Symbol* (Baton Rouge: Louisiana State University Press, 1974); James C. Klotter, *The Breckinridges of Kentucky, 1760–1981* (Lexington: University Press of Kentucky, 1986); Frank H. Heck, *Proud Kentuckian: John C. Breckinridge, 1821–1875* (Lexington: University Press of Kentucky, 1976); Lucille Stillwell, *John Cabell Breckinridge* (Caldwell, Idaho: Caxton Printers, Ltd., 1936); A. J. Hanna, *Flight into Oblivion* (Bloomington: Indiana University Press, 1938, reprinted 1959); Alexander Brown, *The Cabells and Their Kin* (Orig. published 1895; reprint Harrisonburg, Va.: C.J. Carrier Company, 1978).

JOHN MARSHALL PREWITT, an attorney by profession, graduated from the U.S. Naval Academy in 1944 and the University of Kentucky College of Law in 1955.

HANNIBAL HAMLIN (1809–1891)
Vice President, 1861–1865)
(President Abraham Lincoln)

HANNIBAL HAMLIN
(Library of Congress)

By H. Draper Hunt

The U.S. minister to Spain noted wryly that the Russian minister and several other guests at an 1882 Madrid diplomatic dinner stood in awe of the fact that he had once been vice president of the United States. Little did they know Hannibal Hamlin's low opinion of the "second office of the land," a post devoid of power and patronage. Yet, such is the fleeting nature of political fame that the only thing for which Hamlin is remembered even in his native state of Maine (he is virtually unknown elsewhere) is the fact that he was Abraham Lincoln's first vice president. And this was a statesman who served as a U.S. senator for twenty-five years!

Hannibal Hamlin was born on August 27, 1809, in an imposing white house overlooking the White Mountains in Paris Hill, Province of Maine. His roots lay buried deep in New England soil. His grandfather Eleazer

Hamlin, sire of seventeen children by two doubtlessly weary wives, lived in Barnstable, Massachusetts. Geographical and ancient world interests mingled to produce sons named Asia, Africa, Europe, and America, and twin sons Cyrus and Hannibal. Cyrus Hamlin, a physician, and his wife Anna Livermore settled in Paris Mill, where the doctor did some farming and served as sheriff of Oxford County. Hannibal, named after his paternal uncle, nearly died during his first winter. Tradition has an Indian princess and healer named Mollyockett traveling through driving snow to save the baby with ointments, healing herbs, and a diet of cow's milk—and Dr. Hamlin was a pediatrician!

Young Han grew up surrounded by forests, streams, and mountains and came to know them well. He grew up tall and muscular, with black hair and eyes and an extremely swarthy complexion. Educated locally, Han spent a happy year at Hebron Academy (1826–27) studying the classics, math, and history, his favorite. His formal education ended when elder brother Cyrus became ill and Hannibal returned to run the family farm. He subsequently enjoyed a brief stint clerking in a Boston fruit store and flirted with the idea of a theatrical career, but his father summoned him home; this ended his stage aspirations.

Dr. Hamlin's financial situation worsened, and his youngest son had to earn money for college. Training briefly as a surveyor in an 1827 expedition deep in the Maine woods, he then combined surveying with schoolteaching in Paris Hill. His students ran the gamut in size and deportment, some of the bigger boys threatening to toss their eighteen-year-old teacher out the window, but the brawny Hamlin sternly announced, "You will find I will be the master." He proved an effective teacher during his brief career.

College plans went glimmering when Dr. Hamlin died unexpectedly in 1829. As a precaution in case higher education proved impossible, Hannibal had begun to read law even before his father's demise. Now he pressed on with his legal studies as he ran the family farm and cared for his mother and sisters.

He also plunged into politics. Influenced by Portland's Democratic *Eastern Argus,* which he had devoured in his late teens, Hamlin became an enthusiastic Jacksonian Democrat, delivering stump speeches during the 1829 state campaign. In 1830, he scraped together enough money to purchase the *Oxford Jeffersonian,* the Jacksonian weekly of Paris Hill. Its circulation proved disappointing, and Hamlin pulled out after less than a year, intensifying his legal studies. He combined potato-hoeing with law-book reading, a colorful but impractical method. But opportunity came knocking in 1832, and Hamlin journeyed to Portland to read law with the celebrated firm of Fessenden and Deblois. A serious fellow law student was William Pitt Fessenden, General Samuel Fessenden's son and future colleague of Hamlin's in the U.S. Senate.

Sam Fessenden, Maine's premiere abolitionist, discussed slavery at length with Hamlin, but the young man rejected the abolitionist solution. He loathed human bondage but felt that this radical approach simply made matters worse. Scotching the spread of slavery because of its inhumanity and his belief that free white labor could not flourish in slave territory became Hannibal Hamlin's approach as the slavery issue encroached increasingly on his future political career.

Fortified by a year's splendid legal training, Hamlin returned to Paris Hill. Easily admitted to the Maine bar, he won his first case on the same day against famed attorney Judge Stephen Emery. On December 10, 1833, he married Sarah Jane Emery, the judge's daughter, whom he had courted for some time.

A brief sojourn in Lincoln was followed by a move to Hampden, south of Bangor, where Hamlin hung out his lawyer's shingle and served as town attorney. Four Hamlin children were born in Hampden: George, Charles, Cyrus, and Sarah Jane.

As his law practice grew gratifyingly, Hamlin's long-time interest in politics bore its first fruits. Symbolically speaking, Captain Hamlin marched into the Maine legislature in 1836 at the head of his militia company, the green-clad Hampden Rifles, because his men unofficially "nominated" him for the house of representatives. He soon crossed swords with cranky, red-faced old John Holmes of Alfred, earlier Maine's first U.S. senator, who sneered at Representative Hamlin's dark skin. The captain neatly skewered his irascible antagonist: "If the gentleman chooses to find fault with me on account of my complexion, what has he to say about himself? I take my complexion from nature; he gets his from the brandy bottle. Which is more honorable?" From then on, Hamlin was treated with respect and emerged as the leader of younger legislators. He won the house speakership in 1837 and served as speaker twice more, with skill and authority. His aplomb only deserted him once. Governor John Fairfield, the recipient of a 400-pound cheese from an admirer, gave the bulk of it to the legislature, which added cider and brown bread for a collation. Some joker spiked the cider with brandy, and Hamlin, unable to adjourn his drunken colleagues, deserted the podium in confusion.

A true Jacksonian, Hamlin favored sound currency, coin over paper. He fought unsuccessfully to abolish capital punishment in Maine "on general humane principles, and also because it does not serve as a deterrent, finally, because it is not in accordance with the great and fundamental truths of the Sacred Book." Fifty years on, the death penalty would be rescinded, with Hamlin's enthusiastic support.

Hamlin's antislavery views were thoroughly aired as a member of the house committee charged with receiving abolitionist petitions. He loathed slavery, he said, and longed for its ultimate extinction. The peculiar institution "blights all it touches. . . . It is a curse, a moral wrong." He felt it should be bottled up, prevented from spreading, but abolitionists, although wrongheaded, had every right to be heard.

In 1840, amid the hoopla of the "Tippecanoe and Tyler, Too" campaign, Hamlin ran for Congress, losing by a tiny margin to Whig Elisha Allen. A reapportionment of the Penobscot congressional district delayed the next election until 1843, when Hamlin buried Allen in an avalanche of Democratic votes. And so, by a wearying combination of stagecoach, boat, and train, Mr. Hamlin went to Washington. For some thirty-three years, Hannibal Hamlin would make Washington his second home, dwelling in boardinghouses and hotels during congressional sessions.

Hamlin's four years in the federal House proved eventful, even turbulent. He supported rescinding the "gag rule" that effectively consigned antislavery petitions to legislative oblivion, arguing that the people had a right to have petitions of every kind heard and acted upon. "Old Man Eloquent" John Quincy Adams welcomed a fresh ally in his long and lonely fight, and both New Englanders rejoiced at the final destruction of the gag rule in 1844.

Hamlin took firm Jacksonian ground on banking, denouncing "that monster institution" the Second Bank of the United States and applauding Martin Van Buren's subtreasury plan; further, he opposed protective tariffs on principle. But the Maine congressman tempered ideology with pragmatism, pushing hefty duties for such Maine products as cordwood and potatoes.

In an expansionist decade, with the cry "Manifest Destiny" ringing across the land, Hamlin urged the immediate termination of joint British–U.S. occupation of Oregon and the acquisition of as much of that rich territory as the United States could legitimately claim. He favored the annexation of Texas, too, but balked at the slavery-expansion implications of admitting a single massive slave territory. He had hoped to "secure at least half of the territory as free" and voted against the Texas annexation joint resolution because it failed to provide this.

In 1846, Hamlin made his first run for the U.S. Senate. He had political friends all over Maine but powerful and resourceful enemies, too. The latter, so-called pro-slavery Democrats, in many cases enjoyed important shipping and other economic ties to the South and loathed men like the antislavery Penobscot congressman, whom they deemed troublemakers. They defeated Hamlin by the narrowest of margins in the Maine senate.

When the Mexican War came in 1846, Hamlin supported the war effort and voted military supplies, but he bitterly resented what he deemed a southern power play to expand, slavery into fresh territory. Consequently, he vowed to rob the slave states of the "fruits of victory." An original "father" of the Wilmot Proviso barring slavery from any territory ceded by Mexico, Congressman Hamlin even introduced the proviso once when David Wilmot arrived in the House late. The proviso never became a law, but Hamlin enhanced his antislavery reputation.

Hamlin retired from Congress in 1847 but won election to the Maine house for service that same year. He offered powerful antislavery resolutions the thrust of which was that Maine stood adamantly opposed to slavery expansion because "the influence of slavery upon productive energy is like the blight of mildew; that it is a moral and social evil; that it does violence to the rights of man as a thinking, reasoning, and responsible being." All passed almost unanimously.

The following year, after the sudden, shocking death of U.S. senator John Fairfield at the hands of a medical quack, Hamlin moved with lightning speed and incredible energy to line up legislative votes for the succession. This time, he won, beginning what would be twenty-five years as a U.S. senator.

Picture a big, dark-skinned man, wreathed in smoke from his favorite cigar, sitting at his hotel-room desk surrounded by huge bags of public documents for franking to send to constituents. See him in trademark tailcoat and neck stock, without an overcoat even in frigid weather, hurrying through the streets of Washington, visiting government departments in his relentless pursuit of patronage for Mainers. Thus stood Hannibal Hamlin in the 1850s, a self-styled "working" rather than "talking" senator.

Much of his work stemmed from his prestigious chairmanship of the Committee on Commerce, involving shipping, customs and revenue, marine services, river and harbor improvements, lifesaving, and coastal survey. As a senator from a great maritime state, Hamlin was an obvious choice for this powerful, patronage-rich position.

The 1850s posed enormous challenges for Hamlin, with 1850 being a particularly trying year. Filling an interim term, he faced reelection for a full term in spring 1850. His enemies, those opposing the Wilmot Proviso and referred to variously as "Wildcats" (one of their leaders hailed from remote Aroostook County), "Mormons," and "Hunkers," had marked Maine's leading opponent of slavery expansion for political death. These "pro-slavery" legislators boycotted the Democratic legislative caucuses where Hamlin was the heavy favorite and refused to support him when the full legislature balloted. Deadlock ensued, only broken at last by timely aid from enough Free-Soil legislators to give the incumbent U.S. senator the narrowest possible victory. (One doughty Hamlinite, ill with typhoid fever, had his bed carried into the House chamber to help put his hero over the top.)

On the national scene, stormy debate over what became the Compromise of 1850 transfixed Congress. Senator Hamlin wrote to a Maine supporter:

> I shall be as glad as you or any one can be to see all vexed questions fairly settled, and that can and should be done in such a way as to preclude the extension of slavery. We have had some excitement here [i.e., Washington] but far less I apprehend than is supposed. We have disunion men here certainly, but they are few & harmless. I set them down with our abolitionists. And the disunionists of the South will destroy our Govt just about as soon as the abolitionists of the North. It is and has been all stuff, gasconade & bluster.

Hamlin bitterly opposed any comprehensive compromise package, holding out for admission of California as a free state, period. He dubbed Henry Clay's "Omnibus Bill" "a vicious log rolling scheme, which compelled one to vote for what was obnoxious to get at what he wanted." The senator from Maine voted against applying popular sovereignty (that is, allowing the people in each federal territory to decide to allow or bar slavery) to the territories of New Mexico and Utah because he believed that only the Wilmot Proviso approach would surely keep the peculiar institution from spreading.

In 1854, the Kansas-Nebraska Bill controversy convulsed the country and struck the American party system like an earthquake. Under powerful southern pressure, Senator Stephen A. Douglas of Illinois, chairman of the Senate Committee on Territories, reported a bill that, in its final form, specifically repealed the 1820 Missouri Compromise interdicting slavery in Louisiana Purchase territory north of the line 36°30′. It created two separate territories—Kansas and Nebraska—the former due west of the slave state of Missouri and presumably vulnerable to slavery expansion.

Hamlin asked:

What say the good people of Maine? Shall we repeal the Missouri Compromise line of 1820 to let it [Kansas] be made a slave country? Where will this spirit end? Shall we repeal freedom and make slavery? It comes to that.

The Maine Legislature seconded Hamlin's views by strongly condemning the Nebraska bill. The senator defied party discipline, including direct pressure from Democratic President Franklin Pierce, and voted against the bill, which passed notwithstanding.

Antislavery Whigs and Democrats deserted their parties in droves to form anti-Nebraska coalitions, which joined together to create a new free-soil organization called the Republican Party. In 1855, Maine's first Republican governor, Anson P. Morrill, pleaded with Hamlin to desert the foundering Democrats and join the Republicans, but Hamlin bided his time, hoping the party that he had served loyally since his youth would come to its senses. It did not: At its 1856 national convention in Cincinnati, the Democratic Party endorsed the Kansas-Nebraska Act and popular sovereignty.

On June 12, 1856, Hamlin took the Senate floor to resign the commerce committee chairmanship, symbolically severing his ties with his old party. Pressure mounted in Maine for him to become the Republican gubernatorial candidate, thus ensuring a huge state victory and helping elect Republican presidential nominee John C. Frémont in November. The governorship, a part-time job with a minuscule salary and a single-year term, held no charms for Hamlin, but his duty here was clear. To "sweeten the pot," a private understanding was reached that if he made the governor's race, he would be returned to the Senate in 1857.

Hamlin made ninety-nine speeches from "Kittery to Quoddy Head" and won an enormous September victory, becoming an instantaneous Republican celebrity nationwide. That same month, he married Ellen Vesta Emery, half-sister of his first wife, Sarah Jane, who had died in 1855. Young enough to be his daughter, Ellen would make him an ideal wife and the doting father of two sons, Hannibal Emery and Frank.

After less than two months in office, Governor Hamlin resigned to begin a full term as U.S. senator. During the next three years, he blistered his old party for its pro-slavery stance, especially its Kansas policy. As the presidential election of 1860 approached, Hamlin looked over the field of potential Republican nominees and ultimately rejected front-runner Senator William H. Seward of New York as unelectable. Abraham Lincoln of Illinois seemed a better choice, and so the senator told Chicago-bound Maine convention delegates, but he expected Seward to prevail.

Lincoln's surprise nomination stunned the Sewardites, who were offered the vice presidential spot as a consolation prize. They demurred but raised no objections to the nomination of Hannibal Hamlin when eager Maine delegates, sensing a golden opportunity, put his name forward. Hamlin's chief opponent, Cassius M. Clay of Kentucky, a legendary political abolitionist and formidable bowie-knife fighter, was deemed too radical by a majority of delegates. Hamlin won easily on the second ballot.

To say that Hamlin was horrified to learn of his nomination by euphoric Republicans, who stormed his Washington House room saluting him as "Mr. Vice President," would be a gross understatement. The powerless "second office of the land" seemed a one-way ticket to political oblivion to a powerful political leader like Hamlin. Farewell to influence and patronage! Later he declared that had he been at the convention, he would have declined the honor, but it was too late: He would have to run. The Republicans of his hometown of Bangor rejoiced at the Lincoln-Hamlin ticket. Some well-liquored celebrants began to fire cannon salutes, one man sacrificing his trousers for cannon-wadding until only the waistband remained. "You can fire *me* out of the cannon," he emoted, "if only it will kill the Democratic Party!"

The nomination of a prominent former Democrat from new England to balance former Whig Lincoln from Illinois made excellent sense politically, but Lincoln played no role whatever in the choice of his running mate. The two men had never even met. They corresponded during the campaign but, true to the tradition of the day, made no joint speeches or public statements. Hamlin's dark complexion became a minor issue when Southern ultras accused the perfidious "Black Republicans" of putting a mulatto on the ticket with Lincoln.

After their November victory, the president-elect summoned Hamlin to Chicago to discuss Cabinet appointments. The vice president-elect vowed to himself to do everything possible to get along well with his chief. Lincoln impressed him favorably, especially when he left the choice of the New England cabinet member to Hamlin. Working from a list the president-elect gave him, he finally designated

former Democrat Gideon Welles of Connecticut, who became secretary of the navy. Hamlin also played a key role in the intricate negotiations by which Seward assumed the secretary-of-state position, but he failed to keep Simon Cameron out of the cabinet, despite his frank advice that the appointment of the allegedly corrupt Pennsylvanian would be damaging to the Republican Party.

Hamlin's February journey to Washington for the inauguration proved eventful. In New Haven, excited Republicans literally pulled him off the back of the train, and he had to run down the track to board again. He and Mrs. Hamlin rendezvoused with the Lincolns in New York. In Baltimore, an angry mob roiled outside the train, and liquored-up rowdies, searching for Lincoln, peered into Hamlin's compartment but failed to recognize the vice president-elect.

The new vice president fulfilled his sole constitutional function of presiding over the. Senate for two-and-a-half weeks before leaving for Maine "in conformity with established usage, and with a view of affording the Senate an opportunity of choosing a President *pro tempore*. . . ." Back home, he learned of the firing on Fort Summer ten days later left for New York City, apparently to be available in case something untoward happened to President Lincoln. He itched for service. The national emergency and his own hardworking nature compelled him to action. But the vice presidency is not, by its nature, an activist office. Only the president could vest him with even a modicum of authority, and Lincoln's only request was that Vice President Hamlin inform him of troop movements in and out of New York. The vice president had returned to Maine before this message arrived. His reply foreshadows four years of frustration:

> I went to New York in the hope that I might be of some little service to you or the Gov't. I felt it my duty to contribute even a mite, if I could, for I thought I could feel something of the responsibilities you had to meet. I remained

in N.Y. two weeks, and not hearing from you in any way, I came to the conclusion there was nothing for me to do. I even began to fear my motives might be misunderstood. . . . Had I read your note before I left, I would promptly and gladly have performed that service, or any other.

Hamlin concluded by vowing loyally to *"at once* repair to N.Y. or to any place you may desire and perform as well as I can that or any other service you may require." He journeyed to New York and Washington, but it is not known what, if anything, he did for the president in either place.

The impotent vice presidency chafed and galled its Civil War incumbent. President Lincoln seemed well disposed toward Vice President Hamlin personally but, despite his legendary sensitivity and kindness, seems not to have sensed Hamlin's unhappiness and gave him no significant role to play during the war. When Jessie Benton Frémont urged the vice president to help her husband, General John C. Frémont, gain a new command in summer 1862, Hamlin replied with brutal frankness:

What can I do? The slow and unsatisfactory movements of the Government do not meet with my approbation, and that is known, and of course I am not consulted at all, nor do I think there is much disposition in any quarter to regard any counsel I may give much if at all.

Hamlin grumbled that he was the most insignificant man in Washington, neglected by president, cabinet, and Congress. When Congressman William A. Wheeler of New York came to take Hamlin to lunch, he found the vice president asleep in his chair, worn out by an interminable Senate debate. "Wheeler, I will take lunch with you on condition that you promise me you will never be vice president. I am only a fifth wheel of a coach and can do little for my friends." Ironically, Wheeler became Rutherford B. Hayes's vice president in 1877.

One suspects that most vice presidents have found their one Senate duty boring, but Hamlin could have done without the excitement of tangling with drunken Senator Willard Saulsbury of Delaware, whose bitter denunciations of Lincoln and inebriated antics on January 27, 1863, forced the vice president to place him in the custody of the sergeant-at-arms.

Patronage, the lifeblood of Hamlin the politician, was conspicuously lacking during the war years. Having no power, the vice president's pleas for jobs and other government favors could be, and often were, safely ignored. Navy Secretary Welles considered Hamlin "rapacious as a wolf" for patronage, and the former's coldness and unhelpfulness angered the man largely responsible for Welles being in the cabinet.

Vice President Hamlin wanted to make the destruction of slavery an early Union war aim. He applauded President Lincoln's Emancipation Proclamation and his decision to use black troops, but he played only a peripheral role in these landmark policy decisions and others concerning the conduct of the war. Only the removal of the president by death or Confederate capture could have brought Hamlin to power. When President Lincoln took to his bed with a mild strain of smallpox immediately after returning from Gettysburg (he joked that now he had something he could give everybody), anxious discussion of the possible succession of the vice president ensued. But Lincoln recovered quickly, and Hamlin once again became anonymous. As to assassination, Lincoln rarely worried about it. Do you think, he quipped, alluding to the vice president's radicalism on the slavery issue, that "the Richmond people would like to have Hannibal Hamlin here any better than myself? In that one alternative, I have an insurance on my life worth half the prairie land in Illinois."

The seizure of Washington by the Confederates seemed a real possibility after the Southern victory at Second Manassas in August 1862. "Should the emergency . . . arise," Hamlin wrote from Bangor in September, "[be] assured I will be ready to act at once with all the energy and efficiency I possess." Washington remained safely in Union hands.

But Hamlin would have become the seventeenth president of the United States had he won renomination at the National Union Party Convention in June 1864. (The Republicans had temporarily adopted a new label to stress their premier war aim and to woo Democratic votes). Despite the second office's many frustrations, the vice president clearly anticipated a second term to validate his wartime fidelity to Union and party and to provide a secure post for the next four years. The substitution of Andrew Johnson of Tennessee for the doughty Mainer had momentous consequences and has been a source of considerable historical controversy. Lincoln's role has been the center of contention. Did he, as he indicated to some, intend not to interfere with the vice presidential nomination? Certainly he wrote exactly that to his private secretary, John C. Nicolay: "Wish not to interfere about V.P."

But other Lincoln intimates swore he favored Johnson and asked them to work for the Tennessean behind the scenes at Baltimore. Two political realities argue powerfully for this view. First, President Lincoln feared for his own reelection in June 1864, and strengthening the ticket by replacing Hamlin with a Southern war Democrat like Johnson made excellent sense. Second, as a Lincoln supporter and delegate from New Jersey pointed out ". . so perfect was Abraham Lincoln's control of the Baltimore Convention. . . , that he need only have pointed his index finger toward the State of Maine to have had Hannibal Hamlin on that ticket." The president's secret efforts for Johnson doubtless proved decisive.

Hamlin put on a brave front in defeat but four years later voiced his anger and pain. When urged to run for the 1868 Republican vice presidential nomination, Hamlin wrote to a friend in a letter marked "For your eye only":

> One thing I can say very distinctly. My name must not be draged [sic] into the canvass to be defeated. I am sure you will concur in that. I was draged out of the Senate, against my wishes—tried to do my *whole* duty, and was then unceremoniously "whistled down the wind." While I have *never* complained to any one, I did not fail to *feel* and *know* how I was treated. I do not want my name used to such an end again.

During the war, Vice President Hamlin had frequently absented himself from Washington, engaged in such activities as, stripped to his shirtsleeves, harvesting hay and doing other chores on his Maine farm. During the summer of 1864, he served as color corporal in the Maine Coast Guards, a militia unit stationed at Fort McClary in Kittery. Corporal Hamlin stood guard for the first three nights until relieved and appointed company cook. In his biography of Hannibal Hamlin, this writer sums up his military service as follows:

> There is considerable charm and picturesqueness in Hamlin's brief tour of duty. Nothing, however, illustrates more graphically the insignificance of the Civil War vice presidency than the spectacle of its incumbent toting a musket, cooking up fish chowders, and generally playing at being a soldier for two months during one of the most critical periods of the war.

Inauguration Day, March 4, 1865, featured the most notorious vice presidential swearing-in in U.S. history. Vice President Hamlin had banished liquor from the Capitol's Senate wing, but he procured a bottle for his shaky successor, who was slowly recovering from a bout of typhoid fever and was hungover from a party the previous evening. Excitement, an overheated Senate chamber, and two stiff drinks converted the usually dignified Johnson into an inebriate with red face and waving arms, delivering a Tennessee-style stump speech to the stunned dignitaries before him. The *Bangor Jeffersonian* harrumphed:

> His whole manner and speech were the inspiration of a brain crazed by intoxicating liquors.

There was not a respectable man in that whole assemblage . . . from the President to the humblest page, who did not hang his head for shame at such conduct and on such an occasion. Every decent man in the nation feels disgraced.

A few days after the inauguration, Hamlin said goodbye to President Lincoln and headed for Maine. The *New York Herald*'s March 10, 1865, issue carried a story headed "Going Home Disgusted" in which it described the former vice president as "thoroughly disgusted with every thing and almost everyone in public life, excepting the President." Among his gripes was William Pitt Fessenden's refusal to remain in the cabinet as treasury secretary "and leave Hamlin a clean track for his place in the Senate" (Fessenden was returned to the U.S. Senate in January 1865).

Hamlin last saw Lincoln in his coffin in the crepe-hung White House East Room. President Johnson completed a process begun by his predecessor by appointing the former vice president collector of the Port of Boston. The income of the office proved somewhat disappointing, but when Hamlin resigned in 1866, he did so on a matter of principle. He deplored Andrew Johnson's Reconstruction policy, which he believed turned the former Confederate states over to unrepentant rebels and completely abandoned the freed blacks to their fate. When the House impeached, and the Senate tried, President Johnson for high crimes and misdemeanors in 1868, Hamlin made clear that had he held the Senate seat, he, unlike Fessenden, would have voted to convict.

In 1869, Hamlin defeated incumbent Senator Lot M. Morrill by a whisker. He served until 1881, eventually rising to the chairmanship of the Senate Foreign Relations Committee. Senator Hamlin got along famously with President Ulysses S. Grant but clashed with President Rutherford B. Hayes over patronage and the ending of Reconstruction. Hamlin and James G. Blaine dominated the Maine Republican Party in the 1870s, and the senator labored

for Blaine's nomination as president in both the 1876 and 1880 Republican National Conventions. In 1881, Blaine became secretary of state and engineered his political cohort's appointment as minister to Spain. Hamlin found Europe fascinating, touring cathedrals and art galleries, meeting dignitaries, and comparing the Old World with the New:

> While absent, I was in, and saw much of the different nationalities, which enabled me to form opinions of the Governments and people of Europe. And while I tried to judge fairly of all that I saw, I must say that I love our Govt and its plain republican character all the better for what I saw.

During his nine retirement years, Hamlin farmed, fished, attended Grand Army of the Republic encampments, read biographies, novels, and poetry, and enjoyed the comforts of his Bangor home. On July 4, 1891, he suffered a fatal heart attack while playing cards at Bangor's Tarratine Club, the month before his eighty-second birthday.

Hannibal Hamlin could scarcely be described as a great vice president. The office itself has no greatness in it. But during the Civil War he served his nation, his president, and his party with all the dedication and activism his painfully circumscribed role allowed. One should also not forget his significant role as a premier antiexpansionist in the 1840s and 1850s and his status as a mover and shaper of the Republican Party.

REFERENCES

H. Draper Hunt, *Hannibal Hamlin of Maine: Lincoln's First Vice-President* (Syracuse, N.Y.: Syracuse University Press, 1969); Charles Eugene Hamlin, *The Life and Times of Hannibal Hamlin* (Cambridge, Mass.: Riverside Press, Published by Subscription, 1899); Lewis Clinton Hatch, ed.-in-chief, *Maine: A History,* 3 vols. Centennial Edition (New York: The American Historical Society, 1919); Lewis C. Hatch, *A History of the Vice Presidency of the*

United States, revised and edited by Earl L. Shoup (New York: The American Historical Society, Inc., 1934).

H. DRAPER HUNT retired in 1997 as professor of history at the University of Southern Maine, where he taught since 1965. He received his A.B. degree from Harvard College and M.A. and Ph.D. degrees from Columbia University. From 1962 until 1965, he taught at Hunter College of the City University of New York. In addition to his biography of Hannibal Hamlin (above), Professor Hunt's publications include *The Blaine House: Home of Maine's Governors* (1974; rev. ed. 1994) and *Dearest Father: The Civil War Letters of Lt. Frank Dickerson, a Son of Belfast, Maine* (Unity, Maine: North Country Press, 1992).

ANDREW JOHNSON (1808–1875)

Vice President, March 4–April 15, 1865

(President Abraham Lincoln)

ANDREW JOHNSON
(Library of Congress)

By Richard Zuczek

Andrew Johnson, one of the most enigmatic figures in American nineteenth-century politics, had only a brief tenure as vice president, yet his experience dramatically illustrates two important roles of the office. In 1864, the Union Republican Party and Abraham Lincoln selected Johnson for the political advantage he could bring in the election, demonstrating the vital, if supporting, role vice presidents play in campaigns. Only months later Johnson, following the assassination of Lincoln, was thrust into the executive chair, providing an object lesson in the vice president's ultimate function. For Johnson, those few months also marked a rupture in his political career; his subsequent intransigence and short-sightedness as president eclipsed his earlier achievements and destroyed the reputation he had struggled his entire life to build.

That reputation may never be resuscitated, although historical opinion concerning Johnson—and in particular his presidency—has not remained constant. Many historians of the late nineteenth and early twentieth centuries saw a man valiantly protecting the Constitution from the radical designs of northern capitalists and ignorant blacks. Later, revisionists came along and beheld only a racist southerner, nearly traitorous in his support for former confederates and their outmoded values. The latest view lies somewhere in between, depicting an intense man of limited vision who never understood that in a society undergoing revolution, his zealous dedication to conservative principles was not only unproductive, but serf-destructive.

Both the principles and the stubborn attachment to them were rooted deep in Johnson's past. Born in 1808 in Raleigh, North Carolina, Johnson knew hard times. His father, a porter, had died in 1811, forcing Johnson's mother to support the family by weaving. Johnson never attended school but at age fourteen was apprenticed to a tailor from whom he learned the rudiments of reading and writing. Perhaps believing Raleigh too constricting and hoping to improve his standing—once before he had run off to South Carolina with his brother—Johnson sought his future in East Tennessee. He finally settled in Greeneville in 1827, where he met and married Eliza McCardle (1810–1876) and became well regarded as a skilled tailor. He prospered both personally and professionally: He had five children (Martha, Charles, Mary, Robert, and Andrew) and continued his education under the tutelage of his better-educated wife. His commanding physical presence, frank opinions, and appealing oratorical style soon made him popular in the local debating society.

Johnson was a magnet for the town's younger artisans, a man who seemed to embody the Jacksonian Democracy of the 1820s and 1830s. (That Johnson's middle name was Jackson is a myth; he had no middle name.) Before long he started to look toward local politics.

His humble roots, honest egalitarianism, strict constitutionalism, and distrust of government and the wealthy gained him enough admirers to win election as alderman in 1829 and mayor of Greeneville in 1831, but these principles also alienated many townspeople. His stoic adherence to principle caused Johnson political damage throughout his career; for instance, he was elected as a Democrat to the state legislature in 1835, 1839, and 1841 but was defeated in 1837 because he opposed—on constitutional grounds—the state aid to railroads that his constituents demanded. Among the Tennesseans who opposed his rise was William "Parsons" Brownlow, who attacked Johnson as much for his policies as for his admittedly "unaffiliated" religious stance.

Intelligent and ambitious, Johnson hoped to reproduce his local success at the national level. He won election to Congress in 1842 and served five consecutive terms until gerrymandered out of office by the Whig-controlled Tennessee legislature in 1852. In Congress, as in Tennessee, his devotion to his own narrowly defined principles won him both respect and derision. While Johnson opposed most Whig programs, including the tariff and government funding of internal improvements, he was also at odds with Democratic President James K. Polk. Johnson criticized patronage, military academies, the electoral college, and even the Smithsonian Institution. Johnson, who won praise as the defender of the "common man," saw such entities as elitist, costly, and dangerous to democracy.

Johnson's ouster from Washington in 1852 only redirected his energies. He spoiled Tennessee Whig celebrations by being elected governor in both 1853 and 1855. In 1857, when the Democrats retook control of the legislature, he returned to Washington, this time as senator.

Although the growing sectional crisis clouded the background of Johnson's rise to national prominence, it provided opportunities as well. The Tennessean seemed destined to be a major player in the national drama, for he embodied the contradictions and qualities of not only his idol Andrew Jackson but of the nation itself. A southern Democrat and slaveholder, Johnson was also a devout Unionist. A former critic of the Whigs who now saw Republicans as dangerous agitators, Senator Johnson nevertheless advocated the Homestead Bill, which would grant 160 acres of land to those willing to work it; this met with caustic opposition from southern Democrats but hearty support from Free Soilers and Republicans. Yet, while despising southerners' aristocratic pretensions and secessionist rhetoric, he was a long-time defender of states' rights and openly attacked Republicans in the wake of John Brown's raid on Harper's Ferry in 1859.

As the sectional crisis came to a head, Johnson found his values coinciding more with northern interests than southern ones. Above all else, Johnson believed in the sanctity of the Union and the Constitution. Hoping that his peculiar blend of values would merge with his ambition and Unionism, he saw himself as a compromise candidate for the Democrats in the 1860 presidential campaign—he, a man who had built a career on an unwillingness (or inability) to compromise. Realizing he lacked any real support, Johnson then backed Stephen A. Douglas, which further alienated southern Democrats; not even his last-minute support of John C. Breckinridge could repair the damage. The final break came in the winter of 1860–61, following the election of Republican Abraham Lincoln. Johnson adamantly opposed secession, worked furiously (but unsuccessfully) to keep Tennessee in the Union, and found himself allied with former enemies—Whigs like William Brownlow—against former friends. Johnson's support for Abraham Lincoln and his refusal to leave the Senate when Tennessee seceded (he was the only Southern senator who did not go out with his state) made him a hero among Republicans and Northern war Democrats.

A Tennessee Unionist, Johnson was the obvious choice for military governor when federal forces moved into central Tennessee in early 1862, but the attempt to rekindle latent Unionism and reinstate a civil government met with numerous obstacles, including Confederate forces, squabbles over authority with military commanders, and divisions within the pro-Union population. Although civil government was not restored until spring 1865, Republicans had liked what they had seen of Johnson. He had dealt severely with Confederates and sympathizers, and his no-nonsense approach to secessionists and advocacy of emancipation won wide acclaim. But many in the North overlooked other issues that would return after the war: Johnson's belief in *individual* disloyalty, rather than state disloyalty, and his overriding conviction in civil supremacy over the military.

Johnson's defiant stance toward secession and what he termed the "so-called Confederacy"—defiance would always be a character trait—made him an overwhelming choice as Lincoln's running mate in 1864. Carrying the new "Union Party" designation, Republicans hoped to attract as many war Democrats as possible, and the selection of Johnson for vice president increased their chances for bipartisan support. As the Tennessean campaigned during the election (it was rare for vice-presidential candidates to campaign, but Johnson was ever the political maverick) he became even more radical, driving home his stubborn save-the-Union-at-all-costs philosophy. He consistently pushed for emancipation in Tennessee and even admitted blacks to military service in a September militia call. Yet, other messages bothered some Republicans, especially those led by House power Thaddeus Stevens. According to Johnson, his status as a candidate from Tennessee proved his claim that secession was impossible and the states had not left the Union, an approach that would cause considerable conflict during Reconstruction.

The Union ticket of Lincoln and Johnson rode roughshod over the candidates of conservative Unionism, George B. McClellan and George Pendleton, but the November victory and Johnson's contribution to it were tainted by an embarrassing performance at the March inauguration. Exhausted from a rigorous campaign and a celebration the previous night, Johnson sought to steady himself with some whiskey; a packed Senate chamber listened in shock as the veteran stump speaker and new vice president babbled on incoherently, delivering a tirade of self-serving remarks and alienating nearly the entire Cabinet. It was not the first time Johnson had acted without careful thought to consequences, nor would it be the last.

Unfortunately for Johnson and the nation, the Tennessean would not have the opportunity to learn the intricacies and nuances of functioning at the executive level. Abraham Lincoln was assassinated a month after his second inauguration, and on April 15, 1865, Johnson took the oath of office as the seventeenth President of the United States. At first many Republicans believed that Johnson might be more to their liking than Lincoln; a brilliant war leader and politician, Lincoln nonetheless opposed many of the more radical policies favored by some in Congress. Judging by Johnson's hard-line approach during the war, Radicals hoped they had found an ally ready to punish the South and levy a severe penance. In a way, the Radicals were correct, for Johnson was not Lincoln. Impatient, tactless, and egotistical, Johnson lacked his predecessor's ability to observe, assess, and then act, ever mindful of when to conform to the political climate and when to manipulate it. But neither did Johnson understand the men who would oppose him; the choice of the Republican Party and, by implication, of the northern population, he failed to realize the debts he owed. Moreover, he held widely differing views on the Constitution, the role of government, and the status of blacks in American society.

Johnson's first weeks in office gave little indication of the storm to come. Doing his best to ease the sudden transition, the new president retained Lincoln's cabinet and permitted Mary Todd Lincoln to stay in the Executive Mansion for several weeks. He backed Secretary of War Edwin Stanton's hunt for the assassins, even posting a $100,000 reward for the capture of Jefferson Davis. Johnson then coolly sentenced the conspirators—excluding Davis but including Mary Surratt, whose complicity was questionable at best—to their deaths. Radical mirth was short-lived, however, for Johnson's policies were even more war-oriented than Lincoln's: with the war over and the assassination conspiracy exposed, the new president was eager to get on with business as usual.

But business as usual was unlikely until the South was brought back into proper alignment with the rest of the nation. Johnson understood that the southern states needed to make certain concessions before their representatives would be readmitted to Congress. With Congress in recess, Johnson was free to act on his belief that Reconstruction was an *executive* function, and he readily offered his own plan of restoration, rooted in his values as a limited-government southerner. The president appointed provisional governors to oversee the abolition of slavery, the writing of new state constitutions, the repudiation of secession and Confederate debts, and the election of new members of Congress and governors. Beyond this, Johnson required former Confederates to concede little, holding to the concept that *individuals,* and not states, commit treason. He did not require black suffrage or any economic assistance for the freed people and readily offered pardons to former Confederates who applied. In fact, few states even complied with his meager requirements; most refused to repudiate the Confederate debt, and some found clever wordings to avoid nullifying the principle of secession.

By fall 1865, with the passage of restrictive "black codes," the rise of antiblack and anti-Republican violence, and the election of former Confederates to local and national offices, Republicans in Congress decided Johnson was not the man they expected. The South did not appear penitent or remorseful, yet the president seemed unconcerned and even pleased. Battle lines were drawn in December 1865, when Congress, invoking its prerogative, refused to seat the newly elected members of Congress from the former Confederate states. This rejection and the subsequent formation of the Joint Committee on Reconstruction underscored the fundamental difference between the executive and the legislature. Johnson believed that the states held direction over their citizens and that it was the president's responsibility to protect states in their rights. Congress, on the other hand, was wallowing in the extension of federal power that grew out of the Civil War and fully intended that it determine the nature of a state's society.

Because Johnson was unwilling to push for real change in the South, Congress in 1866 attempted to provide the protection for former slaves that the South and the president would not. Through the Freedmen's Bureau Act, the Civil Rights Act, and the Fourteenth Amendment, Republicans hoped to protect blacks in their civil rights, limit southern power in Congress, and bolster the new southern Republican party. To Johnson these measures were unconstitutional infringements on states' rights and the fundamental precepts of American federalism, especially considering that Congress was making laws for states that were not represented! The president vetoed each bill—Congress overrode each veto—and actively campaigned against the ratification of the Fourteenth Amendment. His antagonistic veto messages and belligerent attitude toward Congress drove moderates into the radical camp, further fueling Johnson's own persecution complex.

As had happened before, Johnson's rigid adherence to principle would cost him dearly. His support for emancipation was a war measure, and he had no intention of granting black suffrage or, worse yet, allowing the federal government to impose it. But Johnson's conservative constitutionalism placed him firmly in the South's camp, which alienated him from his base of support in the North. Politically obtuse at times, Johnson could not see that he was binding his future to that of an impoverished, politically bankrupt region that was clutching at the last vestiges of a dying lifestyle. His callousness in the face of southern violence—in particular the New Orleans Riot in July 1866—and his formation of a new party for the fall congressional elections only increased the distance between himself and northern voters. Adding insult to injury was the debacle of his "Swing around the Circle," a speaking tour from New York to the Midwest that demonstrated just how out of touch he had become. The elections hammered the point home, as Republicans took control of two-thirds of each house, assuring them of a free hand in administering their own Reconstruction program. Despite the warning signals, Johnson not only stayed his course but took the offensive; he tinkered with the idea of replacing radical Secretary Of War Stanton with General William T. Sherman, and delivered an annual message critical of Congress and its unconstitutional measures.

Congress responded by embarking on its own plan of Reconstruction. Bolstered by Republican successes at the polls, Congress in the spring of 1867 passed two military reconstruction acts that provided the blueprint for new governments in the South. Under the watchful eye of the army, new elections would be held, but without a white monopoly; blacks and whites would elect new governments, select new national officials, and write new state constitutions. Congress also planted the seed of Johnson's demise with the Tenure of Office Act (designed to prevent the president from removing Republican officeholders) and curtailed his authority by requiring that all orders to the army pass through General of the Army Ulysses S. Grant.

Johnson's reaction was immediate and hostile. Although Congress easily overrode his vetoes, the president found other ways to hamper what he believed were unconstitutional measures that illegally punished some people while dangerously elevating others. He encouraged opposition to the laws in communications to southerners, nurtured opposition in the North, and removed military commanders who he felt had transgressed against civil supremacy.

His recall of commanders Philip Sheridan, Daniel Sickles, and later John Pope angered Radicals and worried Grant, who had been supporting them in their liberal approach to Congress's rulings. Congress matched the president move for move, and in summer 1868 the House Judiciary Committee held impeachment hearings but was unable to produce evidence of any criminal wrongdoing.

The final break with Congress came over the suspension of Secretary of War Stanton. For two years the president and the secretary had been at odds, yet Johnson had vacillated and procrastinated about Stanton's future despite his duplicitous actions and obvious complicity with Radical generals and congressmen. In late summer, during the congressional recess, Johnson suspended Stanton and appointed Grant Secretary of War *ad interim,* but Johnson's few victories—the purchase of Alaska from Russia and the Democratic resurgence in northern states in the fall elections, for instance—could not shield him from Republican wrath. Had Johnson moved more decisively earlier, he might have been spared impeachment, but now Republicans were armed with the Tenure of Office Act. The House Judiciary Committee decided in favor of impeachment in late November, and while the House as a whole rejected impeachment in December, the Senate in January 1868 voted not to concur with the president's suspension of Stanton. Continuing to side with Congress over the president, Grant vacated the position, happy to avoid being crushed between the two warring branches of government.

Johnson, not without Congress's help, had worked himself into a corner with the Senate, General Grant, and Stanton allied against him. When Stanton resumed his old post (and barricaded himself in his office), Johnson formally removed him and appointed General Lorenzo Thomas interim secretary. Johnson's first choice, William T. Sherman, had succeeded in refusing his commander in chief; like Grant, another powerful potential ally had slipped through Johnson's fingers. Johnson's removal of Stanton

only exacerbated the situation. Thomas was unable to take possession of the secretary's office, and Stanton's removal (as opposed to a suspension) convinced the House to vote in favor of impeachment on February 24. The same day, Johnson nominated Hugh Ewing, Sr., to take over the War Department (instead of the inept Thomas), but new affairs took precedence.

On March 30, the galleries were packed as the Senate, with Chief Justice Salmon P. Chase presiding, convened to decide whether the president was indeed guilty of "high crimes and misdemeanors." Benjamin Butler, Thaddeus Stevens, and the other five prosecutors attempted to prove that Johnson had violated both the Tenure of Office Act and the Army Appropriations Act of 1867 and had failed to execute the laws of Congress. The five defense counsels had their hands full, not only refuting Republican charges but keeping Johnson as inactive as possible (he did not even appear at the trial), trying to avert some other blunder that might antagonize Republican fence-sitters. While Johnson was convinced that the trial would vindicate his policy, his chief counsels, Attorney General Henry Stanbery (who resigned to defend Johnson) and noted attorney William Evarts, created a defense based on the legal details of the charges, deliberately avoiding the controversial larger issues of Reconstruction.

Arguments closed nearly a month and a half later, and on May 16, senators began to vote on the individual articles of impeachment. They began with Article 11, the refusal to faithfully execute the laws and found Johnson guilty by a vote of 35 to 19, one vote shy of the two-thirds required for conviction. Ten days later two more articles followed the same pattern. Sensing it was over, Republicans conceded, and the Senate adjourned without voting on the other charges.

Although Johnson attributed his acquittal to the righteousness of his course, other factors were at work. His counsels ably dismantled the prosecution's central charges, those involving the Tenure of Office Act, by showing that it covered officials only during the term of the president under which they were originally appointed. Thus, it was irrelevant here because while Stanton had been appointed under Lincoln, Johnson was now president. Timing also helped Johnson's cause; with his term nearly over and most southern states already readmitted, there was little left to win. Facing such meager rewards at best, many Republicans would rather stick with Johnson than turn the executive chair over to Benjamin Wade, president of the Senate. Since there was no vice president, Wade would succeed if Johnson were convicted, and his rabidly Radical politics were too controversial for many Republicans, who also feared he might complicate matters for the chosen successor, Ulysses S. Grant.

Historians like to believe there was also an element of "constitutional caution" at work, some last-minute fail-safe that stopped the wheels of party politics, and forced senators to consider the significance of their actions. Never before or since has American government come so close to disintegration, so near to setting a disturbing, irrevocable precedent. Just as secession struck at the heart of democratic politics in general, impeachment struck at the heart of democratic government. The trial of Andrew Johnson demonstrated some admirable qualities of American politics: determination, loyalty, perseverance, adherence to principle. Unfortunately both sides lost sight of principles in the face of personalities and paranoia, nearly doing irreparable damage to the structure each intended to protect.

Although the final ten months of Johnson's presidency were relatively uneventful, Johnson still behaved with characteristic intransigence. He trusted to the end that he would receive the Democratic nomination for president (he did not) and in his last annual message reiterated his opposition to the Reconstruction Acts. Always a proponent of his own lost cause, Johnson even sought political office after he returned to East Tennessee in 1869, but as had happened in the past, Johnson fell between party stools:

he remained a Republican enemy, while Democrats clearly remembered his defection during the Civil War. Not until 1874 did his political horizons brighten, when he was elected to the U.S. Senate—the only former president to earn this distinction. The years had not mellowed the man or his temperament, and in a special March 1875 session he attacked President Grant for his support of Reconstruction governments in Louisiana. His return to the national arena was short-lived: On a visit to Greeneville he suffered a stroke and died two days later on July 31, 1875.

Historians will continue to debate Johnson's policies and his legacy. Rather than condemning or justifying him, scholars should be content to try to understand him, a man trapped within his principles, unable to see beyond the past and into the future. Johnson had risen to prominence by challenging conservative views during the Jacksonian period, yet could not see how during the Union crisis, new times again required new thinking. His racism, constitutional conservatism, and shortsightedness were common among whites of the time, but many came to realize that the Civil War had forever altered the country: Revolutionary times required revolutionary thinking. To Johnson, liberty could only be protected if people served the Constitution, rather than vice versa. That the Constitution was a "living" document, capable of growing and changing with the nation, escaped him. To be sure, his administration exacerbated the trauma of the period and damaged the presidency as both an institution and a symbol. Ironically, however, his obstinacy also unified the North and the Republican Party and forced his opponents to tear down the Constitution he so revered and erect a greater one in its place.

REFERENCES

Michael Les Benedict, *The Impeachment and Trial of Andrew Johnson* (New York: W.W. Norton and Co., 1973); *The Papers of Andrew Johnson,* Paul H. Bergeron, LeRoy P. Graf, and Ralph Haskins, eds.

(Knoxville: University of Tennessee Press, 1967–2000); Albert Castel, *The Presidency of Andrew Johnson* (Lawrence, Kans.: Regents Press of Kansas, 1979); Glenna R. Schroeder-Lein and Richard Zuczek, *Andrew Johnson: A Biographical Companion* (ABC-Clio, 2001); Richard B. McCaslin, *Andrew Johnson: A Bibliography* (Westport, Conn.: Greenwood Press, 1992); Eric McKitrick, *Andrew Johnson and Reconstruction* (Chicago, Ill.: University of Chicago Press, 1960); Hans Trefousse, *Andrew Johnson: A Biography* (New York: W.W. Norton and Co., 1989).

RICHARD ZUCZEK, an associate professor at the U.S. Coast Guard Academy, teaches American history, European history, and various military studies courses. He is the author of *State of Rebellion: South Carolina during Reconstruction* (University of South Carolina Press, 1996) and coauthor of *Andrew Johnson: A Biographical Companion* (ABC-CLIO, 2000). He is editor of the two-volume *Greenwood Encyclopedia of the Reconstruction Era* (Greenwood Press, 2006). For the Coast Guard and Department of Homeland Security, he has written and given presentations on such topics as military organizations in transition, the history of American military strategy and policy, and technology and war. He also previously worked on the Johnson papers at the University of Tennessee.

SCHUYLER COLFAX (1823–1885)

Vice-President, 1869–1873

(President Ulysses S. Grant)

SCHUYLER COLFAX
(Library of Congress)

By Patrick J. Furlong and Ann Leonard

Schuyler Colfax, though always associated with Indiana, was born in New York City on March 23, 1823. He was named for his father, who had died of tuberculosis six months earlier. Hannah Stryker Colfax, a widow at seventeen, struggled to support and educate her son. Schuyler Colfax was born into very modest circumstances, but earlier members of the family had distinguished themselves: His paternal grandfather was General William Colfax, who had served as commander of George Washington's Life Guard during the Revolutionary War, and his maternal grandmother, Hester Schuyler, was a cousin of General Philip Schuyler, whose name passed into the Colfax family.

Hannah Colfax lived with her mother and provided for her fatherless son until he reached the age of ten, when her resources were exhausted. Schuyler then went to work clerking in a store to help support his mother. On November 6, 1834, Hannah Colfax married George Matthews of Baltimore. Matthews was only fourteen years older than his stepson, and the two developed a lifelong attachment. Two years later, the family moved to the newly settled village of New Carlisle, Indiana, where Schuyler clerked in his stepfather's general store. In 1841, Matthews was elected auditor of St. Joseph County on the Whig ticket and the family moved to the county seat, South Bend. Matthews appointed his stepson deputy auditor, although Colfax was not yet of legal age when he began his public career. He remained deputy auditor until 1849, but the position was not time consuming.

From 1842 to 1844, Colfax served as assistant enrolling clerk of the Indiana senate. During this period he also studied law intermittently but never qualified as a lawyer. Colfax idolized Henry Clay, and he campaigned for him in the presidential election of 1844, addressing crowds in New York City as well as Indiana. On October 10, 1844, he married his childhood sweetheart, Evelyn Clark of Argyle, New York. From all accounts they had a happy marriage, though Evelyn Colfax suffered from ill health and was a semiinvalid for years until her death on July 10, 1863.

Religion was an important influence on Colfax from his earliest years, and his humanitarian principles of equality for all and his passion for justice grew out of Christian precepts and early training. He began and ended his life as a member of the Dutch Reformed Church, and though sincere, he was not doctrinaire. For a short time, he was a Presbyterian until expelled from that church for driving his horses on Sunday to an Episcopalian wedding. He spoke frequently on the evil of strong drink and encouraged establishment of a total abstinence society in South Bend.

Colfax began to contribute articles to local newspapers when he was only sixteen, and within a few years became a frequent contributor to Horace Greeley's *New York Tribune*, one of the nation's leading Whig newspapers. While working for the state senate he serve also as legislative correspondent for the *Indiana State Journal*, the state's leading Whig newspaper. In 1845, at the age of twenty-two, he was able to secure enough money to purchase a half-interest in a struggling South Bend weekly, which he soon renamed the *St. Joseph Valley Register*. Its circulation was only 250 copies, and it required several years of hard work for Colfax to increase its average weekly sale to 1,000 and to repay the money he had borrowed to buy the newspaper.

The *Register* was a good example of a smalltown midwestern newspaper. It offered the usual selection of European and national news, heavily political of course, with a variety of fiction and human interest stories. Local news, except for politics, received little attention, for word-of-mouth was much faster than a weekly newspaper. Colfax energetically supported development of the St. Joseph Valley, praising the fertility of its soil, the healthy nature of its climate, and the industrial advantages of its streams. He was a vigorous advocate of railroad construction and frequently published long descriptions of his eastern travels by steamboat and railroad. Colfax continued as editor of the *Register* until 1864, with a deputy in South Bend while he attended congressional sessions. From Washington he sent regular reports of the debates in Congress and the social life of the nation's capital.

Politics continued to absorb Colfax's interests outside of journalism. In 1848, he was chosen as a delegate to the national Whig convention. He favored General Winfield Scott, but when General Zachary Taylor won the nomination Colfax worked energetically for his election. He voted with the majority to endorse the Wilmot Proviso, which prohibited the extension of slavery into the western lands acquired after the Mexican War.

Colfax often took time from his editorial duties to attend political gatherings. He was a leading Whig delegate to the Indiana Constitutional Convention in 1850. The Whig minority won few motions, but Colfax argued eloquently against the article that prohibited further black immigration into the state. He favored exempting debtors' homes from seizure for payment of debts and supported the majority in limiting the legislature's power to borrow. Much of the credit for an improved banking system in Indiana goes to Colfax and his ability to encourage compromise among the members of the convention.

Though liberal in his views regarding blacks, Colfax showed himself rigidly opposed to measures intended to protect the property of married women, widows, and orphans. This stand with respect to women is somewhat curious when Colfax is credited with being the leading spirit in the establishment of the Degree of Rebekah, the ladies' auxiliary to the Independent Order of Odd Fellows. In 1850, he was appointed chairman of a committee to consider accepting women, and he wrote the minority report favoring the proposition. When the proposal was accepted by the membership a year later, Colfax drafted the articles of incorporation for the Rebekah.

Slavery was never far from the public and private conscience of Colfax. Colfax disliked slavery on moral principle and opposed its expansion, without moving as far as favoring outright abolition. Henry Clay was his political idol, but he regarded the fugitive slave provisions of the Compromise of 1850 as "unnecessarily harsh and summary." On the other hand, Colfax did not believe that Congress possessed the power to abolish slavery in the District of Columbia without the consent of its residents.

Colfax's political views were firmly Whig, in favor of high protective tariffs and internal improvements. In 1847, he served as secretary of the Rivers and Harbors Convention in Chicago. This was the beginning of his association with a young Whig from Illinois, Abraham Lincoln, who made a stirring impromptu speech at the convention.

Colfax ran unsuccessfully for Congress on the Whig ticket in 1851. The next year at the party's national convention he helped to secure General Winfield Scott's nomination. Colfax declined the Whig nomination for Congress in 1852, but when the party broke apart on the slavery question two years later, he played a significant role in the organization of the new Republican Party in Indiana. He was nominated for Congress in 1854 and elected in a vigorous campaign across a sprawling district in northern Indiana. In 1855, Colfax attended a national convention of the Know-Nothing Party, a serious mistake on his part. When accused afterward of being a Know-Nothing himself, he pretended that he had attended only as a newspaper reporter.

As a member of Congress, Colfax was soon embroiled in the Kansas-Nebraska controversy. He denounced Stephen A. Douglas's scheme to allow settlers in the newly organized Kansas Territory to vote on the admission of slavery to an area long closed to slavery by the Missouri Compromise of 1820. Colfax's stirring denunciation of the oppressive Kansas slave code, delivered in the House on June 21, 1856, greatly advanced his reputation as an orator. More than a million copies of his speech were circulated in pamphlet form by the Republican Party.

In 1858, Colfax was appointed chairman of the Post Office Committee, and he performed his most significant work in Congress in this capacity. He reorganized the postal service and reformed gross abuses, while consolidating routes and extending daily overland mail service to California. He shepherded bills through Congress that greatly improved mail service to the Western mining regions and provided for both the return of undelivered mail and the delivery of articles in addition to letters. During the Civil War, Colfax was responsible for the establishment of the system that made recipients of mail from soldiers and sailors liable for postage.

During the Illinois senatorial election of 1858, Colfax gave Lincoln lukewarm support and met with Douglas on more than one occasion to discuss the latter's break with President James Buchanan over the troubles in Kansas. Colfax did not take an active role in the

Republican convention of 1860, aside from his efforts to encourage the candidacy of the conservative former Whig Edward Bates of Missouri. Once Lincoln received the Republican nomination, Colfax campaigned enthusiastically for him, speaking in Illinois, Iowa, Missouri, and Michigan.

With Lincoln's victory and his own reelection, Colfax and his friends besieged the new president for a cabinet position, preferably postmaster general. Lincoln's political managers had promised the job to someone else, and the popular Colfax was passed over. Colfax faithfully supported Lincoln's war policies, except when Lincoln removed General John C. Frémont from command in Missouri because of his imprudent proclamation freeing the slaves. He said that Frémont "was like a man asked to make bricks without straw." Colfax urged the president to issue an early emancipation proclamation and even detailed the most effective methods of releasing the news to the Northern press.

Colfax and Lincoln attended many social events together, especially theater outings. Years later Colfax recalled that he and Lincoln "often went to Ford's opera house" to relieve the strains of the war. They found pleasure and relaxation watching "those southern girls with their well rounded forms, lustrous hair and sparkling voices," dancing and singing. One night in January 1863, soon after the release of the Emancipation Proclamation, a very dangerous situation developed outside Grover's Theater when an angry crowd surrounded the carriage carrying Colfax and the Lincolns as their coachman lay drunk on the sidewalk. The guards had left the president unattended, and the theater owner grabbed the reins and rescued them. It was Colfax who persuaded the president to attend the Baltimore Sanitary Fair on April 18, 1864, and he acted as host when Lincoln delivered his moving address on liberty.

In later years Colfax noted that two of the most important days of his life were concerned with Abraham Lincoln. He regarded February 1, 1865, the day he signed the House resolution for the Thirteenth Amendment outlawing slavery, as the happiest day of his life. As fate would have it, Colfax was the last public figure to shake Lincoln's hand the night he was assassinated. The two men met that morning to discuss the collapse of the rebellion and Lincoln's plans for Reconstruction. Colfax intended to leave early the next morning for the Pacific coast, and Lincoln gave him a personal message to deliver to the western miners. Colfax declined the president's invitation for the theater that evening but returned to the White House for a promised half-hour visit. He walked the president to the door when it was time for the Lincolns to leave for Ford's Theatre and said his farewell there. Colfax was summoned to Lincoln's deathbed and traveled to Springfield on the solemn funeral train.

The Republican majority chose Colfax as Speaker of the House on December 5, 1863, and reelected him in 1865 and 1867. As Speaker, Colfax was very popular, and though strongly partisan, he was not personally harsh to the Democratic minority. He preferred to use courtesy, tact, and his considerable parliamentary knowledge to guide his rulings. Thaddeus Stevens of Pennsylvania was the dominating figure in the House, and Colfax collaborated with him regularly, both because of Steven's power and because they shared many of the same ideas. Colfax was severely criticized, however, when he left the chair on April 8, 1864, and introduced a resolution to expel Representative Alexander Long of Ohio on the charge that "he had given aid, countenance and encouragement to the enemy." Colfax had to accept a modification of his resolution, and Long was censured rather than expelled.

Originally favorable to President Andrew Johnson, Colfax lost confidence in him when the president appeared to favor former Confederate officers. Johnson took charge of the process of Reconstruction himself, rather than calling a special session of Congress to deal with the defeated South. Soon after Congress convened in November 1865, Colfax made an important speech on Reconstruction policy in which he asserted the constitutional right of the Congress to judge its members' qualifications. He also insisted that Congress would add its own requirements to those of President Johnson for restoration of the southern states. His speech received wide publicity and gave notice to the southerners that their newly elected representatives would not be seated.

Colfax also contended that a clear majority of the people of a state must give evidence of their loyalty before that state could be fully restored to the Union, that blacks as well as whites needed to be protected in their persons and property, and that the Declaration of Independence must be recognized as the law of the land. "Let us make haste slowly," was the dominant theme of this speech which ended with the hope that the executive and legislative departments would "cordially cooperate."

Colfax was again elected Speaker in December 1865, and the newly elected members from the seceded states were indeed refused their seats. When Thaddeus Stevens carried his motion to create a Joint Committee on Reconstruction, the speaker named nine Radicals to represent the House, including Stevens. Colfax also appointed Stevens as chairman of the newly created Committee on Appropriations, and another Radical, Justin S. Morrill of Vermont, as chairman of the important Ways and Means Committee.

For the next few months, Colfax tried to avoid a public split with President Johnson. Reports of southern whites working defiantly against the rights of newly freed slaves inflamed Colfax's prejudice against southerners and hardened his resolve to solidify the Union victory that had cost the lives of so many. The president's belligerence and lack of tact made powerful enemies in Congress. Colfax helped overturn Johnson's veto of the Freedman's Bureau Bill, and the break between the legislative and executive branches became complete by April 1866. Later in the session, the Joint Committee on Reconstruction reported pro-posals that eventually became the Fourteenth Amendment.

As a candidate for reelection in the fall of 1866, Colfax vigorously defended both Radical Reconstruction and the Fourteenth Amendment, while his Democratic rival appealed to the tradition of white supremacy. Back in Washington, Colfax again set the tone for the new session with a speech on December 31, 1866. He paved the way for more Radical legislation, including bills to enfranchise the blacks in the District of Columbia and to extend black suffrage to the territories. Naturally Colfax supported the drastic Reconstruction Act passed over a presidential veto in March 1867. That same day Congress passed the Tenure of Office Act over another presidential veto.

Two days later the Thirty-ninth Congress adjourned with a resolution of thanks to the Speaker and then immediately convened as the Fortieth Congress, the only time Congress, rather than the president, called a session. Elected Speaker for a third term, Colfax within the same hour gave both a valedictory and an inaugural address. President Johnson played into the hands of the radicals when he asked for Secretary of War Edwin M. Stanton's resignation on August 5, 1867, and then suspended him a week later because he refused to resign. There was already talk of removing the president, and in November the judiciary committee unsuccessfully recommended impeachment. Colfax urged Stanton to defy the president and continue in office.

When Thad Stevens moved for impeachment in February 1868, Colfax directed the clerk to call his name so that he too could vote for impeachment, although as Speaker he did not usually vote except in cases of a tie. Colfax allowed himself to be drawn into the hectic confrontation and privately urged the president's conviction and removal. The law of presidential succession then in force provided that when the vice presidency was vacant, the Senate president pro temp ranked before the Speaker of the House. Thus Senator Benjamin F. Wade would have become president had Johnson been removed, not Colfax, although the Speaker was more widely respected and trusted. Colfax was rather surprised when the Senate failed to convict the president.

The 1868 presidential campaign began before the impeachment trial ended, but it was already clear that General U.S. Grant would lead the Republican ticket. There was no clear favorite for the vice presidential nomination. When Colfax's name was placed in nomination, he knew that his strongest competitor would be Senator Wade. The Republican convention in Chicago required six ballots to decide that Colfax would be the party's choice for vice president. Republican newspapers portrayed him as reliable and experienced, and he was well known for his many speeches in support of Republican candidates. Democrats remonstrated with Colfax for his earlier connection with the antiforeign and anti-Catholic Know-Nothings, and he in turn waved the bloody shirt and reminded voters that disloyal Democrats were the ones responsible for the deaths of thousands of Union soldiers. Colfax spoke often during the campaign throughout the Midwest, while Grant remained quietly in Washington.

Senator Carl Schurz described with painful accuracy the general Republican view of Grant's running mate:

> Colfax is a very popular man and on that account a strong candidate. His abilities are not distinguished but are just sufficient to make him acceptable to the masses. They are fond of a happy mediocrity.

The genial "Smiler" Colfax, as he was known in Washington, had few illusions and knew well that his active political career was ending as he became vice president on March 4, 1869. An Indianapolis newspaper quoted an unnamed friend who spoke of "the dignified impotence of his present office," an apt description of the vice presidency during the Gilded Age. With his long experience as Speaker of the House, Colfax presided over the Senate effectively and with great dignity, but he was never

part of the Republican leadership in Congress, and as vice president he was not invited to the party caucus. Colfax did remain active as a party orator, appearing often to speak in favor of Republican candidates, lecturing for Odd Fellow lodges and church groups and still turning down hundreds of speaking invitations each year of his vice presidency.

Impossible to satisfy were the hundreds of deserving Republicans who sought his help in securing government jobs. The vice president had no positions to fill on his own and little influence at the White House. So far as possible, Colfax recommend deserving Hoosiers for federal appointments.

Always of cheerful disposition, Colfax had long enjoyed Washington society, and his receptions as Speaker and vice president were always crowded, although he never served wine or liquor. Shortly after the 1868 election, the widowed Colfax married Ellen Wade, a niece of his convention rival, Ben Wade. His first marriage had been childless, but with the birth of Schuyler Colfax, Jr., two years later, the vice president became a doting father.

As editor and then as a member of Congress, Colfax supported internal improvements, particularly railroads. His western tour in 1865, which he often described in his lectures, enhanced his interest in railroad projects. Two years later he traveled to California on the newly completed Pacific railroad, delivered several speeches, and toured Yosemite and other scenic locations. In 1871, he was invited by Jay Cooke, the leading banker of Philadelphia, to participate in the Northern Pacific Railroad—Colfax replied that he was indeed interested in finding some such position when his term expired. To his surprise, Cooke immediately offered him employment as the railroad's chief lobbyist in Washington, if such a position would not conflict with the vice presidency. Cooke assured Colfax that the Northern Pacific did not seek federal funds or favor. The vice president wisely declined the offer, although he was indeed in financial need because the cost of housing and official entertaining in Washington exceeded his salary.

No vice president had been elected to a second term since 1828, and Colfax spoke often of retiring to private life when his term ended in 1873. He never enjoyed comfortable relations with President Grant, although he vigorously defended the administration against the growing talk of scandal. Their differences were clearly personal rather than political, and although their relationship became strained, both Grant and Colfax avoided public disagreement. "I *do* love the party and its unity, far, far more than any selfish advancement . . . ," Colfax assured a friend. In 1871, Grant asked Colfax to consider resigning from the vice presidency and accepting appointment as secretary of state, but he declined and later joined with Republican senators to persuade Hamilton Fish to remain at the State Department.

For reasons never explained even in his private correspondence, Colfax changed his mind early in 1872 and sought renomination for a second term. Senator Henry Wilson had already won wide support among the Republican convention delegates, and Colfax struggled to make up for lost time. He lost to Wilson on the first ballot by a margin of 364½ to 321½, defeated but certainly not disgraced.

In the 1872 campaign Colfax loyally supported the Republican ticket of Grant and Wilson, although he did not speak as widely as usual, but instead of a graceful descent into retirement, the lame-duck session brought bitter controversy and accusations of corruption. Colfax, Wilson, and other prominent Republicans were accused of accepting bribes from the Crédit Mobilier, a construction company secretly owned by the directors of the Union Pacific Railroad. Oakes Ames, a Republican representative from Massachusetts and director of the Union Pacific, revealed that he had paid generous bribes to win political favors for the railroad.

Vice President Colfax first denied that he had received anything from Ames but was soon forced to concede that in 1868 he had briefly accepted shares in the Crédit Mobilier. As soon as he realized that the Crédit Mobilier might become controversial, Colfax said, he had returned the stock and forfeited his $500 down payment. Investigating committees discovered a deposit in Colfax's bank account that matched the amount of a payment Ames claimed to have made, and there was also a mysterious check payable to "S. C." that Colfax swore he had never seen. He desperately explained that the money he deposited came from an anonymous campaign contribution and the sale of the family piano, but nothing he could say ever cleared his reputation of the shadows of corruption.

When the Poland Committee in the House heard Ames's confusing account of bribes offered and received, Vice President Colfax voluntarily appeared to defend himself against every particular. He denied each of the accusations and then personally cross-examined his accuser. In his own sworn testimony, Colfax insisted: "I never did receive a dollar . . . no one ever gave, or offered to give me, any shares of stock in the Crédit Mobilier, or the Union Pacific Railroad." Still, Colfax had to admit that Ames had proffered Crédit Mobilier shares and that he had initially accepted the offer. Neither court nor congressional committee ever passed judgment on Colfax, and his fate was left to public opinion.

At the end of his term in March 1873, Colfax returned home to South Bend, where he was greeted by a cheering crowd. He was then only fifty years of age, despite his long service in Congress, and for the rest of his life he made his living as a public lecturer, earning far more than his vice presidential salary. He generally avoided politics, speaking most often about his western travels or his memories of Abraham Lincoln. Colfax died of a heart attack on January 13, 1885, at the railroad depot in Mankato, Minnesota, waiting for the train to take him to his next speaking engagement.

Although he presided over House and Senate for ten years during a tumultuous period in American politics, Schuyler Colfax was never among the leaders of the Republican Party. A faithful supporter of radical Reconstruction, Colfax played no role in shaping his party's policy. Easygoing, eloquent, and generous, "Smiler" Colfax fully satisfied his party's expectations: he was a competent presiding officer who upheld Republican principles as defined by the party leaders, as well as a stirring orator willing to travel great distances to speak in support of Republican candidates. Except for the Crédit Mobilier scandal during the final months of his political career, Colfax was always regarded as unusually honest for a political figure of his era. It was the great misfortune in the life of a former newspaper editor that his one political lapse, whether of memory or judgment, appeared prominently in every newspaper in the country. Colfax never blamed anyone but the lying Oakes Ames for his misfortune. He denied participation in the Crédit Mobilier affair as long as he lived, but he could never escape the suspicion of guilt. The public remembered nothing else of his term as vice president.

References

Willard H. Smith, *Schuyler Colfax: The Changing Fortunes of a Political Idol* (Indianapolis: Indiana Historical Bureau, 1952); O.J. Hollister, *Life of Schuyler Colfax* (New York: Funk & Wagnalls, 1886, republished by Gardeners Books, 2007); W. Allan Wilbur, "The Crédit Mobilier Scandal, 1873," in *Congress Investigates: A Documented History, 1792–1974,* ed. by Arthur M. Schlesinger, Jr., and Roger Bruns (New York: Chelsea House, 1975).

PATRICK J. FURLONG is retired as professor of history at Indiana University–South Bend. He has long studied the American Congress as well as Indiana history and politics. He is the author of *Indiana: An Illustrated History* (Windsor Publications, 1985), as well as articles in historical journals such as the *William and Mary Quarterly.*

ANN LEONARD is a graduate of Saint Mary's College in Notre Dame, Indiana. She wrote the entry on Sister Mary Frances de Sales Monholland in *Women Building Chicago, 1790–1990: A Biographical Dictionary* (Indiana University Press, 2001) and has published several historical articles in the *Lincoln Herald,* including "Red Rover, the Civil War, and the Nuns" (1991), "Smiler Colfax and President Lincoln" (1995), and "Catholic Sisters and Nursing in the Civil War" (2000). She wrote business histories for the Northern Indiana Center for History and a weekly column for the *South Bend Tribune.*

HENRY WILSON (1812–1875)

Vice President, 1873–1875

(President Ulysses S. Grant)

HENRY WILSON
(Library of Congress)

By Richard H. Abbott

Henry Wilson, the son of Winthrop Colbath, Jr., and Abigail Witham Colbath, was born on February 16, 1812, near Farmington, New Hampshire, and christened Jeremiah Jones Colbath. His mother quickly bore four more sons, and her husband, an unskilled laborer who was indolent and often drunk, proved unable to provide an adequate living for his growing family. Jeremiah later recalled that "want" sat by his cradle. When he reached the age of ten, his father apprenticed him to a local farmer, for whom the young man worked for the next eleven years. On his twenty-first birthday young Colbath, apparently hoping to escape both a dismal future and a humiliating past, changed his name to Henry Wilson and left New Hampshire in search of a better life.

Wilson's subsequent career, which carried him from the rocky soil of New Hampshire to the halls of the United States Senate and eventually to the vice presidency, provides a case study of the rise of the common man in early nineteenth-century America.

Although Wilson would overcome the handicaps posed by his origins, his early experiences shaped his life. Resolved never to be like his father, he would work hard, avoid alcohol, and strive relentlessly to improve himself. He would identify with other working men and devote his career to helping remove the handicaps that threatened their paths to success. Eventually this course would lead him to champion the abolition of slavery and the achievement of equal rights for African Americans, causes that would earn him his place in history.

When Wilson left Farmington in 1833, he headed for Massachusetts, eventually settling in Natick to learn the shoemaking trade; it remained his home for the rest of his life. In New Hampshire he had had little time for school; in Natick he managed to squeeze out a month here and there to attend local academies, giving him probably not more than a year of formal education in total. In 1840, he married Harriet Malvina Howe, who bore their only child, a son, six years later. Wilson had little time, however, to devote to his family, for his shoe business claimed most of his attention. He was quite successful at it, and by 1847 employed more than 100 workers.

Wilson was not satisfied simply to be a successful shoemaker. Manufacturing brogans provided him with an income but not with an outlet for his powerful ambition. In 1840, he was elected to the lower house of the Massachusetts legislature, and from that time on he sacrificed all else in order to build a successful political career. Between 1840 and 1852, he served for eight years in either the upper or lower house of the state legislature. Political activity seemed to suit Wilson's personality. He enjoyed courting voters and reveled in building coalitions and controlling elections, but he also

was drawn to politics because it offered him a chance to use government to achieve the social and moral reforms that he championed. A self-made man himself, he wanted to help others to achieve similar successes in their own lives, so he worked to abolish imprisonment for debt, reduce the poll tax, institute a secret ballot, enact a mechanic's lien law, secure legislation to limit the consumption of alcohol, and promote free public schools.

It was the cause of the slave, however, that claimed most of Wilson's attention. Wilson had first seen slavery on a visit to Washington, D.C., in 1836, and the experience left him firmly resolved to do whatever he could to eradicate the institution. When he returned home he became an abolitionist, and later in his career one of his proudest moments came when, as a U.S. Senator; he sponsored legislation emancipating the slaves in the nation's capital. Probably Wilson's early experiences as a hardworking apprentice in New Hampshire had given him a sympathy for the oppressed blacks, a sympathy increased by the social ostracism that he experienced because of his own lowly origins. Of all laborers, he said, the slave was the most helpless and the most degraded. He recognized in slavery the absolute antithesis of the free-labor system that had enabled him to rise, and he warned that the same prejudices of class and race that subjugated blacks could also oppress white workers. Although slavery did not exist in Massachusetts, Wilson recognized that racism persisted there, and he sought to abolish segregated schools in the state, to repeal laws banning blacks from the militia and prohibiting interracial marriage, and to enact a state civil rights law.

Of all the northern states, the abolitionist movement was strongest in Massachusetts, where its chief spokesman was William Lloyd Garrison. Wilson shared Garrison's moral objections to slavery but disagreed with his insistence that abolitionists abstain from political action against the institution. Wilson believed that the political power southern slaveholders wielded in Washington helped to perpetuate slavery, and he was determined to break their hold on the national government. Wilson deeply resented the political influence of the southern planters, whom he decisively termed the Slave Power, and warned that this influence was undermining the foundations of republican government. From the time he entered politics, Wilson sought to organize an antislavery party strong enough to gain control of the U.S. government, terminate the baneful influence of the Slave Power, and ultimately abolish slavery itself.

Initially Wilson joined the Whig Party. He was not impressed with the party's economic views, which he believed favored banks and corporations, and frequently he voted, with the Democrats on measures before the state legislature. The Whigs, however, controlled the state, and he thought their party was much more likely than the Democrats to take a stand against slavery. To ensure that it did, Wilson became a leader of the "Conscience Whigs," a group of antislavery advocates that encouraged the party to oppose the further expansion of slavery in the western territories of the United States. In 1848, when it had become clear that the Whig Party had not measured up to his expectations, Wilson left it to help found the Free-Soil Party, which was dedicated to keeping slavery out of lands taken from Mexico after a war with that country, and for three years (1848–51) he edited the Boston *Republican,* a Free-Soil newspaper. In 1851, while a member of the state legislature, Wilson was instrumental in organizing a coalition of Free-Soilers and Democrats that sent an outspoken critic of slavery, Charles Sumner, to the United States Senate.

By 1854, the Free-Soilers had collapsed, and Wilson then joined the newly organized American or Know-Nothing party, which had seized control of the Massachusetts government by exploiting nativist and anti-Catholic sentiment in the state. Wilson quickly became a power in the party, and in 1855 the Know-Nothing legislature sent him to Washington to join Charles Sumner in the U.S. Senate, a position he would hold until he became vice presi-

dent in 1873. Although Wilson soon disavowed the American Party's nativist doctrines, his decision to join the Know Nothings, followed so quickly by his elevation to the Senate, left him open to charges of crass opportunism and helped create an image of him as a political manipulator that he never was able to shake. He remained firm in his antislavery convictions, however, and tried to turn the American Party into a vehicle for unseating the Slave Power in Washington. Instead, the Know-Nothings, who had support in both the North and the South, split over the slavery issue and soon dissolved.

Fortunately for Wilson, another party had appeared in the North by 1855 that would signal an end to his fifteen-year search for an antislavery political organization that he could support. The new party, which took the name Republican, was firmly opposed to slavery expansion, and Wilson willingly left the Know-Nothings to join it. He helped to organize the new party in Massachusetts and remained a loyal Republican for the rest of his life. Because of his strongly antislavery views, Wilson became a member of the newly organized party's radical wing. From 1855 to 1858 he spent much of his time in the Senate trying to keep slavery out of the Kansas Territory, a struggle that convinced him anew of the political power the South held in Washington. In 1856, in the middle of heated debates over Kansas, irate Representative Preston Brooks of South Carolina beat Wilson's colleague Charles Sumner senseless with a cane, furnishing Wilson with even more evidence of the arrogance of the Slave Power.

Two years later, Wilson received much applause in the North for his vigorous denunciation of a speech by South Carolina's James Hammond, who suggested that white workers functioned as slaves in northern society. Proudly Wilson identified himself as a manual laborer, and insisted that while the northern free-labor economy allowed men like himself to rise, in the South slavery kept poor whites in a servile condition. But while Wilson voiced the sentiments of northern workers, he realized that the

Republican Party needed the support of farmers and businessmen if it was to gain control of the government, so he courted the support of such Massachusetts industrialists as Amos A. Lawrence and in the Senate cast votes for railroad land grants, tariffs, bounties for New England fishermen, and homesteads for western farmers. He also spent a great deal of time campaigning for the party: in 1860, he gave more than 100 speeches for Republican presidential candidate Abraham Lincoln.

Lincoln's election immediately precipitated a crisis, when eleven Southern states seceded from the Union to form the Confederate States of America. Both Massachusetts senators, along with other radical Republicans, refused to support compromise proposals that some hoped would resolve the crisis. In April 1861, Confederates fired on U.S. Fort Sumter in the harbor in Charleston, South Carolina, plunging tile nation into a civil war. In July, a large Union army moved into Virginia to engage the Confederates, and in the ensuing battle near Bull Run Creek, the Union force was defeated and retreated hastily back to the capital. As people in Washington searched for answers for this disaster, some suggested that a Confederate spy, Rose Greenhow, had gained information about the Union advance from Senator Wilson. Although the senator was certainly embarrassed by these rumors, no one produced conclusive evidence of their veracity, and the charges were most certainly false.

Later that summer Wilson, who was eager to prosecute the war against the Confederacy, returned to Massachusetts, accepted a colonel's commission, and proceeded to recruit 2,300 men for the Twenty-second Massachusetts Volunteers. He might have been tempted to stay with the regiment, for he was fond of the military. During his political career in the Bay State, Wilson had taken an active role in the volunteer militia and, by 1846, had become a brigadier general. From that time on he relished being called "General Wilson." He decided to resign his colonel's commission, however, to resume his place in the Senate, for he had important

responsibilities there as chairman of the Senate Military Affairs Committee. This post gave him the opportunity to play a major role in organizing the Union war effort. His solicitous attitude toward Union Army officers may account for the fact that when Republicans in Congress established the Committee on the Conduct of the War in December, 1861, which was intended to investigate the operations of the Union Army, Wilson was not named to it.

Drawing on all of his considerable political and legislative skills, Wilson guided a number of manpower procurement laws through the Senate during the war, including the 1863 Enrollment Act. In securing this legislation, which instituted the first federal conscription in the United States, Wilson had to protect both the interests of state governors, who were jealous of their prerogatives, and northern businessmen who feared that either they or their labor force would be drafted into the Union Army. One of the most controversial provisions of the enrollment measure allowed men to pay a $300 commutation fee to escape the draft, which Wilson ardently defended until it was repealed in 1864. He also introduced legislation authorizing the federal government to stimulate volunteering by paying bounties to recruits. These measures, while not producing an efficient national draft, nonetheless deflected criticism of the law, which helped raise and organize the armies that brought victory to the North.

When representatives of the seceding Southern states left the Congress, depriving the South of its political influence in Washington, Wilson realized that the long-sought opportunity to end slavery had arrived. The fact that the Southern states had taken up arms against the Union had given Washington a reason to abolish slavery, and Wilson and his fellow Radical Republicans were quick to urge this upon President Lincoln. He often visited the president to discuss the issue and sought to organize public opinion to pressure Lincoln as well. Not content with waiting for presidential action, Wilson sought congressional legislation to achieve the same end. In 1862, he proudly sponsored legislation abolishing slavery in the District of Columbia, and in the same year he drew up a militia draft bill that authorized the federal government to enlist African Americans, both free and slave, in the Union armed forces. In January 1863, Wilson rejoiced when Lincoln issued his Emancipation Proclamation, but noted that the president had exempted the border slave states from its effects. He urged Congress to compensate border state slave owners if they would emancipate their slaves, and when this effort failed, he secured legislation drafting border slaves into the army and granting them and their families freedom. An ardent advocate of the use of black soldiers, Wilson also secured legislation granting them the same bounty and pay as whites.

In 1865, as the war came to an end, Wilson saw the final realization of a dream when Congress passed the Thirteenth Amendment abolishing slavery everywhere in the nation and sent it to the states for ratification. He and his radical Republican colleagues in Washington, however, realized that the overthrow of slavery did not settle the question of the ultimate status of the almost four million freedmen. Before the war ended, he and Charles Sumner had obtained legislation granting equal civil rights for blacks in the District of Columbia. In 1864, Wilson had also played an important role in creating the Freedmen's Bureau, a federal agency charged with protecting the rights of blacks during the difficult transition from slavery to freedom. The war had only been over a few months before some southern states began to pass Black Codes severely restricting the rights of the former slaves; a horrified Wilson warned Congress that these laws demonstrated that the dark spirits of slavery still lived. In 1866, he and other Radical Republicans pushed through a Civil Rights Act that nullified the Black Codes, and they also obtained new legislation strengthening the Freedmen's Bureau.

Wilson drew back, however, at supporting the recommendations of some Radicals, including his colleague Sumner, that southern planta-

tions be confiscated and their lands divided and given to the freedmen. Nor did he relish the idea of keeping Union troops in the South and governing the southern states by military authority. Instead he, like most of his Republican colleagues, believed granting the freedmen the franchise would be the best way to protect their newly won freedom. They could then vote for public schools, obtain state civil rights laws, and elect sympathetic public officials who would recognize their rights. Enfranchisement would be the capstone that would finish the process of giving laboring African Americans the same rights and opportunities as their white counterparts. It would then be possible, Wilson reasoned, for blacks to rise through the ranks of society as he himself had risen.

Securing suffrage for blacks in the face of resistance from whites not only in the South but in the North presented a difficult challenge to Wilson and his Radical associates. At first, Wilson said he would limit suffrage to blacks who could meet property or literacy tests. When the Republicans won increased control in Congress after the 1866 elections, however, he championed universal manhood suffrage and opposed any restrictions on the ballot. Wilson helped draft reconstruction legislation in 1867 under whose terms the southern states were to be returned to the Union, and he was overjoyed when the first of these laws required these states to enfranchise adult black males. He and most of his Republican colleagues were bitter at the president, Andrew Johnson, who had resisted them every step of the way. They had been forced repeatedly to overcome his vetoes and were upset because he was removing generals in the South who were most active in implementing the Reconstruction acts. In 1868, Wilson became an ardent supporter of the impeachment of Johnson and was bitterly disappointed when the Senate voted not to remove him.

Despite the failure of impeachment, Wilson believed that the work of Reconstruction was nearing a successful conclusion. In 1868, the Republicans nominated northern Civil War hero General Ulysses S. Grant to run for president, and he was elected that fall. The following year Congress passed a Fifteenth Amendment enfranchising black men in the whole country, a step that Wilson and others hoped would forever settle the issue of their rights and freedom. He did try—and fail—to alter the amendment in order to guarantee African Americans the right to hold elective office as well as to vote. Three years after that, he gave firm support to his friend Charles Sumner's civil rights bill, which was designed to prohibit segregation in schools and in public accommodations throughout the United States.

It was Wilson's hope that once equal rights for blacks were spelled out in congressional legislation and in Constitutional amendments, whites would eventually acknowledge the legitimacy of these rights. He believed that former Confederates would be more likely to acquiesce in this new dispensation if they were treated with consideration. Wilson held no vindictive views toward the ex-Confederates, and shortly after the war's end, he endeavored to gain the release of incarcerated Confederate leaders. He opposed inserting provisions in the Reconstruction acts disfranchising them, arguing that coupling universal suffrage with universal amnesty would facilitate national and racial reconciliation. When, despite his opposition, the Fourteenth Amendment did bar some southern leaders from holding office, Wilson voted whenever he could to remove those disabilities.

In 1867, Wilson took a tour of the South, one of the few national Republican leaders to do so. The purpose of his visit was to encourage southern whites to accept the Reconstruction acts, and he promised them that if they did, there would be nothing more asked of them. He encouraged his white listeners to join those freed in supporting the Republican Party, which he believed would work to advance the interests of both races in the South. Constant outbreaks of white violence against blacks in the South, while disappointing to Wilson, did not destroy his hope for a biracial party there, and he continued to work for it the rest of his life. He was outraged by the activities of the Ku Klux Klan

and supported legislation designed to destroy the white vigilante group, but he believed there was a limit to what federal coercion of whites could achieve. Rather than force, he preferred to rely on moral suasion and public education to bring racial harmony to the South.

Buoyed by the fervor of a religious conversion he had experienced in fall 1866, Wilson urged Christian churches to combat the spirit of caste and prejudice that still remained. He also wanted the federal government to help finance the expansion of public education in the South. Denied an opportunity for much schooling himself, Wilson had long struggled to guarantee it to others, both black and white. In every Congress after he entered the Senate, Wilson had introduced legislation to finance education for both races in the District of Columbia, and in 1867 he had assisted in the incorporation of Howard University there. In 1871 and again in 1873, he introduced bills in Congress to distribute revenues from public land sales to the southern states to finance public schools, contending that education would be an effective way to overcome the adverse effects of slavery on both races.

None of these efforts for federal aid to education came to fruition, but they did reveal the depths of Wilson's commitment to a society that afforded all of its citizens equal rights and opportunities. In the early 1870s, sensing that the Republican party was losing sight of its purpose and warning that it was in danger of falling into the hands of a new class of wealthy men, which he now characterized not as the Slave Power but as the Money Power, Wilson called on his colleagues to awaken the party's dormant reform zeal and to take on new challenges. For example, he supported an eight-hour day for government workers and called for the creation of a government commission to investigate laboring conditions in the country. In addition, he championed civil service reform, temperance legislation, and the enfranchisement of women.

Wilson had little success in convincing his Republican colleagues to take up these new issues. His influence in the party, which had been strong throughout the 1860s, was waning by that decade's end. Younger men, more interested in tariffs and banking legislation than in humanitarian reform, began replacing the older generation of antislavery leaders. Wilson became increasingly dissatisfied with the Grant administration: Evidence of corruption among some of Grant's appointees had led Wilson to champion civil service reform. He was also unhappy with the president for pushing a scheme to annex Santo Domingo, a proposal that led to a breach between Grant and Wilson's colleague and friend Charles Sumner, Senate Foreign Affairs Committee chairman.

By 1872, a number of discontented Republicans, including Sumner, formed a "Liberal Republican" Party to nominate and elect someone other than Grant. Wilson, however, refused to join the new movement; instead he tried to mitigate some of the discontent by praising the administration, and he urged Grant's reelection. Wilson's course was probably influenced not only by a strong sense of party loyalty but also by his own ambition because in 1872 many Republicans were talking of nominating him for vice president. The incumbent in that post, Schuyler Colfax, had declared that he would not run again, allowing Wilson to express interest in replacing him. When Colfax then changed his mind, Wilson chose not to withdraw his own name. As a result, the Republican convention, while easily renominating Grant, had a contest for second spot on the ticket, which Wilson won on the first ballot. During the ensuing campaign, Wilson had to defend himself against charges of bigotry arising from his earlier association with the Know-Nothings.

He also faced even more damaging charges when a newspaper revealed that in 1868 he was among several congressmen who had received stock from the Crédit Mobilier, a construction firm that was receiving federal aid to build a transcontinental railroad. As it turned out, Wilson had indeed obtained some of the stock for his wife but a few months later had canceled the deal. Because his long public career provided

ample evidence of his incorruptibility, the charges had little effect, and the Republicans easily won the election. Early the following year, as Wilson relinquished his Senate seat to assume his new office, he was without a dollar in his pocket; he had to borrow money from Sumner for a suit of clothes for his inauguration.

Wilson's nomination and eventual election to the post of vice president brought his career to its culmination. The honor awarded him by the Republicans, however, was made more in appreciation for past services than in anticipation of future contributions. To his frustration, he found he had little influence either with the president or with the Republican Congress. His relentless ambition allowed him little rest, for he harbored dreams of succeeding Grant in 1876. Wilson was critical of the president's Reconstruction policy and still hoped to build the Republican Party in the South on the votes of both races. In 1875, he took another trip through the South and came back convinced that hundreds of thousands of southern ex-Whigs could be made into Republicans if the president would offer them representation in his cabinet and if Congress would provide assistance in building southern railroads. Wilson's suggestion anticipated the southern policy that would be implemented not by Grant but by his successor, Rutherford B. Hayes, in 1877.

Wilson would not live to see that happen. Having lost his political influence, he spent his remaining years in Washington, working on a multivolume history of the rise and fall of the Slave Power. By the time he had become vice president, both his wife and son had died, followed soon by colleagues and friends like Sumner who had shared his struggle against the Slave Power. Feeling lonely and forgotten, Wilson was determined to write a history that would record his own role in the great events of his era. By 1868, he had already produced several legislative histories chronicling the passage of the various military, antislavery, and reconstruction measures that he had either authored or supported. He then began to collect material for a three-volume history, portions of which he began to publish in newspapers in 1870. In spring 1872, the year he was elected vice president, Wilson published the first volume. Desperate to finish the work and hopeful of additional income from its sale, Wilson devoted up to sixteen hours a day to his writing, even though his physical condition was failing. On May 19, 1873, Wilson suffered a stroke that partially disabled him. Invoking a friend's aid to help him with his writing, he plunged ahead, and in 1874, the second volume appeared, and the third neared completion. In October 1875, he suffered a second, more-serious paralytic attack, and in November, yet another. He died later that month, lying on a bed in the plain surroundings of the vice president's room in the Capitol.

The nation grieved Wilson's passing. During his career, Wilson had probably campaigned more than any other prominent politician. He had traveled hundreds of thousands of miles, had crisscrossed the North, and had visited the South on two occasions. By the time he died, he was one of the most well-known politicians of his day. Many eulogists took note of his rise from lowly origins, and while they quarreled about the quality of his statesmanship and recalled his penchant for political manipulation, most agreed that his legislative achievements and his devotion to the cause of freedom and equality were unparalleled. A year after his death, the third and final volume of his history appeared to stand as a monument to Wilson's life and achievements. Although his election as vice president brought him to the second highest office in the land, he is best remembered for his leading role in the political antislavery movement, for his work to organize the Union effort during the Civil War, and for his struggle to secure for African Americans the rights and opportunities accorded to whites.

REFERENCES

Richard H. Abbott, *Cobbler in Congress: The Life of Henry Wilson, 1812–1875* (Lexington, Ky.: The University Press of Kentucky, 1972); Ernest McKay, *Henry Wilson, Practical Radical: Portrait of a Reformer* (Port Washington, N.Y.: Kennikat Press, 1971); John L. Myers, "The Writing of the Rise and Fall of the Slave Power in America," *Civil War History,* 31 (June 1985), 144–162; John L. Myers, *Senator Henry Wilson and the Civil War* (Lanham, Md.: University Press of America, 2008).

RICHARD H. ABBOTT passed away in 2000, shortly before his scheduled retirement from the history department at Eastern Michigan University. In addition to *Cobbler in Congress,* his 1972 biography of Henry Wilson, Abbott was author of a number of other books and articles on the Civil War period, including *The Republican Party and the South, 1855–1877* and *Cotton and Capital: Boston Businessmen and Antislavery Reform.*

WILLIAM A. WHEELER (1819–1887)
Vice President, 1877–1881
(President Rutherford B. Hayes)

WILLIAM A. WHEELER
(Library of Congress)

By Frank P. Vazzano

William A. Wheeler was born on June 30 1819, in Malone, the seat of Franklin County in upstate New York, an area dominated geographically by Lake Saranac, some 60 miles from the Canadian border. Wheeler's Puritan ancestors had settled first in Concord, Massachusetts, then in Fairfield, Connecticut, and finally in Vermont. Both of his grandfathers fought in the Revolutionary War. Wheeler's father, Almon, a lawyer, died in 1827, too young to have left his family an estate or any other means of support, and his widow Eliza sustained herself and her three children by boarding students enrolled in Franklin Academy in Malone.

At best, Wheeler was an average student, although sharp in mathematics. From the common school in Malone, he moved on to highly regarded Franklin Academy, from which he graduated in 1838. Wheeler then attended the University of Vermont but dropped out after two years. He returned to Malone to study law with Franklin County District Attorney Asa Hascall. After a five-year apprenticeship, Wheeler was admitted to the New York bar. In that same year, 1845, he married Mary King.

While honest and sure, he was not a spectacular lawyer, but he was politically ambitious and won election to various town and school clerkships. When Hascall's failing health forced him to relinquish the district attorneyship in October 1846, Franklin County officials appointed Wheeler to the post. Subsequently, county voters elected him to the job, which he held for three years.

Wheeler used the district attorneyship as a political springboard. Running as a Whig, he was elected to the New York Assembly in 1849. He seemed a born parliamentarian and was also quick to grasp public issues. He so impressed some of his fellow legislators that they suggested he seek the speakership in 1850, although he had already agreed to support another for the post. Wheeler resisted the enticement. The next year, during his second term in Albany, he was named chairman of the Ways and Means Committee, a singular distinction for so junior an assemblyman.

Despite his success, Wheeler spurned a third term and returned to Malone. He became cashier of the newly organized State Bank of Malone, a position that he kept for fifteen years. Solid and honest as cashier, Wheeler attracted the attention of officers of the Ogdensburg and Rouse Point Railway, part of the Northern New York Railroad Company that passed through Malone. Eventually, he became a trustee and then president of the line. Re was so astute a financial manager that he retained the latter office for eleven years.

While Wheeler enjoyed much personal success in the 1850s, the nation was rent, North and South, over the issue of slavery. Passions kindled by the "peculiar institution" helped spawn the Republican Party in 1854. Antislavery forces of all stripes, particularly old Whigs, found its philosophy attractive. Wheeler was among those drawn to the party. He helped organize the Franklin County Republicans in 1855 and supported the soldier-explorer John C. Frémont for president in 1856.

Frémont's defeat at the hands of James Buchanan did not sour Wheeler on Republican politics. In 1857, urged on by friends who persuaded him to run for the good of the fledgling party, Wheeler campaigned as a Republican and won a seat in the New York Senate from the Seventeenth District, representing Franklin and St. Lawrence counties. Recalling Wheeler's reputation for honesty and efficiency as an assemblyman, his fellow partisans elected him president pro tempore in both 1858 and 1859.

By 1860, Wheeler was ready and eager for a larger political stage. While the Union was disintegrating, he campaigned for and won election to the United States House of Representatives from New York's Sixteenth District. This Thirty-seventh Congress began the formal prosecution of the Civil War. It supported President Abraham Lincoln's recognition that a state of war existed and approved his requisition of militias and volunteers from the loyal states. The same Congress abolished slavery in the District of Columbia and passed a measure calling for the death penalty or fine and imprisonment for those convicted of treason against the United States. In all this, Wheeler voted a strict Republican line.

The frenzy of the Thirty-seventh Congress convinced Wheeler that one term was enough. In 1863, he retired to private life and spent the next four years quietly in Malone with his wife. Only his banking and railroad interests intruded upon the tranquility of the lake and mountain life.

Politics, however, remained in Wheeler's blood. In 1867, when New York State prepared to draft a new constitution, the still-popular Wheeler won election as a delegate to the convention. His fellow Republicans, predominant at the convention, nominated him for presiding officer, and he won. His new honor enabled him to appear as more the statesman than the partisan because he was now removed from debate but yet could still direct his colleagues on the convention floor. Even his friends expressed surprise at how easily and effectively he assumed the executive's role.

Heartened by his successful reentry into politics at the constitutional convention, Wheeler in 1868 once more ran for Congress. He won easily and did so again in 1870, 1872, and 1874. His continuous service spanned from March 3, 1869 to March 3, 1877. House Speaker James G. Elaine, acknowledging Wheeler's railroad experience, named him chairman of the Pacific Railroad Committee, a post he filled until 1873. Later, Wheeler served on the Appropriations Committee.

George Frisbie Hoar of Massachusetts, who befriended Wheeler when both entered the House in 1869, said of the New Yorker that he had "little respect for the devious and self-seeking. . . ." Hoar recalled how Wheeler's unwavering honesty provoked a storied confrontation with Roscoe Conkling, the consummate spoilsman and unquestioned martinet of the United States Senate. Conkling, attempting to entice Wheeler to his side in state politics, propositioned his fellow New Yorker: "Wheeler, if you will act with us, there is nothing in the gift of the state of New York to which you may not reasonably aspire." An indignant Wheeler snapped: "Mr. Conkling, there is nothing in the gift of the state of New York which will compensate me for the forfeiture of my self-respect."

That kind of bravery in the face of pressure from one of the most powerful and vindictive politicos of the day not only established Wheeler's independence but also spoke eloquently to his character. Fortifying his reputation as an honest man, Wheeler spurned the infamous "Salary Grab" of 1873. While many of his congressional colleagues embraced the proposal that increased their salaries from $5,000 to $7,500 a year and gave them an additional two years of the raise as back pay, Wheeler, who had opposed the measure from the beginning, returned the money to the United States Treasury.

It was Louisiana politics that gave Wheeler the national reputation needed to enter the lists for the vice presidency. Difficult though Reconstruction was in any of the seceded states, nothing could match the fraud, intimidation, and violence that dominated Louisiana electioneering in the 1870s. In trying to regain control of their state's political machinery, the so-called Redeemers had virtually declared open season on their opponents, whom they considered to be carpetbaggers and scalawags. In 1874, after Democrats concluded that the Republicans had cheated them out of the recently contested governorship, gunfire broke out in the streets of New Orleans. Fifty-six people died before the military, acting upon direct orders from President Ulysses S. Grant, restored order.

Grant's intervention, however, only temporarily eased tensions. Later in the year, Congress sent Wheeler as part of a committee to Louisiana to arbitrate the angrily contested gubernatorial election. Under Wheeler's lead, the contending forces worked out a compromise in 1875, allowing Republican Governor William Pitt Kellogg to keep his office. In return, Democrats received most of the nineteen disputed seats in the lower house of the state legislature. The Wheeler Compromise restored as much peace to Louisiana politics as was possible in that fractious state and, by enhancing Wheeler's reputation, opened the way to his vice-presidential nomination in 1876.

Republican politics in America's centennial year were muddled. The scandal-scarred but still popular Grant dared not risk the nation's traditional aversion to a third-term and stepped aside. Among the possible successors, James G. Blaine of Maine seemed the favorite, although several other aspirants, including Benjamin Bristow of Kentucky, Oliver P. Morton of Indiana, Roscoe Conkling of New York, and Rutherford B. Hayes of Ohio, all hoped to win Grant's presidential mantle. The Republicans at the Cincinnati nominating convention chose Hayes on the seventh ballot.

The din of Hayes's nomination had scarcely subsided when the convention's presiding officer, Edward McPherson of Pennsylvania, called the vote for a vice-presidential nominee. Wheeler nominated by Luke P. Poland of Vermont, surged immediately to the front and remained there when the roll call reached New York. The Conkling-supported candidate, Stewart L. Woodford, recognizing that his chance for nomination was slim, stepped aside for Wheeler. New York's delegates then promptly cast their seventy votes for the man from Malone. Shortly thereafter, the convention bowed to the inevitable and moved for the unanimous nomination of William A. Wheeler for vice president of the United States.

At the moment of his triumph, Wheeler was two weeks short of his fifty-seventh birthday. He stood taller than most of his nineteenth-century contemporaries and, despite his fifty-seven years, was ramrod straight and strong of limb, although he frequently complained of ill health. Clean shaven and crisply turned out, in sharp contrast to the bushy-bearded and typically rumpled Hayes, Wheeler looked more "presidential" than the chief nominee himself. Moreover, his life could bear any scrutiny, *The New York Times* declared in its postnomination assessment. His geography was right too: A New Yorker on the ticket with an Ohioan assured widespread support in both the Northeast and the Midwest. Both sections of the country were essential to victory in November.

Within days of his nomination, Wheeler began to offer Hayes advice. The Democratic presidential nominee, Samuel Jones Tilden, the millionaire governor of New York who had fashioned a reform reputation for himself by smashing the notorious Tweed Ring, Wheeler warned, was a "wonderful organizer and manipulator" and would gladly put his considerable wealth to "unscrupulous use." "But his foes are many and bitter. . . ," Wheeler continued, and if "Ohio and Indiana swing out right in October, we shall not despair of New York."

Wheeler also had sound thoughts about the organization of the Republican National Committee. Do not let Conkling control the committee by engineering the election of his lieutenant Alonzo B. Cornell as chairman, he cautioned, and sage advice this was, because Cornell's allegiance to Conkling would have boded ill for Hayes. The senator from New York, unable to forget his failure and Hayes's success at Cincinnati, bore a perpetual grudge against the Ohioan and constantly tried to undermine his presidency.

Wheeler proffered other advice as well. Knowing that civil service reform and sound money were Hayes priorities, he suggested that "capacity and character" ought to be prerequisites for government appointment and that there was no need of enlarging on Hayes's well-known fiscal conservatism. Regarding treatment of the South, Wheeler was sufficiently radical to appeal to those Republicans who were still mentally fighting the Civil War.

As the campaign of 1876 began to crystallize, Wheeler disappeared from the public eye. He begged off active campaigning, informing Hayes that poor health, perhaps accentuated by his wife's death earlier in the year, prevented him from taking to the stump. He was quick to add, however, that he did "not intend by any means to be an idle spectator. New York is to be fought inch by inch, and there is work to be done here far more effective in results than speech making." What Wheeler had in mind was working with New York State Republicans to nominate a gubernatorial candidate who would strengthen the national ticket in November.

Interestingly, pressures to campaign, although not coming from Hayes, soured Wheeler on his vice-presidential nomination. In August, when James G. Blaine asked Wheeler to stump Maine, the nominee once again pleaded ill health. Typhoid fever in 1872 had weakened him, and he suffered constantly from insomnia as well. Of the latter affliction, he complained: "No resident of the grave or a lunatic asylum has suffered more from this cause than I have. Speaking, and the presence of crowds, excite me and intensify my wakefulness. I regret that I was nominated."

By September his enthusiasm seemed to return. From his home in Malone, he wrote Hayes that he was optimistic about New York in the coming election. Republicans there had a few weeks earlier nominated Edwin D. Morgan for governor, not the Conkling-run Alonzo B. Cornell, and close Democratic friends had confided to Wheeler that they held little hope of carrying New York in the presidential canvass.

Three weeks before the election, Wheeler noted that the Democrats were desperate in New York, even trying to convince the Catholic French of the northern part of the state that the Democratic party "was a friend of their church." "The contest in this state," he observed, "is the combination of every evil agency within it, in intense action, marshaled by the cunning, adroitness and energy of the devil himself, against its intelligence, conscience and decency."

Wheeler was more prescient than he knew. The presidential election of 1876 did indeed combine "evil agencies" and "intense action" as Republican and Democratic managers sank to new depths of chicanery and deceit.

The heated campaign in New York—and everywhere else for that matter—served as a prelude to one of the most notorious presidential elections in U.S. history. Three southern states, Florida, Louisiana, and South Carolina, submitted dual sets of votes, one for each candidate. Conflicting returns were problem enough, but the absence of a constitutional or traditional procedure to determine which ballots were valid complicated the situation. Tilden had already beaten Hayes by more than 250,000 popular votes and led in the electoral count, 184 to 165. But the three southern states, and Oregon where a Republican postmaster—in violation of the Constitution—served as an elector represented twenty disputed votes. If Hayes captured them, he would win.

In January 1877, Congress compromised its way to a solution. Both houses agreed to the creation of an Electoral Commission of five members each from the House, the Senate, and the Supreme Court; those fifteen commissioners would determine the validity of the disputed returns. The Democratic House named three Democrats and two Republicans; the Republican Senate selected three Republicans and two Democrats. With a congressional representation of five men from each party, it was hoped that a fair judgment could be assured with the appointment of two Republican and two Democratic justices and the neutral David Davis. However, the partisan balance tipped toward the Republicans when the Illinois legislature elected Davis to the United States Senate. He stepped aside and was replaced by Joseph P. Bradley, a Republican. During the deliberations over Electoral Commission, Wheeler, like Hayes, deliberately faded from view.

The Electoral Commission began its work on February 1, 1877. For a month the committee examined the returns and heard arguments from lawyers representing both sides. First Florida, then Louisiana and Oregon, and finally South Carolina were declared for Hayes. In each instance the partisan vote was 8–7.

Congressional Democrats saw the handwriting on the wall after Hayes received the votes from Florida and Louisiana. They threatened to stop his installation by filibustering to prevent the election returns from being officially counted. The resultant interregnum could prove disastrous, especially because rumors of outright revolution already ran rampant in the capital. With Hayes's tacit sanction, some of his supporters, notably James A. Garfield, John Sherman, and Stanley Matthews, met with moderate southern leaders, including John Young Brown of Kentucky and John B. Gordon of Georgia, to effect a compromise. The bargainers were bold and explicit; Hayes's men asked what concessions they would have to make to ensure his inauguration. The reply was equally explicit—withdrawal of all federal troops from the South, the appointment of a southerner to Hayes's cabinet, and government subsidies for internal improvements in a South still reeling from the Civil War. None of the conditions was distasteful to Hayes. Although much was made of the bargain afterward, he was already committed to a conciliatory southern policy. By February 28, 1877, barring revolution, Rutherford B. Hayes and William A. Wheeler were secure in their positions as the next president and vice president of the United States.

Grant's term ended on March 4, a Sunday. Custom dictated that an inauguration could not take place on the Sabbath, so, to avoid a potentially dangerous interregnum, Hayes privately swore the presidential oath on March 3 after slipping off to the Red Room during a White House dinner party hosted by the outgoing president.

Wheeler's inauguration took place during the formal ceremonies on Monday, March 5. Although the country's newspapers tracked Hayes's every movement for the next several days, they reported nothing about the new vice president. Already Wheeler headed into the obscurity that seemed inevitably to stamp the second highest office in the land.

Wheeler, however, stayed close to Hayes. The two discussed the formation of the new cabinet, with the vice president pressing his views. The cabinet, he told Hayes, would set the tone for the new administration and must contain the best possible men. The president should not retain anyone from the previous cabinet because Hayes's administration should stand in marked contrast with Grant's scandal-plagued regime.

Wheeler successfully recommended Charles Devens of the Massachusetts Supreme Court for attorney general. Wheeler ultimately disapproved, though, of William M. Evarts, Hayes's choice for secretary of state because Evarts equivocated too much on patronage appointments, refusing, for instance, to tell aspirants that they stood no chance of gaining a place in the government. Although he appointed Evarts, Hayes agreed with the vice president that candor in patronage was safest and fairest to all.

Where Wheeler could have been most helpful to Hayes, he begged off. The president, in accordance with promises hinted if not sworn in the hectic months while his election was still in dispute, wished to inquire into Louisiana politics with the intention of withdrawing the last federal troops from the state. To that end, in early 1877 he sent a five-man commission to Louisiana. Wheeler, because of his experience in the state, seemed an obvious choice for the commission. By late March, however, the vice president had already left Washington for Malone and was too weary to assume any official responsibilities. Furthermore, Wheeler explained, he had to tend to his invalid sister until she improved. In any case, he told Hayes's secretary, William K. Rogers: "I should be utterly at [a] loss what to advise as to the Louisiana problem."

He was less reluctant to comment about the South in general, though, even when his opinion differed from the president's. In 1878, when Hayes still held hope of reconciling the South, Wheeler warned the president that southerners were not to be trusted, "*I* never had a particle of faith in their beguiling professions," he wrote, "and long before you leave the Executive Mansion any lingering confidence *you* may have in them will be fully dispelled." The next year, when Hayes became embroiled in a bitter appropriations struggle with congressional Democrats, most of whom were southerners, he accepted his vice president's views more readily.

Wheeler's support heartened the president in that contest with his Democratic Congress. In seven vetoes that followed rapidly one upon another, Hayes refused to allow the Democrats to repeal laws calling for federal troops to protect the polls during national elections and requiring a loyalty oath for southern jurors. Hayes's vetoes broke the Democrats' resolve and united a Republican Party badly divided over the president's conciliatory policy toward the South.

Wheeler congratulated Hayes for his determination. He described one of the president's vetoes as "a document impregnable in form and substance and which, alone, would secure [the president] a place in the history of the country." Two weeks later, in response to still another

Hayes veto, be wrote: "It is rarely given to a man to defend the constitution of his country by both sword & pen. . . . [I] rejoice in your marked success."

Wheeler's fidelity continued as Hayes moved into the second half of his term, but his official duties were few, and he was consequently free to chair the Republican state convention at Saratoga, New York, in September 1879. Hayes's and Wheeler's old nemesis, Roscoe Conkling dominating that convention, got his man Cornell nominated for governor. Hayes's earlier purge of Conkling's patronage plum, the New York Custom House, was so complete, however, that he could afford to be generous to the New York senator, even to the point of allowing Secretary of the Treasury John Sherman, Secretary of State Evarts, and a reluctant Wheeler to stump the state for Cornell.

With few formal responsibilities, much of Wheeler's relationship with Hayes was personal. Not only were the president and the vice president warm friends, but their cordiality spread to the entire Hayes family. Wheeler was a regular visitor at the White House, particularly on Sunday evenings when the First Family gathered in the library or Red Room for an evening of song. Typically, the vice president provided copies of *The Presbyterian Hymn and Tune Book* for all. Hayes's Secretary of the Interior Carl Schurz or some other guest accompanied on the piano. The songfests provided a welcome respite from Washington politics and at least a semblance of family life for the widowed and childless vice president.

Lucy Webb Hayes's visit to Malone in the spring of 1878 attested more than anything else to the closeness between Wheeler and the Hayes family. Without her husband but accompanied by her daughter Fanny, Mrs. Hayes spent three weeks as Wheeler's guest traveling in the Adirondacks and fishing Saranac Lake. Not only did she find the vacation itself invigorating, but Lucy also enjoyed testing her angling skills. She virtually gushed at the prospect of landing some of the huge trout for which Saranac was so renowned.

The trip also gave her a chance to see the home of the man who so frequently visited hers. Wheeler's house reminded her of their own in Fremont, Ohio, perhaps even nicer in some respects, she informed her husband. Wheeler, too, enjoyed Mrs. Hayes's visit:

Scarcely an hour of the day passes that some Adirondack experience is not marshalled up in memory. Would that some friendly, artistic hand could have sketched for our own eyes the post-prandial on Flood-wood Pond. The splendor of a White House reception would pale in the contrast,

Lucy's presence in his Malone home, brief though it was, allowed Wheeler to forget momentarily the lingering sadness occasioned by his wife's death. Months later he still reminisced about the excursion.

Hayes not only entrusted his wife to Wheeler for the Adirondack holiday, but he also thought the entire country could be entrusted to his vice president. As a publicly avowed single term advocate, Hayes refused to run for another term, but in late 1879, during a conversation with several journalists and members of the Republican National Committee in the white House library, the President seemed to favor Wheeler as his successor in 1880. Such a man could likely carry the important state of New York, Hayes thought. Too, Wheeler's nomination would validate Hayes's presidency, and considering the longtime hostility between the vice president and Roscoe Conkling, it might also weaken the New York senator's control of politics in the Empire State. John Sherman was Hayes's final favorite, but the prospect of a Wheeler candidacy was appealing.

Neither Wheeler nor Sherman, however, was the Republican Party's choice in 1880. The honor fell to James A. Garfield, the House minority leader and Hayes's chief congressional liaison. With Garfield's narrow victory in the November election, Hayes and Wheeler's term drew to a close. Neither man appeared disappointed at the prospect; indeed, both seemed relieved, as if their service had been more burden than pleasure.

Wheeler's final Washington appearance was at Garfield's inaugural ball on March 4, 1881. He then escaped, with great relief, to a holiday in Tennessee, intending to avoid the late winter snows of upstate New York. Returning finally to his home in Malone, he was greeted by a brass band and hundreds of well-wishers. In April, he wrote a happily retired Lucy Hayes that after his trip to Tennessee he stopped for a day in Washington to gather some personal effects. He lamented:

> Oh how changed everything seemed. I encountered new faces at every hand. I did not go near the White House. When I parted with you on the eve of the 3d. of March, I felt that I should never again enter its portals, nor have I a desire to.

Even during retirement, Wheeler and Hayes stayed close. Through a mutual friend, Hayes learned in 1885 that Wheeler, now sixty-six, looked well but suffered from vertigo. Later, Hayes let their correspondence lapse, but Wheeler remained in contact with various members of the former president's family. In 1886, the former vice president still felt sufficiently familiar with Hayes to complain about his bladder and bowel problems. Although he claimed to be an invalid, Wheeler confessed that most of the time he was up and dressed and able to walk short distances.

Serious illness struck in early 1887. On March 8, Wheeler caught a chill, became feverish, and grew so weak that his doctors thought he was dying. He never fully recovered. On May 30, after weeks of irrationality, he lost consciousness and, save for a few moments here and there, never regained it. Finally, surrounded by friends, members of his deceased wife's family, his physician, and his pastor, Wheeler died. In Malone, and later in the nation's capital, flags fluttered at half-mast. At home in Fremont, a saddened Hayes reflected on Wheeler's perseverance and integrity. He was a "'rare man,' sound and true. In character he was sterling gold," the retired president confided to his diary as he made plans to attend the funeral.

The immediate assessments of Wheeler's life and career were neither untrue nor exaggerated. The New York *Tribune* described him as "not a man of brilliant, showy parts" but of "natural sagacity, and sturdy common-sense with unswerving moral rectitude." The *New York Times* judged him similarly: "He had the confidence of those who knew him. He was not an orator or great leader. . . . But he was above all things trustworthy." His old friend George Frisbie Hoar recalled how adroitly Wheeler had run the Senate, a body not known for its self-restraint or altruism during Hayes's stormy term. Wheeler, Hoar claimed, kept testy senators in check with "as little show of force as if [he] were presiding over a company of guests at [his] own table."

In retrospect, Wheeler's professional relationship with Hayes, unlike his personal one, seemed distant. Certainly in the nineteenth century, by tradition and function, the first and second officers of the land shared few official duties. On one occasion, Wheeler actually had to write the president to learn if the latter intended to call the Senate into special session during the appropriations crisis of 1879. Hayes, too, at times had to resort to correspondence with his vice president for information about Senate proceedings. Once the president waited four months for records of the Senate's executive sessions before asking Wheeler: "Can you make the waters move?"

Wheeler never considered the vice presidency as a stepping stone to the White House, nor did he use the position for personal gain. Early in his term, he succinctly described his vice presidential role to Hayes: "no advice to proffer, no positions to seek, but always at your command, with my best energies to do anything within my power in furtherance of your great purpose." Such a promise, ardently expressed and genuinely fulfilled, was refreshing in a day when the likes of Blaine and Conkling, who felt political and personal gain were natural prerequisites of office, dominated politics.

Wheeler's penchant for hearth and home bespoke a sensitivity almost antithetical to the rough and tumble of late nineteenth-century political life. In his leisure he read Shakespeare and, too often for his own good, brooded over personal tragedies, particularly the passing of his wife Mary in 1876 and his sister Delia in 1879. With their deaths, Wheeler seemed to lose much of his zest for politics and life itself.

Given Wheeler's temperament, the vice presidency was probably best suited for him in 1876. He had long been a political animal and likely was unprepared to abandon the public calling to which he had already devoted most of his life. The vice presidency was visible enough to provide him comfortable ingress to retirement and welcome repose in his beloved lake and mountain country.

REFERENCES

Frank P. Vazzano, "Who Was William A. Wheeler?" *Hayes Historical Journal: A Journal of the Gilded Age,* IX, 4 (Summer 1990), 5–23; James T. Otten, "Grand Old Partyman: William A. Wheeler and the Republican Party, 1850–1880" (Ph.D. diss., University of South Carolina, 1976); James T. Otten, "The Wheeler Adjustment in Louisiana: National Republicans Begin to Reappraise Their Reconstruction Policy," *Louisiana, History,* XIII (Fall 1972), 349–367; Frederick J. Seaver, *Historical Sketches of Franklin County* (Albany, N.Y.: J.B. Lyon Company, 1918).

FRANK P. VAZZANO is professor emeritus of history at Walsh University in North Canton, Ohio where he began teaching in 1971. His research interests are in the Hayes presidency, the Great Depression, and immigration and ethnicity. His articles have appeared in *Louisiana History, Ohio History, The Hayes Historical Journal, Congress & the Presidency,* and in various publications of the American Italian Historical Association.

CHESTER ALAN ARTHUR (1829–1886)

Vice President, March 4–September 19, 1881

(President James A. Garfield)

CHESTER ALAN ARTHUR
(Library of Congress)

By Justus D. Doenecke

When the Republican Party convention, meeting in Chicago in early June 1880, chose Chester Alan Arthur as its vice-presidential candidate, the move was widely perceived as a cynical political bargain.

Arthur had been a prominent lieutenant of New York Senator Roscoe Conkling, head of the Grand Old Party's Stalwart faction and the epitome of spoils politics. The party's presidential candidate, James A. Garfield, had been backed by the rival Half-Breed group, led by Maine senator James G. Blaine. Hence Republicans deemed it necessary, indeed urgent, to unite the party by giving the vice-presidential slot to the defeated wing.

When Arthur was first notified that he was in the running for the nomination, Conkling commented: "Well, you should drop it as you would a red hot shoe from the forge." Garfield, predicted the New York State boss, was bound to be defeated at the polls. Arthur, however, accepted the bid, saying: "The office of the Vice-President is a greater honor than I have ever dreamed of attaining." Perhaps he saw the nomination as vindication of his conduct as collector of the Port of New York, a post from which he had been removed by President Rutherford B. Hayes on the grounds that he tolerated illegal conduct. Perhaps he sought to enhance his own political standing within New York State party ranks.

The reformist weekly *The Nation,* in commenting on the ticket, expressed a kind of ironic relief, finding

> no place in which [Arthur's] powers of mischief will be so small as in the Vice-Presidency. . . . It is true General Garfield, if elected, may die during his term of office, but this is too unlikely a contingency to be worth making extraordinary provisions for.

As a political candidate, Arthur played a crucial role in the campaign, coordinating scores of rallies and securing contributions from scores of public servants. As vice-president elect, however, he undercut his own running mate Garfield on a crucial matter as he vehemently backed Conkling's efforts to push Stalwarts into the major government positions. Even after Garfield and Arthur were inaugurated respectively as president and vice president of the United States, Arthur fought his own president on a crucial matter, the collectorship of the Port of New York, a major patronage plum.

In a shocking turn of events, Garfield was shot early in July 1881 and died on September 19. The general reaction was later recalled by Cornell University President Andrew Dickson White: "It was a common saying at the time among those who knew him best, 'Chet' Arthur president of the United States. Good God." That Arthur ended up a competent president was one of the nation's great political surprises.

Chester Alan Arthur was born on October 5, 1829, in a small log cabin in Fairfield, Vermont. Arthur's father, William, an Ulsterman born in Dreen, Ireland, was an itinerant Baptist minister who served parishes in Vermont and New York State. His mother, Melvina Stone Arthur, was of English descent; her father had fought in the Revolution.

In 1845, Arthur entered Union College, where he chose the traditional classical curriculum and coedited the school newspaper. By now a tall, strikingly good-looking youth, Arthur was elected to Phi Beta Kappa. Upon graduating in 1848, he taught in rural schools and in 1851 became principal of a small academy located in his father's church basement in North Pownal, Vermont. A year later he became a principal in Cohoes, a village near Troy, New York.

But Arthur's real interest lay in law, and in 1854—after private study—he was admitted to the New York City bar and made a partner in the firm of Culver, Parker, and Arthur. As an attorney, he participated in the famous Lemmon Slave, Case of 1858, centering on the rescue of eight slaves passing through the city, and also in a test case that led to the racial integration of the New York streetcar system. In 1859, Arthur married Ellen ("Nell") Lewis Herndon, a Virginian who could trace her ancestry to colonial times and whose late father, Captain William Lewis Herndon, had been a prominent explorer.

Originally a Whig, Arthur became active in the newly organized Republican Party. He was a protégé of the wealthy New York merchant Edwin D. Morgan, who was elected governor in 1858. Three years later, Morgan appointed Arthur state engineer-in-chief. When the Civil War broke out, Arthur was made brigadier general, being given the task of representing the quartermaster general's office in New York City. His task: the feeding, housing, and equipping of thousands of troops. Sometimes working on no more than three hours sleep per night, Arthur proved to be an effective administrator.

In February 1862, Arthur was appointed inspector general and in July quartermaster general, in which capacity he established thirty-two recruitment camps in the state. He was an efficient and respected leader, known for his firmness and integrity. In some ways, these two years were the high point of his life.

Yet, a new governor assumed office on January 1, 1863, an event that caused Morgan and his staff, including Arthur, to lose their commissions. Arthur did not reenlist but left the service the day Lincoln issued the Emancipation Proclamation. Speculation remains as to his motives: the possible influence of his wife, whose close relatives were fighting for the Confederacy; the possible fear that the war might turn into an antislavery crusade; the possible desire for additional income.

All this time, Arthur was keeping his political fences mended, and he was closely affiliated with the conservative wing of the Republican Party, headed by Thurlow Weed and William Henry Seward. A dutiful functionary of the Weed-Seward machine in the 1864 election, Arthur collected assessments (that is, compulsory contributions) from postmasters and tapped donations from army contractors. By 1868, he chaired the executive committee of the Republican State Central Committee. In addition, he served as chairman of the Central Grant Club and again raised funds for the party. A year later, Arthur—whose law practice was now slipping—became counsel to the New York City Tax Commission, a plush job that came through the influence of Democratic boss William Marcy Tweed.

By now Arthur was becoming Roscoe Conkling's chief political lieutenant. Tall, vain, and dressed like a dandy, Conkling was a ruthless boss who suspected all men's motives but his own. He once summarized his political statement in a single sentence: "I do not know how to belong to a party a little."

In 1871, President Ulysses S. Grant appointed Arthur collector of the New York Customhouse. The Customhouse was the largest single federal office in the nation, collecting about 75 percent of the nation's customs receipts, and was also the greatest source of patronage as well. The collector directed appointments and removals, guided the assessment of hundreds of employees, and in the process held the highest-paying job in the federal government. Arthur tolerated, at times encouraged, the illegal conduct that made the office a national scandal. He had a better command of office tasks than several predecessors but still devoted most of his time to machine politics. Although popular with businessmen, subordinates, and politicos, he discreetly bypassed civil service rules and gave party supporters the lucrative positions. For Arthur, politics had remained a struggle for spoils.

By now Arthur was a corpulent figure, though always dressing in subdued elegance. He ate, drank, and smoked cigars with Republican cohorts until 3:00 A.M. As Arthur biographer Thomas C. Reeves notes, the world of Arthur was

> the world of expensive Havana cigars, Tiffany silver, fine carriages, and grand balls; the "real" world where men manipulated, plotted, and stole for power and prestige and the riches that bought both.

In 1876, Arthur was a delegate to the Republican national convention, in which capacity he pushed Conkling for president. Once Governor Rutherford B. Hayes of Ohio was nominated, however, Arthur threw himself into the presidential race, engaging in his usual drive for assessments and possibly assisting Republican leaders in influencing the outcome of the disputed election.

Yet if Arthur hoped for continued support from the White House, he was soon disappointed, for within a year Hayes ordered an investigation of customs corruption. By the middle of 1878, in a move that became a *cause célèbre*, the president suspended Arthur. True, Secretary of the Treasury John Sherman, in specifying the reasons for Arthur's removal, stressed matters of efficiency and fiscal responsibility, but partisan use of the office was obviously at stake. When in February 1879, Arthur's replacement was confirmed by the Senate, the humiliation was complete. Again a mere lawyer, not a civil servant, Arthur collected assessments for his party in the 1879 New York gubernatorial campaign, an effort that cemented Conkling's control of the governor's office, the state legislature, and the state Republican Party.

Despite the glitter, however, Arthur's life was becoming marred by tragedy. When Arthur was thirty-four, a son died; when he was fifty, his wife passed away. The latter event in particular caused him grief, for he realized how often he had neglected her for the late hours devoted to machine politics. The marriage, in fact, was on the verge of dissolution when in 1880 she succumbed to pneumonia.

Arthur again found national visibility at the Republican convention of 1880, meeting in Chicago. Part of the New York delegation, Arthur worked with fellow Stalwarts to try to gain a third-term nomination for Grant, who had been out of office for four years. Members of the Stalwart faction of the party, led by Roscoe Conkling and Senators J. Donald Cameron and John A. Logan, were united by their hostility to the South and their "stalwart" allegiance to Grant. Opposing the Stalwarts within the Republican Party were the Half-Breeds (a pejorative label affixed by their Stalwart enemies), led by James G. Blaine and Whitlaw Reid. While each side claimed to have significant differences from the other, in truth the split was more on matters of personality and control of the party than on policy or doctrine. Both sides were vehemently opposed to civil service reform, for example.

The party rejected Grant however, and Senator James A. Garfield of Ohio, a dark horse with Half-Breed leanings, was chosen as standard bearer, with Arthur put forward as running mate to appease the Stalwarts. Garfield had not authorized the overture to Arthur and indeed turned pale when he heard of the bid. Yet, he realized that any successful candidacy needed the cooperation of the Stalwarts and therefore acquiesced.

Arthur was soon chosen, receiving the blessing of the New York caucus in a session chaired by Conkling (who had strong misgivings) and of the convention as well. On the only ballot conducted, he won 468 of the 611 votes cast. The nomination, however, was declared unanimous.

In his letter of acceptance, Arthur supported suffrage for black Americans. He praised Hayes's vetoes of army bills, as they contained riders that would have prevented federal troops from keeping peace at the polls. In addressing himself to the spoils system, a major political controversy of the post–Civil War era, Arthur opposed civil service examinations: "They have seemed to exalt more educational and abstract tests above general business ability, and even special fitness for the particular work in hand." Yet, he continued, "positions of responsibility should, so far as practicable, be filled by the promotion of worthy and efficient officers." Indeed "the punishment of all official misconduct should be prompt and thorough."

If, during the campaign, Arthur's tasks as running mate were minimal, he ably served the Republican machine. He coordinated many mass meetings and took charge of tours made by Conkling and Grant throughout the Middle West. Indeed, he might have been the first "advance man" in American political history. More important, as chairman of the New York State Republican Committee, he collected assessments from city, state, and federal employees, with the normal request being 3 percent of an annual salary. Arthur played a particularly crucial role in collecting a secret fund aimed at securing a Republican victory in Indiana, an important state that had gone Democratic two and four years before.

When on November 2, 1880, Arthur was elected vice president, he refused to stand aloof from the party's still warring factions. Rather he strengthened his ties to the Conkling machine. Indeed, so anxious was he to bolster Stalwart power that he journeyed to Albany to fight over a Senate slot. On February 11, 1881, at a meeting of the Union League Club at Delmonico's famous restaurant in New York, Vice President-elect Arthur boasted of his role in paying for Indiana voters and thereby securing that crucial swing state for the Republicans. Obviously somewhat inebriated, he said: "If it were not for the reporters present I would tell you the truth, because I know you are intimate friends and devoted adherents to the Republican Party."

Upon hearing the day before the inauguration that Garfield had not slated a Conkling protégé as postmaster general, which was a powerful major patronage position, Arthur, Conkling, and New York Senator Thomas Platt stormed to the president-elect's Washington hotel room. There Conkling castigated the president-elect for more than an hour, claiming that Garfield deceived his friends and betrayed his party. Arthur sat on the edge of Garfield's bed, listening in silent approval. To Arthur, tacit or overt support of a man about to be president meant far less than continued loyalty to a party faction. Far from thinking that he was acting treacherously, he saw himself as obedient to the political code upon which he had been raised.

After his inauguration on March 4, 1881, Arthur as vice president presided over the Senate. Party strength in the upper chamber was practically even; both Democrats and Republicans had thirty-seven members. One independent, David Davis of Illinois, sided with the Democrats. Virginia's William Mahone, a former Democrat who won his seat as a "readjuster" of his state's debt, agreed to support the Republicans in return for control over state patronage and GOP pledges to keep the party ticket off future state elections. Within this deadlocked Senate, Arthur cast deciding votes, though at one point he was so nervous his hands shook and he called a tally incorrectly.

By this time, Garfield sought a showdown with the Stalwarts, who were continually demanding more lucrative patronage positions. On March 23, he appointed William H. Robertson, a Half-Breed who was president pro tem of the New York senate, to the collectorship of the New York Customhouse. Garfield sought to make the issue one of presidential prerogative, writing a friend: "This brings on the contest at once and will settle the question whether the President is registering clerk of the Senate or the Executive of the United States." Because Half-Breed leader Blaine, now secretary of state, was really behind move, nothing could have insulted the Stalwarts more.

As the controversy developed, Arthur made little secret of Ms loyalty to Conkling. In a petition to the president dated March 28, Arthur joined with Postmaster General Thomas James, Conkling, and Platt in accusing Garfield of violating senatorial courtesy. Visiting the White House on April 14, the vice president implored Garfield to withdraw Robertson's name, arguing that the move could only lead to the Republican's national defeat. Along with Conkling, Arthur pushed a petition among New York importers: It criticized Robertson's record in the state legislature and called for the retention of the current reformist collector, General Edwin A. Merritt. Arthur's New York home was the center of several anti-Robertson strategy meetings.

On May 16, Conkling and Platt resigned their senate seats. Were they to be sent back by the New York legislature, the Stalwart cause—they believed—would be vindicated. Conversely, were the legislature to turn them down, their political machine would be weakened beyond repair. Arthur personally opposed the move, no doubt doing so in the realization that the New York legislature had earlier endorsed Robertson. Once, however, Platt and Conkling made their move, he backed them to the hilt.

The U.S. Senate had long been tied up over a Democratic filibuster, one not centering on the Robertson imbroglio but over a different controversy: whether to offer favors to renegade Virginia Senator Mahone. Once, however, the Republicans abandoned the effort to back Mahone, the Senate could vote on Robertson. On May 18 he was easily confirmed. Arthur continued his support of the two recalcitrant

New York senators, journeying with Conkling to Albany on May 24 to rally the Stalwart forces. His efforts did little good, for on May 31 the legislature turned down both Conkling and Platt.

Not surprisingly, Arthur's moves were tarnishing his image even further. Democrats, Half-Breeds, and independents alike portrayed him as a man of sheer expediency. Arthur might well have resented such attacks, but he would not let them interfere with his opposition. Arthur told the Stalwart editor of the *New York Herald* that Garfield, "spurred by Blaine, by whom he is easily led, has broke every pledge made by us; not only that, but he seems to have wished to do it in the most offensive way."

Biographer Thomas Reeves ably captures Arthur's thinking:

He had been a Stalwart too long to surrender an inch—much less the war—to Blaine and those he controlled. If he could not be popular, at least he could be true to his friends; and if Conkling regained his political power there would soon be admirers enough.

On the morning of July 2, Arthur and Conkling had barely stepped off the steamer from Albany to New York when they heard that the president had been shot. Charles Guiteau, a lunatic who felt slighted in his quixotic quest for major office, had shot Garfield at Washington's Baltimore and Potomac Station. Upon arrest, Guiteau said: "All right, I did it and will go to jail for it. I am a Stalwart, and Arthur will be president." Arthur took the midnight train to New York. Conkling carried his bags to the depot.

Over the ensuing weeks, Garfield steadily grew weaker. A bullet had lodged near his spinal column, and his physicians deemed him too weak for a probe. In genuine agony, Arthur was overwhelmed by the prospect of becoming chief executive, stunned by the situation that had brought him to Washington, and crushed by savage press attacks. Old friends had not found him so moved since the death of his wife.

Secretary Blaine was obviously no friend of the Stalwarts but feared that Garfield might linger incapacitated for months, perhaps years. On August 27, the cabinet sounded out Arthur on his willingness to serve as acting president. Despite Blaine's support, Arthur refused, finding the proposal improper. Having returned to New York City in mid-July, he refused to go back to Washington.

There was also the matter of the U.S. Senate, where there was again fear of Democratic control. The resignation of Conkling and Platt had given the Democrats a majority, and the party undoubtedly desired to elect Maryland's Thomas Bayard its president pro tem. Arthur prevented the move by refusing to vacate his chair, so the Senate adjourned without a constitutional successor to the presidency if the vice president was incapacitated. Bayard in particular was far from pleased with such crude partisanship, and he wrote to reformer Carl Schurz: "May heaven avert the contingency of Arthur's promotion."

Bayard was not alone. To many, Arthur represented, a bit unfairly, the worst of the spoils system, and Guiteau was seen more as a disappointed office seeker than a certified madman. The press did give Arthur credit for conducting himself with propriety during the assassination crisis, but his unsavory reputation remained. E.L. Godkin, editor of the *Nation,* wrote: "It is out of this mess of filth that Mr. Arthur will go to the Presidential chair in case of the President's death." Ex-president Hayes wrote in his diary: "Arthur for President! Conkling the power behind the throne, superior to the throne!"

On September 19, Garfield died at Elberon, a village on the Jersey shore. At 2:15 A.M. the following day, a judge administered the oath of office to Arthur. Three days later, he again took the presidential oath, this time before Chief Justice Morrison R. Waite. He gave a brief inaugural speech, referring to his predecessor's "example and achievements" and the "pathos of his death." He called attention to the nation's prosperity and, as a hard-money man, praised its "well-grounded" fiscal policy. There was, he said, "no demand for speedy legislation," and as president he would never find any.

Few then realized that a man of such limitations would take the presidency seriously. Ohio Governor Charles Foster was almost alone in claiming that "the people and the politicians will find that Vice-President Arthur and President Arthur are different men."

Once he became chief executive, Arthur made some strong appointments, even if most were Stalwarts: Former U.S. senator Frederick T. Frelinghuysen became secretary of state; Charles J. Folger, chief justice of the New York State Supreme Court, was made secretary of the treasury; Pennsylvania's former Attorney General Benjamin Harris Brewster served as attorney general. Arthur sought prosecution of a postal scandal—the star route affair—though he knew full well that former cronies were among the guilty. Indeed, he was extremely embarrassed when the courts found the defendants not guilty.

The Stalwart faction received so few favors that one member complained of Arthur: "He has done less for us than Garfield, or even Hayes." Arthur did ask Conkling, who was an able attorney, to serve on the U.S. Supreme Court, but "Lord Roscoe" had his eye on the State Department and refused. Eventually Conkling found the Hayes administration by comparison "reputable, if not heroic." As former old Arthur cronies of customhouse days mourned: "He isn't: 'Chet' Arthur any more; he's the president."

Arthur could not entirely escape his shady past. Both William E. Chandler, his secretary of the navy, and Timothy O. Howe, his postmaster general, were perceived as typical spoilsmen. The removal of reformer Silas Burt, naval officer to the New York Customhouse, was a spiteful act against an able administrator, and certain other appointments—such as Arthur's first choice for chief examiner to the Civil Service Commission—aroused the ire of reformers.

In his first annual message, Arthur endorsed civil service reform. Only, however, after the congressional elections of 1882 was the cause taken seriously. The Democrats had won the House and almost captured the Senate. It was better, realized the lame-duck Republican Congress, to back the civil service bill advanced by Ohio's Democratic senator George Hunt Pendleton titan to take the blame for delaying the inevitable; indeed, by moving quickly, the GOP could protect the tenure of their own incumbent officeholders before any ax fell.

With his second annual message, Arthur became a vocal reformer par excellence, and on January 18, 1883, he signed the Pendleton Act. On the plus side, the bill provided for a five-member Civil Service Examination Board, with authority to hold competitive examinations for positions on a classified list. On the minus side, it exempted the vast majority of federal employees and all municipal and state ones. Indeed one Democratic senator caustically called the measure "a bill to perpetuate in office the Republicans who now control the patronage of the Government."

Like other Gilded Age presidents, Arthur used his veto power generously. In 1882, he successfully vetoed a Chinese exclusion bill that would have excluded Chinese laborers from entry into the United States for twenty years and denied U.S. citizenship to Chinese residents. While conceding that unrestricted Chinese labor might threaten American livelihoods, he claimed in his veto message that twenty years—"nearly a generation"—was unreasonable. Moreover, the bill violated a treaty made with China in 1880, disdainfully ignored those Chinese laborers who had contributed to the U.S. economy, and risked a lucrative Far Eastern trade. Arthur also vetoed a steamboat safety bill, claiming that the wording contained several technical errors, and a rivers and harbors bill that was heavily weighted in favor of one section—the South.

Arthur promoted naval development to such a degree that he could be called one of the fathers of the modern navy. In his annual message of 1881, he referred to the protection of "the highways of commerce, the varied interests of our foreign trade." Furthermore, he said: "We must be prepared to enforce any policy we think wise to adopt." His secretary of the navy, William E. Chandler, was a ruthless party organizer who had been judge advocate under Lincoln and was the only pronounced Half-Breed (though a strong Arthur partisan) in the cabinet. With Arthur's full approval, Chandler instituted a surprising number of reforms: a much-needed Naval War College at Newport, Rhode Island; the closing of superfluous navy yards at Pensacola, Florida, and New London, Connecticut; and a new naval advisory board that recommended the construction of armor-plated cruisers. In March 1883, Arthur signed a bill that gave the nation its first three steel-plated cruisers and a new dispatch boat.

In some areas, Arthur was quite limited. As with most Gilded Age presidents, he so believed in laissez-faire that he was unable to cope with a declining economy. In 1883, the Supreme Court found unconstitutional the Civil Rights Act of 1875, a law that provided that all persons, irrespective of race, were entitled to equal access to "inns, public conveyances on land or water, theaters, and other places of public amusement." In response to the decision, the president said he would unhesitatingly support any "right, privilege, and immunity of citizenship" that Congress might pass. Yet, when congressional Republicans introduced five different bills to replaced the defunct 1875 Civil Rights Act, Arthur offered little support. His annual messages spoke only of educational needs.

Arthur also had some major setbacks. Congress, for example, overrode his veto of a rivers and harbors bill. When examining his foreign policy, it is hard to find a single success. His administration was unable to mediate the war between Peru and Chile, to alter the Clayton-Bulwer Treaty of 1850 that recognized British rights over any canal built through Central America, or to secure a treaty with Nicaragua that would give the United States co-ownership of any canal strip there. The Germans and French blocked the entry of American pork. Congress tabled the Berlin agreement of 1885,

a treaty that formally recognized the Congo Free State; it also refused to act on reciprocity efforts concerning Mexico, Cuba, Puerto Rico, and Santo Domingo.

Within a year after assuming office, Arthur became extremely lethargic. Much of his apparent listlessness was caused by Bright's disease, a fatal kidney ailment that led to spasmodic nausea, mental depression, and inertness. His deteriorating condition, however, was probably the best-kept secret of his administration. A courageous man, he refused to court public sympathy, and in fact found it undignified to burden others with his plight. All the time he was failing, he carried on his official duties, refusing to go into seclusion. He realized that the performance of official tasks was hastening his end, but he did not want to be remembered as a caretaker executive. In 1884, he made a nominal bid for election to a term in his own right, but he was simply going through the motions. Reluctance would merely raise suspicions about his health, competency, and courage. After leaving the White House, Arthur moved back to New York City where he assumed the position of counsel to his a old law firm. Within a year, he was an invalid. On November 17, 1886, Chester Alan Arthur died in New London, Connecticut.

REFERENCES

Justus D. Doenecke, *The Presidency of James A. Garfield and Chester A. Arthur* (Lawrence, Kans.: Regents Press of Kansas, 1981); George Frederick Howe, *Chester A. Arthur: A Quarter-Century of Machine Politics* (New York: Dodd, Mead, 1935); David M. Pletcher, *The Awkward Years: American Foreign Relations under Garfield and Arthur* (Columbia, Mo.: University of Missouri Press, 1962); Thomas C. Reeves, *Gentleman Boss: The Life of Chester Alan Arthur* (New York: Knopf, 1975).

JUSTUS D. DOENECKE is the author of *The Presidencies of James A. Garfield and Chester*

A. *Arthur* (1981) and has written numerous other books and articles. In 2000, he won the annual Herbert Hoover Book Award from the Hoover Presidential Library Association for his book, *Storm on the Horizon: The Challenge to American Intervention* (2000). In 1991, he received the Arthur S. Link Prize for Documentary Editing from the Society for Historians of American Foreign Relations. He received his Ph.D. from Princeton. He is professor emeritus of history at the New College of Florida.

Thomas Andrews Hendricks (1819–1885)

Vice President, March 4–November 25, 1885

(President Grover Cleveland)

Thomas A. Hendricks
(Library of Congress)

By Thomas Burnell Colbert

It was probably the largest funeral ever in Indianapolis, Indiana. On December 1, 1885, a mass of mourners came to lay to rest Thomas A. Hendricks, the twenty-first vice president of the United States. For more than three decades, Hendricks had been one of the state's most prominent political leaders. Four times he had been a candidate for the Democratic Party's presidential nomination, and twice he had been the party's candidate for vice president. Indeed, Hendricks had played a conspicuous role in state and national politics during a tumultuous period in American history.

As with any notable politician, any attempt to assess his career, achievements, and qualities confronts conflicting viewpoints. To his many admirers, Hendricks was an admirable person. This understanding of Hendricks was summed up well by historian Louis Clinton Hatch, who wrote: "Personally, Hendricks was thoroughly honest, a man of culture but without hauteur, fond of mixing with his fellows, agreeable and conciliating." Furthermore, present-day Indiana historian Ralph D. Gray has concluded that Hendricks "had talent, firm convictions, a simple but powerful style of oratory, and the common touch. He was indeed a most eloquent spokesman for the Indiana Democracy, and for Democrats everywhere, during a critical two decades." To his critics—in both national parties—Hendricks lacked commitment to defining political policies. To them, he was more of a political operator, an office seeker rather than a statesman. Consequently, Whitelaw Reid, the editor of the Republican *New York Tribune,* called Hendricks "the Professional Candidate," and Oliver P. Morton, Indiana's powerful Republican leader, caustically said that Hendricks's "thirty years of nonachievement in office set some sort of record." A brief review of his life shows how all these views have basis.

Thomas Andrews Hendricks was born on September 7, 1819, in Zanesville, Ohio, to John Hendricks and his wife, Jane Thomson Hendricks. In 1822, John Hendricks moved his family to Shelby County, Indiana. Thomas grew up in Shelbyville, first in a log cabin and then in a brick house his increasingly successful father built. John Hendricks, a staunch Presbyterian who helped found the First Presbyterian Church in Indianapolis, sent Thomas to Hanover College, a Presbyterian school, in Hanover, Indiana, in 1836. After spending one year in the preparatory courses, Thomas began college work, graduating in 1841. He decided to study law, first with Judge Stephen Major in Shelbyville and then with his uncle, Judge Alexander Thomson, who conducted a law school in Chambersburg, Pennsylvania. In 1843, Hendricks was admitted to the Indiana bar.

For the next few years, Hendricks worked to develop a practice. On September 26, 1845, he married Eliza Morgan. In 1848, their only child, Morgan, was born; sadly, the boy died in 1851. Eliza gave much attention to helping Thomas advance his career, becoming not only a social hostess but also a trusted advisor.

In 1848, Hendricks entered politics and was elected as a Democrat to the Indiana assembly's lower house. His family had a history of political life: His grandfather, Abraham Hendricks, had been elected to four terms in the Pennsylvania assembly, but more important, his uncle, William Hendricks, was a bulwark of the Democratic Party in Indiana, having served as Indiana's first member of the U.S. House of Representatives, as the second governor of the state, and then as a two-term U.S. senator. Ironically, though, Thomas did not distinguish himself in the legislature. Apparently, his interest was not piqued, and he refused renomination.

What did propel Hendricks into a leadership role was the state constitutional convention. Indianans in 1850 prepared to revamp their state constitution, and Shelby Countians sent Hendricks to the convention. As a Jacksonian Democrat, Hendricks attracted notice for his critical views on paper money and banks. Additionally, he was also outspoken in his opposition to allowing blacks to enter Indiana. While he claimed to be no friend to slavery, he called for separation of the races—an attitude held by many Indianans who approved the new constitution and its exclusion article.

In 1851, buttressed by his new-found popularity, Hendricks was elected to the U.S. House of Representatives from the Indianapolis district. In Congress, Hendricks fulfilled the expectations of his supporters, and in 1852, having to run so soon because of the new constitution's election-date changes, Hendricks was easily reelected. During this term, Hendricks more closely aligned himself with Senator Stephen A. Douglas of Illinois. In particular, as a Western Democrat, Hendricks supported the Homestead Bill to open free land to settlers and Douglas's controversial Kansas-Nebraska Act to nullify the Missouri Compromise on the extension of slavery through popular sovereignty. Consequently, in 1854, Know-Nothings, old Whigs, prohibitionists, and other non-Democrats fused to defeat Hendricks for reelection.

Much to Hendricks's surprise, newly elected President Franklin Pierce asked him to become commissioner of the General Land Office. Initially, Hendricks wanted to refuse the offer, for he suspected that Pierce wanted to gain approval of Indiana Democrats more than having any particular desire for Hendricks in the administration. However, John Hendricks convinced his son to accept the post, and Pierce informed Thomas that he did indeed desire him for the office because of his strong support for the Homestead Bill.

As commissioner, Hendricks proved an able and efficient administrator. Many land claims were processed under his leadership, and when James Buchanan became president in 1857, he asked Hendricks to continue in the job. Unfortunately, Buchanan and Hendricks did not get along. Hendricks resisted the president's efforts to use clerkships in the Public Land Office for patronage payoffs. Furthermore, not only did Buchanan not endorse the Homestead Bill, but he was also at odds with Douglas, his rival in the Democratic Party. Therefore, in 1859, Hendricks resigned.

After returning to Indiana, Hendricks was nominated for governor by his fellow Democrats in 1860. The growing Republican Party, however, won many contests in Indiana that year, and Hendricks lost by 25,000 votes. Following his defeat, Hendricks moved from Shelbyville to Indianapolis to practice law.

By 1862, the political situation had changed somewhat. Abraham Lincoln's winning of the presidency had led to Southern secession, the creation of the Confederacy, and finally the Civil War. While some Northerners with Southern ties and sympathies in Indiana opposed the war, most Indianans were unionists; however, many were not emancipationists, including Hendricks. Moreover, the war effort at first went poorly for Union forces, especially in the East. All of this fostered a frustration played out at the state Democratic convention in 1862.

Hendricks was chosen as president of the convention, and he and others spoke out against the possible emancipation of slaves and the recruitment of black soldiers. (Several years later; in 1880, he conceded that he was wrong in opposing the abolition of slavery during the war.) Hendricks opined that it would hurt the morale of white Indianans to be joined by blacks, for he maintained that blacks were inferior to whites and that the races should be kept unequal and separated. Later that year, a mass state convention was held, and Hendricks was elected its president by acclamation. Once more, he voiced his views and concerns, and certainly, he had become one of the Indiana Democratic Party's major leaders. The efforts of Hendricks and other wheelhorses paid off when Democrats gained control of the state legislature. In turn, on January 14, 1863, they elected Hendricks to the U.S. Senate.

Throughout the Civil War, although accused by Republican enemies of being a Copperhead (one of a group of Democrats who worked actively to end the war and whom many regarded as traitors), Hendricks remained a staunch Unionist. In fact, contrary to the carping of his opponents, he strove to curb Copperhead activities. Although he opposed conscription (he favored enlistment and the payment of bounties), emancipation, high taxes, and the issuance of greenback currency, he always admonished Indianans to obey the laws—he denounced civil disobedience and treason. At the same time, he supported legislation in the Senate for prosecuting the war. Most notable, perhaps, was his opposition to the Thirteenth Amendment to the Constitution. Again arguing that blacks were inferior to whites, he said that while he did not like slavery, the issue should be calmly and judiciously resolved by all the states, not just those in the North. He argued that the states in rebellion had not left the Union; they were merely not at the time capable of considering the amendment, which should be withheld from consideration until after the war. In all, Hendricks became a leading Democratic spokesman in the

Congress at a time when his party was in the minority. At the same time, he professed to enjoy a friendly cordiality with President Lincoln despite their disagreements.

When Andrew Johnson became president following the assassination of Lincoln, Hendricks took a lead in supporting Johnson's Reconstruction actions. He opposed the Radical Republicans' Freedmen's Bureau Act, the Civil Rights Bill, reapportionment legislation with the destruction of the three-fifths clause, the Fourteenth Amendment, and the Fifteenth Amendment. He continued to argue that the southern states had never left the Union and should have a say in any future constitutional amendments. As for civil rights, he offered that the term was vague, and with his well-known views on race relations, he expressed his fear of black suffrage and potential interracial marriages. Additionally, while he had nothing against opening federal lands to black homesteaders, he did oppose confiscating land to be given to former slaves.

On issues not directly connected to Reconstruction policies, Hendricks was more pragmatic. Indeed, his detractors said he was a "trimmer," an opportunistic and unprincipled politician. Thus, for example, he could cooperate with like-minded Western Republicans in opposition to high tariffs or could modify his position on greenbacks ("soft money") when farmers in the West desired inflation after the war.

Hendricks's strength as a Democratic leader was evinced in January 1868, when he was nominated for governor of Indiana. At the state convention, he again assailed black suffrage but then implied that he could accept gradual and restricted enfranchisement for qualified freedmen. He had supported such a policy with his votes in the Senate.

More important, at that year's national Democratic convention Hendricks sought the presidential nomination. The leading contender from the West before the convention was George H. Pendleton of Ohio, who had gained prominence as a result of his opposition to reducing the amount of greenbacks in circulation. With the war's end, the economy had soured. In Indiana and in the West, farmers faced low prices on their produce, coupled with heavy debt from high-interest loans that had been made in depreciated greenbacks. Nonetheless, the administration's fiscal conservatives wanted to make the economy more monetarily sound by reducing the amount of paper money, which would deflate prices even more and make repayments even harder. Many westerners, both Republicans and Democrats, opposed "contraction" (as it was called) of the money supply. Consequently, Pendleton proposed not only the curtailment of contraction but also that the principal of government bonds be redeemed in greenbacks in order to place more paper money in circulation. On the basis of this so-called Ohio Idea, Pendleton cast his eyes toward the presidential nomination. Eastern Democrats, however, who did not care for Pendleton, looked to Hendricks as an alternative, even though the Indiana delegation came to the convention committed to Pendleton and Hendricks had accepted the Democratic gubernatorial nomination in Indiana.

Hendricks's position on soft money was ambiguous. Before and during the war, he had opposed the issuance of greenbacks. In 1866, when the Contraction Bill came before the Senate, he did not vote. But in 1868, when Indianans of both parties voiced opposition to contraction, he voted to repeal the act. Thus to some he was at heart a hard-money man; to others he was an advocate of soft money. Consequently, Hendricks's name was placed in nomination, and he seemed to have a chance at victory as Pendleton's support peaked. On the twenty-first ballot, Hendricks had the most votes. At that point, Pendleton's Ohio delegation moved to defeat Hendricks by nominating Horatio Seymour, the hard-money governor of New York. The convention was being held in New York and Seymour was chairman. On the fourth ballot, his name had been offered, and he had it removed. Seymour did not, however, stop the stampede for his candidacy on the twenty-second ballot.

After Hendricks failed in his surprise bid for the presidential nomination in 1868, he also lost in the Indiana governor's race. His apparent early lead dissipated, and he lost by 961 votes. On the other hand, his personal popularity was equally evidenced by the fact that Republican presidential candidate U.S. Grant carried the state by more than 20,000 votes.

Although Hendricks retired to private life and his partnership in a very successful law firm in 1869, he remained active in politics. In 1872, after the national Democratic convention merged with the new anti-Grant Liberal Republican Party and endorsed its presidential candidate, Horace Greeley, some "straight-out" Democrats who were opposed to Greeley looked to Hendricks as a possible presidential candidate. Hendricks, however, announced at the Indiana Democratic state convention that he would be willing to support Greeley. Following the lead of Hendricks and his ilk of Democrats, the party both wrote a state platform that adopted much of the Liberal Republican positions and ran Hendricks for governor. At the same time, the rumor spread that if the Democrats gained control of the state legislature, Hendricks would be sent to the U.S. Senate, which he desired more than the governorship. The Republicans, however, carried the state except for the offices of governor and superintendent of public instruction. Hendricks thus in 1872 became governor in his third attempt. His victory had been determined by the support of temperance advocates, for he said that he would sign a local option liquor law if the legislature passed one, even though he personally preferred a license law.

His gubernatorial victory again made Hendricks important in national Democratic politics. He had become one of the first Democrats to lead a northern state after the Civil War. In fact, the degree of his new importance was symbolized when the Electoral College met in 1869. Greeley died not long after the presidential election, and of his eighty-one electoral votes, the electors gave forty-two of them to Hendricks.

In 1873, the nation headed into an economic depression, and once more the agitation for greenbacks and inflation began. The so-called Inflation Bill to put more greenbacks in circulation was passed by both houses of Congress in 1874, but President Grant vetoed it. This action raised the ire of western Democrats, and at the Indiana Democratic convention Hendricks half-heartedly accepted soft-money planks for the state platform. However, when the Democrats gained control of the legislature, Hendricks supported the senatorial candidacy of hard-money Democrat Joseph E. McDonald. McDonald's main competitor for the office was Congressman Daniel Voorhees, an outspoken advocate of soft money. Supposedly, Hendricks had rejected Voorhees for McDonald on the condition that McDonald and other conservative Indiana Democrats endorse Hendricks for president in 1876.

By 1875, the money controversy took a new turn when the Republican-controlled Congress passed the Resumption Bill, which called for the resumption of specie payments by the government in 1879. President Grant signed the measure, and opposition to the Resumption Act made a strong issue for soft-money Democrats. As for Hendricks, he said that gold and silver were true money and that resumption was necessary. However, he also said that because it should not be accomplished so quickly as to hurt businesses and farms, the Resumption Act should be repealed at this point. Hendricks proposed instead that bonds be sold for the government to build a stock of gold over a longer period of time than four years. Furthermore, he offered that an increase in production and rebuilding the South would do much more to enhance the national economy than the premature resumption of specie payments.

To the astute, it seemed clear that Hendricks was hedging on the money issue, sounding paradoxically like both a hard-money; and a soft-money advocate. Hendricks, however, was trying to position himself for the Democratic presidential nomination in 1876.

Hendricks did not attend the Democratic national convention that year; rather, the Indiana delegation, led by Senator McDonald, was pledged to Hendricks's presidential candidacy. Furthermore, he let it be known that he would accept nothing less than the head of the ticket. At the convention, however, Samuel J. Tilden, the reform-minded governor of New York, received the nomination, and despite his wishes, Hendricks was unanimously nominated for vice president. His selection was based on geography. Democratic strategists hoped that Hendricks could at least carry the important state of Indiana and perhaps some others in the West with his financial views, and that Tilden could carry New York, and then with victories in the "redeemed" Democratic states in the South, Tilden would win. Regardless of the political logic behind his selection, Hendricks only reluctantly acquiesced to accepting the nomination, and then only after the strenuous urging of political allies.

Tilden and Hendricks, unfortunately, were not overly agreeable with each other. Tilden termed the call for repeal of the Resumption Act a "barren promise," while Hendricks campaigned for repeal, although conservative Eastern Democrats working for Tilden promoted Hendricks as a proponent of hard money. Moreover, Hendricks openly felt snubbed by not receiving the presidential nomination. The final controversy came with the results of the election. Twenty electoral votes were in dispute and claimed by both parties. Tilden and Hendricks needed only one of the votes to claim the election, in which they had outpolled the Republican ticket by more than 200,000 votes. The impasse was resolved when a special electoral commission was established. It consisted of eight Republicans and seven Democrats who voted on partisan lines on every questioned electoral ballot. Republican Rutherford B. Hayes thereby became president. Tilden begrudgingly accepted the decision of the commission. Hendricks, however, chided Tilden for his passivity in the controversy. He believed that Tilden should have demanded that he be declared president and then asked the Supreme Court to act on the electoral count question.

In 1877, Hendricks again returned to private life while still thirsting for a presidential candidacy. In 1880, the Indiana delegation to the national Democratic convention was instructed to support Hendricks for president. However, Senator McDonald, who also harbored presidential aspirations, likewise had a following in the delegation. Nonetheless, Daniel Voorhees nominated Hendricks, and the Indiana delegation stayed solidly behind him, though he garnered few other votes. General Winfield Scott Hancock won the nomination, and to placate some Indianans and to carry the state, W.H. English, a Conservative banker from Indianapolis, was chosen as his running mate. Hendricks took no pleasure in English's selection. As congressmen in the 1850s, the two had split between supporting Douglas and Buchanan, and they had not gotten along well since then. Indeed, it was even said that English was nominated for the vice presidency, in part, just to upset Hendricks.

In another close election, the Republican ticket won again. More personal to Hendricks, though, was a blow to his health. He suffered a stroke, which left him with some paralysis in his right arm. Two years later, he endured a second stroke. This one left him lame.

Regardless of his deteriorating health, Hendricks did not forsake politics, especially as he experienced popularity on the Democratic speakers' circuit. Again in 1884 he and Tilden were mentioned for another national ticket. Hendricks, however, now could not abide Tilden, and they no longer even spoke to each other. Tilden said he was too old and sick to consider another run. As for Hendricks, that spring he publicly professed his distaste for civil service reform and his support for tariff reductions, as well as reminding everyone that he and Tilden had been cheated out of office in 1876.

The Democratic national convention of 1884 was the largest such political gathering held in the United States up to that. Hendricks was a delegate-at-large from Indiana, and he had agreed to place Senator McDonald's name in nomination for the presidency, although McDonald and his supporters more realistically viewed the senator as a contender for the vice-presidential slot. The strongest contender for the presidential nomination, however, was Grover Cleveland, the governor of New York. Cleveland had a reputation as an efficient administrator and an advocate of civil service reform. As such, however, he did not enjoy the backing of the patronage-based Tammany Hall New York City Democratic machine. John Kelly, "the Grand Sachem of Tammany," was not only opposed to Cleveland but also a friend of Hendricks. He and his cohorts tried to turn the convention toward Hendricks when, on the second ballot, a delegate from Illinois cast his vote for Hendricks just as he appeared dramatically in the doorway. The hoopla that followed did not change the outcome: Cleveland was nominated easily. However, the memory of the "old ticket" of 1876 helped lead to Hendricks being nominated for vice president. The reasons for Hendricks's selection were much the same as before: he could carry an important state; he was a soft-money man while Cleveland was for hard money; he had the support of machine politicians who opposed Cleveland on civil service reform. Moreover, he carried the martyr's baggage of having been defrauded of the vice presidency.

Hendricks was reluctant to accept the nomination. His health was poor, and he had earlier declared his support for McDonald. Nor was Cleveland enthusiastic about Hendricks. Nonetheless, Hendricks agreed to run; campaigned well in New York, Ohio, Illinois, and Indiana; and even joined in the mudslinging for which the contest became infamous by charging the Republican Navy Department with corruption. However, as with Tilden, not only were there political differences between Hendricks and Cleveland but also personal ones. In particular, when it was discovered that Cleveland was supporting an illegitimate son, some thought he

should surrender the nomination. (Reportedly, Hendricks was one who uttered such a view.) However, in a public letter, Hendricks stated that it was too far into the race for Cleveland to bow but. Besides, Hendricks offered; this "moral" issue was not so great as to disqualify Cleveland for the presidency.

Cleveland and Hendricks won a majority of electoral votes although they outdistanced the Republican ticket by only 20,000 popular votes. When asked about the contest, Hendricks remarked: "It's very unpleasant. . . . This is the fourth time that an election in which I was a candidate has been so close that both sides claimed it, until the official count was declared." Furthermore, the relationship between Cleveland and Hendricks, who met for the first time after the election, did not improve. Cleveland cared little for the patronage concerns of Hendricks and his wing of the Democratic Party, but probably more distancing was Cleveland's resentment of Hendricks's propensity for compromise and especially his equivocating monetary views. The situation was further exacerbated when it was reported that inasmuch as Cleveland was a bachelor, Mrs. Hendricks intended to oversee social functions at the White House. Hendricks was compelled to show the press his telegram to Cleveland saying there was "no truth in the assertion."

Regardless of any strained relations, both men took their oaths of office on March 4, 1885, and Hendricks turned to presiding over the Senate. The task lasted for only a month while the senators considered cabinet appointees. Hendricks attended every Senate meeting and did not allow the Republican majority to select a president pro tem to preside in his absence. He probably not only wanted to perform his one official duty faithfully, but he also chose to deny the Republicans the opportunity to advance one of their own.

Soon, however, Hendricks and Cleveland became embroiled in a dispute over patronage. Cleveland both wanted to fulfill his promise of civil service reform in government appointments and didn't care to spend his time dealing with office seekers. On the other hand, Hendricks wished to put his supporters into patronage jobs. This difference spilled into a public controversy over who would become the postmaster for Indianapolis. Hendricks backed Aquila Jones for the position, but Indiana congressman William D. Bynum wanted someone else. Hendricks won out, but not before a congressional committee investigated the matter. At the same time, Hendricks faced the hostility of Senator McDonald, who claimed that Hendricks had kept him from receiving the Democratic presidential nomination in 1880 and now had Cleveland deny him either a cabinet post or a foreign mission. (He did not mention Hendricks gaining the vice presidential nomination in 1884!) For his part, Hendricks complained: "The Democratic party isn't in power. Grover Cleveland is making a party of his own." When asked by a reporter if he and Cleveland did not get along, he replied "Our relations when we meet are decidedly cordial. I have not seen the President in four months, but I have no doubt when I meet him it will be on terms of the most cordial Democratic fellowship."

While waiting for the Senate to reconvene in December, Hendricks not only rested but also accepted speaking engagements at Yale and Harvard, following which the *New York Times* reported that he looked "worn." Nonetheless, despite his age and health, Hendricks was again mentioned as a possible presidential candidate in 1888 by some who disliked Cleveland. Hendricks, however, confided to a close friend that

> all the talk about my being a candidate in 1888 is the veriest twaddle. I shall never be a candidate for that or any office again. I was not a candidate for Vice President last year, but having been elected, I am satisfied, more than satisfied. A happier man than I am today you never saw.

Hendricks died suddenly a week later on November 25, 1885, in Indianapolis, after attending a major reception in his honor.

Thomas Andrews Hendricks served as vice president of the United States for only nine months. He did little to distinguish himself in that office. On the other hand, he had been a major player in the Democratic Party for three decades. Perhaps he merited some of the invective heaped upon him by his political enemies. Hendricks certainly found no solace in observations such as Oliver P. Morton's that Hendricks had "fearlessly refused to commit himself upon any question until after his party has taken a position on it." Yet, that was a characteristic that many party brokers sought in candidates. Hendricks could, when advantageous, comfortably compromise on party concerns. He spoke well, he made many friends, and he worked the spoils system. In all, he functioned creditably at politicking and electioneering. Therefore, while Hendricks's time as vice president was brief, his role in national politics had been established for many years, and the vice presidency was only the capstone to his place in history.

REFERENCES

John W. Holcombe and Hubert M. Skinner, *Life and Public Services of Thomas A. Hendricks with Selected Speeches and Writings* (Indianapolis, Ind.: Carlon and Hollenbeck, 1886); *American Biographical History of Eminent and Self-Made Men in the State of Indiana, District 7* (Cincinnati, Ohio: Walden & Stowe, 1880); Ralph D. Hayes, ed., *Gentlemen from Indiana: National Party Candidates 1836–1940* (Indianapolis: Indiana Historical Bureau, 1977); Emma Lou Thornbrough, *Indiana in the Civil War Era 1850–1880* (Indianapolis: Indiana Historical Bureau and Indiana Historical Society, 1965); G.R. Tredway, *Democratic Opposition to the Lincoln Administration in Indiana* (Indianapolis: Indiana Historical Bureau, 1973); William G. Carleton, "The Money Question in Indiana Politics 1865–1890," *Indiana Magazine of History*, 42 (June 1926), 107–150; Edward L. Gambill, *Conservative Ordeal: Northern Democrats and Reconstruction 1865–1869* (Ames: Iowa State University Press, 1981); James Rawley, *The Politics of Union: Northern Politics During the Civil War* (Lincoln: University of Nebraska Press, 1974). While obviously biased, a sense of Hendricks and the politics of the times can be found in the several presidential campaign biographies in which he was featured.

THOMAS BURNELL COLBERT is professor of social sciences and humanities at Marshalltown Community College in Iowa. He holds a B.A. and M.A. in history from the University of Iowa and a Ph.D. in history from Oklahoma State University. One of his main areas of research and publication is nineteenth-century political history of the West and Midwest. He has written several articles for historical journals and encyclopedias as well as numerous book reviews and professional papers. He was a contributor to *Enduring Nations: Native Americans in the Midwest* (Champaign: University of Illinois Press, 2008).

LEVI PARSONS MORTON (1824–1920)

Vice President, 1889–1893

(President Benjamin Harrison)

LEVI PARSONS MORTON
(Library of Congress)

By Robert S. La Forte

Timing is everything in politics. With it, Levi Parsons Morton could have been president of the United States. James A. Garfield wanted him as his running mate in 1880, but Morton refused because Roscoe Conkling, his faction's party boss in New York State, asked him to. Eight years later Benjamin Harrison gave Morton a second chance to be vice president, and he accepted, but unlike the ill-fated Garfield, Harrison served a full four years. If Morton had wished, he could have been on the Republican ticket with William McKinley in 1896, but having been beaten for the top spot, he eschewed second place. Had he been nominated and later renominated, he, not Theodore Roosevelt, would have become president in 1901.

The presidency was not the only office to elude Morton's grasp. He wanted to be United States senator from New York but failed to win enough support on at least four occasions when his party controlled the state legislature. But while his fondest political goals eluded him, he was, nevertheless, an important Republican leader in the late nineteenth century. In addition to his vice presidency, he was twice elected to Congress, served four years as United State minister to France, and was a one-term governor of New York.

Morton was the person censured by the famed Populist orator, Mary Elizabeth Lease, who allegedly advised Kansas farmers to "raise less corn and more hell!" In her best-known speech at Kansas City in March 1891, she denounced American government as "a government of Wall street, for Wall street, and by Wall street," noting that "Money rules and our vice president is a London banker." By then, Morton was a senior partner in the English banking firm of Morton, Rose and Company.

But what makes Morton truly significant is that he personifies the successful businessmen who cast aside class aversions to politics to dominate the Republican Party during its early years as a national political organization. These are the men discussed by Robert Marcus in his admirable study, *Grand Old Party: Political Structure in the Gilded Age, 1880–1896* (1971). Although Morton was not the supreme leader at any national convention, he used his wealth to be close to those who were. In 1880, he headed the Republican Party's national finance committee, and on other occasions, notably in 1888, he raised impressive amounts for the party, donating freely of his own riches.

Morton was allied with the Stalwart Republican faction in New York headed by Conkling until 1881 and by Thomas C. Platt in the 1890s. He united with these men to make certain that the party continued "to foster and to protect" America's "business interests and industries." A nationalist and tariff protectionist, Morton believed that business and industrial prosperity meant a higher standard of living for the majority of Americans and a strong and peaceful nation. He said so when he accepted the vice-presidential nomination in 1888.

Born in Shoreham, Vermont, on May 16, 1824, Morton was descended on both his mother's and his father's sides from Puritan families that arrived in the Massachusetts Bay Colony during the 1620s and 1650s. His father, the Reverend Daniel O. Morton, was a Congregational preacher, and his mother, Lucretia Parsons, a housewife. Even after assuming a new ministry in Springfield, Vermont, in 1833, Daniel Morton's salary never exceeded $600 a year, and, as a result, he could provide his son with only a common school and academy education. Thus, the youth left school at fourteen to take a job at a country store in Enfield, New Hampshire, for $50 a year.

In 1841, the younger Morton taught briefly in the Boscawen common school but left the next year for a clerkship at a general store owned by a Mr. Esterbrook in Hanover. A Boston merchant, James M. Beebe, took control after Esterbrook's business failed and allowed Morton to run the store until eventually selling it to him. During these years Morton learned the fundamentals of commerce and prospered, but not as much as he wished. With a fortune of $13,000 he left New Hampshire in 1849 to join the wholesale dry-goods firm of James M. Beebe and Company in Boston. Two years later, it became J.M. Beebe, Morgan and Company, with Junius Spencer Morgan added as a partner, Here, Morton made the acquaintance of J. Pierpont Morgan, who had been brought into the business by his father.

During the next several years, Morton became knowledgeable in more than the textile trade, as Beebe, Morgan and Company added railroads, private banking, and insurance to their interests. Despite an improved business position, in 1855 Morton moved to New York and, with F.B. and W.F. Grinnell, nephews of a business associate, began the wholesale dry-goods commission house of Morton, Grinnell and Company. Until the Civil War, the firm profited, doing considerable business in the South, but after 1861, unable to collect debts owed it by Southern merchants, it failed. Reorganized following bankruptcy, Morton and

Grinnell initially paid its creditors fifty cents on the dollar but within two years Morton was reportedly able to host a banquet at which he placed under each creditor's plate a check for payment-in-full with interest.

Having put his affairs in order, in 1863 Morton formed the banking concern of L.P. Morton and Company. Among his partners was J.S. Morgan's son-in-law, Walter H. Burns, who opened a London branch of the firm, Morton, Burns and Company. Six years later Morton and Company increased its capital and membership, adding George Bliss and John Rose as partners. As reconstituted, the firm became Morton, Bliss and Company in the United States and Morton, Rose and Company in London. Rose, who had been Canada's finance minister, returned to England to head the London branch of the business.

From its beginning, Morton's financial house did both private and public business, helping to finance the closing years of the Civil War. Morton, who had married Lucy Young Kimball in 1856, began a friendship with General Ulysses S. Grant, and at Grant's behest he began to dabble a bit in politics. His earliest political associations had been as a Whig, but with the party's demise he supported John C. Frémont in 1856. He remained a Republican for the rest of his life and began to help finance some of the party's campaigns. His wife, who wanted him to enter electoral politics, died in July 1871, delaying, perhaps, his actively seeking office.

By then Morton was immersed in affairs surrounding the settlement of the *Alabama* Claims, which were preferred against Great Britain for depredations caused by Confederate commerce raiders built in England during the Civil War. His partner, Sir John Rose, was instrumental through unofficial talks with Secretary of State Hamilton Fish in setting the stage for creation of the Joint Anglo-American High Commission of Ten, which negotiated the Treaty of Washington of 1871. Rose's role in helping settle outstanding difficulties between the United States and England and Morton's friendship with President Grant undoubtedly contributed to Morton, Rose and Company being appointed as an agent in the arbitrational award payment to the United States of $15.5 million for the *Alabama* Claims and $5.5 million to Great Britain for the subsequent Halifax award to continue American fishing liberties in Canadian waters.

At about this time, Morton, Rose and Company could have replaced the Baring Brothers' as managers of the London account of the U.S. State Department. Not wanting to offend Barings, they eschewed the offer, but at the failure of Jay Cooke's banking house, which had taken the account, Grant gave it to Morton and Rose. When Secretary of the Treasury John Sherman began to resume specie payments in 1879, under the law of 1875, Morton's bank in conjunction with several others formed a syndicate to take 4 percent government bonds so that resumption might be possible. By this time, Morton had become a man whose financial advice was sought by government and Wall Street; indeed, J.P. Morgan and he were considered the nation's premier financiers.

Two years after his first wife died, Morton married Anna Livingston Read Street in 1873. She too was interested in politics and may have contributed to his decision to run for Congress from Manhattan's "silk-stocking" Eleventh District in 1876. He was supported by both of the party's important factions. Conkling's pro-Grant Stalwarts and Whitelaw Reid's anti-Grant Half-Breeds.* Unskilled in oratory, his few campaign speeches dealt with the money question then being agitated by Greenbackers and silver money advocates. A banker, Morton supported a sound currency, that is, gold, and favored the resumption of specie payments under the 1875 law. He was attacked by his opponent, Benjamin A. Willis, the incumbent Democrat, as a "plutocrat" who was merely "a tool of Wall Street." Although defeated, Mor-

---

*Editor's note: See CHESTER A. ARTHUR for further explanation of the Stalwarts and the Half-Breeds.

ton ran well ahead of the Republican presidential candidate in the district. He also trimmed Willis's margin of victory from 2,500 votes in 1874 to only 500 in 1876.

Smitten by politics, Morton bean to prepare for the 1878 congressional election. He helped to finance the ailing Republican New York *Evening Mail* and became a charter member of the New York Civil Service Reform Association. He also gained recognition when President Rutherford B. Hayes appointed him honorary commissioner to the Paris Exhibition of 1878. Morton had helped raise money to hire the lawyers who argued the Republican case in the contested election of 1876. But Internal difficulties in the Democratic Party helped Morton most of all, and he defeated Willis by 7,018 votes. In 1880, he was reelected over James W. Gerard, Jr., by an even larger margin. Irving Katz, in a brief biography of Morton, quotes Morton's daughter as saying that "in New York society the prejudice against politicians was very great, so that when my father first entered public life, his friends behaved as if my father had almost committed a crime and as if he were abandoning respectability."

As a member of the Forty-sixth Congress, Morton was appointed to the Committee on Foreign Affairs, addressing those issues that rose naturally from this position: immigration, the tariff, and the building of an isthmian canal in Nicaragua. He spoke in support of immigration but wanted laws excluding paupers, destitutes, criminals, and lunatics enforced; he was a tariff protectionist, who later helped organize the Protective Tariff League, a group of 1,000 "defenders" of American industry who each contributed $100 annually to advance their cause; the New Yorker also wanted a canal constructed in Central America that would be controlled by the United States. To this end, several American politicians, naval officers, and financiers, including Morton, organized the Provisional Inter-Ocean Canal Society to obtain concessions from Nicaragua. This group was ultimately restructured as the Maritime Canal Company of Nicaragua.

Morton joined the debate on the use of silver as money, endorsing the gold standard as the only fair means of coinage. He opposed a silver dollar that contained only "84 cents worth of silver" at open market prices and was against a move to make the trade-dollar, which was silver, legal tender. As created, trade-dollars, authorized in February 1873 and put into use in 1876, were not to circulate in the United States but were to be used only for export.

Although Morton was not an orator, he spoke on a variety of topics during his time in Congress, supporting an effort to convince the Czar of Russia to allow U.S. citizens of Jewish ancestry to own property in Russia. He advocated the repeal of taxes on bank checks and bank deposits, and favored official United States support for the Argentine Republic.

Morton's most active moment in Republican politics came during the election of 1880. His friendship for General Grant caused him to accept the leadership of Roscoe Conkling, who favored Grant's nomination while opposing a second term for Hayes. Despite considerable work by the Stalwarts at the Chicago convention, Grant failed to win sufficient backing, and James A. Garfield, a candidate of conciliation, was nominated by the Republicans. Knowing that New York would have to be placated if the Republicans were to win, Garfield and his Ohio backers offered the vice presidency to Morton. The banker-congressman accepted before checking with his friends.

The vice presidency was not what Conkling wanted for New York's support. The "boss" wished to control all patronage in the state and hoped to name the secretary of the treasury, who along with the postmaster general and secretary of state supervised most national patronage. Apparently, Conkling informed Morton that he hoped "no sincere friend of mine" would accept the vice presidency, and cleverly recommended that Morton seek advice from George S. Boutwell, former governor and then senator from Massachusetts. As expected, Boutwell advised Morton to reject the offer. Some historians think that Conkling also hinted that he thought the Wall Street tycoon should be appointed secretary of the treasury. After Morton withdrew, Garfield's supporters offered the vice presidency to Chester A. Arthur, another New York Stalwart of the Conkling faction. Before Conkling knew what had transpired, Arthur accepted and would not later forswear the opportunity when told to do so by the New York boss.

That Morton was interested in becoming secretary of the treasury became apparent in the few months after the national convention. With Garfield's campaign lagging and his position in New York appearing weak, the Republican nominee agreed to meet with leaders of the Empire State's Stalwart faction to enlist their aid, specifically, to ask Morton to raise money. Morton later claimed that at a meeting in the Fifth Avenue Hotel he was promised the treasury position if he would take charge of the campaign's finances—a task he performed to almost everyone's satisfaction, the president-elect later telling him that he had been of "great and effective service." Additionally, other New York Stalwarts, including Conkling and Thomas C. Platt, believed that Garfield had promised to allow them to name all federal appointees in New York State.

With Morton's help, Garfield carried the pivotal states of New York and Ohio, in part through the use of a "special fund" that Morton raised. Garfield's plurality was only 9,000 votes, but he defeated Democratic candidate Winfield Scott Hancock 214 to 155 in the electoral college. What happened next is subject to different interpretations by historians. As the president-elect dillydallied in naming his cabinet, Morton grew apprehensive, finally confronting Garfield directly about the treasury appointment. To his dismay, the future president said: "I will not tolerate nor act upon any understanding that anything has been pledged to any party, state, or person." Among the several reasons given for the decision not to appoint Morton, the most important seems to be that Garfield did not think it politic to name a major Wall Street banker as the secretary of the trea-

sury. Moreover, the Stalwart' chief enemy, James G. Blaine, had been made secretary of state and was apparently exercising considerable influence in selecting the cabinet. Morton's judgment of what happened, which he later passed on to a friend, was "that an Ohio man cannot be relied on to stand by his pledges."

The new president's unwillingness to allow Stalwarts a determining role in New York appointments and his selection of a Half-Breed as collector of the Port of New York eventually led to a bizarre turn of events when Conkling and the recently elected Platt foolishly decided to resign in protest from the Senate, assuming that they would be reelected. When they were not reelected, Morton may have made his second unsuccessful bid for the United States Senate. He had tried a few months earlier, in January 1881, when Platt replaced Senator Francis Kernan. Just before Conkling and Platt resigned, Morton accepted the position of secretary of the Navy, but when Conkling denounced him for betraying the Stalwarts, the congressman reversed himself and asked Garfield to release him from the commitment.

While the president may have misled Morton regarding the treasury, he was grateful to him and apparently fond of the New Yorker. After his 1892 defeat, the only time, Garfield appeared publicly for a candidate was at the Carnegie Music Hall during Morton's 1894 gubernatorial campaign. More immediately, at Blaine's suggestion, Morton was made minister to France, an assignment he gratefully and graciously accepted. He resigned from the House of Representatives, put his private affairs in order, and presented his credentials to the French on August 5, 1881. He served until May 14, 1885, when President Grover Cleveland replaced him with Robert M. McLane.

Morton enjoyed his duties in Paris, although when he first arrived the embassy was located over a laundry and a butcher shop on the Rue de Chaillot, a dingy area that the new minister found distasteful. He moved it to a mansion in the Place de la Bitche, which the French renamed the Place des États-Unis. As was the case in

New York and Washington, Morton had the wealth to entertain lavishly, and he did, both at the embassy and at his palatial summer residence, the Château Champ Fleuri, near the forest of St.-Germain. His tour of duty became memorable as a social success for the United States.

On July 4, 1884, Morton drove the first rivet into Frédéric-Auguste Bartholdi's Statue of Liberty ("Liberty Enlightening the World"), which he accepted on behalf of the American people from the Franco-American Union. He subsequently helped arrange for its shipment to Bedloe's (now Liberty) Island in New York Harbor. He also represented the United States at Le Pui, the birthplace of the Marquis de Lafayette, when a statue of that patriot was unveiled.

Politically, Morton convinced the French government to modify its commercial regulations so that U.S. businesses could place agencies in France; saw them recognize as U.S. citizens the sons of Frenchmen born in the United States; and, although nothing of importance happened, played a role in trying to convince the French to accept America's good offices to settle their difference with China. He was modestly involved in trying to mitigate French colonialism in the Congo and Madagascar. Fearing French imperialistic moves in areas of American interest, he discussed with them potential commercial violations in Hawaii and infringements against the Monroe Doctrine in Venezuela.

The most controversial development during Morton's stay in France dealt with exclusion of American pork from French markets. The ban was part of difficulties American packers faced throughout Europe, as nation after nation asserted that U.S. pork was diseased and blocked access to their markets during the 1880s. Scientific and medical studies disproved the allegations, but American officials realized that Europeans feared cheap bacon and lard, not the trichina worm, as they claimed.

Morton abandoned the tactics used by his predecessor, Edward F. Noyes, who, on the advice of Secretary Blaine, had hinted at retaliation against French wine, which was frequently adulterated when sold in the United States. Morton set out to ingratiate himself with French leadership, trusting in his ability to reason with them. He did succeed in getting France's president, François P.J. Grévy, to withdraw the decrees momentarily, only to have the Chamber of Deputies reverse the president's action. Even though Morton failed, he laid some of the groundwork that allowed Whitelaw Reid, another New Yorker who subsequently represented the United States in Paris, to get the ban lifted later.

Although Morton's ministry lasted officially until May 14,1885, he returned to New York in October 1884 to take part in that year's presidential election. Despite promising Secretary of State Frederick T. Frelinghuysen that he would not be involved in the race, he raised funds for Blaine, who lost the election when he failed to carry New York. After the Republican defeat, Morton reentered banking and spent time developing his country estate, "Ellerslie," near Rhinecliff, a village on the Hudson River, about seventeen miles north of Poughkeepsie.

Politics still occupied much of his time, and he made his two most serious efforts at becoming U.S. senator after his return from France. In March 1885, when the term of Elbridge C. Lapham ended, Morton seemed to be the favorite to replace him; however, New York reformers opposed Morton because of Platt's role in the campaign. At the last minute they were able to push forward former Secretary of State William M. Evarts, a man not aligned with any wing of New York's Republican party. The final tally when taken was not even close: Evarts 61, Morton 28, and Chauncey M. Depew, a noncandidate, 3.

Morton seemed to be Platt's candidate for governor at the New York State Republican convention in 1886, although this was a ploy: It was the U.S. Senate that he coveted. In 1887, three men emerged as important senatorial candidates in the January elections: Morton, Warner Miller, the incumbent, and Congressman

Frank Hiscock. As balloting commenced, Hiscock, who ran third, held the balance of power, the vote running about 35 for Morton, 44 for Miller, and 12 for Hiscock. Senator Miller was the candidate who had defeated Platt when he ran alter resigning his seat in 1881. Sometime before the sixteenth ballot, Platt became convinced that Morton could not win. Not wanting the much despised Miller to be reelected, he had the banker's supporters switch their votes to Hiscock, who was nominated, 50 to Miller's 43.

Having lost what he most desired, Morton became something of an object of pity, and many party members momentarily put aside their differences to advance him as a favorite son for president in 1888. He was not terribly interested in the matter until talk, coaxed by Platt, developed in favor of a Harrison-Morton ticket, Such a combination had tremendous advantages. It assured the campaign of adequate funding and united candidates from the key states of Indiana and New York, both of which were needed for an electoral college victory.

After Harrison was nominated on the eighth ballot in the Chicago Republican convention, the New York delegation advanced their favorite son for second place. Despite opinions such as those of Wisconsin Senator John Coit Spooner that Morton "would be denominated all over the country as a boodle candidate," he was selected on the first ballot; the vote was Morton 592, William W. Phelps of New Jersey 119, William O. Bradley of Kentucky 103, and 11 votes scattered. Harrison wired him: "Let me assure you that the association of your name with mine upon the ticket gives me great satisfaction."

Morton played what for him was an active role in the campaign. Harrison, an accomplished orator, did most of the public speaking, but Morton was important in articulating the party's commitment to the protective tariff, the main issue in 1888. Republicans, also, raised a multimillion-dollar war chest, and Morton's presence on the ticket was one of the reasons they were so successful. Knowing that he would be attacked for his wealth and business connections, he resigned from Morton, Bliss and Company, from his directorship of the Canadian Pacific Railroad, and from the Pacific Postal Telegraph Cable Company. Despite his efforts, he was attacked by *The New York Times* and *Nation* for his alleged involvement in what was billed the "Peruvian guano scandal." They claimed he used his governmental and political connections to secure a lucrative contract to sell guano at a high commission for the Société Générale de Crédit Industriel et Commercial. The Crédit Industriel was a European financial group that held large amounts of Peruvian government bonds and was forcing the sale of the country's immense guano deposits to secure repayment.

Despite losing the popular vote—Grover Cleveland and Allen G. Thurman 5,540,050; Harrison and Morton 5,444,337; with 399,830 for third-party candidates—the Republicans won the electoral vote: Harrison 233 and Cleveland 168. In his inaugural statement to the Senate on March 4, 1889, Morton acknowledged that he lacked experience as a presiding officer and asked for the body's "indulgent consideration." He added that he hoped to "administer the rules of procedure with entire fairness, and to treat each senator with courtesy and consideration." "I hope," he concluded, "that our relations officially and personally will prove mutually agreeable."

Morton is best remembered for his social role as vice president. He and his wife entertained lavishly at their Scott Circle home in northwest Washington, D.C. One of his daughters recalled a typical Wednesday during his tenure: "In those days hordes of people went from one official house to another . . . [Mother] used to have as many as two thousand people pass through her rooms on an afternoon." He did have trouble with prohibitionist groups because of his less than abstinence, particularly when the Women's Christian Temperance Union discovered that liquor was served in the Shoreham Hotel, a property he purchased in Washington.

Morton was considered a gentlemanly, evenhanded, competent presiding officer, and several important pieces of legislation passed during his years as Senate president, including the Dependent Pension Act, McKinley Tariff, Sherman Antitrust Act, and Sherman Silver Purchase Act. North Dakota, South Dakota, Montana, Washington, Idaho, and Wyoming were also admitted to the Union in 1889 and 1890. In fact, Congress passed 1,100 bills, a record for its time; however, Morton's legislative participation in these actions was inconsequential, his only crucial role was during consideration of the Federal Elections, or Force, Bill.

The Force Bill began in the House under the sponsorship of Congressman Henry Cabot Lodge of Massachusetts. It provided that bipartisan election supervisors, appointed by U.S. district judges, inspect registration books and attend to elections in all congressional districts. In towns of 20,000, the supervisors were to make house-to-house canvasses, informing registrants of the mechanics, place, and time of elections. A three member board of canvassers was to certify the results of elections, checking the voter turn out of each district every November 15. Designed primarily to protect African American voters in the South, the so-called Lodge Bill passed the house during the first session of the Fifty-first Congress, 155 to 149; all affirmative votes were Republican and only two members of the G.O.P. voted in the negative.

In the Senate, opposition from Democrats, "mugwumps," silver interests, and commercial groups stalled the legislation. Nevertheless, its proponents were able to secure a promise that the bill would be given priority in the second session, which convened in December 1890. When debate began on the measure, Democratic senators used a variety of parliamentary tactics to delay a vote, including a thinly disguised filibuster. At this juncture, western Republicans who were dissatisfied with existing legislation and wanted greater expansion of the currency joined Democrats to set aside the Federal Elections Bill to consider a new silver-coinage measure, which passed but as predicted was buried in the recently elected Democratic House.

In January 1891, a motion was introduced to make the Force Bill an order of business. It passed when Vice President Morton cast the tie-breaking vote. Once again Democrats filibustered, but this time Republican leaders decided to force a vote on an ad hoc cloture rule that Senator Nelson Aldrich had cleverly devised to allow a majority to stop debate. To achieve their ends, Republicans needed Morton's support, expecting it because President Harrison made passage of the legislation one of his main considerations. To their dismay, the vice president refused to force a vote on the Aldrich rule: He maintained that his duty required him to be nonpartisan, impartially enforcing all existing rules, and that until the new cloture was adopted he could not stop debate. Republicans tried to get him to step down temporarily from the chair, suggesting on one occasion that he take a vacation to Florida. Morton refused, even abandoning his custom of going out for lunch. One New York newspaper declared that Republican leaders might "wail," or "tear their hair, in impotent rage, but Morton will not surrender." Inevitably, by a vote of 35 to 34, the Senate moved to other legislation; there would be no Force Act in 1891.

Morton's action was critical in defeating the Federal Elections Bill, which may have changed the course of American history and, if administered as planned, would have effected a major change in southern elections. The episode illustrated how much the Civil War Republican Party had changed and was perhaps the last gasp of what some call "bloody shirt" Republicanism. Born in part as an economic reform group, the party was now almost wholly engrossed in matters of the marketplace.

Perhaps it is understandable that Morton was not chastised for his inaction, albeit one historian suggests that he was dropped from the ticket in 1892 because of it. Actually, his failure to be renominated seems to have had little to do with the Force Bill. He failed to state clearly a desire to be renominated by Republicans at a time when continuation of vice presidents was not the tradition it is today. Moreover, his New York opponents wanted the publisher of the *New York Tribune,* Whitelaw Reid, to replace him. Further, Platt was disenchanted with Harrison because of the latter's patronage practices. He felt Morton would help the president's reelection. Senator Spooner, a Republican supporter of the Force Bill, wrote that if the nomination "had been left to the Convention without the influence of the New York delegation your support would have been in my judgment overwhelming." His main biographer says that Morton received the news of Reid's nomination at Minneapolis, Minnesota, "without the least appearance of resentment," but another described him as being "chagrined, but dignified."

In February 1893, the Senate honored Morton with an unprecedented banquet at the Arlington Hotel in Washington, D.C. At the gathering, Charles F. Manderson, Nebraska Republican and president pro tempore of the Senate, said: "Our tribute to the genial gentleman who has for four years presided over the Senate is not an empty compliment. It is given to him out of the fullness of our affection for him." A few days later, the Senate passed a resolution thanking him "for the dignified, impartial, and courteous manner" in which he presided over its deliberations. Congratulations arrived from many quarters, including the nation's press. After Harrison's failed reelection *The Washington Post* suggested that the Republicans lost because Morton was not on the ticket; in fact, his absence had little to do with the defeat.

When Morton returned to New York he expected his time in public life would be over—he was sixty-eight years old—but Tom Platt had other ideas and convinced him to run for governor in 1894, telling him the job was not very demanding. By attacking Democratic corruption, Morton defeated David B. Hill, 673,818 votes to 517,710, with 84,173 scattered. For the next two years, Morton proved to be what Theodore Roosevelt maintained was "far and away the best Governor we have had for many a long day."

Morton's relationship with Platt was interesting. While he often followed the boss's advice on patronage, he also championed the state's recently adopted merit system of civil service appointments, nor did he slavishly accept Platt's recommendations on policy. When the mayors of New York and Brooklyn objected to creation of a Greater New York City by the legislature, his response was dilatory maneuvering, which incensed Platt. Supporting Morton's presidential ambitions in 1896 and realizing that the banker depended on him, Platt wrote that if Morton continued stalling: "I will not feel like taking off my coat and doing the work I contemplated in the presidential matter. I might as well be frank with you now." Greater New York City was ultimately created, and within a few years it satisfied almost everyone. On the whole, Platt considered the former vice president, "the safest governor New York ever had."

Other important changes that Morton championed and secured for New York included adoption of the Australian ballot, regulation of horse racing, creation of a four-man bi-partisan New York City police board, and the Raines Liquor Law. The Raines Act established state regulation and taxation of traffic in alcohol beverages and eventually removed liquor as an issue from New York politics. He also improved the existing civil service system.

Morton could have been renominated for governor in 1896 but chose not to be. His defeat as a presidential contender that year convinced him to leave public life. In truth, he never had the slightest chance of beating McKinley, who overwhelmed his opposition at the St. Louis Convention.

Morton remained interested in politics and the Republican Party for most of the rest of his life. He was opposed to war with Spain in early 1898, but as a good nationalist supported the country's effort once war was declared. His feelings toward Theodore Roosevelt are illustrated by his opinion that a conservative Democrat could beat the president in New York in 1904 because of the "the direction in which . . Roosevelt's economic policies were aimed."

In 1897, Morton, Bliss and Company became the Morton Trust Company. Thirteen years later, the former vice president reached what might be considered the pinnacle and end of his financial career when Morton Trust merged with J.P. Morgan's Fifth Avenue Trust to form Guaranty Trust. Although Morgan arranged the merger, Morton became chairman of the board of the new organization. The position was more honorary than functional, but Morton was now recognized as the "Grand Old Man" of Wall Street. Morton almost died in 1913, but recovered to live seven more years, passing away on his ninety-sixth birthday, May 16, 1920.

REFERENCES

Robert McElroy, *Levi Parsons Morton: Banker, Diplomat and Statesman* (New York: G.P. Putnam's Sons, 1930); Irving Katz, "Investment Bankers in American Government and Politics: The Political Activities of William W. Corcoran, August Belmont, Sr., Levi P. Morton, and Henry Lee," (Ph.D. diss., New York University, 1964); *Testimonial to Vice-President Levi P. Morton Upon His Retirement from Office March 4, 1893; Proceedings at the Banquet, Given to the Vice-President by the United States Senate* . . . (Concord, N.H.: Monitor Press, 1893); Justus D. Doenecke, *The Presidencies of James A. Garfield and Chester A. Arthur* (Lawrence: Regents Press of Kansas, 1981); Brigham Duncan, *Whitelaw Reid: Journalist, Politician, Diplomat* (Athens: University of Georgia Press, 1975); Harold F. Gosnell, *Boss Platt and His New York Machine, A Study of the Political Leadership of Thomas C. Platt, Theodore Roosevelt and Others* (Chicago, Ill.: University of Chicago Press, 1924); Stanley P. Hirshson, *Farewell to the Bloody Shirt: Northern Republicans and the Southern Negro, 1877–1893* (Bloomington: Indiana University Press, 1962); David M. Jordan, *Roscoe Conkling of New York: Voice in the Senate* (Ithaca, N.Y.: Cornell University Press, 1971); John D. Long, ed., *The Republican Party: Its History, Principles, and Policies* (New York: M.W. Hazen Co., 1888); Robert D. Marcus, *Grand Old Party: Political Structure in the Gilded Age, 1880–1896* (New York: Oxford University Press, 1971); Richard L. McCormick, *From Realignment to Reform: Political Change in New York State, 1893–1910* (Ithaca, N.Y.: Cornell University Press, 1979); David M. Pletcher, *The Awkward Years: American Foreign Relations Under Garfield and Arthur* (Columbia: University of Missouri Press, 1962); Thomas C. Reeves, *Gentleman Boss: The Life of Chester Alan Arthur* (New York: Alfred A. Knopf, 1975); Thomas Clarke Smith, *The Life and Letters of James Abram Garfield* (New Haven, Conn.: Yale University Press, 1925); Homer E. Socolofsky and Allan B. Spetter, *The Presidency of Benjamin Harrison* (Lawrence: University Press of Kansas, 1987); William O. Stoddard, *Men of Business* (New York: Charles Scribner's Sons, 1904); Richard E. Welch, Jr., *George Frisbie Hoar and the Half-Breed Republicans* (Cambridge, Mass.: Harvard University Press, 1971); Beckles Willson, *America's Ambassadors to France (1777–1927): A Narrative of Franco-American Relations* (New York: Frederick A. Stokes Company, 1928). Congressional Record, 1st, 2nd, and 3rd sess., 46 Cong.; 1st and 2nd sess., 51st Cong.; *The New York Times,* 1888–1920.

ROBERT S. LA FORTE, former department chair and professor of history at the University of North Texas, retired in 2000. He is the author and editor of *Leaders of Reform: Progressive Republicans in Kansas, 1900–1920* (1974), *Down the Corridor of Years* (1989), *Remembering Pearl Harbor* (1991), *Building the Death Railway* (1993), *With Only the Will to Live* (1994), and *Our Nation's Heritage* (1995).

ADLAI EWING STEVENSON (1835–1914)

Vice President, 1893–1897

(President Grover Cleveland)

ADLAI EWING STEVENSON
(Library of Congress)

By Leonard C. Schlup

Adlai E. Stevenson, patriarch of a political family, experienced a rewarding but sometimes frustrating career in politics that spanned nearly half a century. While he has usually been relegated to a footnote in history, in his day he achieved recognition as a shrewd politician. A highly sociable person and master raconteur who respected his opponents, Stevenson, the quintessential gentlemen who avoided making personal enemies of political adversaries, was a political insider who forged alliances with disparate groups while deflecting insensitive comments-with humors and skillfully turning political setbacks to his advantage. He sought harmony in an era of transformation and intense partisanship, offered soothing words to heal intraparty dissension, and refused to indulge in personal vendettas. The vice president was a coalition Democrat who preached the politics of accommodation. Emerging on the right side at the right time, Stevenson, a consummate survivor, was an American Talleyrand and a political rarity. His political genius lay in a careful mix of principle and pragmatism.

Born in Christian County, Kentucky, the son of John Turner Stevenson, a farmer, and Eliza Ann Ewing Stevenson, the young Adlai Stevenson moved to Bloomington, Illinois, with his parents in 1852. There he worked at his father's sawmill and taught school to earn money to attend Illinois Wesleyan University and later Centre College in Danville, Kentucky. Upon the death of his father in 1857, Stevenson returned to Bloomington, studied law under Robert E. Williams, and was admitted to the bar in 1858, the year in which the Lincoln–Douglas debates stimulated his interest in politics. He began his practice in Metamora, where on occasion he rode circuit with Abraham Lincoln. In 1860, Stevenson and Robert G. Ingersoll, a lawyer, traveled the state in support of Steven A. Douglas for president. During the Civil War, Stevenson served as a master in chancery of Woodford County's circuit court, helped to organize the 108th Regiment Illinois Volunteer Infantry, and was a presidential elector in 1864 for the Democratic ticket of McClellan and Pendleton. After the war, from 1865 to 1869, he was prosecuting attorney for the Twenty-third Judicial District. In 1866, at Chenoa, Stevenson married Letitia Barbour Green, the daughter of Lewis Warner Green, a former Presbyterian clergyman and college president.

In 1869, Stevenson and his wife returned to Bloomington, where they raised their four children in a Victorian home on Franklin Square. Stevenson and his double cousin, James Stevenson Ewing, formed a law partnership that prospered over a period of twenty-five years. Stevenson was the politician and office lawyer, while Ewing was the trial lawyer who promoted his colleague's political career. In one sensational case, they won a $50,000 damage verdict for an attractive young woman who claimed that a Bloomington physician had contributed to her downfall through the use of drugs. Stevenson also served as president of the McLean County Coal Company, a family operation, which was the city's largest industry, with nearly 300 employees. A successful businessman and lawyer, Stevenson gained the respect of his neighbors and friends, including David Davis, associate justice of the United States Supreme Court, who urged him to pursue a political career.

Stevenson entered national politics in 1874 when the Democrats of his congressional district nominated him for a seat in the U.S. House of Representatives. Endorsed also by the Greenback Party, Stevenson defeated the Republican incumbent. Two years later, he lost his bid for reelection, but he regained the House position in 1878, only to lose again in 1880 and 1882. Serving in Congress for two nonconsecutive terms and representing a rural Republican constituency, Stevenson in large measure managed to win a House seat due to his persuasive skills, political instincts, and ability to make politics out of the issue of nonpartisanship. Assiduous salesmanship on his part sustained his image of evenhandedness among his constituents Yet, he won only in off-year contests that coincided with national Democratic victories and majority control of the lower chamber, and he narrowly lost reelection bids in presidential years when he suffered the effects of high voter turnout, intense partisanship, and Republican presidential coattails. These defeats tempered Stevenson as a politician and bred a cautious outlook, making him cognizant of his political vulnerability and the patterns of ticket splitting in subpresidential voting.

A member of the Forty-fourth and Forty-sixth Congresses, Stevenson earned a reputation for honesty, commitment to service, and exceptional talent for making friends. He advocated laissez-faire policies, tariff reduction, low taxes, balanced budgets, railroad regulation, agricultural growth, antitrust legislation, electoral college reform, and immigration restriction. Stevenson differed from party conservatives and spokesmen for business in that he favored silver coinage to reduce indebtedness and to provide for a more elastic currency. In the process of balancing interacting forces, he applied on the national level the lessons he learned from prairie Republicans to camouflage differences among Democrats. These years constituted a preparatory period on which he built his reputation as a flexible accommodationist.

A turning point in Stevenson's career occurred in 1884 when, as a delegate to the Democratic national convention in Chicago, he endorsed the presidential nomination of Governor Grover Cleveland of New York. He also formed a crucial political association with William F. Vilas, a Wisconsin lawyer whom Cleveland appointed to head the Post Office Department. Shortly after assuming the presidency in 1885, Cleveland selected Stevenson for the position of first assistant postmaster general. While functioning in this role, Stevenson removed nearly 40,000 Republican postal employees across the nation, replacing them with Democrats. He relished this assignment, for he typified the spoilsman of the 1880s who earned the wrath of civil service reformers such as Carl Schurz. For a short time, Stevenson was acting chief of the Post Office Department in the absence of Vilas and attended cabinet meetings during this interlude. While performing his patronage duties as first assistant postmaster general for four years, Stevenson collected valuable IOUs from Democrats across the nation and in one case established a local post office in order to fill the vacancy. His duties and responsibilities gave him a new sense of purpose and whetted his appetite for higher office. He had become infatuated with Washington life. After Cleveland's defeat for reelection in 1888, he selected Stevenson for an associate justiceship on the Supreme Court for the District of Columbia, but Republicans, who controlled the Senate, blocked the nomination.

Stevenson returned to his law practice in Bloomington in 1889 but remained an astute observer of political events. A clever political practitioner and political chameleon who could take on the characteristics of diverse constituencies, Stevenson preached the politics of pacification while campaigning for Democratic congressional candidates in 1890. He communicated with Cleveland and traveled the country in spring 1892 to enlist support for the former chief executive's presidential bid that year. Tying his own political aspirations to Cleveland, Stevenson carefully laid the foundation for his vice-presidential nomination. His failure to obtain second place on the ticket with Cleveland in 1888 only enhanced his fierce sense of ambition and determination to succeed in 1892.

Stevenson played an important role at the 1892 Democratic national convention in Chicago. At the Hotel Richelieu on June 17, he chaired a session of pro-Cleveland delegates. Chairman of the Illinois delegation, Stevenson persuaded his colleagues to cast all their votes for Cleveland, which contributed to his first-ballot victory. Stevenson also delineated clear directives regarding the vice presidency, mentioned his availability and encouraged a small coterie of friends to work in his behalf. He easily won the coveted prize on the revised first ballot, securing support from all regions of the nation. Although Cleveland considered several possibilities for his running mate, he did not contribute in any direct way to Stevenson's victory but wholeheartedly approved the outcome.

Stevenson's vice-presidential nomination, a political development based on the demands of practical politics, stemmed from several factors: Foremost among these was the meticulous planning by Stevenson and his cohorts both before and during the convention; a second reason concerned his ability to unite discordant elements within the party. A political moderate of unquestioned personal integrity, Stevenson did not antagonize diverse internal groups and found himself in the advantageous position of being a compromise choice. Lacking ideological rigidity, Stevenson fashioned a career of centrist positions, espousing the politics of consensus. He emerged in 1892 as the Great Conciliator.

Stevenson provided both philosophical and geographical balance to the Democratic ticket. Cleveland forged a political alliance in 1892 in order to strengthen his chance of carrying Illinois and to placate southern farmers, upset with his sound-money policies, who were flirting with the Populist Party and its stand on transportation, land, and currency. Because Cleveland and Stevenson held divergent views on the volatile currency question, Stevenson wisely sidestepped the matter, preferring to concentrate on tariff reform. Even though, on Cleveland's insistence, he pledged his approval of the hard-money plank in the Democratic platform, Stevenson Continued to cherish his associations with soft-money advocates who favored the free and unlimited coinage of silver at a ratio of 16 to 1 with gold. The vice-presidential nominee pursued a policy of reticence that would neither offend nor threaten Cleveland while preserving his own independence. In his acceptance speech at Madison Square Garden in July, Stevenson appealed to the sober judgment of the people. He later wrote his acceptance letter in Charleston, West Virginia, with the assistance of George F. Parker, a journalist and close Cleveland confidant.

To counteract the Populist threat to Democratic success in the South, which was a solid part of the Democratic presidential coalition, Stevenson met with Cleveland in a postconvention strategy session at the former president's summer home in Buzzard's Bay, Massachusetts. There they devised a carefully crafted plan for a conservative counterattack. This compromise of 1892 consisted of five parts: First, southern Democrats who refrained from voting for the Populist Party would be rewarded by victorious Democratic opposition to Republican efforts in Congress to enact a federal elections law to protect African American suffrage; second, the Democratic administration would continue to direct economic benefits to the South; third, the Democrats would demonstrate their appreciation for southern support through patronage; fourth, the new administration would resume its past endeavors to reinstate the South to a proper place in the Union by harmonizing relations between sections; and fifth, the Democrats would lower the tariffs and practice frugality in government. Together these proposals constituted a significant challenge to the Populist danger, and with this program the Democrats bargained to hold a wavering South.

Stevenson functioned as the main proponent of this strategy in the presidential campaign of 1892. The Democratic plan for economic and political revitalization, he argued, would compensate for the more radical programs of the Populists. To consolidate Democratic strength and thwart the third-party movement, Stevenson visited several midwestern, border, and deep southern states, including Indiana, Kentucky, Tennessee, Alabama, North Carolina, Maryland, West Virginia, and Virginia. In these appearances, Stevenson sought to generate support for the Democratic platform and convince discontented Democrats that too many votes for the Populists would only concede the presidential election to Benjamin Harrison, the Republican standard bearer. While touring these states, he assured Cleveland by letter that nothing was being left undone and that he was putting into operation, in private talks with party leaders and public speeches, the principles outlined in the compromise that year between the national party and the; southern electorate.

Opposed to federal interference in elections, Stevenson contended that a Republican Congress and White House would attempt to implement a new federal elections law. Its passage, he theorized, would lead to economic calamities, heavy taxes, and the election of Republican congressmen from the South. He easily translated this personal belief into public rhetoric to squash the Populists and Republicans by recalling the bleak era of Reconstruction. Raising his hands in a gesture for emphasis, he scolded his audience in the manner of a stern father. Working closely with local conservative southern leaders, Stevenson, concerned that a new West-South agrarian alliance might replace the old East–South

Bourbon alignment, provided them with the oratorical justification for the compromise package of 1892, which enabled these groups to exploit their opposition and repair their tenuous position in countless speeches throughout the region. Although warning southerners of the direct threat that awaited their interests should Harrison recapture the White House, Stevenson prudently avoided mentioning the race question in his prepared statements. Nor did he comment; about black rights and opportunities. In common with Democratic politicians of his era, he made no effort to protect African Americans, who voted overwhelmingly Republican.

Stevenson did his part to help the Democrats win the presidential election of 1892. The chairman of the Democratic National Committee, William F. Harrity, thought that Stevenson's work had contributed largely to the result. A dedicated and competent public servant, Stevenson attained stature in the Democratic Party in 1892 and brought a broader trend toward personal campaigning in American politics. His most fundamental political skill revolved around an ability to charm audiences and attract support, regardless of geographic area. Stevenson championed party loyalty and regularity, intertwining Democratic fortunes with his own destiny and endeavoring through compromise to ease the transition from the politics of the antebellum era to that of the Gilded Age. Having fought for years to define the center, Stevenson in 1892 created a political posture in the middle of the spectrum that enabled him to avoid crossfires between Democratic factions. It was perhaps the defining event of Stevenson's political life.

Stevenson received the news of his victory in Bloomington, where he had begun and ended the campaign. He immediately wired a congratulatory telegram to Cleveland. Neighbors and friends welcomed the vice president-elect at a public reception. There Stevenson accepted the cheers while putting partisanship aside for the moment. He reminded the crowd that the glory attached to the American name and flag belong exclusively to no party or section but was instead the common heritage of all the people. Shortly thereafter, Stevenson contacted Vice President Levi P. Morton to make arrangements for a smooth transition. In late February 1893, the Stevenson family left Bloomington by train for Washington and the inaugural ceremonies.

In a brief ceremony conducted in the Senate chamber on March 3, 1893, Stevenson took the oath of office as vice president. The next day, in a special session of the Senate, he delivered a short inaugural address in which he pledged to discharge the important duties as president of the Senate with impartiality, courtesy, and fidelity. After witnessing Cleveland's inauguration on March 4 and attending an inaugural ball at the Pension Office, Stevenson and his family went to their temporary living quarters, a large suite on the second floor of the Normandie Hotel. Later, they moved to the Ebbitt House.

Stevenson entertained frequently and earned a prominent place in Washington's social circle. He presided over several banquets, including dinners for Secretary of the Treasury John G. Carlisle and Secretary of War Daniel S. Lamont. Two of Stevenson's children married during his vice-presidential tenure. Stevenson's wife, president of the Daughters of the American Revolution and member of other organizations, was also active socially in Washington as the nation's second lady. On more than one occasion she assisted Frances Folsom Cleveland with receptions at the White House.

In addition to social responsibilities, Stevenson maintained his interest in politics. He regarded the vice presidency as an important office and accepted his position despite its constitutional shortcomings. Although he did not attend the cabinet meetings and voted only twice on minor bills to break a Senate tie, Stevenson never wavered in his belief that he was a representative of all the people. He opened his office door to reporters, allowing them easy access for interviews and questions, so that they could inform the citizenry of his activities. The vice president usually went to his office in the Capitol in the morning to work on his mail before presiding over the Senate, a parliamentary procedure with which he was familiar and liked immensely. His son, Lewis Green Stevenson, served as his clerk for a time.

Nearly four months after taking office, President Cleveland underwent surgery to remove a malignant growth on the roof of his mouth. His precautions for secrecy were so elaborate that only his wife, doctors, a close friend, and Secretary of War Lamont had any knowledge of the president's serious condition. The clandestine operation occurred aboard a slowly cruising yacht on Long Island Sound, while doctors worried about the effects of an anesthetic upon the corpulent chief executive and the possibility of a stroke of apoplexy occurring without a properly equipped hospital. Cleveland neglected to inform Stevenson of this event; in fact, Stevenson was a "near president" without ever learning the events that could have catapulted him into power. Cleveland's enigmatic reticence may have prevented a sudden fluctuation in the economy, but he was guilty of concealing a presidential illness from both his colleagues and the people. By denying Stevenson, who was then in Illinois, the right to important information and not providing him with the necessary briefings to assure a continuation of governmental activity in case of temporary incapacitation, Cleveland adopted principles that were inconsistent with the national interest and displayed a limited view of presidential prerogatives.

Stevenson was vice president during a severe economic depression. Rising unemployment and distressed conditions spawned political protest and social unrest, including a march on Washington in support of a public works relief program by an "army" led by Jacob Stevenson Coxey. To restore public confidence and strengthen the economy, Cleveland asked Congress to repeal the Sherman Silver Purchase Act of 1890. Sentiment in the Senate ran strongly in favor of compromise, but Cleveland refused to consider alternative legislation. Some western and southern senators thereupon engaged in a filibuster to resist the revocation. Displaying no feelings of disloyalty toward Cleveland or secret sympathies with the silverites, Stevenson, who regarded the Sherman law as an ill-advised enactment, did nothing to break the filibuster. Although supporting repeal, he permitted the verbal marathon to continue because of his deep regard for the established tradition of unlimited debate in the Senate. He contended that his oath bound him to obey the traditions of the upper chamber. Personally believing that wise legislation and good government resulted from debate, Stevenson worried that hasty legislation without reasonable discussion could imperil the public welfare. In the end, the bill repealing the Sherman measure passed Congress in 1893.

Stevenson's political endurance was greatly tested in 1894. He was caught in the middle that year in a dispute between Cleveland and Governor John Peter Altgeld of Illinois. Cleveland dispatched federal troops to Chicago to safeguard the mail, protect interstate commerce, and restore order during the Pullman Strike, an action called by the American Railway Union under Eugene V. Debs that immobilized railroads in the Midwest. The president's decision to quell the disturbance by force met with opposition from Altgeld, who angrily condemned Cleveland. Wishing to antagonize neither Cleveland nor Altgeld, the governor of his home state, Stevenson remained silent on the issue, though his secret sympathies probably were with Cleveland.

Other issues confronted Stevenson in 1894. Democrats had pledged in 1892 to reform the tariff, and the House of Representatives in 1894 passed a measure to reduce taxation. Projectionist senators, on the other hand, added numerous amendments to safeguard certain items, which emasculated the original purpose of the legislation. The Wilson–Gorman Tariff of 1894 became law without Cleveland's signature, for he disliked the final version and denounced those Democrats who had contributed to protectionism. A disappointed Stevenson chose not to condemn fellow Democrats;

instead, he blamed selfish interest for the defeat of reform. He also rationalized that the Democratic tariff was a step in the direction of lowering duties and that it was better than the Republican McKinley Tariff of 1890. As the depression deepened and farmers grew more restless, Cleveland's popularity plummeted, and he remained virtually secluded in the White House, shunned by segments of his own party.

During the congressional elections of 1894, Stevenson campaigned for Democratic candidates. The outcome reaffirmed his apprehensions: The Democratic Party sustained a stinging rebuke in one of the most profound off-year electoral routs in American history. A voter rebellion swept Republicans into power in Congress, which reconfigured political leadership. The stunning Republican revolution transformed the nation's political landscape, producing a political realignment outside the South. The nation's long electoral and ideological leaning toward the Republican Party since 1860 reached its watershed in 1894 when Democrats lost 113 seats in the House and 5 in the Senate. This enormous redistribution was such that Democrats failed to elect a single member of Congress in twenty-four states. Without much of the Democratic infrastructure left standing, demoralized Democrats recognized that there existed a widening sectional division between East and West and a shrinking base of Democratic political power.

During his four years as vice president, Stevenson traveled extensively across the nation. He and Cleveland attended the opening of the Chicago's World Fair in 1895. In 1893, Stevenson and his wife, accompanied by the chief justice of the Illinois Supreme Court and other guests, boarded a private car of the Great Northern Railroad to tour several western areas. After seeing the Dakotas and Rocky Mountains, the entourage passed through the territories of New Mexico and Arizona, stopped at Los Angeles, and then arrived in San Francisco. A flotilla in the bay greeted the vice president, along with a nineteen-gun salute and a formal reception. There he met with Governor Henry M. Markham of California. After departing San Francisco, the group went home by way of Oregon, Montana, and Minnesota.

Stevenson also did a great deal of traveling in 1895. He and Altgeld were present at the dedication of the Chickamauga National Park, where Stevenson addressed the issue of healing sectional wounds and emphasized the indivisible union of indestructible states. Certainly the vice president's most notable trip that year was his train ride across the nation to Washington and his excursion by ship to Alaska, where he spent several days sightseeing and conferring with local officials. When he visited the state of Washington, people there wanted to know if he thought their majestic mountain should be called Mount Rainier or Mount Tacoma. Not wishing to antagonize anyone on this important but divisive local matter, Stevenson adroitly resolved the dilemma his own way: In a speech from the rear platform of the train, he devoted his peroration to discussing the beauty of the mountain, pledging not to rest until the mountain had a name. Then the vice president pulled a secret cord to notify the engineer. As a result, his last words, at-the very point when he was supposed to mention his choice regarding this northwestern nomenclature, were drowned out by the noise of whistles and steam as the train pulled away from the station, leaving Stevenson, white of mane and dressed in a Prince Albert coat, bowing graciously to a cheering crowd, with his position still unknown.

Although Cleveland and Stevenson shared a mutual friendship and high regard for each other, the two never became close confidants. The president did not allow the vice president to share in decision making, but on one occasion Cleveland did ask Stevenson to review a Thanksgiving proclamation. Despite being on the outside, Stevenson loyally defended his chief's decision in both domestic and foreign affairs. This was apparent in speeches and writings in which he supported Cleveland's stand with regard to the Venezuelan boundary controversy with Great Britain, the maintenance of the Monroe Doctrine, and opposition to the annexation of Hawaii. Yet, it was the division within the Democratic Party in 1895 and 1896 over the money issue that tested Stevenson's ability as a versatile politician.

Neglecting to comprehend the political situation in 1895, Stevenson failed to seize the advantage he enjoyed that year over potential presidential rivals. He had reached his zenith and needed to create a national feeling for his presidential candidacy, as well as to generate a groundswell of support among Democrats that would make opposition to his presidential ambitions unpalatable. With Altgeld's blessing and with endorsements from the South, where he counted numerous political allies, Stevenson would have been in good shape to try for the nomination without directly attacking Cleveland's policies. Instead, he found himself in a quandary in 1896 and in the position of bearing ultimate responsibility for his own actions.

The most trying time politically for Stevenson occurred in 1896 when the contentious currency question strained his relationship with sound-money and free-silver friends. There existed a conflict inside the vice president—a contest between the gentlemen and the politician. The problem was how far Stevenson, dexterous accommodator, could go without antagonizing the Cleveland conservatives to perpetuate his political viability. Stevenson's instinct told him to keep his two jobs—vice president and practicing politician—distinct, but this was a self-defeating policy that crippled his chance for the presidency. An aura of invulnerability clouded his judgment and prevented him, until it was too late, from seeing the danger that he faced from opponents. Eager to please, Stevenson not only misjudged the political situation early in 1896, but everything he did prior to the Democratic convention seemed desperate and insincere. In short, Stevenson's style of leadership was both his strength and his undoing.

In spring 1896, a handful of free-silver senators, including James K. Jones of Arkansas, George G. Vest of Missouri, and Isham G. Harris of Tennessee, planned to promote Stevenson's presidential candidacy and urged the vice president to postpone announcing his intentions until an appropriate moment. While these senators were working to line up support for Stevenson's nomination on a free-silver platform, the vice president quietly met with sound money Democrats to gauge their sentiment concerning his possible presidential bid. In April 1896, Stevenson attended a dinner-table conference in New York at Wolfert's Roost, the home of Senator David B. Hill of New York. Present on this occasion were Senator Calvin Brice of Ohio, Senator Arthur P. Gorman of Maryland, Judge Alton B. Parker of New York, and John R. McLean, owner of the *Cincinnati Enquirer* and *The Washington Post*. While conferring with this group, Stevenson considered the possibility of stopping the free-silver movement from overtaking the badly divided party.

Stevenson was looking in two opposite directions in his quest to gain the nomination and heal intraparty wounds. He desired the endorsement of conservative and free-silver-coinage Democrats, talking unostentatiously with each side in an endeavor to gauge his strength, mollify differing factions, and endanger nothing. The vice president sought to emerge as the compromise choice of both Democratic factions and to compete for the presidency on a moderate platform. Ever eager to please, Stevenson showed a preference for compromise that by 1896 displeased all sides. His reputation as a dexterous accommodator always concerned with preserving his political viability raised questions that year about his leadership. Stevenson's strong point was empathy, but many wondered if it was adequate for the times.

The growing strength of the free-silver crusade and the Republican nomination of William McKinley on a sound-money platform weakened Stevenson's chance of obtaining the Democratic nomination on any kind of platform. By the end of June, when it had become obvious that prosilver forces would control the Democratic National Convention, Stevenson's free-silver allies in the Senate abruptly withdrew their support of his candidacy, and their cabal collapsed before the onslaught of free-silver ideologues determined to choose a more acceptable candidate.

An incensed Stevenson purportedly took umbrage over the unexpected turn of events and notified his cohorts that he would make his own fight for the nomination. Resenting the manner in which he had been used and then discarded when radical silverites gained control of the convention, Stevenson, instead of backpedaling to the safety of his vice-presidential suite, accused the senators of political cowardice and complained of the contemptible manner by which he had been deserted by his friends. Stevenson thereupon used the press as a vehicle to enhance his prospects and dispel the fear that he was not loyal to silver, conveniently forgetting his 1892 declaration in favor of sound money. Newspapers quickly capitalized on the beleaguered vice president's activity. The plan failed to generate enthusiasm, leaving Stevenson in a political quagmire. Radical silver ideologues, such as Altgeld, viewed Stevenson as an unlikely patron of change, accusing him of straddling the currency issue and being incapable of rebuilding a winning coalition. At the Democratic national convention in Chicago, Stevenson received no votes from either Kentucky or Illinois, and only a small handful from other states. Secluded in his Bloomington home, the vice president experienced a rapid fall from grace.

Stevenson's innate political cautiousness, a successful trait in the past, proved calamitous in the tumultuous arena of Democratic politics in 1896. It was the ultimate irony for a lawyer who had achieved success in the political world with his talent for fashioning compromises. Disliking divisive politics, Stevenson preferred to merge groups into the middle ground of happy consensus. Regrettably, the explosive political situation in 1896 put the vice president in a position that did not play to his natural strengths. He ultimately had to displease one group or the other by stating what kind of monetary system he envisioned for the nation. Unable to escape the cloud of discontent hanging over the Cleveland administration, the vice president, practicing the politics of preservation to immunize himself from extremism, endeavored to play politics for the silver vote but lost while trying to deflect criticism that he had not done enough for free silverism. Caught between the vacuum that was Cleveland and the resentment that was William Jennings Bryan, Stevenson faced his worst political identity crisis.

Struggling to reconcile a divided party by using his outmoded conciliatory style, Stevenson tried to appease all factions with concessions but went down to a humiliating defeat. His presidential ascendancy in 1896 would have been the result of deep intraparty wrangling, fueled by a policy clash over the money issue, a deadlocked convention, and an ultimate Stevenson coronation as a compromise choice. It did not happen. Vice President Stevenson lacked the personal dynamism to energize Democrats with frenzied enthusiasm; he was not the heroic figure that the occasion demanded. Instead, Bryan steamrolled his opposition, crushing Stevenson in the process. An older group of party stewards exited while the torch was passed to a new generation of Democrats. Stevenson quickly joined the group and wholeheartedly endorsed Bryan as the Democratic presidential nominee.

Although he failed to obtain the Democratic presidential nomination in 1896, Stevenson worked for party unification in a way that Bryan refused to do in the postconvention period. Unlike Bryan, whose victory infuriated conservatives, Stevenson did not make the Chicago platform a litmus test of faith, and he rejected all unyielding positions on party purification and attempts to purge those Democrats who refused to pledge their loyalty. Unalterably opposed to the principle of excommunication from the party, Stevenson minimized differences, preached assimilation, and warned that Democratic divisions would result in Republican control of Congress and the White House. The vice president was the highest official in the Cleveland administration supporting Bryan, who, along with the new chairman of the Democratic National Committee, miscalculated badly by neglecting to use the soothingly sensible Stevenson in the national campaign to ease the clash among party factions. Stevenson's careful blend of pragmatism and partisanship constituted an important counterpart to the more ideologically charged agenda of Bryan. Nevertheless, Stevenson campaigned for Bryan, introduced him to the crowd when the nominee visited Bloomington, and decided against discussing his stand with Cleveland, who supported the independent presidential candidacy of Senator John M. Palmer, an Illinois sound-money politician chosen in Indianapolis by bolting Democrats. Although Palmer, Cleveland, and Stevenson remained friends, the vice president did not endorse Palmer on a separate third-party ticket, nor did he question the sincerity of his conservative colleagues who favored Palmer over Bryan.

At the end of September 1896, before participating in the quadrennial convention of the National Association of Democratic Clubs in St. Louis, Missouri, Stevenson went to Burlington, Iowa, to represent the administration in the semicentennial celebrations of that state's admission to the Union. In the midst of this festival, the reviewing stand on Main Street, hastily erected against the wishes of some local businessmen, suddenly collapsed from the crowd's weight, sending dignitaries and guests falling to the rain-soaked ground. Stevenson, seated near the center of the stand, was thrown into a wildly struggling mass of people. His left leg was badly bruised, and his knee was slightly sprained. He appeared dazed for a moment by the force of the fall, and concern grew when he was unable for a time to leave the scene of the accident. Eventually, the vice president entered his carriage for the ride to the hotel, where he recovered after a short rest. Stevenson took the incident good naturedly and only seemed concerned about the injuries of those who fell about him.

After leaving Iowa and Missouri, Stevenson returned to Illinois to await the results of the presidential election. William McKinley, the Republican presidential standard bearer and former governor of Ohio, easily won the presidency on a conservative platform. Stevenson immediately dispatched a congratulatory telegram to Vice President-elect Garret A. Hobart of New Jersey. He then made preparations for his final months in office. Members of the U.S. Senate individually and collectively expressed their appreciation to Stevenson for his fairness and efficiency in presiding over the upper chamber. They unanimously passed a resolution of thanks and presented the vice president with a handsome silver service and a signed testimonial.

On March 3, 1897, Stevenson administered the oath of office to his successor, Vice President Hobart. He then delivered his farewell address, in which he thanked the senators for their courtesy and urged that they extend the same spirit of cooperation to Hobart. Stevenson stated that it had been a great honor and a rewarding experience to preside over the Senate, and that he carried with him no feelings of unkindness toward any senator. Adding that he had endeavored to interpret and execute faithfully the rules of the Senate, Stevenson reiterated his support of its rules and traditions.

After attending McKinley's inaugural ceremonies at the Capitol on March 4, 1897, Stevenson returned to his home in Bloomington. He resumed his legal career and duties as president of the McLean County Coal Company. The former vice president also served for a time as president of the Interstate Building and Loan Association of Bloomington and as director of the People's Bank of Bloomington. He looked forward to a relaxed life with his family and neighbors.

In April 1897, one month after he left office, Stevenson was back in Washington to accept the invitation of President McKinley to serve as one of three members of the Bimetallic Monetary Commission, headed by Senator Edward O. Wolcott of Colorado. McKinley chose Stevenson to represent the Democratic Party, but the two men had long been good friends. The three commissioners immediately sailed to Europe to discuss with world leaders the monetary question and to explore the possibility of bimetallism, which would establish the proper mint ratio between gold and silver. Stevenson secretly believed the Democrats would not be able to convert the nation to free coinage and that the only hope for silver rested with an international agreement. With this goal in mind, he discussed international bimetallism with British and French spokesmen.

While wailing for final negotiations and a decision from India, Stevenson and his wife visited Norway, Sweden, Denmark, Italy, and Switzerland. Upon returning to London, where he was presented to Queen Victoria, Stevenson learned that European leaders had declined the American offer.

The following year Stevenson and McKinley renewed their relationship when they shared a platform at a Peace Jubilee Banquet in Chicago. On that occasion Stevenson warmly praised McKinley's successful conduct of the Spanish–American War, referring to the brief conflict in 1898 as the marvel of the closing century.

Stevenson surfaced again politically in 1900, when events took a surprising turn at the Democratic National Convention in Kansas City. There, delegates extricated Stevenson from political retirement by choosing him as a vice-presidential candidate to run with Bryan. Mayor Carter H. Harrison II of Chicago assumed the initiative by presenting Stevenson's name to the Illinois delegation. Altgeld's gubernatorial defeat in 1896 had created a Democratic void in Illinois, and Stevenson's friends again controlled the political machinery. Easily eliminating other contenders, Stevenson triumphed on the first ballot. He received the vice presidential nomination in 1900 because he was the most available man in the Democratic Party to provide the stability and harmony that the party needed that year. Nominated in 1892 as a liberal to balance a slate led by a conservative, the rehabilitated Stevenson, a spokesman for traditional Democratic nostrums, obtained a second nomination in 1900 as an elder conservative statesman to stabilize a ticket headed by a progressive who championed reinvented government.

The Democrats changed presidential leaders and philosophical direction in eight years but kept Stevenson, who also received the vice-presidential nominations of the Silver Republican and Populist parties, which had fused with Bryan. The belated attempt of the Bryanites to assuage differences with Democratic conservatives by selecting Stevenson would have been more useful and effective had they chosen Stevenson as Bryan's running mate in 1896. In any event, Bryan, who had preferred another candidate, did nothing to prevent Stevenson's nomination in 1900, praising him as a person of splendid character and, in an unprecedented move, announced his determination to increase the importance of the vice presidency by having the incumbent attend cabinet meetings.

In 1900, Stevenson regarded the vice presidency as a suitable conclusion to his long career of public service. His nomination, which marked the first time that a vice president had recaptured his party's nomination after having left office, propelled him once again into the political spotlight, and the prospect of serving his party and country prompted him to campaign widely. Again conferring with Bryan in Lincoln, Nebraska, on campaign strategy and following his acceptance speech in Indianapolis, Stevenson visited several states, including Maryland, Delaware, New York, New Jersey, and West Virginia. He denounced monopolistic growth and the trusts but avoided mentioning the currency issue, which he did not regard as paramount in the campaign of 1900.

Stevenson took special interest in foreign affairs in 1900. He was particularly opposed to the provision in the Paris peace treaty of 1899 for acquiring the Philippine Islands. An implacable opponent of overseas expansionism, Stevenson predicted that the acquisition and retention of the Philippines would compromise America's original altruistic purpose. He presented a number of constitutional, political, economic, diplomatic, historical, and radical reasons to substantiate his opposition to imperialism. A product of the isolationism that flourished in the midwestern heartland, Stevenson repeated the warnings of George Washington and Thomas Jefferson regarding alliances and internal involvement. Although Stevenson espoused continental containment, he lacked the xenophobic paranoia and pessimism characteristic of some rabid antiimperialists. In essence, he was a traditionalist who tried to steer the country away from permanent entanglements and belligerent interventionism. To Stevenson, isolationism meant maintaining maximum freedom of action and not total withdrawal from world affairs. He advocated a coherent foreign policy for the future while fully recognizing America's aversion to interventionary politics. Stevenson also hoped for the establishment of a tribunal of all nations, including the United States, that would resolve issues and preserve peace. Ironically, his grandson and namesake, Adlai E. Stevenson II, Democratic presidential nominee in 1952 and 1956, served as United States ambassador to the United Nations from 1961 to 1965.

After the defeat of the Bryan-Stevenson ticket in 1900 at the hands of McKinley and Roosevelt, Stevenson returned to Bloomington. There he lived a quiet but active life as a respected elder party spokesman. He addressed various groups, delivered lectures, and favored New York Democrat Alton B. Parker for the presidency in 1904. In 1908, after handily winning the Democratic primary, Stevenson narrowly lost the Illinois gubernatorial election, but he ran ahead of Bryan, who unsuccessfully sought his third try at the White House. Vote frauds in Chicago wards controlled by Republican Mayor Fred A. Busse may have cost Stevenson, who commanded the backing of Republican Congressman William Lorimer, the governor's office. Four years later, in a letter to President-elect Woodrow Wilson, Bryan suggested Stevenson as a possibility to fill a position in the new Democratic administration. The offer never materialized, and Stevenson died shortly thereafter in a Chicago hospital.

Stevenson must be analyzed in connection with the complicated political context in which he lived and the ambiguities of his beliefs and policies, for he embodied the contradictions of an age that was simultaneously resisting and welcoming ongoing changes in society. Like most Gilded Age politicians, Stevenson suffered from an inability to recognize that the major problem of his generation reverberated around the adjustment of American politics to the enormous economic and social transformations imposed on the United States by industrialization and urbanization, which brought the nation to a new stage of self-awareness. Stevenson, whose politics combined a generally conservative social and political agenda with a strong dose of moralism, was a Gilded Age Jeffersonian who lived in the agrarian Midwest. His fidelity was to the Democratic Party, whose faithful servant he tried to be throughout his career. Partly progressive and partly conservative, both a reformer and a conformer, he sought the society of Old Guard security but often registered dissenting opinions. Admittedly, he was a complex political figure who zigzagged across stereotypes, both naturally and by calculation.

Although not in the first rank of great men of his generation, Stevenson was a good vice president and an honest politician in an era when the public neither expected nor sought great political leaders. He also served as a transitional figure in bridging the passing of the Democrats from the conservatism of Cleveland to the progressivism of Bryan and Wilson. Like many nineteenth-century vice presidents, however, Stevenson failed in his quest for lasting fame. His glory, like that of many who preceded him, rested in achieving, rather than holding, high political office. On the other hand, as the founder of a political dynasty whose grandson ran for president in 1952 and 1956, he thrust his family onto the political stage where they remained for the next three generations. Stevenson's contribution to the American political tradition was a legacy for his family and the nation.

REFERENCES

Leonard C. Schlup, "The Political Career of the First Adlai E, Stevenson" (Ph.D. diss., University of Illinois at Urbana-Champaign, 1973); Leonard C. Schlup, "The American Chameleon: Adlai E. Stevenson and the Quest for the Vice Presidency in Gilded Age Politics," *Presidential Studies Quarterly*, 21 (Summer 1991), 511–529; Adlai E. Stevenson, *Something of Men I Have Known: With Some Papers of a General Nature, Political, Historical, and Retrospective* (Chicago, Ill.: A.C. McClurg and Company, 1909).

See the entry for Garret Hobart for a biographical note on Leonard C. Schlup.

GARRET AUGUSTUS HOBART (1844–1899)

Vice President, 1897–1899

(President William McKinley)

GARRET AUGUSTUS HOBART
(Library of Congress)

By Leonard C. Schlup

Garret A. Hobart was one of the nation's first modern vice presidents. Although he entered office with a modest résumé, he demonstrated that conventional credentials are not always the main indicators of political success. Hobart gave a new distinction to the vice-presidential office, increased its stature, served as a loyal personal friend and political companion to President William McKinley, skillfully presided over the United States Senate, and performed duties assigned to him by McKinley. Because of his important role and responsibilities, combined with his close relationship with McKinley, Hobart was often referred to as the "assistant president." In the public mind, he was clearly identified with the administration. Hobart was more than the titular president of the Senate with a reversionary right to the presidency; he was for more than two years a factor in the political and social life of the nation.

231

Born in Long Branch, New Jersey, the son of Addison Willard Hobart, a teacher and farmer, and Sophia Vanderveer Hobart, Garret Hobart attended elementary and preparatory schools before graduating third highest in his class with honors in mathematics and English from Rutgers College in 1863. He taught school for a short time before relocating to Paterson, New Jersey, where he studied law in the office of Socrates Tuttle, whose daughter, Jennie, he married in 1869, the year of his admission to the bar. Hobart became a counselor at law in 1871 and a master in chancery the following year. He advanced quickly in the fields of law, business, and politics. In 1871, he was chosen city counsel of Paterson, and in both 1872 and 1873, Hobart won a seat in the lower chamber of the New Jersey state legislature, becoming speaker of the house in 1874. Elected state senator in 1876 and 1879 by large majorities, he served as president of the senate in the sessions of 1881 and 1882, thereby becoming the only person in New Jersey history ever to be both speaker of the state assembly and president of the senate.

Early in his career, Hobart developed interests in national politics. Chairman of the New Jersey State Republican Committee from 1880 to 1891, he was a delegate-at-large to five successive Republican national conventions, where he made many friends. In 1884, he joined the Republican National Committee. Unsuccessful as the Republican candidate for the U.S. Senate in 1883 in an age when state legislators selected senators and Democrats then controlled the New Jersey legislature, Hobart, declining to run for a seat in the U.S. House of Representatives, refused to allow his defeat to terminate his political interests. In 1888, he dispatched letters to Republican presidential nominee Benjamin Harrison to outline the political situation in New Jersey and offer his advice.

A constructive moderate from an important eastern state, Hobart supported sound-money principles, a protective tariff to safeguard American industry, expanded markets, development of transportation systems, and federal spending for projects of regional and national importance. He accepted the industrial United States and the ethic of the day. Eager to see the country grow, Hobart was a nationalist who possessed the emotional attitude for increased governmental action. The dogmas of localism, retrenchment, and antifederalism were foreign to him as he embraced his party's growing nationalism and the rapid social and economic changes in the nation. In New Jersey he represented an industrial constituency of business, agriculture, labor, and the professional middle class.

Hobart's political and business Interests were intertwined; he regarded himself as a businessman who engaged in politics for recreation. In 1885, he assumed the presidency of the Passaic Water Company. A director of several banks and a receiver for the New Jersey Midland Railroad and the First National Bank of Newark, Hobart earned a reputation for business sagacity, eventually having connections with sixty corporations. In the process, he accumulated a fortune and surfaced as a leading Republican of northern New Jersey. The practicing businessman/politician in 1895 secured the Republican gubernatorial nomination for his friend, John W. Griggs, and managed the campaign. Griggs's election ended a long reign of Democratic control and heralded a new era of Republican rule in the state.

The beginning of a long Republican reign in the Garden State began when the GOP took control of the state legislature in 1894 and the governor's mansion the next year. Several factors were responsible for this emerging Republicanism, among them the severe depression that engulfed the nation, the decrease in the number of farms, the increase of the conservative commuter vote, the support for tariff protection, and the disapproval of the free-silver movement. Republican domination of New Jersey opened the door to Hobart's vice-presidential nomination.

The depression that gripped the nation following the panic of 1893 weakened the Democratic Party. Legions of unemployed workers and scores of failed businesses contributed to a bleak picture of the American economy. This economic distress spawned political protest and social unrest. President Grover Cleveland's popularity plummeted, and he was shunned by segments of his own party. His handling of the currency issue, among other actions, divided Democrats, with southern and western free-silver advocates aligned against the East in a battle of the monetary standards. As a result of overwhelming Republican victories across the nation in the off-year congressional elections of 1894, Republicans felt confident of success in 1896.

Hobart also sensed a Republican victory in 1896. His duties as a Republican National Committee member and as a delegate-at-large from New Jersey occupied his time in the immediate weeks prior to the party's state and national conventions. Endorsed by the New Jersey convention as a vice-presidential favorite son, Hobart left Paterson on June 8 to entertain the New Jersey delegation at the Lawyer's Club in New York City and make arrangements for the national convention. He also conferred with Senator Matthew S. Quay of Pennsylvania, who endorsed Hobart for the vice presidency. On his way to the national convention in St. Louis, Hobart stopped at McKinley's home in Canton, Ohio, to discuss politics with the former congressman and governor who was the front-runner for the presidential nomination. Meanwhile, the stage was being set for his vice-presidential nomination. Confident of Hobart's nomination, Senator John M. Thurston of Nebraska, Republican national convention chairman, arrived in St. Louis wearing a McKinley-Hobart button. Senator Redfield Proctor of Vermont also sported a similar ornament. Illinois lawyer, banker, and businessman Charles G. Dawes, who later served as vice president, lined up the Illinois delegation for Hobart.

At first dismayed and overwhelmed at the thought of his possible nomination, Hobart expressed his innermost feelings and trepidations in letters and conversations with his wife and close friends. His concerns centered mainly on the work, the worry, and the loss of home life connected with political office. He was also cognizant of the impenetrable vacuum that characterized the vice president, a person usually viewed as the trailer to the ticket, a fifth wheel in the national bandwagon who rolled painlessly into oblivion. Knowing that McKinley needed a running mate from an eastern-seaboard state, Hobart hoped that Thomas B. Reed, Speaker of the House of Representatives, would consent to accept second place, but Reed adamantly refused to consider this possibility. Although he approached the convention with misgivings, Hobart ultimately decided that he would neither seek nor avoid the vice-presidential nomination; he would allow events to take their own natural course.

Republican delegates convened in St. Louis on June 16, 1896, for their quadrennial national convention. McKinley easily triumphed on the first ballot to become the party's presidential standard bearer. The platform, which called for a protective tariff and sound money, contained ideas and words offered by Hobart; in fact, his unwavering endorsement of the gold standard helped to influence the party's position on that vexatious issue.

When delegates began to consider vice-presidential possibilities, Thomas C. Platt, the recognized leader in New York Republican politics, attempted to force upon the convention the name of Governor Levi P. Morton of New York, who had served as vice president from 1889 to 1893, during the administration of Benjamin Harrison. Because there was no one candidate from New York upon whom the Republicans could agree, the delegates needed to look elsewhere. Mark Hanna, a wealthy Ohio industrialist who shrewdly managed McKinley's campaign, preferred Hobart, and he used his powerful influence to further the ambitions of the New Jersey contender. United States Senator William J. Sewell, the boss of New Jersey Republicanism, also favored Hobart for the vice presidency, contending his presence on the ticket would guarantee Republican success in the Garden State. The New Jersey delegation thereupon presented Hobart as the state's candidate for the vice presidency. Hobart was nominated by Judge John Franklin Fort, later to serve as governor of New Jersey, who emphasized that his politically regenerated state merited the recognition. J. Otis Humphrey, an Illinois attorney who later served as a federal district judge, seconded Hobart's nomination. Hobart scored an easy victory on the first ballot over his nearest competitor, Henry Clay Evans of Tennessee.

McKinley and Hanna joined forces with Hobart in 1896 for a variety of reasons. First, Hobart was politically acceptable to and ideologically compatible with McKinley. Hobart and McKinley belonged to the same wing of their party; neither political doctrine nor a separate allegiance divided the two men. Second, Hobart entertained no presidential ambitions and carried no burdensome baggage. Although he had not been governor or senator and was without a national reputation, Hobart was a moderate and noncontroversial politician who possessed personal integrity and wealth although he lacked political enemies. In short, he did little to strengthen the ticket, but he did nothing to weaken it either. Third, Hobart lived in a region that provided geographical balance to the ticket in an era when both parties, by prevailing practice, selected their presidential and vice-presidential nominees from the Midwest and East. As a native of New Jersey, Hobart was expected to help carry that pivotal state for the Republican slate and add vigor to the ticket in the East. For these reasons, Hobart, a conservative pragmatist, emerged as a national political leader in the Republican coalition of 1896.

After receiving the vice-presidential nomination, Hobart thanked his New Jersey colleagues and the Republican delegates for their expression of confidence in his ability to discharge the duties of the vice presidency. He pledged to employ his best efforts to further McKinley's election. Hobart thereupon returned to New Jersey, where on July 17 the Committee appointed by the convention to notify Hobart of his nomination arrived at his Paterson home. Charles W. Fairbanks of Indiana, chairman of this committee, who would later serve as senator and vice president, remarked that the vice presidency had been graced by eminent statesmen who had contributed to the upbuilding of the strength and glory of the nation.

In his reply, Hobart accepted the nomination. He promised to help the party achieve electoral success and reaffirmed his support for the gold standard and protective tariffs as sound principles on which to restore the nation's prosperity. The nominee pointed out that monetary uncertainty or instability could lead to serious consequences and that the gravity of the financial question could not be overestimated. Because gold was the one standard of value among all enlightened commercial nations, Hobart declared that the issue could not be compromised.

The presidential election of 1896 was a crucial contest in U.S. history, constituting a fundamental turning point in American electoral politics and demonstrating the periodicity of political realignment. By 1896 the economic depression had led to an erosion of living standards for many, including farmers who watched their incomes plummet and their debt skyrocket throughout the course of the national malaise. A crisis of confidence gripped Cleveland's presidency at the time of the campaign. Years of violence, sectional antagonisms, class conflicts, social unrest, political protest, and economic disillusionment, combined with the problems of growing urbanization and industrialization, fostered frustration and triggered national anxiety. These forces climaxed in the campaign of 1896, the most significant election in the Gilded Age, a term coined by Mark Twain to describe a post-Civil War generation characterized by excess.

Hobart assumed an active role in the 1896 presidential campaign. He delivered speeches, corresponded with McKinley, visited the most important cities of New Jersey, helped to manage the campaign from an office in New York

City, and received delegations of visitors on the front lawn of his home in New Jersey. Like McKinley, who conducted a front-porch campaign from his home in Canton, Hobart abstained from the national barnstorming method identified with the Democratic and Populist presidential nominee, William Jennings Bryan, who ran on a free-coinage platform. Maintaining that the Republican Party was right in its principles and that issues were more important than personalities, Hobart emphasized that he was not fighting the old Democratic Party but rather a new group that had seized power and overturned traditional party nostrums. The new group's proposal of such fiscal alterations and heresies, Hobart warned, would lead to a financial revolution, inflation, and the collapse of sound money; in a speech at Newark, he predicted that the election's outcome would teach the greatest lesson in political morality that had ever been taught in America.

Twice during the campaign, Hobart journeyed to McKinley's home to confer with the head of the ticket. On the second visit, he brought his letter of acceptance with him. Hobart met McKinley and Herman H. Kohlsaat, editor and publisher of the *Chicago Times-Herald*. The New Jersey Republican read his letter of acceptance while McKinley, who had supervised its preparation, smoked a cigar and offered suggestions. McKinley was exceedingly cautious about the exact wording, but Hobart gladly accepted the revisions.

Hobart's formal letter of acceptance, dated September 7, was addressed to Fairbanks and other members of the notification committee. The letter, devoted chiefly to the monetary issue, contained several graphic illustrations of the horrendous consequences of free silver, referring to this question as the supremely important subject in the campaign. Hobart claimed that the money standard of a great nation should be as fixed and permanent as the nation itself and that the free coinage of silver at the ratio of 16 to 1 was a policy that no country had ever before proposed. Noting that the foundation of a house is not always in sight but

that the house would not stand without its foundation, Hobart warned that any depreciation in the value of the dollar would defraud those who had accumulated savings and would hurt the pensions of Civil War veterans, a situation that would be tantamount to war upon the people. He believed that no person should be made homeless because a political party wanted to experiment with the money standard for its own selfish purposes. Contending that the country could not afford to give its sanction to wholesale spoliation, Hobart wrote that it was neither wise nor patriotic to make a political platform the medium of assault upon property, the peace of society, and civilization itself. He equated the Democratic platform with revolutionary propaganda embodying a menace of national disintegration and destruction, and he urged all men regardless of political affiliation to unite in defense of individual and institutional rights and of the nation's endangered interests.

Although he emphasized the currency issue, Hobart did not neglect the tariff question. Reminding Americans that their paralyzed industrial system had resulted from a mistaken economic system deliberately enacted by Democrats, he stressed that the duty of government was to protect and encourage in all practical ways the development of domestic industries, the elevation of home labor, and the enlargement of prosperity. Hobart remained convinced that the voters would understand the issues during the campaign and would choose safe and sure remedies rather than trust the Democratic Party, winch under Bryan had dishonored its pledges and repudiated its past principles and policies.

McKinley and Hobart made the election of 1896 a contest between the forces of law and decency versus those of radicalism and violence. Their supporters distributed American flags, thereby making the nation's banner a symbol of conservative politics. Mounting a great publicity and mass-marketing effort, Hanna raised millions of dollars on behalf of the McKinley-Hobart team, whose campaign was the first to be professionally run. A new era had dawned in American politics.

McKinley triumphed nationally to win the presidency in 1896, while Republicans retained control of both houses of Congress, further cementing the political realignment that had begun two years earlier. Republican nationalism scored an impressive victory in that McKinley, a safe midwesterner, represented the conscience of the country and symbolized the ideals of nationality in an age of industrial growth and uncertainty. A political collision of two ideologies occurred in 1896. The fuel that, fired the political revolution that seminal year was a blend of anger and fear that adverse economic, and social forces were slipping out of control. The outcome demonstrated that business and industrial groups had conquered agrarian forces, and the result, plus the passage of the Gold Standard Act of 1900, helped to destroy free silver as a powerful political issue. The immediate result marked a victory for conservatism and the politics of census, the very cornerstone of McKinleyism. From this election, Republicans built a presidential coalition that, with the exception of eight years of Woodrow Wilson, dominate American politics until the Great Depression.

A few days after the election, in which the Republican ticket swept New Jersey with 60 percent of the popular vote, Hobart acknowledged his victory in a spirit of nonpartisanship. He said that he did not consider the election a personal victory; rather, it was a triumph of American patriotism that belonged to no party. The vice president-elect observed that many voters had abjured their past political affiliations and had voted as their consciences dictated for the supremacy of law and to maintain the national honor. Seeking to assuage campaign wounds, Hobart magnified principles and patriotism instead of personalities.

During the postelection period, Hobart prepared himself for his new position. He studied the history of the vice presidency, mastered and memorized the rules of the Senate, and learned the names of all the senators. He arrived in Washington on March 2, 1897, establishing his headquarters and temporary living quarters at the Arlington Hotel. Vice President Adlai E. Stevenson paid a courtesy call on his successor. Hobart returned the nicety by visiting with Stevenson at the Ebbitt House the next day.

On March 4, 1897, Stevenson administered the oath of office to Hobart as the nation's twenty-fourth vice president. The ceremony occurred in the Senate chamber with members of Congress, President Cleveland, President-elect McKinley, governors, cabinet officers, and other dignitaries present for the occasion. After taking the oath, Hobart delivered a brief inaugural address in which he promised to abide by a conservative, equitable, and conscientious construction and enforcement of the upper chamber's rules while at the same time conserving the precedents and established traditions that had contributed to making that tribunal the most distinguished of the world's legislative bodies. He pledged to assist the senators to move expeditiously in the interests of good government and positive legislation, maintaining that any attempt to obstruct the regular course of wise and prudent legislative action after the fullest and freest discussion was neither consistent with true senatorial courtesy nor conducive to the welfare of the people. Hoping to form genuine friendships with members of the Senate, the vice president announced his intention to discharge his duties in such a manner as to lighten their labor and promote the pleasant and efficient transaction of the public business in such a way that their work would redound to the peace and honor of the country and the prosperity and happiness of all the people. Upon the conclusion of Hobart's speech, Cleveland leaned over to McKinley and whispered that it was the sweetest oration he had heard in a long time.

Although abhorring unnecessary procrastination and prolonged debates, Hobart entertained no plans to usurp the prerogatives of the Senate, to change its rules and customs, or to claim unconstitutional powers; instead, he frankly expressed his views, promising to set an example of facilitation in his endeavor to conduct sessions in a businesslike fashion. A business-politician oriented toward goals and achievements, Hobart wanted to see concrete results in ways similar to those he had witnessed in his private business transactions over the years. Moreover, he propounded the idea that the results of the presidential election demonstrated that the people demanded action from their elected representatives.

Skillfully presiding over the Senate, using a gavel made from his father's apple tree, Hobart took his duties seriously and prepared assiduously for the legislative agenda. Regularly attending Senate sessions, the vice president became known as a chronic audience. He enjoyed sitting in the presiding officer's chair, listening to the debates, strolling the corridors, visiting committee sessions, lunching with senators, attending afternoon smokers, holding dinner parties, and smoothing things over for McKinley in the upper house. He was somewhere between the powerful Speaker of the House Thomas B. Reed on the one hand and passive insignificance on the other. With his quick perception and keen memory for legislative details, Hobart speeded proceedings by providing rapid answers to parliamentary questions, in the process, he surfaced as a popular president of the Senate who avoided making political enemies. A kindly gentleman with modest dignity and a good conversationalist who was known for his charm and his willingness to compromise, he gave new meaning to the vice presidential office, gained the respect of the Senate and the president, influenced the Senate to promote the administration's policies, and sought harmonious feelings between the executive and legislative branches. McKinley had an invaluable ally in Hobart.

The Hobarts leased the Cameron Mansion at 21 Lafayette Square, which stood diagonally across from the White House. Often called the Cream White House, the home was owned by Senator James D. Cameron of Pennsylvania, who at first wanted a $10,000 rental agreement, which Hobart, whose salary was only $8,000, refused outright. Fortunately, the two Republicans came to an agreement. The proximity of the Cameron Home to the White House facilitated frequent social meetings between the McKinleys and the Hobarts. Jennie T. Hobart often served as the White House hostess for Ida S. McKinley, an invalid who experienced seizures of unconsciousness. Unable to fulfill all her social duties, Mrs. McKinley often turned to Mrs. Hobart for assistance. The vice president's charming wife, who popularized the title "second lady," thoroughly enjoyed her role as a Washington hostess with a busy social calendar. From these frequent contacts, a close personal relationship developed between the two families. On more than one occasion, they vacationed together at Bluff Point on Lake Champlain and shared certain holidays, including Thanksgiving Day 1898 in the White House. Hobart even served as an investment counselor to the president and manager of McKinley's income.

Hobart loyally supported McKinley's programs. In 1897, he endorsed the Dingley Tariff, a high protectionist measure. Later that year, upon the resignation of Attorney General Joseph McKenna, Hobart persuaded McKinley to appoint Governor Griggs of New Jersey to the vacant cabinet spot. Although McKinley did nearly everything possible to promote Hobart as a vital part of the administration, such as soliciting his views on issues and consulting with him on affairs of state, he neglected to invite the vice president to attend cabinet meetings, a surprising oversight. Socially, Hobart was the first vice president to assert predominance over Sir Julian Pauncefote, dean of the diplomatic corps in Washington, who previously had claimed a position next to the president in receiving lines. Recognizing Hobart as the second-highest official, McKinley, asserting unmistakably that second place at diplomatic receptions belonged to the vice president, ordered Hobart to stand next to him instead of the British ambassador.

As presiding officer, Hobart had the opportunity to address the Senate on various occasions in which he related his personal impressions of the character and scope of the upper chamber. At the close of the session in which the Dingley Tariff had been approved in 1897, he conceded that his inaugural remark about Senate promptness had been made in innocence and that he had since learned that his definition of reasonable expedition differed considerably from the Senate's conception of the meaning of that phrase. He praised Senate Democrats for refraining from abusing the rules of the Senate and congratulated Republicans for their endeavors to promote the public welfare by passing legislation designed to restore healthy industrial and economic conditions, adding that senators represented well the desires of their Constituents. Defining the Senate as a remarkable body and the sine qua non of legislation, Hobart asserted that the smallest state was just as powerful as the largest one in the upper house. He opined that the cloud of depression and distrust was evaporating and then bluntly lectured U.S. socialists on the work ethic, telling them that no industrial rewards existed for the idle.

In 1898, Hobart turned his attention to foreign affairs. The desire of the Cubans for independence from Spain received his warm blessing. After the sinking of the U.S. battleship *Maine,* Hobart joined the president, the secretary of state, and Catholic archbishop John Ireland in a meeting on March 10 at the White House, where they reviewed the Cuban situation. Hobart used that occasion to notify McKinley of the growing pressure for war that was prevalent in Congress and to express his belief that the nation had no alternative except to declare war on Spain. Congress approved the war declaration on April 25. The swift military triumphs in the popular Spanish-American War of 1898 heightened Hobart's patriotic and nationalistic sentiments. He boasted of the brilliant military victories; yet he opposed annexing a free Cuba to the United States. Like McKinley, Hobart was not an imperialist by inclination but a reticent expansionist eager to gain new markets for American business and industry. He favored the annexation of Hawaii in 1898, scoffing at the impassioned rhetoric and warnings of antiimperialists over American acquisition of distant lands.

The single casting vote of Hobart as president of the Senate took place on February 14, 1899, eight days after the Senate had ratified the Treaty of Paris, the formal document concluding the war with Spain. Democratic Senator Augustus O. Bacon of Georgia proposed a resolution to limit American control over the Philippine Islands, which the United States had acquired from Spain, urging that the United States disclaim any intention to exercise permanent jurisdiction over the islands and affirming that the United States would withdraw once a stable independent government had been formed by the people. McKinley disapproved this restriction, suggesting that it would place restraints on his conduct of foreign policy in the region. Because some Republicans were absent when the resolution came up for a vote in the Senate, the outcome resulted in a tie of 29 votes for each side. Empowered by the Constitution to break a tie vote, Hobart cast his vote against the resolution, thereby relieving McKinley of an embarrassing situation. When Hobart administered the coup de grâce by voting to defeat the resolution, he opened a new political struggle in the United States between imperialists and antiimperialists.

On March 4, 1899, before declaring the Senate adjourned, Hobart addressed the members. Recalling the Spanish–American War as a conflict undertaken in the interest of humanity and conspicuous for the brilliant deeds of the army and navy, he bragged that an imperial domain had been added to American possessions. The vice president expressed confidence that future Congresses would also meet grave questions with wisdom and patriotism and would resolve them properly. Hobart also confessed that he cherished a profound faith in the spirit of the American people and that his confidence in the strength of American political institutions had been increased during his tenure in office.

No doubt the most difficult personal assignment Hobart completed for McKinley occurred in the summer of 1899. Public outcry over unpreparedness, mismanagement, and incompetence in the army during the Spanish-American War led to an investigatory commission and public requests for the resignation of Secretary of War Russell A. Alger, a former governor of Michigan whom McKinley had appointed to his cabinet in 1897. Blamed for wartime mistakes and sins of omission, Alger, who tried to shuffle the blame, became the scapegoat and an embarrassment to the McKinley administration. Several daily newspapers severely censured his conduct. At first the president showed no inclination to dismiss Alger, but everyone except the secretary knew that the end was near. McKinley's baffling silence, which led Alger to believed he had been vindicated, only compounded the tense situation and lengthened the tortured affair.

In June, Alger offered to resign, effective January 2, 1900, when he planned to run for the U.S. Senate from Michigan, but the president demurred. Demonstrating surprisingly squeamish behavior, McKinley refused to demand his secretary's immediate resignation under fire to placate public feeling or to unburden the administration from a ticklish dilemma or a potentially dangerous political problem. Rather than meet Alger face to face, McKinley devised a surreptitious scheme to remove the secretary of war: He asked Secretary of State John Hay to notify Alger that he must resign his position. Hay tactfully declined to perform this disagreeable duty, and McKinley then gave to Hobart, Alger's close friend, the delicate task of requesting the secretary's resignation from the cabinet. Attorney General Griggs journeyed to New Jersey as the president's messenger to inform an ailing Hobart of McKinley's decision. The vice president accepted the unpleasant burden out of duty and friendship for his chief. He immediately summoned Alger to visit him at his summer home at Norwood Park, where, assisted by his wife, he told the secretary that the president wanted him to resign at once. Alger received the news with surprise and pain, leaving the house deeply chagrined. After reflecting on the episode, Alger returned to Hobart's home the next morning. Seeing the sick vice president sitting on the piazza, Alger ran toward his friend and threw his arms about him.

Hobart found his task doubly painful in that he was desperately ill at the time and had long been friends with Alger. Still, he performed the job with such understanding and finesse that the New York *Sun* called the vice president a man of crystal insight and velvet tact. Happily, neither the Hobarts nor the Algers allowed this pathetic incident to mar their friendship. In an attempt to console Alger, Hobart dispatched a telegram, assuring the deposed secretary that he would appreciate his freedom more and more each day.

When Alger returned to Washington, he confronted McKinley. He remonstrated against the president's failure to see him directly and deplored the roundabout method of forcing his resignation, which he submitted to the president, effective August 1, 1899. Alger had a valid point: On this issue McKinley showed weakness, indecisiveness, and an absence of common sense, which were totally out of character with his administration. He should have handled the matter forthrightly from the beginning rather than delegating an unpleasant presidential duty to his terminally ill vice president. McKinley's action was inexcusable. Grateful in the end for Hobart's services, McKinley wired his thanks to the vice president. The drama officially ended when Elihu Root of New York entered the cabinet as secretary of war.

The battle in the Senate over the ratification of the controversial peace treaty with Spain and the Alger affair took their toll on the vice president. Long hours of hard work and a weak heart exhausted him, resulting in a physical collapse in spring 1899 from which he never recovered. He went to Long Branch, New Jersey, to recuperate and stayed at Norwood Park, his seaside home on the coast. Failing to improve, he returned to his Paterson home, where McKinley visited him. The two corresponded that autumn: Hobart wrote of his sleepless nights, nervous indigestion, the diagnoses, and the remedies the doctors has prescribed to give him relief. He grew weaker and weaker in October, knowing that he would not live much longer.

Hobart died in Paterson on November 21, 1899, from complications resulting from a heart attack. He was the sixth vice president to die in office. A grieving McKinley attended the funeral. Hobart was buried at Cedar Lawn Cemetery in Paterson. Following his death, John Hay became next in line of succession to the presidency, while Republican senator William P. Frye of Maine, president pro tempore of the Senate, presided over that chamber. Senators eulogized Hobart in speeches from the floor. In 1903, the citizens of Paterson erected a bronze statue of the vice president next to that of Alexander Hamilton on the City Hall plaza.

Although not an outstanding national leader or orator in the first rank of his generation, Hobart was a competent and cautious government official. He shared with Vice President Charles W. Fairbanks many of the same personal and political qualities. Hobart's short term as vice president was soon overshadowed by the presidential election of 1900, the assassination of McKinley, and the presidency of Theodore Roosevelt. Yet, during his nearly three years in office, Hobart laid the foundation for twentieth century vice presidents from Theodore Roosevelt to Albert Gore. A model presiding officer of a deliberative assembly and adviser to the president, Hobart made the vice-presidential office what the framers of the Constitution properly intended it to be and lifted the office to the dignity and importance it deserved in the Gilded Age. Massachusetts Republican senator Henry Cabot Lodge argued that Hobart restored the vice presidency to its proper position. By honoring the office Hobart honored himself. A successful businessman with a vision and an individual possessed of a tremendous capacity for hard work, Hobart was a man of conscience who brought a business-oriented pragmatism to the vice presidency. He also mirrored McKinley's attitudes and proved loyal to his chief. His personal integrity exerted a healthy influence in late nineteenth-century American politics. Hobart's death in 1899 paved the way for Theodore Roosevelt.

REFERENCES

Jennie Tuttle Hobart, *Memories* (Paterson, N.J.: privately printed, 1930); David Magie, *Life of Garret Augustus Hobart, Twenty-Fourth Vice-President of the United States* (New York: G.P. Putnam's Sons, 1910); Leonard Schlup, "Republican Nationalist in the McKinley Era: Garret A. Hobart of New Jersey and His Political Career and Letters," *The North Jersey Highlander,* 32 (1996).

LEONARD SCHLUP earned a B.A. degree from the University of Akron, an M.A. from Kent State University, an M.L.S. from Indiana University, and a Ph.D. from the University of Illinois at Urbana-Champaign. He is coeditor of *American Economic Developments in the Gilded Age: Eyewitness Accounts* (Midwest Press, 2008) and coeditor of *The Historical Dictionary of the Gilded Age* (M.E. Sharpe, 2003) and *It Seems to Me: Selected Letters of Eleanor Roosevelt* (University Press of Kentucky, 2001). He wrote fifty biographical essays for *The American National Biography*. He has also written entries for the *Encyclopedia of the United States Congress* and the *Tennessee Encyclopedia of History and Culture*.

THEODORE ROOSEVELT (1858–1919)

Vice-President, March 4–September 14, 1901

(President William McKinley)

THEODORE ROOSEVELT
(Library of Congress)

By John Allen Gable

Vice President Theodore Roosevelt became the twenty-sixth president of the United States on September 14, 1901, taking the oath at the home of his friend Ansley Wilcox in Buffalo, New York, after the death of President William McKinley, who had been shot by an anarchist while attending the Pan American Exposition in Buffalo. Theodore Roosevelt won the presidential election of 1904 and was the first vice president to become president because of the death of his predecessor who then went on to be elected president in his own right. TR was the fifth vice president elevated to the presidency by the death of his predecessor; the eighth man to serve as vice president to become president; and the third vice president to become president due to assassination.

Theodore Roosevelt was born on October 27, 1858, in a fashionable brownstone at 28 East 20th Street, Manhattan, and is the only president of the

United States born in New York City. His ancestors were an immigrant couple, Claes Martenszen van Rosenvelt and his wife, Jannetje, who came from the Netherlands to what was then New Amsterdam in the 1640s, and their descendants became wealthy importers, merchants, bankers, and holders of real estate. Many members of the family held public office over the years. Theodore Roosevelt's father, also named Theodore Roosevelt, was an importer, merchant, and philanthropist. The future president's mother, Martha Bulloch, was from Roswell, Georgia, the daughter of a noted family of the old South.

The Civil War was a personal crisis for young Theodore's household. Martha's brothers were officers in the Confederate Navy, but Theodore, Senior, was an ardent supporter of Abraham Lincoln, the Republican Party, and the Union. Out of deference to his wife's feelings, Theodore, Senior, did not join the army, but he was active in war work. Theodore, Junior, watched Lincoln's funeral procession in 1865 and Lincoln became TR's hero and Lincoln's democratic nationalism became TR's creed. Because of his family heritage and his years as a cattle rancher in the Dakota Territory, TR claimed to be a son of both the North and the South, a westerner as well as an easterner. These claims were useful politically, but they also reflected the importance and centrality of nationalism to Roosevelt's philosophy and politics.

Theodore Roosevelt was a politician most of his adult life, but he found time and had the talents to be the kind of American admired by a wide spectrum. "Roosevelt was a many-sided man and every side was like an electric battery," said his friend, the nature-writer John Burroughs. "Such versatility, such vitality, such thoroughness, such copiousness, have rarely been united in one man." Brander Matthews, literary critic and professor at Columbia, once wrote: "The more closely we scrutinize Theodore Roosevelt's life and the more carefully we consider his many ventures in many totally different fields of human activity, the less likely we are to challenge the assertion that his was the most interesting career ever vouchsafed to any American. . . ." In 1915, the writer Julian Street published a portrait of Theodore Roosevelt and entitled his little book, simply, *The Most Interesting American.*

For Julian Street, as for Brander Matthews, it was TR's many-sidedness that made him supremely interesting. Only Benjamin Franklin and Thomas Jefferson among his countrymen seem obvious rivals to the multiplicity of TR's roles and accomplishments. His entertainment value has never been in doubt. The question of his greatness, however, is another matter—one that has been endlessly debated.

Theodore Roosevelt was a naturalist, hunter, conservationist, historian, explorer, soldier, winner of the Nobel Peace Prize, rancher in the "Wild West," intellectual, deputy sheriff in cowboy country and head of the New York City Police Department, author of more than thirty books on a wide variety of subjects, politician, magazine editor and newspaper columnist, and founder of his own political party. He was Phi Beta Kappa at Harvard, one of the original members of the National Institute of Arts and Letters, and one of the first fifteen elected to the American Academy of Arts and Letters. He was a founder of the Boone and Crockett Club, the National Municipal League, the Bird Club of Long Island, and the National Collegiate Athletic Association. He was president of the American Historical Association. He spoke French and German fluently. He put a river on the map in Brazil. He climbed the Matterhorn and led troops into battle. He wrote essays and reviews on a dazzling variety of topics, ranging from primeval man to polar exploration and from poetry to politics. A.A. Norton in a recent study of Roosevelt as a writer has said that TR was "perhaps the outstanding generalist in his era."

As a child, TR suffered from asthma and other ailments and was seldom able to attend school or lead a normal life. At the urging of his father, young Theodore took up body building and then sports. TR's youthful struggle for health eventually became part of the Roosevelt saga that served as inspiration to generations of American boys. "He was frail; he made himself a tower of strength. He was timid; he made himself a lion of courage," asserted the memorial resolution passed by the Boy Scouts of America when TR died in 1919.

TR's devotion to physical fitness, outdoor adventure, sports, and strife on behalf of noble causes became a philosophy of living that TR called the "strenuous life." TR said in 1899:

> I wish to preach, not the doctrine of ignoble ease, but the doctrine of the strenuous life, the life of toil and effort of labor and strife; to preach the highest form of success which comes, not to the man who desires mere easy peace, but to the man who does not shrink from danger, from hardship, or from bitter toil, and who out of these wins the splendid ultimate triumph.

For TR the "ultimate triumph" was that he became a hero to millions of his countrymen in his time and since.

From early boyhood, TR was deeply interested in natural history. He learned taxidermy as a boy, and eventually the bird specimens he collected in his childhood and teenage years enriched the collections of museums all over the world. He published papers on ornithology while in college and in his twenties became an authority on North American big game. His books on hunting and his adventures in wild places won a wide audience, were reprinted again and again, and earned the respect of the scientific community. During his lifetime, TR hunted, collected, and wrote about wildlife in North America, the Near East, Africa, and South America. His many outdoor books include *Outdoor Pastimes of an American Hunter* (1905), *African Game Trails* (1910), *Through the Brazilian Wilderness* (1914), and *A Book-Lover's Holidays in the Open* (1916). In the 1890s, TR was George Bird Grinnell's coeditor and contributed to three volumes published by the Boone and Crockett Club: *American Big-Game* (1893), *Hunting in Many Lands* (1895), and *Trail and Campfire* (1897). In 1914, TR was co-author with Edmund Heller of *Life-Histories of African Game Animals,* published in two volumes. TR's love and knowledge of nature found further expression through his leadership in the conservation movement.

Roosevelt wrote history before he made it. While a senior at Harvard, he began work on what would become his first book on any subject, *The Naval War of 1812.* The 500-page scholarly work was published in 1882 when TR was in his early twenties. Roosevelt went on to write biographies of Thomas Hart Benton (1887), Gouverneur Morris (1888), and Oliver Cromwell (1900); a history of New York City (1891); and an epic study of the westward movement, *The Winning of the West,* published in four volumes, 1889–1896.

Both *The Naval War of 1812* and *The Winning of the West* were in print in the 1990s and still consulted by scholars. TR's biographies of Senator Benton and Gouverneur Morris were volumes in the prestigious "American Statesmen" series, edited by John T. Morse, Jr. Other contributors to the series included Henry Adams, William Graham Sumner, and Moses Coit Tyler. TR's biographies of Benton and Morris have been attacked by later critics as superficial and opinionated, but at the time they were favorably reviewed, and both volumes were widely used and cited by historians for many years. TR's concise history of New York City was part of the noted and classic "Historic Towns" series, edited by E.A. Freeman. Roosevelt's work on the naval aspects of the War of 1812 was so respected that he was asked to contribute the section on the War of 1812 for the English history of the Royal Navy edited by William Laird Clowes, but nobody on either side of the Atlantic ever has had much to say in praise of TR's biography of Oliver Cromwell.

TR's work on naval history predated Alfred Taylor Mahan's books, and the first volumes of *The Winning of the West* came out before the publication of Frederick Jackson Turner's frontier thesis. TR influenced Mahan and Turner.

He knew both historians, conducted a continuing dialogue with them, and was influenced in turn by their thinking.

Roosevelt's views on the writing of history were eloquently expressed in his famous inaugural address as president of the American Historical Association in 1912, "History As Literature," which is a defense of history as a didactic epic, or story with a moral, and an attack on the German school of "scientific" history. "History As Literature" is still widely cited in works on historiography. Although TR did make his mark as an historian, he is of course remembered more as a maker rather than a writer of history.

Theodore Roosevelt graduated from Harvard in 1880, and that year married Alice Hathaway Lee of Chesnut Hill, Massachusetts. He studied law at Columbia for a time but soon became a lawmaker rather than a lawyer. TR was elected a Republican member of the New York State Assembly from Manhattan's Twenty-first District in 1881, shortly after his twenty-third birthday. There were annual elections at that time, and TR was reelected in 1882 and 1883. He was the Republican minority leader in one session during his tenure and the youngest member of the state assembly. He won a reputation as a reformer and was a nationally known figure in the Republican Party by 1884.

TR and historian Henry Cabot Lodge, his friend and fellow Harvard graduate, gained much attention at the Republican national convention of 1884 for their opposition to James G. Blaine, whom they considered corrupt. However, when Blaine won the nomination, both TR and Lodge backed the Republican ticket, refusing to bolt the G.O.P. in company with reform-minded independents known as the "Mugwumps" who went over to Grover Cleveland and the Democrats. Roosevelt's refusal to bolt confirmed his status as a professional politician.

On February 14, 1884, devastating personal tragedy struck TR when his wife and mother died on the same day in the same house.

TR's mother died of typhoid, and Alice Lee Roosevelt succumbed to Blight's Disease after giving birth, on February 12, to a girl, named Alice. TR turned from politics for a time and became a cattle rancher, near Medora, in the Badlands of western Dakota Territory. Roosevelt's trilogy on his western experiences, *Hunting Trips of a Ranchman* (1885), *Ranch Life and the Hunting Trail* (1888), and *The Wilderness Hunter* (1893), became classics, promoted the careers of such artist-illustrators as Frederic Remington, and helped formulate the images of cowboy life and the "Wild West" that have come down to us.

In 1886, Roosevelt returned east to run for Mayor of New York City against labor leader Henry George and the winning Democrat, Abram S. Hewitt. TR came in a poor third. Shortly after the election, TR married a childhood friend, Edith Kermit Carrow (1861–1948), in London on December 2,1886. After an extended European wedding trip, the Roosevelts returned to live at Sagamore Hill, the house TR had built in 1885 at Cove Neck in Oyster Bay, New York, on the North Shore of Long Island, where the couple were to raise a lively brood of six children, Alice (born to TR's first wife), Theodore, Kermit., Ethel, Archibald Bulloch, and Quentin.

Having campaigned loyally for the Republican Party over the years, TR was rewarded in 1889 when he was appointed to the U.S. Civil Service Commission by President Benjamin Harrison. He continued in the post during part of Democrat Grover Cleveland's second term and served from 1889 to 1895.

On the Civil Service Commission, Roosevelt did much to replace the traditional spoils system of partisan appointment to government jobs with the merit system that had been authorized by the Pendleton Act in 1883. While enforcing the law, TR fought with spoilsmen from both political parties. He put the cause of civil service on the front page of the newspapers and reestablished his credentials as a reformer. During TR's tenure on the commission, the number of jobs covered by the civil service more than doubled. The historian William H. Harbaugh writes:

> His imaginative and energetic enforcement of the laws had virtually institutionalized the civil service system; and had he never performed another service for the American nation, that alone would have assured perpetuation of his memory as a secondary figure of substantial accomplishment.

Theodore Roosevelt was appointed to the four-member board of police commissioners of New York City in 1895 and was chosen president of the board. In two years as president, he revolutionized the New York Police Department and made his mark in the history of American law enforcement. He attacked corruption in the NYPD; hired women and Jews; enforced the law rigidly, regardless of political consequences; and transformed police work through civil service reforms and the use of modern techniques and technologies. TR set minimum professional standards for recruits (height, weight, age, ability to do basic arithmetic, and so on); published a manual of rules and regulations; adapted the use of the Bertillion system for identification; started a much-publicized bicycle squad; and established a school for training in the use of firearms. The New York School of Pistol Practice, founded in 1895, was at the time one of the two schools for police training that existed in the United States. There was a dramatic increase in arrests and a systematic attack on graft under Roosevelt.

As usual, TR was front-page news on virtually a daily basis. Probably most Americans knew the name of the police commissioner of New York City and what he was doing, but Roosevelt was attacked by the leaders of both political parties, and his enforcement of the Sunday closing law for saloons and other unpopular laws alienated much of the public. Frustrated by growing opposition to his police policies, TR sought a new job when the Republicans again won the White House in 1896.

President William McKinley appointed TR to the post of assistant secretary of the Navy in 1897. Roosevelt was in the Navy Department for a year, and during his tenure, Roosevelt sought to prepare American naval forces for the war he saw coming with Spain over the independence of Cuba, the last remnant of the Spanish empire in the New World. Biographers have given TR much credit—probably too much—for the subsequent spectacular American naval triumphs in the Spanish–American War, and TR's influence in bringing about the war has been exaggerated by both his admirers and his severest critics. Yet, that assistant secretary is remembered while his superior, Secretary of the Navy John Davis Long, is forgotten, and TR went on to become one of the most famous heroes of the Spanish–American War.

After protracted quarreling over the future status of Cuba between the United States and Spain, on April 24, 1898, Spain declared war on the United States. The next day, Theodore Roosevelt was appointed lieutenant colonel, and his good friend Leonard Wood, an office in the regular army, was named colonel of the First United States Volunteer Cavalry Regiment, soon popularly known as the Rough Riders. The Rough Riders, who assembled at San Antonio, Texas, in May, were composed in large part of cowboys and Indians from the West, and Ivy League athletes and eastern aristocrats. These men represented Roosevelt's Knickerbocker–Harvard background and his days as a cattle rancher in the West. What did these groups have in common? They could ride and shoot, were fit, and needed relatively little training to be ready for battle.

The Rough Riders were shipped out from Tampa, Florida—without their horses, thus turning them into infantry—and landed at Daiquiri, in Cuba, on June 22. They defeated the Spanish at the Battle of Las Guasimas on June 24. On June 30, the day before the major advance on Santiago, Leonard Wood was promoted in the field to brigadier general, and TR was made colonel of the Rough Riders. On July 1, 1898, TR and the Rough Riders charged uphill into immortality at the Battle of San Juan Hill. He led the assaults on first Kettle Hill and then San Juan Hill on the ridges overlooking the city of Santiago. The U.S. forces won the day, and soon Santiago fell. The Rough Riders had the highest casualty rate of any regiment in the war.

After the fall of Santiago, the Rough Riders, many suffering from yellow fever and other ailments, were shipped to Montauk Point, at the eastern end of Long Island, to rest and recuperate. There at Montauk, Colonel Roosevelt was approached about becoming the Republican candidate for governor of New York State, and there the Rough Riders mustered out, on September 16, 1898, after 137 days in the army.

Senator Thomas Collier Pratt, the boss of the Republican Party in New York State, mistrusted Roosevelt because the Rough Rider's reputation as a reformer and an independent. But there was a big scandal with the Erie Canal in 1898, and the Republicans dared not run their incumbent governor for reelection. It was thought that only Roosevelt the war hero could win. Accordingly, TR was nominated for governor of the Empire State on September 27, and after a spirited campaign, in which Colonel Roosevelt emphasized national issues and the glories won by his regiment, he was elected on November 8, receiving a vote of 661,715 to his opponent Democrat Augustus Van Wyck's 643,921 votes.

The year 1898 had indeed been busy for Theodore Roosevelt: In January, he was in the Navy Department in Washington, working to prepare for war with Spain; in July, he was leading the Rough Riders at the Battle of San Juan Hill; and in November, he was elected governor of New York. He had seized and made the most of every opportunity. Fortune seemed to smile on TR in his youth; events seemed to break in his direction. In his last years, the reverse appeared to be the case, but to a considerable extent Theodore Roosevelt made his own luck.

By 1898, TR had been a political celebrity for more than fifteen years, but the governorship of New York was really the first top-level job Roosevelt had. He had been head of the police in New York City but was defeated for mayor. He had been a civil service commissioner and an assistant secretary but never a member of the cabinet. He made it to colonel but not general in the Spanish-American War. Yet, he was famous, quoted, and admired, and he influenced events and shaped public policy from the time when he was in his midtwenties. TR's career up to the governorship seemed to follow one of Roosevelt's favorite adages, "Do what you can, with what you've got, where you are."

In his inaugural address as governor, on January 2, 1899, TR declared:

> It is only through the party system that free governments are now successfully carried on, and yet we must keep ever vividly before us that the usefulness of a party is strictly limited by its usefulness to the State, and that in the long run, he serves his party best who most helps to make it instantly responsive to every need of the people, and to the highest demands of that spirit which tends to drive us onward and upward.

In other words, TR was a professional partisan politician, but he was also a reformer. To fellow partisans he preached the need for honesty and a positive program. To reformers he spoke of the necessity of working "through practical methods and with a readiness to face life as it is, and not as we think it out to be."

As governor of New York, Roosevelt brought about the passage of legislation taxing corporate franchises, strengthening the state's civil service system, setting up a tenement commission, increasing the power of factory inspectors, raising teachers' salaries in New York City, limiting working hours for drug clerks and state employees, and other reform measures. He did much for conservation, working to preserve the Palisades and reforming the forest, fish, and game service. He saw to it that factories in the state were not allowed "to make bird-skins or bird feathers into articles of ornament or wearing-apparel."

TR regularly consulted with Senator Platt and avoided any open breach with the Republican machine, but Platt was displeased when the governor refused to accept the senator's orders on job appointments, nor was he happy with most of the governor's reform measures. Platt therefore decided to rid himself of Roosevelt by making him the next vice president of the United States. Vice President Garret A. Hobart, elected with McKinley in 1896, died on November 21, 1899, and thus Republicans needed to find a new running mate for President McKinley in 1900.

TR wanted to be reelected governor in 1900, and as for the vice presidency: "The more I have thought it over the more I have felt that I would a great deal rather be anything, say a professor of history, than vice-president," he said. At the time, the vice presidency was seen as a dead end for politicians, a high honor, no doubt, but also the end of the line, Yet, TR's close friend Henry Cabot Lodge urged TR to take the job and was certain that the vice presidency would be Roosevelt's stepping stone to the White House.

Senator Mark Hanna of Ohio, Republican national chairman and President McKinley's closest friend and advisor, was strongly opposed to Roosevelt for vice president, as was McKinley. But McKinley refused to repudiate Roosevelt openly or make known any choice for the vice presidency. Republicans from the West wanted the Rough Rider on the ticket to counter the appeal of westerner William Jennings Bryan, Democratic presidential candidate in 1896 and again in 1900, and many party leaders saw TR as a match against Bryan's dynamic campaigning.

Both Hanna and McKinley considered TR unstable and dangerously independent of party discipline. Hanna warned G.O.P. delegates to avoid Roosevelt. He asked them to consider that with TR as vice president there would be "only one life between that madman and the White House." But Senator Platt found an ally in Senator Matthew Quay, the powerful boss of Pennsylvania, who disliked Mark Hanna. Platt and Quay deftly outmaneuvered both Hanna and their candidate at the G.O.P. convention in Philadelphia, the western delegates had their way, and the Rough Rider was nominated.

The campaign of 1900 was largely a running debate between William Jennings Bryan and Theodore Roosevelt, who both strenuously stumped the country. In 1896, McKinley, in contrast to Bryan's whistle-stop campaign, had spoken to visiting delegations from his front porch in Canton, Ohio, and in 1900, the president wanted to maintain the same style. It was TR who was sent out to whistle-stop for the G.O.P. TR ignored his opponent for vice president, sixty-five-year-old Adlai E. Stevenson of Illinois, who had been vice president in Cleveland's second term.

Bryan attacked the Republicans on imperialism, the high tariff, and the trusts, and, as in 1896, he advocated freesilver inflation. TR pointed with pride to prosperity and to "full dinner pail," the results of the protective tariff and a stable gold-standard dollar. TR embraced the responsibilities of world leadership and overseas commitments brought about by victory over the Spanish empire. He denounced the evils of the trusts, surrendering no ground to Bryan and the Democrats on that issue, and attacked free silver and the Democrats' irresponsibility on foreign and domestic policy. According to observers then and since, the outcome of the election was never in doubt because the incumbent administration presided over good times and had just won a war. The ticket of McKinley and Roosevelt defeated Bryan and Stevenson in a landslide, 292 electoral votes to 155.

Theodore Roosevelt was inaugurated as vice president of the United States on March 4, 1901. He presided for four days over a special session of the Senate, and that, as it turned out, ended the only official duties he was to have as vice president. Senator Platt happily remarked on his way to the inauguration that he was going "to see Teddy take the veil."

As vice president, TR felt that he had little influence in the administration. He explained to office seekers that he now had less power over federal appointments than when he was the governor of a large state. To Leonard Wood, Vice President Roosevelt wrote on April 17, 1901: "You know that the Vice-Presidency is an utterly anomalous office (one which I think ought to be abolished). The man who occupies it may at any moment be everything; but meanwhile he is practically nothing."

To occupy his time, and with an eye to future employment, TR made plans to study law and seek admission to the bar. TR also worked on an innovative program to educate college students about politics and draw them into public life. He held a seminar for selected undergraduates and recent graduates from Harvard and Yale at Sagamore Hill on June 29, 1901. An unexpected dividend of the seminar was that one of the Harvard men, Richard Derby, later married TR's daughter Ethel Roosevelt. In 1901, as his correspondence clearly reveals, Roosevelt also began to work to line up support for himself for the 1904 Republican presidential nomination.

On May 20, 1901, Vice President Roosevelt opened the Pan American Exposition at Buffalo, New York, delivering a speech entitled "The Two Americas." President McKinley visited the exposition on September 6 and at a public reception was shot twice by an anarchist, Leon Czolgosz. TR was attending an outing of the Fish and Game League at Isle la Motte, Vermont, when he was notified of the shooting. The vice president hurried to Buffalo, where he stayed at the home of his friend, the attorney and reformer Ansley Wilcox. McKinley seemed certain to recover, said the doctors, and TR left Buffalo on September 10, soon taking his family for a vacation at the Tahawus Club in the Adirondacks. On September 13, the vice president climbed Mount Marcy, and while returning, late in the afternoon, he saw a man coming toward him on the trail. TR later recalled: "When I saw the runner I instinctively knew he had bad news, the worst news in the world."

The news was that McKinley appeared to be dying. TR headed for North Creek, New York, to board a special train. He traveled all night on country roads, and when he reached North Creek at dawn he was informed that President McKinley had died at 2:15 A.M. After TR's train reached Buffalo, he went to offer his condolences to Mrs. McKinley and then took the oath of office at the Wilcox Mansion, on Delaware Avenue, from U.S. District Judge John R. Hazel at about 3:30 P.M. on September 14. He was forty-two years old, the youngest president in history, before or since. In 1904, TR was elected in his own right. TR served as president from September 14, 1901, to March 4, 1909.

Theodore Roosevelt was a prolific phrase-maker and wordsmith, enriching the public discourse with such terms as *muckrakers, nature fakers, weasel words, Ananias Club* (whose members were liars), *malefactors of great wealth, race suicide* (birth control), *clean as a hound's tooth, mollycoddlers,* and *hyphenated Americans.* TR felt as fit as a "bull moose" as he led the "strenuous life" and preached to Americans from the "bully pulpit" of the White House about a "square deal" in domestic policies, while advocating in foreign affairs a policy of "speak softly and carry a big stick."

TR's square-deal policies emphasized the conservation of natural resources and the regulation of big business. He sought to reverse the traditional policy of laissez-faire and to bring order, social justice, and fair play into the workplace and the marketplace. When he entered the White House, virtually his only instrument for dealing with big business was the Sherman Antitrust Act of 1890, which had been made a dead letter by the rulings of conservative courts.

Shortly after becoming president, TR brought the Sherman Act back to life with a suit against the Northern Securities Company, a holding company owned by J.P. Morgan, E.H. Harriman, and James J. Hill. After a lengthy fight in the courts, the Supreme Court by a five to four decision dissolved the Northern Securities trust, thereby reversing earlier court rulings that weakened corporations and monopolies. The Roosevelt administration launched antitrust suits against American Tobacco, Du Pont, Swift and Company, Standard Oil, and other giants, forty-five antitrust suits in all, most won by the government.

TR said that government by lawsuit left much to be desired. What was needed, TR insisted in every annual message, was continuous regulation of all important aspects of economic life by commissions, but a Congress dominated by "standpat" Republican conservatives and Bourbon Democrats rejected most of the president's recommendations for comprehensive legislation to regulate big business. TR was able, however, to get through Congress an impressive list of laws, including the Elkins Antitrust Act (1903) and the Hepburn Act (1906) to regulate railroads; the Pure Food and Drug Act and the Meat Inspection Act, both signed on June 30, 1906; and the Federal Employers Liability Act (1908). The Pure Food and Drug Act and the Meat Inspection Act were the beginning of consumer protection by the federal government.

TR's conservation policies were broad and multifaceted. He worked for the preservation of wildlife, natural beauty, and wilderness areas and also promoted the planned use, development, and control of natural resources. Under the Newlands Act of 1902, TR started the first twenty-one federal irrigation projects, including what became Theodore Roosevelt Dam in Arizona. Under the Antiquities Act of 1906, the president preserved eighteen national monuments, the first being Devil's Tower in Wyoming, set aside on September 24, 1906. TR's other national monuments include the Grand Canyon, Muir Woods, Mount Olympus, and Arizona's Petrified Forest. He also expanded the forest reserves from about 43 million acres to 194 million acres, doubled the number of national parks, and set up the first federal wildlife preserves, including the National Bison Range in Montana and some fifty-one reservations. TR's work for conservation also included the first inventory of natural resources, the appointment of commissions, and the calling of conferences to promote conservation. If he had done nothing else, surely TR could be called a great president on the basis of his conservation legacy.

His record on conservation has won universal praise from posterity, but the Rough Rider's conduct of foreign affairs has always been controversial. Historians have been highly critical of Roosevelt's dealings with Colombia and Panama in building the Panama Canal and of the Roosevelt Corollary to the Monroe Doctrine, which defined the role of the United States as a police officer for Latin America. Yet, the record shows that TR worked hard on behalf of peace.

TR was the first world leader to submit a case to the Court of Arbitration at The Hague and to call for holding the Second Hague Peace Conference, which met in 1907. Successfully mediating an end to the Russo-Japanese War in 1905 led to his being awarded the Nobel Peace Prize in 1906. He prevented a war from starting between France and Germany in 1906 by resolving the Moroccan Crisis through the Algeciras Conference. Roosevelt firmly upheld the Monroe Doctrine, preventing European occupation of first Venezuela and then the Dominican Republic over debts. At the Second Hague Peace Conference, the Roosevelt administration secured the adoption of the Drago Doctrine, which outlawed the use of force in the collection of foreign debts. The Roosevelt administration also was responsible for setting up the Central American Court of Justice.

In foreign affairs, TR's "big stick" was the Navy. Under him, the U.S. Navy was expanded greatly, and by 1909 the United States was second only to Great Britain as a naval power. The voyage of the U.S. "Great White Fleet" around the world in 1907–1909 showed that American national interests and military capabilities were now global.

The Democrats nominated William Jennings Bryan, the "Great Commoner," in 1896, 1900 and 1908, but in 1904 the party turned from progressivism and nominated for president a conservative, "safe and sane" eastern Democrat, Alton B. Parker, the chief justice of the Court of Appeals of New York State. For vice president, the Democrats chose an elderly millionaire, Henry G. Davis of West Virginia.

TR drafted as his running mate in 1904 Senator Charles W. Fairbanks of Indiana. The choice was a case of traditional ticket balancing. Fairbanks was a conservative from a midwestern state running with a progressive reformer from the East. In an article published in 1896, commenting on the vice-presidential candidates of that year, Roosevelt wrote: "It is an unhealthy thing to have the Vice-President and the President represented by principles so far apart that the succession of one to the place of the other means a change as radical as any possible party overturn." So it had been in 1901 when TR followed McKinley, and yet in 1904 Roosevelt was guilty of doing the "unhealthy thing" by choosing a running mate at odds with the president's philosophy. In his 1896 article, TR had also suggested that the vice president be included in cabinet meetings, but he did not give Fairbanks, as Arthur M. Schlesinger, Jr., puts it, "a seat in the cabinet or anywhere else."

In 1904, the Roosevelt-Fairbanks ticket received 7,628,834 popular and 336 electoral votes to the Parker–Davis totals of 5,084,491 popular and 140 electoral votes. TR had won by the greatest popular-vote majority to that time, and Parker had carried no states outside the South.

In his seven-and-a-half years in the White House, TR had transformed the presidency to the center of a powerful federal government and made the president a world leader. The man for whom the Teddy bear was named had entertained and inspired the public as few presidents before or since. TR's view was that the president "was a steward of the people bound actively and affirmatively to do all he could for the people." he was an activist on behalf of the public, recognizing no bounds except the specific prohibitions of the Constitution and the statutes. "Is there any law that will prevent me from declaring Pelican Island a Federal Bird Reservation?" TR asked his attorney general in 1903. No legal barrier could be found. "Very well, then I so declare it," said TR, thus creating the first federal bird refuge. He would establish fifty more by 1909.

TR is generally seen as the first "modern president," and historians and political scientists rate him among the greatest of the presidents. When the experts are polled, TR always makes the top ten presidents, and recently he has been found in the top five. His importance is as obvious as his visage on Mount Rushmore.

There was nothing of the anticlimatic in Theodore Roosevelt's last years, but there was frustration, defeat, and tragedy.

Returning to the United States in 1910, after a postpresidential expedition to Africa and tour of Europe, TR found the Republican Party seriously divided between conservative and progressive factions. TR's own handpicked successor, the former secretary of war, President William Howard Taft, sided with the conservatives, abandoning his promise to follow the Roosevelt policies. Progressive Republicans looked to TR for leadership. TR responded with his "New Nationalism" speech in 1910, which the historian George E. Mowry says is "probably the most radical speech ever given by an ex-president."

In 1912, with the progressive movement at high tide, Roosevelt opposed President Taft for the nomination. TR swept the newly instituted popular primaries, but the Taft forces prevailed at the Republican national convention. TR's followers then bolted the Republican Party and founded the Progressive Party, which nominated him for president and Governor Hiram W. Johnson of California for vice president. The new party was popularly known as the Bull Moose Party, after its robust presidential nominee. Roosevelt ran on a detailed and advanced reform platform that advocated most of the major reforms adopted since 1912, including old-age pensions, unemployment and health insurance, the graduated income tax, wages and hours laws, and women's suffrage. In the midst of the campaign, Roosevelt was shot by an anti-third-term fanatic. The Bull Moose insisted on making his speech before going to the hospital and was back on the campaign trail in a few weeks.

In the November election, Democrat Woodrow Wilson was elected due to the split in the normal Republican vote. TR came in second, and for the first and only time in history the Republican candidate came in third. During the next four years, the Wilson administration co-opted much of the 1912 Bull Moose platform. In defeat Roosevelt had firmly established the presidential primary system—the voters had strongly rebuked the G.O.P. leadership—and he had provided his opponent and nemesis Woodrow Wilson with a program for the next four years.

World War I began in 1914, and soon Roosevelt was the leading advocate in the United States for military preparedness and a hard-line policy toward Germany. Wilson preached neutrality and at first did little to strengthen the army and navy. Seeing Wilson's defeat as the prime national need, the old Rough Rider turned down a second Bull Moose nomination in 1916 and backed the Republican candidate, Charles Evans Hughes. Wilson was narrowly reelected and asked for a declaration of war a few weeks after his second inauguration. TR volunteered for military service; Wilson turned him down.

TR's last years were a time of frustration for the old Rough Rider: He was unable to regain office and tasted defeat again and again. Yet, in those final years, with both major parties against him most of the time, without office, Roosevelt still set the agenda, still decided what issues were to be faced by the politicians and the people, and usually his view prevailed in the end.

On July 14, 1918, TR's youngest son, Quentin Roosevelt, an army pilot, was shot down and killed behind German lines in France. After Quentin's death, the boy in TR died, as his friend Hermann Hagedorn observed. The man soon followed. Theodore Roosevelt died in his sleep in the early morning hours of January 6, 1919, at the age of sixty.

REFERENCES

William H. Harbaugh, *Power and Responsibility: The Life and Times of Theodore Roosevelt* (New York: Farrar, Straus, and Cudahy, 1961); David McCullough, *Mornings on Horseback* (New York: Simon and Schuster, 1981); Paul Grondahl, *I Rose Like a Rocket: The Political Education of Theodore Roosevelt* (New York: Free Press, 2004); Edmund Morris, *The Rise of Theodore Roosevelt* (New York: Coward, McCann and Geoghegan, 1979) and *Theodore Rex* (New York: Random House, 2001); Aïda DiPace Donald, *Lion in the White House: A Life of Theodore Roosevelt* (New York: Basic Books, 2007); Frederick W. Marks, III, *Velvet on Iron: The Diplomacy of Theodore Roosevelt* (Lincoln: University of Nebraska Press, 1979); John Allen Gable, *The Bull Moose Years: Theodore Roosevelt and the Progressive Party* (Port Washington, N.Y.: Kennikat Press, 1978); Lewis L. Gould, *The Presidency of Theodore Roosevelt* (Lawrence: University of Kansas Press, 1991); Joshua D. Hawley, *Theodore Roosevelt: Preacher of Righteousness* (New Haven, Conn.: Yale University Press, 2008); James R. Holmes, *Theodore Roosevelt and World Order: Police Power in International Relations* (Washington, D.C.: Potomac Books, 2005); John Allen Gable, "Theodore Roosevelt: A Selected and Annotated Bibliography," in *Theodore Roosevelt: Many-Sided American,* edited by Natalie A. Naylor, Douglas Brinkley, and John Allen Gable (Interlaken, N.Y.: Heart of the Lakes Publishing, 1992), 645–654; Joseph Bucklin Bishop, *Theodore Roosevelt and His Time, Shown in His Letters,* 2 vols. (New York: Charles Scribner's Sons, 1920); Elting Morison, John M. Blum et al., eds., *The Letters of Theodore Roosevelt,* 8 vols. (Cambridge, Mass.: 1951–1954); Hermann Hagedorn, ed., *The Works of Theodore Roosevelt: Memorial Edition,* 24 vols. (New York: Charles Scribner's Sons, 1923–1926).

―――――――――

JOHN ALLEN GABLE, who died in 2005, graduated from Kenyon College and received a

Ph.D. in history from Brown University. He was the executive director of the Theodore Roosevelt Association, a historical society and public service organization for more than thirty years and an adjunct professor of history at Hofstra University. He was the editor of the quarterly *Theodore Roosevelt Association Journal* and the author and editor of numerous books and articles on the twenty-sixth president.

CHARLES WARREN FAIRBANKS (1852–1918)

Vice President, 1905–1909

(President Theodore Roosevelt)

CHARLES WARREN FAIRBANKS
(Library of Congress)

By Ray E. Boomhower

A conservative former railroad attorney and senator from Indiana, Charles Fairbanks was selected by the Republican convention in 1904 to balance the ticket with the more progressive Theodore Roosevelt. In 1916, Fairbanks made a second try for the vice presidency by running with G.O.P. presidential candidate Charles Evans Hughes but lost to fellow Hoosier Thomas Marshall and his presidential candidate, Woodrow Wilson.

Fairbanks was a native of Union County, Ohio, born on May 11, 1852. One of the few politicians who could truthfully say that he had been born in a log cabin, the house was owned by his farmer father, Loriston Monroe Fairbanks. According to the younger Fairbanks, he absorbed his abiding interest in politics and political discussion from his father, a waggonmaker and an abolitionist who often built "liberty wagons" for political rallies and parades held at the county seat.

During his youth Fairbanks displayed the same quiet, steady character that marked his subsequent career in law and politics—a demeanor that won for him the unflattering nicknames the "Indiana Icicle" and "Senator Icebanks." In a 1904 campaign biography for the GOP vice-presidential candidate, Fairbanks's uncle, William Henry Smith, said that although biographers often delight in relating exciting stories about their subjects' young lives, there were, unfortunately, "few incidents connected with the boyhood life of Mr. Fairbanks that would interest the reader. He was not bad, as boys go, nor was he especially good." In a sketch prepared on his life for the Indiana State Library in Indianapolis, Fairbanks said of his early days that he was an "active young farmer, with a predominating love of books."

At the age of fifteen, Fairbanks entered Ohio Wesleyan University, a small Methodist institution located in Delaware, Ohio. Although he worked his way through school, the Ohio farm boy still found time to serve as one of three editors for the campus newspaper, the *Western Collegian*. Reminiscing about his college days with a newspaper reporter, Fairbanks noted that he and his roommate subsisted on a diet of "mush and milk and boiled potatoes with an occasional dish of stewed dried apples."

Graduating with honors in 1872 (he ranked eighth in a class of forty-four students) his uncle, William Henry Smith, Western AP general manager, offered Fairbanks a job as a reporter for the Associated Press in Pittsburgh. After a year in Pittsburgh, the young reporter received a transfer to the news service's Cleveland office. While in that city, Fairbanks attended law school for six months, receiving a degree from the Cleveland Law College on July 10, 1874.

In fall 1874, Fairbanks took two important steps in his life: On October 6, he married Cornelia Cole, a fellow editor on his college newspaper and daughter of Judge P.B. Cole of Marysville, Ohio, and he accepted an offer from another uncle, Charles Warren Smith, Chesa-peake and Ohio Railroad System general manager, to become claims attorney for the Indianapolis, Bloomington, and Western Railroad. The young couple moved to Indianapolis, and Fairbanks set out his shingle for a law career that saw him try only one criminal case. Instead, he turned his legal talent to working with railroads, becoming a general solicitor for the Ohio Southern and the Dayton and Ironton railroads; president and principal stockholder of the Terre Haute and Peoria Railroad; and director, general solicitor, and principal stockholder of the Cincinnati, Hamilton and Dayton Railroad.

During his days with these various railroad enterprises Fairbanks amassed a considerable personal fortune, which he made with assistance from relatives who provided him with investment tips. His railroad ties not only made him rich but also made Fairbanks popular with politicians and other public officials—especially because he regularly granted free passes on railroads in which he had a stake to these influential people. In 1888, Fairbanks, at age thirty-six, entered the hurly-burly world of Hoosier politics as manager of his friend Judge Walter Q. Gresham's attempt to capture the Republican presidential nomination. Gresham's effort failed, and the nomination went to rival Indiana candidate Benjamin Harrison. Despite losing out to the former Civil War general, Fairbanks remained true to the GOP, campaigning energetically on Harrison's behalf during the general election, which Harrison won.

Fairbanks's entrance onto the Hoosier political scene came at a time when Indiana played an important role in national politics. With both parties having almost equal strength in the state, the national organizations vied furiously to capture Indiana's fifteen electoral votes in presidential elections. In an attempt to woo Indiana voters to their side, each party often placed Hoosiers on their tickets, earning for the state the designation as the "mother of vice presidents."

With the Harrison faction's loss of control of the Indiana GOP following the president's 1892 reelection defeat, Fairbanks became a powerful force in Hoosier Republican Party circles. "I intended to be a lawyer," Fairbanks told an *Indianapolis News* reporter in 1918, "but out here in the states west of the Alleghenies, politics and the law, you know, somehow run together." Fairbanks began to build an impressive political machine. In 1892, as the Indiana Republican Convention's permanent chairman, he worked to place men loyal to him on the Republican state committee. To help solidify his political power in the Hoosier state, Fairbanks, in 1893, became a silent partner with his uncle William Henry Smith in purchasing the *Indianapolis News*.

It was during Harrison's failed 1892 campaign that Fairbanks first met a man who would do much to advance his political career in the coming years—Ohio politician and future president William McKinley, who told the railroad lawyer that he belonged in the United States Senate. Four years later, with Indiana solidly behind McKinley thanks to Fairbanks's efforts, the Hoosier G.O.P. leader delivered the keynote speech at the Republican national convention in St. Louis. In 1897, with the support of now President McKinley, Fairbanks was elected by the Indiana general assembly to a seat in the U.S. Senate.

Fairbanks's career in the U.S. Senate was less than inspiring. In his biography of the Hoosier politician, *Charles Warren Fairbanks: Conservative Hoosier,* Herbert J. Rissler noted that Fairbanks "spent more time opposing what he considered to be unwise proposals than in formulating new proposals of his own." Fairbanks did serve as a U.S. representative on the United States and British Joint High Commission that was formed in 1898 to settle between the two countries the Alaskan boundary dispute. When the commission failed to come to a final agreement, Fairbanks spoke out against the suggestion of submitting the issue to a foreign arbitrator. His role on the commission

won for him the admiration of Alaskan citizens, who named the community of Fairbanks after the vice president.

Although his political mentor McKinley was assassinated in 1901, Fairbanks remained a potent force in state and national G.O.P. affairs. He harbored hopes that the party would look to him as its presidential candidate in 1904. The increasing national popularity enjoyed by McKinley's successor, Theodore Roosevelt, however, offered a major roadblock to Fairbanks's presidential ambitions. Although conservative Republican leaders were concerned about Roosevelt's crusading tendencies, it seemed likely that the former Rough Rider would be the party's choice for president.

With Roosevelt's nomination all but assured, political insiders began to wonder who might be selected as his running mate. Despite making no public statements about his choice, Roosevelt did admit to his son, Theodore, Jr., that

strictly between ourselves, I very earnestly hope that Mr. [Congressman Robert R. of Illinois] Hitt will be nominated for Vice-President with me. He would be an excellent candidate and if I should be elected he would be of all men the pleasantest to work with.

There were, however, a number of factors working in favor of Indiana's favorite son, Fairbanks. To party insiders, a Roosevelt/Fairbanks ticket made perfect sense as it matched an easterner with a midwesterner and a progressive with a conservative. Even Roosevelt could see the handwriting on the wall. On May 27, 1904, Henry Cabot Lodge wrote Roosevelt to tell him about a visit from Fairbanks that morning in which the Indiana senator indicated

that he was at your service in any way you might indicate. He would not say that he wanted the V. Presidency; held off as before but yet made it perfectly evident to me that he did want it and is after it,—and means to get it. If he pushes for it he will get it.

Fairbanks got it; in June Republican delegates at the GOP national convention in Chicago selected the Hoosier politician as the party's vice presidential candidate.

In congratulating Fairbanks on his selection, Roosevelt offered scant personal enthusiasm for his new running mate: "I do not see how you could refuse [the nomination] in view of the unanimous feeling of the representatives of the Republican party that you were the man above all others needed for the place," Roosevelt wrote Fairbanks, leaving unsaid whether the Indiana politician was his personal choice for the post. Although the two men were never close friends—Roosevelt even once proclaimed that Fairbanks was nothing but a "reactionary machine politician"—their coolness toward each other had no effect on the 1904 election's outcome. As he had in other elections, Fairbanks traveled throughout the country touting the glories of the Republican Party, ending with a whirlwind tour through Indiana. His efforts did not go unrewarded; the G.O.P. national ticket swamped Democratic candidate Alton B. Parker by more than 2.5 million votes (336 to 140 electoral college votes). Hearing about the overwhelmingly Republican election returns, an excited and pleased Roosevelt exclaimed, "How they are voting for me! How they are voting for me!"

After the excitement of a landslide election triumph, Fairbanks settled down into the drudgery of being vice president. Although Roosevelt had once advocated increasing the office's power and responsibilities, he made no such changes. During his four years in office, Fairbanks played little or no role in the Roosevelt administration. In fact, the vice president worked with conservative House Speaker Joseph "Uncle Joe" Cannon to halt Roosevelt's Square Deal program, vowing to delay "all progressive measures in committee so that they [will] never come to vote."

One anecdote highlights the conservative Hoosier's isolation from the more progressive president. Irritated one day by the continued tinkling sound made by a White House chandelier, Roosevelt is reported to have turned to his butler and said: "Take it to the vice president. He needs something to keep him awake." The president often received reminders from others on Fairbanks's ambition to succeed him in office. When Roosevelt planned to inspect a new, and dangerous, device—a submarine—humorist Finley Peter Dunne warned him not to go on the trip unless he took Fairbanks with him. It came as no surprise that Roosevelt turned to Secretary of War William Howard Taft to succeed him as president instead of Fairbanks.

Contributing to the tension between Roosevelt and Fairbanks was an incident in the vice president's home state. Roosevelt had in 1907 agreed to travel to Indiana on Memorial Day to help dedicate a statue honoring Henry W. Lawton, a Spanish-American War general later killed fighting forces opposed to America's control of the Philippines. Problems soon arose, however, when Civil War and Spanish-American War veterans squabbled over their rightful places in the proceedings. A Spanish-American War veteran himself, Roosevelt nevertheless wrote Fairbanks that "both because of their age and because of the infinitely greater nature of the war, our claims must not be put forward against the claims of the Civil War veterans."

A greater controversy resulted from ceremonies before Roosevelt's speech dedicating the statue at the Marion County Courthouse. Arriving in Indianapolis's Union Station a little before 11 A.M. on Memorial Day, the president journeyed to the Fairbanks home at 1522 N. Meridian Street to be guest of honor at what he called "a big political lunch."

The forty guests for lunch were divided into two parties, one hosted by Fairbanks in the dining room, and the second headed by U.S. Senator from Indiana James Hemenway in the library. One item on the menu received nationwide attention—Manhattan cocktails.

A teetotaling Methodist, Fairbanks may not have drunk any liquor himself at the luncheon, but he bore the brunt of nationwide newspaper attacks on his character when they learned of the cocktail incident. Already nicknamed "Buttermilk Charlie" for his advocacy of buttermilk instead of hard liquor, Fairbanks had a brand new moniker after the affair— "Cocktail Charlie." A leading Methodist official proclaimed that the vice president had been "crucified by a cocktail."

At first, Fairbanks took full responsibility for the entire matter, writing a Methodist bishop in Buffalo, New York: "I followed the usual custom in such entertainments. For what was done, I was entirely responsible. I have never had any apologies to make for it." But with the frigid relations between the president and vice president, Fairbanks had some nagging doubts about Roosevelt's role in the affair.

These doubts came to light at a Washington, D.C., Gridiron Club dinner honoring Roosevelt as he prepared to leave office. In his speech, Fairbanks said that although he had often been assailed and misunderstood during his career, he himself had "never thrown a line to trip an adversary." Roosevelt, the next and last speaker, responded in kind to Fairbanks's remarks, telling the audience: "The Vice President says he never threw a line to trip an adversary. In that he and I differ. I have thrown a line to trip an adversary, and I would do it again."

Despite the president's angry words at the Gridiron Club function, earlier he had expressed sincere bewilderment about the uproar caused by the incident. In his memoirs, Indiana Congressman James E. Watson told about a visit he made to see Roosevelt during the controversy. The president told Watson that the treatment afforded Fairbanks had been uncalled for and termed the situation "ludicrous and preposterous." Ironically, Roosevelt confided to Watson: "I don't like cocktails anyhow. I like champagne, and that made the incident at Fairbanks's home all the more gruesome to me." Of course, the negative publicity Fairbanks received on the "cocktail affair" did not in itself cost the vice

president the 1908 Republican presidential nomination. Even with that incident hanging over his head, Fairbanks proved to be a potent force at the convention. He could not, however, prevent Taft—Roosevelt's handpicked successor—from winning the G.O.P. presidential nomination. After leaving office, Fairbanks and his wife embarked on an around-the-world trip. Even though he was out of politics, he made headlines again when the Pope denied Fairbanks an audience after the former vice president tried to address students at the Methodist schools at the American Church in Rome. On his return to Indiana, Fairbanks kept active in Republican Party affairs but failed to exercise the control he once enjoyed. He kept busy by serving as a trustee for his alma mater, Ohio Wesleyan University, and for DePauw University and American University. In 1912, Congress made Fairbanks a regent of the Smithsonian Institution.

The last political hurrah for Fairbanks came in 1916 when he was once again the G.O.P.'s choice as vice president. Although Fairbanks helped his running mate Charles Evans Hughes to carry Indiana, the duo lost in a close race to incumbent President Woodrow Wilson and his Hoosier running mate, Thomas Marshall. The defeat ended Fairbanks's political life. Fairbanks died on June 4, 1918. Today, when Fairbanks is remembered, it more often is not for his political stature but rather for his physical stature. Naming Fairbanks one of Indiana's two greatest senators in 1957 for a selection committee choosing the United States Senate's five most distinguished senators of all time, former President Harry S. Truman could only give this rationale: "It is said that the mirror in the Vice President's office, which once belonged to Dolly Madison, is placed at its present height so that Vice President Fairbanks could see to comb his hair."

References

Herbert J. Rissler, "Charles Warren Fairbanks: Conservative Hoosier" (Ph.D. diss., Indiana University, 1961); James H. Madison, "Charles Warren Fairbanks and Indiana Republicanism," in *Gentleman from Indiana: National Party Candidates, 1836–1940* (Indianapolis: Indiana Historical Bureau, 1977); William Henry Smith, *The Life and Speeches of Hon. Charles Warren Fairbanks: Republican Candidate for Vice-President* (Indianapolis, Ind.: Wm. B. Burford, 1904); *The Letters of Theodore Roosevelt*, Elting E. Morison, ed. (Cambridge, Mass.: Harvard University Press, 1951); James E. Watson, *As I Knew Them: Memoirs of James E. Watson* (Indianapolis, Ind.: The Bobbs-Merrill Co., 1936).

RAY E. BOOMHOWER is senior editor of the Indiana Historical Society's quarterly popular history magazine, *Traces of Indiana and Midwestern History*. Along with numerous articles for that magazine, he has also written for *The Indiana Magazine of History, Outdoor Indiana,* and other historical periodicals. Boomhower is the author of *Jacob Piatt Dunn, Jr.: A Life in History and Politics, 1855–1924* (Indiana Historical Society, 1997); *The Country Contributor: The Life and Times of Juliet V. Strauss* (Guild Press of Indiana, 1998); *Destination Indiana: Travels through Hoosier History* (Indiana Historical Society, 2000); *"But I Do Clamor": May Wright Sewall, A Life, 1844–1920* (Guild Press of Indiana, 2001); *"One Shot": The World War II Photography of John A. Bushemi* (Indiana Historical Society, 2004); *Gus Grissom: The Lost Astronaut* (Indiana Historical Society, 2004); and *Robert F. Kennedy and the 1968 Indiana Primary* (Indiana University Press, 2008).

JAMES SCHOOLCRAFT SHERMAN (1855–1912)

Vice President, 1909–1912

(President William Howard Taft)

JAMES SCHOOLCRAFT SHERMAN
(Library of Congress)

By William H. Cumberland

The nation's twenty-seventh vice president during the administration of William Howard Taft (1909–13) was James Schoolcraft Sherman, a conservative, business-oriented New Yorker. Veteran of nearly two decades in the House of Representatives, Sherman was known more for his parliamentary than his legislative skills. He remained firmly attached to the stand-pat wing of the Republican Party where he played an influential though not dominant role during the Progressive Era. His genial demeanor and civility earned him the name "Sunny Jim." In 1912, Sherman became the first Republican vice president to be renominated since the party's founding in 1856. However, he died a few days before the election was held.

James Schoolcraft Sherman was born in New Hartford village, New York, then a suburb of Utica, on October 24, 1855. His parents were Richard Updike

259

Sherman and Mary Frances Schoolcraft Sherman. The family name was originally spelled *Shearman,* and the first ancestor on his father's side to arrive in America in the seventeenth century was Henry Shearman, son of Sir Henry Sherman of Dedham, Essex County, England. James Schoolcraft Sherman was of the ninth generation of descendants from Henry Sherman, a line also connected to Roger Sherman, signer of the Declaration of Independence, and William Tecumseh Sherman, the Union general during the Civil War.

The family moved from Connecticut to Massachusetts and finally to Oneida County, New York, where James's father, Richard Updike Sherman, was born. Richard's father, Willet Sherman, was a successful glass manufacturer and captain of the steamboat *Burlington,* which was featured in Charles Dickens's *American Notes.*

Richard Updike Sherman was a Democrat and quite prominent in political and civic affairs, serving as a state constitutional convention member in 1867. He was tally clerk of the U.S. House of Representatives for ten years, and in 1853 wrote a legislative manual that remained in use into the twentieth century. He also served for fifteen years as president of the New York State Forest and Game Commission and had worked as a journalist in Rochester, New York.

James S. Sherman was educated in the Utica public schools and at Whitestown Seminary. His advanced education came at Hamilton College in Utica, where he received the B. A. in 1878 and the L.L.B. in 1879. Sherman distinguished himself as a debater and, although not a brilliant student, was popular with both professors and peers. After gaining admission to the bar in 1880, he entered the Utica law firm of Cookinham, Gibson and Sherman. Henry J. Cookinham, a former New York assemblyman, was married to Sherman's sister, Mary Louise.

Sherman's role in the partnership appears to have been that of a business adviser, and he remained with the firm until 1907. Meanwhile,

his father's career stimulated in James an interest in politics, but his decision to enter the political arena as a Republican was contrary to the senior Sherman's advice. An early effort to obtain the Republican nomination to the state senate failed by one vote.

Sherman's first political triumph was his election as mayor of Utica in 1884 at the age of twenty-nine, making him the youngest mayor in the city's history. One of his brothers had been elected mayor of Utica earlier on the Democratic ticket. James Sherman served only one term, declining renomination, as he prepared to move into national politics. Sherman was a supporter of the Half-Breed faction in Republican Party politics and associated with the machine known as the "gang" which for years made its power felt on the Oneida County political scene.

Actually, Oneida County and Utica had been the spawning ground of a number of outstanding political careers—among them Francis Kernan, a prominent Democrat and United States senator, Horatio Seymour, Democratic presidential nominee in 1868, and Senator Roscoe Conkling, powerful Republican leader during the Gilded Age. The area was also the home base for Elihu Root, distinguished lawyer and secretary of state during the administration of Theodore Roosevelt. Root's father and brother taught mathematics at Hamilton College during the nineteenth century, where they were known as Square and Cube. Elihu Root and James Schoolcraft Sherman became warm personal friends. Both men had close ties to Hamilton College and had belonged to the same fraternity.

Although there appears to have been no outstanding municipal achievement during Sherman's one term as mayor, he managed to work his way into position for the Republican nomination for Congress in 1886. He defeated his democratic opponent, Thomas J. Spriggs, who had held the office for two terms. Sherman's congressional election victory started him on a long and successful career in national politics that would culminate only with his death in 1912. However, a strong anti-Sherman faction soon developed over his support of the McKinley Tariff bill and his alleged unwise use of patronage. This led to his only election defeat and caused the often critical *New York Times* to describe Sherman as "a rosy cheeked genial young lawyer whose political pull is based upon a native cunning rather than any reputation for ability." Except for that single election loss by a close margin in 1890, Sherman served in the House, representing the Twenty-seventh (earlier known as the Twenty-third) District, until selected as Taft's running mate in the 1908 election. His career spanned the last phase of the laissez-faire Gilded Age and most of the reform-minded Populist and Progressive Era that followed and during which he never wavered from the principles of the Republican Party's Old Guard wing.

Meanwhile, Sherman's personal life and career were steadily progressing. He had married Carrie Babcock of East Orange, New Jersey, on January 26, 1881. Carrie Babcock Sherman's father, Lewis Babcock, was a prominent lawyer, and her grandfather, Colonel Eliakim Sherrill, had been killed on the third day of fighting at Gettysburg. Carrie and her future husband had attended school together in Utica and had known each other since childhood. They had three sons, Sherrill, Richard U., and Thomas M., all of whom were destined for successful business careers. Carrie Babcock Sherman has been described as a "regal Victorian lady," whose gentle manners made her much respected and loved. She was short of stature, prematurely gray, with attractive, round facial features. She was always solicitous of the well-being and proper accommodations of the Sherman household's servants. When her husband was elected vice president in 1909, Carrie Sherman became the first second lady to accompany her spouse in the inaugural parade. During her husband's tenure as vice president, she founded the Congressional Club for senators' and representatives' wives. When in Utica, the Shermans attended the Dutch Reformed Church, where the congressman was president of the trustees and church treasurer.

Upon his father's death in 1895, Sherman assumed the presidency of the New Hartford Canning Company and was also instrumental in the Utica Trust and Deposit Company's formation in 1899. Sherman served as president of this corporation, one of the most important financial institutions in Central New York.

He was a popular "stump" speaker throughout his career, although during his years in Congress he rarely addressed the galleries. As an emerging politician and successful businessman, Sherman furthered his contacts as a trustee of Hamilton College as well as serving as president of that institution's Washington Alumni Association, as president of the Oneida County Historical Society, and as a member of several golf clubs, the Washington Metropolitan Club, Union League, Chevy Chase, and the Order of Elks. He received honorary L.L.D. degrees from Wesleyan University and the University of Pittsburgh. While vice president, he was on the board of the Smithsonian Institution.

One of Sherman's favorite hobbies was cultivating flowers, and he always wore a boutonniere. It was Sherman's custom to be finished with breakfast before 8:00 A.M. and then take a brief outing either by buggy or in one of the three autos his sons possessed. He enjoyed playing golf and frequently attended baseball games. Sherman's desire to play baseball was only tempered by his stocky, 190-pound frame, which limited his mobility. His amiable disposition soon led to the nickname "Sunny Jim," which was attached early and remained with him throughout his life. It was said that "he was a man of cheerful yesterdays and confident tomorrows."

Sherman's national career began with his election to Congress during the first Cleveland administration in 1886. He was not known as a legislative leader or innovator, and there are few bills that bear his imprint. His main contribution appears to have been as parliamentarian. Here, Sherman developed a reputation for being fair and for his detailed knowledge of parliamentary procedure. He was chairman of the Committee of the Whole during important debates, and there were few men in either party whose parliamentary knowledge was more highly respected.

He often presided over the House during the fierce debate over the Dingley Tariff in 1897. Sherman was entrusted with this position by Speaker Thomas "Czar" B. Reed, a major influence in the congressman's career. Sherman was also a member of the Committee on Interstate and Foreign Commerce and despite the fact that he was not from a western state was appointed Committee on Indian Affairs chairman, a post he held for twelve years. Other committees on which he served were the judiciary, civil service, and census. His leadership was, according to his colleagues, one of firm dignity as he demonstrated both fairness and executive ability.

Sherman gradually worked his way into the Republican Party's upper echelons and was a trusted colleague of House Speakers Thomas Reed, David B. Henderson, and Joseph G. Cannon. When his close friend Thomas Reed died, Sherman eulogized him as "a lofty patriot, the great and representative citizen of the American Republic who has gone into history." Sherman himself was eventually regarded as one of the House of Representatives "big five," which included Speaker Joseph G. Cannon (Illinois), Sereno E. Payne (New York), John Dalzell (Pennsylvania), and James A. Tawney (Minnesota). Champ Clark remarked that Sherman was "the slickest of the bunch."

A successful career in Congress led Sherman to aspire to further political ambitions. In 1899, he was nominated and confirmed for the post of general appraiser for New York. At first Sherman accepted the position, but then he declined because he claimed his constituents wished him to remain in Congress. Shortly thereafter, when Speaker Reed retired, Sherman entered the contest for Speaker of the House. The position went instead to David Henderson of Iowa. At this point in his career,

Sherman may have entertained the prospect of running for the Senate. "Uncle" Joe Cannon, another close colleague of Sherman's, followed Henderson as Speaker in 1903. All three Speakers held enormous power over legislation, which ultimately led to a revolt against Cannon by House insurgents during the Taft administration. Sherman further enhanced his reputation by chairing the New York Republican convention in 1895, 1900, and 1908, was Republican national convention delegate in 1892, and in 1906 chaired the Republican Party's National Congressional Committee.

During the 1906 midterm election, Sherman was instrumental in devising a scheme by which every Republican would contribute a dollar to the campaign. For a time thereafter, "Sunny Jim" was given a new sobriquet, "Dollar Jim." He also endeavored to solicit a political contribution for a good deal more than a dollar from railroad magnate E.H. Harriman, only to be curtly refused. Harriman, not pleased by Roosevelt's reform policies, indicated that he was indifferent to the GOP's electoral success. Republican Congressional Campaign Committee chairman Sherman reported the incident to the president. The dispute that surfaced between President Roosevelt and Harriman had been festering since 1904, when the railroad executive had raised (supposedly at Roosevelt's request) $250,000 to assist the campaign in New York, where GOP success was in doubt. This included Harriman's personal contribution of $50,000. Subsequently, Harriman thought Roosevelt had failed to keep commitments, including a promise to appoint Old Guard Senator Chauncey Depew as ambassador to France. The episode became public in April 1907, when a discharged employee of Harriman's sold to the *New York World* a letter Harriman had written to Sydney Webster, revealing the details of the 1904 arrangement with Roosevelt. Roosevelt denied that he had requested the contribution and produced a letter to Sherman dated October 8, 1906, to validate his position. "Sunny Jim," returning from a cruise on the Spanish Main with House Speaker Joe